# Reviving Growth in India

*Edited by*
Pradeep Agrawal

# CAMBRIDGE
## UNIVERSITY PRESS

4843/24, 2nd Floor, Ansari Road, Daryaganj, Delhi 110002, India

Cambridge Univerisity Press is part of the University of Cambridge.

It furthers the University's mission by disseminating knowledge in the pursuit of education, learning and research at the highest international levels of excellence.

www.cambridge.org

Information on this title: www.cambridge.org/9781107090330

© Cambridge Univerisity Press 2015

First published 2015
Reprint 2016

Printed in India by Thomson Press India Ltd., New Delhi 110001

*A catalogue record for this publication is available from the British Library*

*Library of Congress Cataloging-in-Publication Data*
Reviving growth in India / edited by Pradeep Agrawal.
     pages cm
Includes bibliographical references and index.
Summary: "Discusses some of the unresolved questions relating to reviving growth in India covering various sectors of the economy"-- Provided by publisher.

ISBN 978-1-107-09033-0 (hardback)

1. India–Economic policy. 2.  India–Commercial policy. 3.  Industrial policy–India.
I. Agrawal, Pradeep.

HC435.3.R488 2015
330.954—dc23
2014049625

ISBN 978-1-107-09033-0 Hardback

# Contents

Contents

## Section 4: The supply constraints to growth

## Section  5: Emerging issues in growth: The labour and capital markets

# List of Tables and Figures

## Tables

## Figures

# Preface

Between 2000 and 2011, India's growth rate averaged over 8 per cent per annum. This growth rate raised hopes of a Chinese-type economic miracle, of an escape from the low-income trap India has been in for centuries and of regaining its bygone glory as a leading nation of the world. However, since mid-2011, India's growth rate has been faltering precipitously. This book was conceived in mid-2012 to help discover the latest research finding on ways to revive and sustain higher growth rates in India.

The next 20 years or so is a particularly opportune period for maintaining a high growth rate, because we would have the support of the demographic dividend—in the form of the world's youngest population and one of the highest proportions of working age population to total population in the world. That is why it is important that we revive high growth rates urgently, for, once this demographic dividend is exhausted, achieving 8–10 per cent rates of growth, and escaping from the poverty trap, will become much more difficult.

To discover the latest research ideas for reviving growth, leading economists from India and abroad were invited to a workshop to present research studies pertaining to reviving and sustaining high growth rates in India. The workshop was held on 25–26 July 2013. The inaugural address was delivered by Raghuram Rajan (then Chief Economic Adviser to the Ministry of Finance and currently Governor, Reserve Bank of India). The second day saw a special address by Subir Gokarn (former Deputy Governor of the Reserve Bank of India and currently Director of Research at Brookings India), who also presided over the session on monetary and financial sector issues and commented on the research studies in detail. Based on the feedback during this workshop, the studies were refined. This book is a selection of resulting research studies that address practically all the relevant aspects of reviving growth in India.

If proper attention is paid to these issues, and the right policies are followed, India's growth cannot only be revived but sustained at the 8–10 per cent level for decades. This would turn India into an upper-middle-income country in 15 years and a developed country in about 30 years. Fortunately, the new government seems to be showing keen awareness of these key issues. We hope it delivers on the huge expectations people have from it and takes India to its rightful place as a leading nation of the world. We also expect the research and policy recommendations presented in this book to make useful contribution to this immensely valuable task.

The Think Tank Initiative of the International Development Research Centre (IDRC), Canada at the Institute of Economic Growth, and the Reserve Bank of India, provided generous financial support for the workshop. The Institute of Economic Growth provided invaluable administrative and logistical support. I thank Raghuram Rajan and Subir Gokarn for their generosity in sharing their time and insights. Professors Bishwa Nath Goldar, Ashima Goyal, Sushant Mallick and many others helped me in various ways during the preparation of this book. The excellent assistance provided by Durairaj Kumarasamy and Shruti Tripathi was invaluable in the smooth organization of the workshop. Finally, I thank all the authors, discussants, referees and the editorial team at Cambridge University Press (especially Dhiraj Pandey) for their cooperation and support, without which this important project would not have been possible.

Pradeep Agrawal

# Section 1
# The importance of growth

# 1

# Introduction
## Reviving Growth in India

### Pradeep Agrawal

India has maintained a growth rate of over 6 per cent per annum for the past 30 years. Over the more recent period between 2000 and 2011, the Indian economy grew impressively at an average rate of about 8 per cent per annum, and even exceeded growth rates of 9 per cent per annum for some years. For a while, it seemed that India could repeat the Chinese miracle, and finally escape the low income trap that it has been in for centuries, to regain its bygone glory as a leading nation of the world. However, over 2011–14, inflation reared its ugly head as India struggled to meet rising food demand and deal with rapidly rising prices of crude oil and other commodities. This was compounded by large fiscal deficits and several populist schemes that created excessive demand for which appropriate supply arrangements did not exist. These supply constraints led to increasing inflation.

At this juncture, very careful steps were needed to be taken by the government to ease the supply constraints, especially to argument food supplies whose demand was rising rapidly with rising incomes, and to find imaginative solutions to increasing crude oil and commodity prices by better demand management and greater use of coal (that India has in abundance) and renewable energy. There was also an urgent need to control the fiscal deficits and avoid excessive spending on subsidies that were not well targeted to the poor. However, the United Progressive Alliance (UPA) government got mired in many corruption scams, which led to erosion of public confidence in and support for the government. The country seemed to drift during this period. The political leadership failed to give clear direction, and were often busy fighting political battles within the coalition and from the growing opposition. Senior bureaucrats hesitated to take decisions and sat on files. These conditions led to a 'policy paralysis'. Thus, the supply side steps needed urgently to fight food and commodity price inflation were not taken—at least not with sufficient vigour to make a difference. These conditions and the policy paralysis also led to erosion of the confidence of domestic and foreign investors in the Indian economy, thus further slowing down investment and economic growth.

Under normal circumstances, the Reserve Bank of India (RBI) might have considered lowering the interest rates or undertaking other monetary easing mechanisms to fight the resulting slowdown. But, as the government failed to undertake appropriate supply side measures to fight inflation, the entire burden of controlling inflation fell on the RBI, and it responded by raising interest rates sharply. This double assault of erosion of investment climate and the sharp increase in interest rates led to a sharp decline in investment and growth. The growth slowdown began in interest rate-sensitive sectors, like construction, automobiles and durable goods manufacturing, and eventually spread to the whole economy. Consequently, GDP growth, which was about 9 per cent in 2010–11, declined to under 5 per cent in 2012–13 and 2013–14 for the first time in over 10 years.

The next 20–25 years is a particularly important period for India, because we have the support of demographic dividend in the form of the world's youngest population and one of the highest proportions of working age to total population in the world. In about 20–25 years, once we exhaust this demographic dividend, achieving 8–10 per cent rates of GDP growth and escaping the poverty trap will become more difficult and the escape from the poverty trap much more difficult. But if we can maintain a growth rate of close to 10 per cent, we can become an upper middle income country in about 15–20 years. Since higher income levels tend to slow population growth, high growth rates now should also help slow population growth. This would help to stabilize India's population at a lower level than under a slower GDP growth scenario. This effect will further boost per capita income for a given GDP growth rate.

If we also start educating and skilling our people to world class standards, follow proper industrial policies to free the entrepreneurial energy of our people and have good governance, a growth rate of close to 10 per cent per annum is possible for the next 20–30 years (as the Chinese have achieved). That would set India on the road to becoming a developed country and one of the largest economies in the world. Thus, it is extremely important that India achieve a growth rate of close to 10 per cent per annum and sustain it for the next 20–30 years.

Given this importance of reviving and sustaining high growth rates in India, a workshop was organized on this topic at the Institute of Economic Growth, Delhi, India on 25 and 26 July, 2013. The workshop brought together leading economists from India, Europe and the US to analyse the major issues related to this theme and to find solutions to the problems facing India. This book is a selection of papers presented at the workshop.

## ORGANIZATION OF THE BOOK

This book is divided into five sections. The first section discusses the importance of growth; the second section focuses on industrial and trade policy; the third section considers how to deal with growth dampeners like inflations; the fourth section analyses various supply constraints to growth, such as food, energy, social and physical infrastructure, and discusses how to deal with them; and the fifth section deals with some emerging issues in growth relating to the labour and capital markets. A brief summary of each chapter is presented below.

Section 1: The importance of growth

Part 1 discusses the importance of growth. Chapter 1 discusses the importance of maintaining high economic growth in India for it to be able to escape the low income trap and emerge as a developed country in about 20–30 years. It also provides an overview of the various chapters of the book.

Poverty continues to remain a serious problem in India with its consequent toll on human welfare in the form of poor health, low levels of education and a poor quality of life. Unfortunately, about 33 per cent of India's population still lives in acute poverty (less than $1.25 per person per day). Thus, a careful analysis of the determinants of poverty and of various government policies that can help reduce poverty is very desirable. This is the purpose of this chapter.

Thus, in Chapter 2, Pradeep Agrawal empirically examines the various factors that affect poverty and shows that economic growth is the key to rapid poverty reduction in India. He shows that main factors affecting poverty can be decomposed into the growth of income per capita and the distribution of income and then undertakes empirical analysis to show that the poverty rate declines with the growth of GDP per capita and reduced inequality of income distribution. Over the past 20 years, the impact of growth in GDP per capita (which nearly tripled over the past 20 years) in reducing poverty was much larger than that of reduced inequality (which declined by about 10 per cent over the same period). Agrawal shows that growth reduced poverty by leading to increased employment and higher real wages. Further, both government revenue and expenditure increased considerably in real per capita terms, even while not changing much as per cent of GDP. This demonstrates the magic of growth. Government revenue, which has tripled since 1993, was used partly to increase expenditure on education, health and welfare measures. This increased social expenditure has helped reduce poverty as also argued by Amartya Sen and others. . However, the increase in real social expenditure per capita was made possible by rising government revenues due to rapid growth. In fact, social expenditure as a percentage of GDP or as a percentage of government revenue has not increased significantly over the past 20 years. So that, in the absence of growth, even a very well-meaning government would not have been able to achieve much in terms of increasing social services or reducing poverty. This shows that growth is indeed the most crucial element in the fight against poverty—both directly, by creating more employment and raising wages, and indirectly, through increased social expenditure, on education, health, and welfare measures, which are facilitated by increased government revenues as a result of the growth in GDP. Another insight that emerges from our analysis is that given that raising per capita income (or output) is the most crucial factor in reducing poverty, controlling population growth also has a significant role to play in the fight against poverty, at least in a surplus labour economy like India, where the marginal contribution of labour to output is close to zero. The government should, therefore, actively promote smaller family norms and try at the earliest to move the country towards a zero population growth target. Thus, the government's near abandonment of its policy of promoting smaller family norms over the past decade is highly regrettable and needs to be changed.

Section 2: Reviving growth of industry and exports

Given the importance of rapid economic growth, this section deals with policies for sustaining high rates of industrial growth (Chapter 3), growth drivers (ICT and Inclusive Innovations; Chapter 4), and examines the various determinants of services exports (Chapter 5), to help to devise better policies to revive economic growth of industry and exports.

In Chapter 3, B N Goldar examines various aspects of 'Sustaining a High Rate of Industrial Growth in India in the Next 10 Years'. The basic motivation of this chapter comes from India's new National Manufacturing Policy, which aims at raising the share of manufacturing in aggregate GDP from about 15 per cent now to about 25 per cent by 2022, and creating in that process an additional 100 million jobs. Is such an increase in the growth rate of manufacturing real GDP possible and sustainable and, if so, what does it entail? This chapter focuses on these questions. For attaining this objective, the rate in real output growth of the manufacturing sector should be about 13–15 per cent per annum over the next 10 years, which is much higher than the trend growth rate (8.3 per cent per year) in manufacturing real output during the period 1999–2000 to 2011–12 that collapsed to near zero per cent over 2012–14. Thus, even if we ignore the last two years as an abnormality, the annual growth rate in real output growth of the manufacturing sector needs to increase by about 5 per cent.

The overall investment rate of the Indian economy had a clear upward trend since the early 2000s. Assuming similar trend for the future, one may expect the overall investment rate in Indian economy to go up by about 10 per cent in the next 10 years. (Although the share of manufacturing in investment flows in India had a downward trend in the recent period, the long term trend in this ratio is an upward one). Thus, there are reasons to believe that this ratio will increase in the years to come. In 10 years' time it may again reach the peak it reached in 2007–08 (36 per cent). The fixed capital series for manufacturing constructed under these optimistic assumptions has a growth rate of 12.6 per cent between 2013–14 and 2022–23. This hike in the growth rate of capital input will raise the annual growth rate of real GDP of manufacturing by about 2.5–3 per cent. If the annual growth rate in manufacturing real GDP has to go up by 5 per cent, the annual rate of growth in TFP in manufacturing needs to increase by 2–2.5 per cent. Much of this increase has to take place in organized manufacturing. Thus, the rate of TFP growth in organized manufacturing needs to increase from about 1.6 per cent between 1999–2000 and 2011–12 to about 4.5 per cent per year in the next 10 years. This is high, but not unachievable provided major policy initiatives are taken by the government.

In India's organized manufacturing sector, the rate of TFP growth can be improved by greater export orientation of Indian manufacturing firms; substantial improvements in the investment climate, particularly labour market reforms to increase flexibility and productivity; sizeable investment in infrastructure; and large investments in human capital formation. This will also create a favourable environment for investment in manufacturing and, thus, contribute further to growth. However, a mismatch between skilled labour requirements of manufacturing firms and the availability of skilled workers among the youth who would be entering the Indian labour market in the next 10 years may pose a serious obstacle to growth of Indian manufacturing. While 1.7 per cent of the youth of age between 15–24 years have technical education (in 2009), in a majority of industries at least 5 per cent of the workers have technical education. There are several industries (constituting about one-fifth of all three-digit manufacturing industries) in which more than 30 per cent of the workers have technical education. Evidently, only a very small proportion of the youth have the skill levels required by organized manufacturing industry. This is a major problem that needs to be solved.

In Chapter 4, 'Growth Drivers: ICT and Inclusive Innovations', Ashima Goyal explores the contribution of innovations to Indian growth. Innovations are essential to raise productivity and sustain growth. The chapter explores the contribution of innovations to Indian growth. Inclusiveness of innovations is also important to sustain growth, benefit the common man, raise average productivity, and expand the market size. An analytical framework helps to characterize policies that contribute to such innovations, and provide measures against which recent telecommunication, science and technology, and mobile banking policies are examined. While policies can directly encourage it, if innovation depends on market size above a threshold, policies that expand size can be especially useful. These include a general improvement in public services. But in India, the record in expanding even telecom infrastructure has been poor. However, new technical developments that promise more flexibility and convergence can help overcome the last mile problem, provided that enabling policies reduce costs and that implementation improves through better coordination and incentives. The failure to focus on increasing market size was partly responsible for India's failure, compared to other countries, in the more inclusive use of many productivity-enhancing innovations. Mobile banking is a recent example of such failure.

Along with industrial growth, exports growth is also important for promoting faster economic growth. While exports of goods have been analysed by many previous authors, exports of services have not been adequately analysed.

Thus, in Chapter 5, 'Determinants of India's Service Exports', Sahoo, Das and Mitra examine and analyse the factors of India's robust performance in services exports. The chapter argues that sustaining services exports is important for sustaining India's high growth rate and also for maintaining stability in the external sector. It examines and analyses the factors responsible for India's robust performance in services exports. The results reveal that India's aggregate services exports are determined by world income, exchange rate, manufacturing exports and endowment factors like human capital, physical infrastructure stocks and financial development. While factors such as institutions, foreign direct investment and financial development significantly impact the export of modern services, traditional exports are more dependent on limited factors like world income, exchange rate, manufacturing exports and infrastructure levels. Since The world economy is growing at a moderate pace and this might limit growth of manufacturing and services exports of India, India needs to focus on the supply side factors, such as the development of human capital, infrastructure, financial sector development, institutions and broadband tele-density to improve competitiveness of services exports thereby resulting in higher exports.

Section 3: The dampeners to growth – controlling inflation

A major dampener to growth over the past few years has been inflation. Thus, the two chapters in this section discuss whether and how monetary policy can deal with inflation. Both chapters argue that in the presence of supply constraints and commodity price increases, monetary policy cannot be very effective in controlling inflation, as indeed has been India's experience—instead, it is the government that has to work to ease the supply constraints.

In Chapter 6, titled 'Macroeconomic Effects of Monetary Policy in India', S. K. Mallick investigates the macroeconomic impact of the nominal exchange rate and monetary shocks, using quarterly Indian data, along with examining the impact of term-premium and fiscal policy shocks. Within a theoretical setting, the model predictions have been estimated, identifying structural shocks via recursive and non-recursive procedures. Given the rupee depreciation and high inflation, this chapter aims particularly at disentangling the effect of different shocks on a depreciating currency along with the shocks driving high inflation. Supply shocks are found to be more dominant sources of inflation than exchange rate and demand shocks. While monetary policy shocks play a limited role in affecting output dynamics, they also tend to stabilize inflation in the short run. No discernible effect of monetary policy shock was found on inflation in the medium term. This suggests the ineffectiveness of monetary policy in an emerging market economy, where the monetary authority has multiple targets to achieve, and where inflation is largely due to supply shocks. Therefore, the central bank's recent monetary tightening to stabilize inflation via the interest rate channel is unlikely to be effective in the Indian context, because of the modest impact of monetary policy shocks on inflation, and the underlying cause of the inflation, as made evident in this chapter.

In Chapter 7, A. Samanatraya analyses the 'Role of Monetary Policy in Sustaining High Growth' and controlling inflation. The role of bank credit in the monetary transmission mechanism is critical. Given that, this chapter develops a model to understand the dynamics in the determination of bank credit and to objectively assess the role of monetary policy to support economic growth in India. The model explicitly considers the endogeneity between bank credit, deposits and lending rate in a small simultaneous equations framework. Using panel data analysis based on bank-wise data for India during the post-reform period, the estimated results for the above model revealed that credit supply by banks was mainly influenced by monetary policy stance, while the cost of borrowing and overall economic growth were significant to determine the credit demand by the public. It was also observed that lower interest rates on deposits discouraged public demand for bank deposits. Juxtaposed with observed evidence on the heavy dependence of the supply of bank lending on deposits, the above findings do not support the proposition that a lower interest rates regime can engender credit expansion and support economic growth. On the contrary, the estimated results tend to support the view that monetary tightening through raising of interest rates can dampen credit growth due to its adverse impact on credit demand. Thus, the asymmetric impact of monetary policy on the economy becomes evident, and confirms what monetary policy can and cannot do. In assessing the current economic slowdown in India, the policy implications from the present study highlight the limited potency of monetary policy to boost the economy by adopting a lower interest rate regime, but also that monetary policy can contribute to sustain high economic growth in general and a revival from the current economic slowdown indirectly by achieving and maintaining price stability.

Section 4: The supply constraints to growth

The analysis of the previous section on controlling inflation explains that when a country faces supply constraints and the price of commodities increases, a monetary policy is not very effective in controlling inflation. Instead, it is the government that must act and do its best to release the underlying supply constraints (e.g., by increasing food output to control food inflation) and ensure supplies or look for suitable alternatives (as in the case of crude oil and gas). Similarly, the government must ensure development of human capital (through education, vocational training, proper provision of health facilities for the poor) and by developing good infrastructure Unfortunately, this job has not been handled properly so far, and there is an urgent need to pay special attention to these areas of the economy if we are to control inflation and sustain growth over long periods. Thus, the four chapters in this section deals with understanding various supply constraints facing the Indian economy.

In Chapter 8, titled 'Sustainability in Indian Agriculture', Ghosh and Kumarideal with supply constraints in India's agricultural output, needed to feed its large and growing population. It attempts to reflect rationally on the way forward to food security. The chapter reviews and explores future possibilities for Indian agriculture, identifies the concerns that should guide the path to sustainable growth, identifies the limitations of Indian agriculture, and observes the tendencies in India's production pattern from the perspective of the limitations identified. They find that the pattern of shift in agricultural production seems to be inconsistent with India's resource endowments, especially water. Given the expected substantial increase in the production of fruits and livestock products, indirect consumption of cereals and pulses is projected to grow more than the current growth rate of these products. This will increase the demand of water substantially, causing depletion of resources. Growth in Indian agriculture, therefore, needs to be planned with care and caution with an eye for not only food security and consumer demands but environmental, resource endowment and economic sustainability also.

In Chapter 9, titled 'Energy Security for India', Pradeep Agarwal and Shruti Tripathy empirically estimate India's long term demand relations for crude oil and diesel, using careful co-integration procedures, and then use these to project demand for these products until 2025 under various scenarios of GDP growth and oil prices. The projections show that by 2025, demand is likely to increase by about 90 per cent for crude oil and 110 per cent for diesel. This study suggests that to ensure better energy security, India needs to (a) take measures to improve efficiency in the use of petroleum products by using market determined prices; (b) try to enhance supplies within the country and through production-sharing agreements by Indian oil companies with other countries; and (c) increase the use of nuclear, hydro, solar, wind and other alternative energy sources as Western European countries have done. Using the results of demand estimation, this chapter also shows that withdrawing the diesel subsidy will reduce the current account deficit by \$7 billion and the fiscal deficit by about \$12 billion in each subsequent year. The possible immediate spurt in inflation can be avoided by increasing the diesel price gradually.

In Chapter 10, titled 'Social and Physical Infrastructure in India: Constraints to Rapid Growth', Pradeep Agrawal argues that good social and physical infrastructure facilities are crucial for rapid economic growth, rapid human development, poverty reduction, and improvement in living conditions for the population. A comparison with other major emerging economies shows that India's physical and social infrastructure is much poorer and requires major improvement. Average schooling per adult in India is appallingly poor, at only 4.4 years on average, while other emerging economies average at about 7 to 9 years. This is further compounded by the poor quality of education. Survey studies show that Indian elementary school students are typically about three years behind the standard in which they are studying. The condition of higher education is also quite bad. Vocational training could create productive jobs for many with limited education, but it has not received the attention it deserves. A major expansion in education facilities at all levels is urgently needed, along with a significant improvement in the institutional structures to deliver the promised education better. This has to begin with a system of regularly measuring the actual educational attainment at various levels and, then, careful monitoring and experimentation with institutional design to achieve far better performance. In the health sector, the facilities for the vast majority of population are very poor and require urgent attention in both expansion and improvement in institutional mechanisms.

In the sphere of physical infrastructure, India's performance (for its level of per capita income) in the development of roads, railways and telephony is reasonable, though significantly behind China and other emerging economies. However, in the sphere of electricity access and consumption per capita, internet access, level of air travel and quality of seaports, India's performance is quite poor compared to other emerging economies. So, once again, major efforts need to be made to expand and improve the quality of the physical infrastructure and improve the institutional mechanism for faster delivery and less leakage. The new land acquisition law of 2013 has made land acquisition for infrastructure projects too cumbersome. It needs to be revised to make land acquisition for infrastructure and industrial development easier. Regulatory and environmental clearances are another source of major delay in infrastructure projects and need better governance. Thus, Agrawal argues that if proper efforts are made in expanding and improving the quality of education and health facilities and of physical infrastructure through improved budgetary allocation and better governance, it will go a long way in reducing poverty, improving human development as well as reviving and sustaining high rates of economic growth in India.

In Chapter 11, titled 'Infrastructure Challenges in India: The Role of Public–Private Partnerships', Geethanjali Nataraj argues that the lack of international quality infrastructure is a drag on India's development. The goals of inclusive growth and 9 per cent GDP growth can be achieved only if this infrastructure deficit is overcome. Infrastructure development will help in creating a better investment climate in India. To develop infrastructure in the country, the government needs to tackle the issues of budgetary allocation, tariff policy, fiscal incentives, private sector participation, and public–private partnerships (PPPs) with resolve. This chapter discusses the important sources of infrastructure financing in the country, elucidates public private partnerships in India and presents the approach to PPPs as followed in India. The chapter also discusses major challenges and impediments to infrastructure development in the country, and concludes that policies that could lead to the streamlining of procedures and the protection of interests of both investors and consumers are the key to success in infrastructure growth. To make PPPs a success, state governments need to establish full-fledged PPP departments mandated with developing core competencies, policy frameworks and public discourse. A rigorous assessment of the costs and benefits of large projects would also be critical for achieving broader public support for these.

## Section 5: Emerging issues in growth – labour and capital markets

This section deals with some of the emerging issues in growth related to the labour and capital markets and throws light on the reforms needed in these markets to make them more efficient.

In Chapter 12, 'Issues in Labour Cost and Employment', Arup Mitra discusses issues in labour cost and employment in select developing economies. This chapter finds that though productive employment generation is an important objective in most developing countries, this motivation has probably induced firms to adopt capital-intensive techniques. This chapter uses country-specific data on the manufacturing sector in select developing countries to critically examine the argument that high labour cost reduces labour absorption. The effect of labour market regulations on employment has also been assessed. Evidence does not favour labour market deregulation; rather, skill factor reveals a negative impact on employment, and implies a mismatch between the available labour quality and the labour demand in these countries that tend to reduce employment. The wage elasticity of employment does not turn out to be high across countries. Hence, the argument favouring wage flexibility through labour market deregulation is again not empirically justified. The results are also indicative of a weak relationship between productivity and wage, which with labour market deregulations would further weaken these links, leading to gross inequality in income. The effect of labour market regulations on employment, wage elasticity of employment, impact of high cost of labour and relationship between productivity and wage are also critically analysed.

In Chapter 13, titled 'Financial Structure and Growth: A Study of Firms in Indian Private Corporate Sector', Pravakaran Nair discusses the financial structure of firms in the private corporate sector in India. He shows the increasing dependence of such firms on internal rather than external funds in the post-reform period. After the initial boom, funds from capital market sources have declined drastically. A similar picture is seen in the case of total borrowings: a sharp decline in the share of borrowings from financial institutions have led to a significant decline in the share of borrowings as a percentage of firm assets in the post-reform period. Thus, a notable feature of external financing is the re-emergence of bank borrowings as a major source of external financing over the years. In terms of differences across firms of different sizes, Nair finds evidence of strong credit constraints for small firms. He shows that large firms are able to borrow proportionately more than two times as much debt from financial institutions and also benefit from access to cheaper foreign credit. Nair then undertakes an analysis of the relationship between financial structure, debt maturity structure and growth. The results reveal that, on average, Indian manufacturing firms in the private corporate sector depend on debt to finance their expansion and not on capital markets, including equity markets. From the positive and significant impact of the share of bank debt in total debt for all sizes of firms, it seems that the corporate financing strategy of Indian firms is still bank-based in nature. The study found that the growth pattern of Indian manufacturing firms is highly fragile, since it is negatively related with the increase of non-financial debt.

Nair concludes that market imperfections continue to exist in the financial markets that prevent economy-wide efficiency in the post liberalization period. To augment total resources available to firms, there is a need for a greater role of the state regulation of capital markets in terms of evolving suitable accounting standards, preventing insider trading, strengthening fraud laws, and improving provisions for investors' protection. Reforms of banking sector should involve a greater role of private banks and, correspondingly, will require much stronger regulation and supervision to limit moral hazard.

In Chapter 14, titled 'Export Intensity and Dividend Policy of Indian Firms', Goldman and Viswanath argue that the development of export markets for Indian products is important in the resurrection of economic growth, along with internal issues such as infrastructure development and institution building. Developing export capacities will generate employment on the one hand and, on the other, likely generate profits for reinvestment. While some of these profits can be reinvested by exporting firms growing organically, it would be desirable that profits be paid out as dividends to allow the market to direct resources to their best uses. It is, therefore, important to study the dividend behaviour of Indian firms and how it relates to their export intensity. In this study, they use the different theories of dividend determination to uncover the particularities of exporting firms. Their results show that firms that export actually pay higher dividends than non-exporting firms. They find evidence that this is due to a diversification effect caused by the imperfect correlation between domestic and foreign sales that allows exporting firms to have lower cash flow volatility and, thus, be able to pay higher dividends. Finally, they show that firms' exporting behaviour might have a positive effect on valuation in the stock market through its impact on cash flow volatility. Their results can be interpreted as support for export promotion policies.

## MAIN CONCLUSIONS AND POLICY RECOMMENDATIONS FROM THE BOOK

Overall, the studies in the book suggest that a revival of India's growth requires a major push towards industrial revival through increased investment, productivity improvements, and innovations. The industrial sector is still shackled with too many regulations. It needs to be unshackled if we are to achieve major industrial revival that can help create a large number of jobs. The government needs to become a promoter, and not just a regulator, of industry. The industry also requires well trained and skilled workers, which are not available in sufficient numbers. Exports need to be increased to reduce the current account deficit and allow us to meet increasing demand for petroleum and other imports. Export and industrial growth will be facilitated if we improve our physical and social infrastructure and keep a competitive exchange rate.

Inflation has been a sticky problem. The analyses in this book show that it is difficult to lower interest rates until inflation is controlled, because lowering interest rates at this point, when CPI inflation is around 8–9 per cent, is likely to reduce supply of deposits, so that bank credit will begin to dry up if the interest rates are reduced. This will end up hurting, rather than helping, investment. At the same time, it is shown that monetary policy is not very effective when inflation is due largely to supply constraints, commodity price increases and fiscal deficits. This explains why even a large increase in interest rates was not very effective in controlling inflation. What was really needed in this situation was strong action being taken by the government to increase food production to ease food price inflation, other measures to deal with crude oil and commodity price increases, and reining in fiscal deficits. But the government did little on these crucial fronts and passed the burden of inflation control entirely to the RBI, in a situation where monetary policy was not very effective. The results are there for everyone to see: the RBI, forced to raise interest rates excessively in the absence of government action in controlling inflation, has not been able to control inflation effectively, but has contributed considerably to slowing down economic growth.

This episode clearly shows that when inflation is caused by supply side constraints and large fiscal deficits, it is vital that RBI and the government work together to fight inflation, with government doing all it can to release the supply constraints while RBI supporting it, possibly with limited monetary tightening. Had this approach been taken, we might have been much more successful in taming inflation without slowing down the economy nearly as much as has happened in the past three years.

Several studies in the book suggest that India's growth is primarily supply constrained and a concerted effort at improving physical and social infrastructure is needed. For short run revival of growth, urgent attention needs to be paid to increasing agricultural output (especially of vegetables, fruits and dairy products) to fight food price inflation. Simultaneously, we need to work on India's energy security, and on making it less dependent on petroleum imports—by increasing production and use of coal and renewable sources of energy like solar, wind, hydro and nuclear. We also need to increase domestic exploration for oil and gas and participate in exploration and production sharing in foreign fields where possible. Finally, we have to also tread the path of fiscal prudence and minimize the subsidy burden by allowing only those subsidies that are well targeted to the poor and by ensuring that they function better.

For the long-run sustainability of growth, we have to improve our social and physical infrastructure. In particular, we must expand education and vocational training and improve the quality of education available to the masses. If we cannot educate and skill them, we can never hope to eliminate poverty or have inclusive growth. There is no hope that this can be achieved with the status quo or by a simple expansion of the current system, as the current institutional structure is very weak. Survey studies reveal that the quality of education available to the average child in India is very poor. For example, most fifth graders can neither read simple sentences in their native language nor do simple subtraction or division.

Some major new innovations are needed in this area, including possible use of private sector or public private partnership (PPP) arrangements that can deliver quality education to the masses. The situation of higher education is no better and vocational training, which could create productive jobs for so many of our youth with limited education, has simply not received the attention it deserves. A major expansion in education facilities at all levels is urgently needed, along with a significant improvement in institutional structures to deliver the promised education better. This has to begin with a system of regularly measuring the actual educational attainment at various levels and then careful monitoring and experimenting with institutional design to achieve better performance.

Similarly, in the health sector, the facilities for the vast majority of population are very poor and require urgent attention in both expansion and improvement in institutional mechanisms.

Finally, the physical infrastructure needs major improvement. The need is most critical in the electricity sector where our consumption is much below the levels of other emerging economies like China. Roads, railways and seaports could also benefit from improvements and fresh investments. Once again, we need to design better mechanism for effective performance and less leakage so that much more is achieved within our limited resources.

If proper attention is paid to these issues, India's growth can not only be revived but sustained at near 10 per cent levels for decades. This would turn India into an upper middle income country in 15 years and a developed country in about 30 years with one of the largest GDP in the world. Fortunately, the new government seems to be showing a keen awareness of the key issues mentioned here. We hope it delivers on the huge expectations people have from it and takes India to its rightful place as a leading nation of the world. We hope also that the research and policy recommendations presented in this book can make a useful contribution to this immensely valuable task.

# 2

# Economic Growth: The Key to Poverty Reduction in India

## Pradeep Agrawal

## INTRODUCTION

Poverty continues to remain a serious problem in India, with its consequent toll on human welfare in the form of poor health, low levels of education and a poor quality of life. Unfortunately, about 33 per cent of India's population still lives in acute poverty (less than \$1.25 per person per day). Thus, a careful analysis of the determinants of poverty and of various government policies that can help reduce poverty is very desirable. This is the purpose of this chapter.

Many economic studies have emphasized the role of higher economic growth to tackle the problem of poverty. This has been supported empirically by the work of Tendulkar (1998), Ravallion and Datt (1996) and Besley and Robins (2000). Using data from nearly 80 countries, Kray (2006) shows that in the medium-to-long-run, between 66 per cent and 90 per cent of the variation in changes in poverty can be accounted for by growth in average incomes, and all of the remainder is due to changes in relative incomes. The role of economic growth in poverty reduction has also been supported by Deaton and Dreze (2001), Bhagwati (2001) and Datt and Ravalion (2002). Sen (1996) has strongly emphasized the need for higher government expenditure on social assistance to the poor, especially in provision of education, as the most important determinants of poverty reduction. However, since government social expenditure that helps the poor is dependent on government revenue, which in turn grows with economic growth, the key role of economic growth is likely. In this chapter, we examine these issues empirically for India and show that economic growth indeed plays a key role in poverty reduction.

The change in poverty over a period can be broken into two components: the impact of income growth over the period and the impact of change in income distribution over the period. Thus, if the income distribution does not change much (which is often the case with most countries), countries with higher growth rates tend to be associated with more rapid reduction in poverty. We show with the help of national-level data that this result holds for India.

Growth is considered pro-poor if the income share of the poor rises with growth (their incomes grow faster than that of the non-poor). We found evidence that inequality has declined slightly over the recent high growth period in India, and that it has also been accompanied by reduction in the poverty gap and severity. This evidence provides support for the view that the recent high growth period in India has been pro-poor.

We consider how growth might reduce poverty. We show that higher growth was associated with higher employment creation and higher real wages. We also examine whether government revenue and expenditure improved with growth in India, which helped reduce poverty. We show that real government revenue and expenditure per capita increased with growth and, in turn, these translated into a corresponding improvement in expenditure on the social sectors (education, health and welfare expenditures). These contributed to poverty reduction and making growth pro-poor during the recent high growth period.

Given the importance of growth, India needs to follow policies helpful in sustaining high rates of growth. These include the creation of a stable macroeconomic environment, good infrastructure, well functioning education and health services for the poor, well functioning and inclusive financial system and good governance. We also need to pay special attention to the education sector and developing our human resources. Failure to sustain high growth will prove quite disastrous in terms of poverty reduction and development. But if we are able to sustain high growth, it will give India an excellent chance to reduce poverty significantly and meet various development goals, especially if the government takes steps to increase support for infrastructure development, education and health services, etc.

## THE RELATION BETWEEN POVERTY, GROWTH, AND INEQUALITY

This section presents a simple decomposition of the changes in the poverty rate in a country to show that the changes in per capita income and the income distribution are the main determinants of changes in the poverty rate.

The head count ratio of poverty (HCR) is defined as the percentage of the population whose income is below a given poverty line. Thus, HCR will generally depend on average income per capita ($Y^*$) and the poverty line ($\underline{Y}$), *both expressed in constant prices*. It will also depend on the income inequality or distribution ($D$):

$$HCR = HCR(Y^*, \underline{Y}, D)$$

Thus, change in HCR stems from changes in either of the two determinants of Y*, given the constant poverty line.

(a) If income growth is distribution-neutral, or the income of every individual grows by the same proportion, then the Lorenz curve will stay unchanged and change in HCR is due entirely to changes in the mean income.

(a) When the mean income neither grows nor contracts, a change in poverty will occur if and only if the Lorenz curve shifts, i.e., there is income redistribution among some individuals.

The reasoning that change in poverty, $\Delta HCR$, can be separated into two components: growth and distributional effects can be presented mathematically as follows (to keep the notation simple we suppress $\underline{Y}$ from $HCR$ since $\underline{Y}$ is constant over the period 0 to $t$):

$$\Delta HCR = HCR(Y^*_t, D_t) - HCR(Y^*_0, D_0)$$

$$= [HCR(Y^*_t, D_t) - HCR(Y^*_0, D_t)] + [HCR(Y^*_0, D_t) - HCR(Y^*_0, D_0)] \qquad (1)$$

The first term in equation 1 above is the *growth effect*, which measures the change in poverty due to change in the average income over the period 0 to $t$ for a given income distribution. Clearly, for a given income distribution and poverty line, growth in average income of the population would lead to reduction in poverty, since in that case $HCR(Y^*_t, D_t) < HCR(Y^*_0, D_t)$. The second term above is the *distribution effect*, which measures the change in poverty due to the change in the income distribution over the period 0 to t for a given average income. Clearly, for a given average income and poverty line, a more equal income distribution (lowering of income inequality) would lead to reduction in poverty, since in that case $HCR(Y^*_0, D_t) < HCR(Y^*_0, D_0)$.

Given that the income distribution often tends to remain relatively stable in most countries, the above decomposition suggests that the growth in income per capita is the main source of reduction in poverty in most countries. This has been supported by the work of Dollar and Kray (2002), Tendulkar (1998), Ravallion and Datt (1996), Bhagawati (2001), and Datt and Ravalion (2002).

Policies for more rapid poverty reduction

While there is consensus on the relationship between growth, inequality and poverty reduction, there continues to be significant debate on the reasons why countries with comparable growth performances show considerable variation in poverty reduction. This led to considerations of how to conceptualize and measure pro-poor growth. The debate seems to have boiled down to the 'relative' and 'absolute' camps. In the 'relative' sense, growth can only be called pro-poor if the growth rate of income of the poor (suitably aggregated) exceeds the average income growth rate. In other words, growth needs to have a relative bias to the poor in the sense that the income growth of the poor exceeds the average so that inequality (e.g., as measured by the Gini coefficient) declines. This definition has been widely used in the literature due to its intuitive appeal, but it also has some limitations. Concentrating solely on the inequality aspect disregards the absolute levels of growth and might end up favouring growth strategies that are suboptimal for both the poor and the rich. The 'absolute' definition avoids this problem by concentrating on the absolute level of growth for the poor. Growth is considered pro-poor in the absolute sense if the poor population benefits from it in absolute terms, irrespective of how the total gains are distributed within the country in question. Most economists and policymakers, however, consider both absolute as well as relative aspects of poverty, thus recognizing the possible tradeoffs between high growth and distribution of growth according to class.

Why has economic growth been more pro-poor in some countries than in others? Is it mainly due to differences in the rate and sectoral pattern of economic growth, or are there important differences in the poverty-reducing impact of that growth across countries? Is it due to differences in government policies in support of the poor, or is it due to initial conditions (level of literacy, health facilities, etc.) existing across countries/regions? Some economists have argued that a high initial level of inequality can be harmful to the pace of economic growth in poor countries (Gunnar Myrdal, 1968; Aghion et. al. 1999). A plausible argument in this context is that credit market failures mean that the poor are unable to exploit growth-promoting opportunities for investment in human and physical capital. The higher the proportion of poor (and hence credit-constrained) people in the economy, the lower the rate of growth. A support for the argument can be found in Binswanger et al. (1995), Benabou (1996), and Aghion et al. (1999), among others. Some economists, like Dreze and Sen (1995), have argued that effective government intervention in favour of the poor through social welfare policies is most important for poverty alleviation, and growth plays only a minor role (so that government focus should be on education and welfare promotion rather than growth promotion). The World Bank (1993 and 1997) suggests that poverty reduction depends not only on rapid economic growth but also on basic human development, that is, the level of social indicators such as literacy, life expectancy, health facilities, etc., could also be important.

Empirical research has long been trying to analyse the factors affecting poverty in various countries. The factors most often cited as being important for effective poverty reduction include economic growth, inequality and government social expenditure on sectors such as health, education, welfare programmes and social security, which subsidize important services for the poor and reduce vulnerability of elderly, single mothers and children. To examine what factors were significant for reducing poverty in India, the impact of some of these factors for India is evaluated in the next two sections.

## GROWTH, INEQUALITY AND POVERTY REDUCTION: EMPIRICAL EVIDENCE

The analysis of Section 2 showed that poverty reduction should increase with higher economic growth and lower inequality. It also argued that increased social expenditure on education, health and welfare measures should also help reduce poverty. In this section, we will examine these issues empirically.

### Data and econometric procedures

Until 1997, the time series for poverty rate (HCR), inequality (Gini coefficient) and MPCE is taken from Ravalion and Datt (1998). After that, it is author's calculations based on the data from the household expenditure surveys of the National Sample Survey Organization (NSSO) (see Appendix A.1 for details of poverty measurement issues and definitions of poverty measures). The data on GDP are taken from the Handbook of Statistics, RBI. Finally, data on central and state government expenditure on social services and their components are taken from the EPW Research Foundation. While data on macro indicators is available from 1950, composite data on total central and state government expenditure is available only from 1971. The survey periods of the NSSO rounds do not always coincide with the financial year, and all the variables are available only on an annual frequency. Therefore, we have constructed *values corresponding to a given NSSO round* as (a) the value of the variable for the financial year if the midpoint of survey period coincides with the ending of financial year, or otherwise, as (b) a weighted average of the values for financial years overlapping with the survey period of that round.

All econometric relations reported in this chapter are the long run relations estimated from auto-regressive distributed lag (ARDL) co-integration procedure proposed by Pesaran et al. (2001). The procedure is briefly explained in Appendix A.2.

### *Poverty alleviation and economic growth*

Equation (1) derived in Section 2 above implies that as long as average income or GDP per capita increases (i.e., GDP grows faster than the population growth rate), incidence of poverty should decline due to the income growth effect. To present the impact of growth on poverty in India, Figure 2.1 plots real GDP per capita, and incidence of poverty given by HCR (per cent of population with incomes below

21

the national poverty line). The plot of HCR and GDP per capita gives a negative correlation between poverty and income of individuals. As income has increased over the period, HCR has declined correspondingly; this is most evident in the post-1990 period. The figure shows that the incidence of poverty in the country has declined continually, from as high as 57 in 1970 to 20 in 2010. This decline in HCR matches well with the increase in income per capita, and became more rapid after 2003 following the more rapid growth in GDP per capita since then.

**Figure 2.1: HCR, Gini and real GDP per capita, 1951–2011**

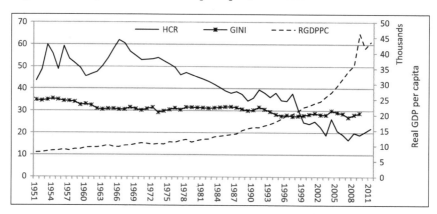

*Source:* RBI and Author's Calculation

To further examine the relation between growth and poverty reduction, econometric analysis was also carried out between (the logs of) poverty rate (LHCR) and GDP per capita (LGDPpc). We used the ARDL co-integration procedure (see Appendix) to obtain the long run relation between poverty rate and GDP per capita. The analysis was undertaken for the period 1955–2010. The following results were obtained (t-statistics of coefficients are given in brackets below them and *, ** denote significance at 5 per cent and 1 per cent levels respectively).

$$\text{LHCR} = 11.16 - 0.78 \text{ LGDPpc}$$
$$(19.7^{**}) \quad (-13.2^{**})$$

$R^2 = .90$; $DW = 2.00$; Serial correlation $[\chi^2(1)] = 0.793$;
Functional form $[\chi^2(1)] = 0.037$
Normality test $[\chi^2(2)] = 0.330$; Heteroskedasticity $[\chi^2(1)] = 13.30$

The estimation results shows that the coefficient of log GDP per capita (LGDPpc) is −0.78 which is large, negative and statistically significant at 1 per cent confidence level. The results imply that an increase in GDP per capita is strongly associated with decrease in poverty and a 1 per cent increase in GD per capita should reduce poverty by about 0.78 per cent. These results imply that that higher GDP growth rate reduces poverty and confirm that the international evidence that higher GDP growth is associated with more rapid decline in poverty is equally applicable for India.

Poverty and population growth

Another insight emerges from the above result that rising GDP per capita is a major factor that helps reduce poverty. Given our surplus labour economy, the marginal product of labour to output in close to zero. Thus, along with raising GDP growth, reducing population growth rates also has an important role to play in raising GDP per capita and thus reducing poverty, especially in the case of labour surplus and land scarce countries like India. Therefore, the government should actively promote smaller family norms and try to move towards a zero population growth target for the country at the earliest. Thus, near abandonment of active government support for smaller family norms over the last decade is highly regrettable and needs to be changed.

### *Poverty alleviation, growth and inequality*

Equation (1) derived in Section 2 above also implies that declining inequality (falling Gini coefficient) is likely to result in a faster decline of poverty for any given level of growth. In a World Bank study of 88 instances where a country achieved positive per capita GDP growth for a decade, inequality improved slightly in about half of the cases and worsened slightly in the other half (World Development Report, 2000). Thus, it is of interest to examine what has happened to inequality in India, especially over the period of growth since 1990, the year marking the beginning of liberalization.

Figure 2.1 also shows the Gini coefficient of expenditure inequality as well as the GDP per capita for India. It is seen that inequality followed a higher path until liberalization, and that there has been a gradual decline in the level of inequality[1],

---

[1]  It may be noted here that this data on inequality relates to expenditure (or consumption) inequality. It is possible, as some economists have argued that the income inequality may have not declined or even increased while expenditure inequality declined (say, due to welfare support for the poor or because the rich consume a smaller proportion of their income). However, to our knowledge, no reliable data is available on income inequality (probably because true income is often not revealed, especially by the rich – to avoid taxes). In view of this problem, we have used the expenditure inequality data, which we believe is acceptable for poverty related analysis, since poverty rates are largely calculated from expenditure on consumption data.

even more so after 1990—the value of the Gini co-efficient has shifted from the 30–31 band to the 27–29 band.

The estimation of the long run relation between (logs of) poverty rate (LHCR), Gini coefficient of inequality (LGINI) and GDP per capita (LGDPpc) using the ARDL co-integration procedure yielded the following result (t-statistics of coefficients are given in brackets below them and *, ** denote significance at 5 per cent and 1 per cent levels):

$$\text{LHCR} = 2.01 \text{ LGINI} - 0.32 \text{ LGDPpc}$$
$$(5.84^{**}) \qquad\qquad (-2.42^{*})$$

$R^2 = .91; DW = 2.07;$ Serial correlation $[\chi^2(1)] = 1.66;$ Functional form $[\chi^2(1)] = 2.36$
Normality test $[\chi^2(2)] = 0.79;$ Heteroskedasticity $[\chi^2(1)] = 5.12$

It is seen that while poverty in India declined with increasing GDP per capita (LGDPpc), it increased with increasing inequality. Note the rather large coefficient of Gini, implying a 1 per cent decrease in Gini would have reduced poverty by an additional 2 per cent. These results are fully consistent with the theoretical predictions of equation (1). The rapid decline of poverty since 1998 is seen to be largely the result of high growth of incomes per capita, aided by some decline in the Gini coefficient of inequality. This is despite the contribution of growth being much larger (since GDP per capita has increased over 150 per cent between 1991 and 2010) than that of decline in inequality (which declined by about 10 per cent from about 0.31 to 0.28).

This estimation was also repeated using the monthly per capita consumption (MPCE) data obtained from the same NSSO household surveys used to measure poverty rates. This data directly measures the average income of the same sample of households and is thus more accurate than the GDP per capita, which is a general proxy for per capita income from nationwide GDP calculations. The result should thus be more accurate using the MPCE measure of household income. The results we obtained are given below (t-statistics of coefficients are given in brackets below them and *, ** denote significance at 5 per cent and 1 per cent levels) .

$$\text{LHCR} = 8.66 + 1.16 \text{ LGINI} - 2.15 \text{ LMPCE}$$
$$(3.01^{*})\ (1.85^{*}) \qquad\quad (-7.54^{**})$$

$R^2 = .98; DW = 2.13;$ Serial correlation $[\chi^2(1)] = 1.41;$ Functional form $[\chi^2(1)] = 3.02$
Normality test $[\chi^2(2)] = 1.23;$ Heteroskedasticity $[\chi^2(1)] = 7.79$

The estimation results show that the coefficient of MPCE and GDPpc came out negative and significant, and that the coefficient of Gini came out positive. This implies that while poverty in India declines with a high GDP per capita and MPCE, it increases with increasing inequality. The coefficient of MPCE came out considerably higher than that of GDPpc, implying that change in the incidence of poverty is more sensitive to change in consumption expenditure than change in total income. Partly, this could also be due to MPCE being a more direct measure of consumer expenditure than GDPpc. Thus, the international evidence that high income and expenditure is associated with declining poverty is found to be equally applicable for India.

Further, that the poverty gap index and the poverty severity index (or squared poverty gap)[2] had improved further suggests that not only the incidence of poverty but also the condition of the population still under the poverty line improved over the high growth period of 1970–2010 (Figure 2.2).

**Figure 2.2: Trend in Poverty Gap (PG) and Squared Poverty Gap (SPG) index**

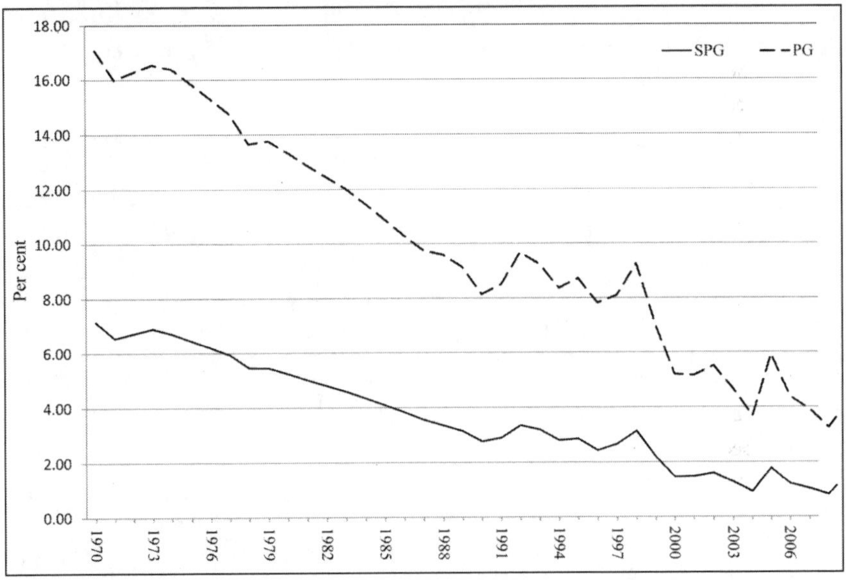

*Source:* Author's Calculation

## *Poverty alleviation, growth, employment, and wages*

How does economic growth reduce poverty? The linkage between poverty and growth can be conceptualized as follows: high rates of economic growth lead to sustained increase in production of various goods and services, which require more

---

[2]  The poverty gap index is a measure of inequality that gauges how far the average income of the poor is below the basic subsistence minimum. The poverty severity index or squared poverty gap shows how poor the poorest of the poor are (see the appendix for definitions).

workers and thus lead to generation of more employment opportunities. With this increased demand for labour, some new workers get employment. At the same time, some workers may be able to get higher wages in their existing occupations, or shift to new occupations, thus also leading to a possible increase in their real wages. Higher levels of earnings can enable workers to spend more on education and skill formation of their children, thus raising the productive capacity of the future workforce, and creating conditions for achieving higher future economic growth. The process would thus complete the virtuous circle of economic growth, leading to poverty reduction via growth of employment and wages, and reduced poverty creating the possibility of further increases in productivity and higher rates of economic growth.

**Figure 2.3: Relation between growth of real GDP per capita and growth of employment in India 1971–2011**

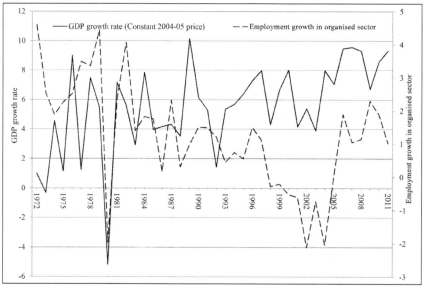

*Source:* Author's Calculation

Figure 2.3 plots the growth rates of employment in the organized sector (reliable annual data was not available for the unorganized sector) and of the growth rate of real GDP for 1971–2011. The figure shows a significant correlation between the two variables, and higher GDP growth is generally associated with a faster increase in employment, albeit with an additional negative trend. There appears to be a general decline in organized sector employment, due to structural changes in the economy (including greater use of contractual labour). We also carried out an econometric analysis of the long run relation between employment growth (EMPLOYgr) and GDP growth (GDPgr) and time trend (T) using the ARDL co-integration procedure. The results were as follows (t-statistics of coefficients are given in brackets below them and *, ** denote significance at 5 per cent and 1 per cent levels):

$$EMPLOYgr = 3.83 + 0.85 \, GDPgr - 0.17 \, T$$
$$(4.37)^{**} \quad (3.71)^{**} \qquad \quad (4.88)^{**}$$

*$R^2 = .66$; $DW = 1.93$; Serial correlation $[\chi^2(1)] = .09$; Functional form $[\chi^2(1)] = 0.48$*
*Normality test $[\chi^2(2)] = 0.97$; Heteroskedasticity $[\chi^2(1)] = 1.60$*

The results show that various diagnostics tests for a good fit are satisfied. Each 1 per cent additional GDP growth is seen to lead to 0.85 per cent increase in employment in the organized sector, but at the same time, it is seen that there is indeed a significant negative trend in the employment in this sector.

**Figure 2.4: Trend in real GDP per capita and average daily wage rate**

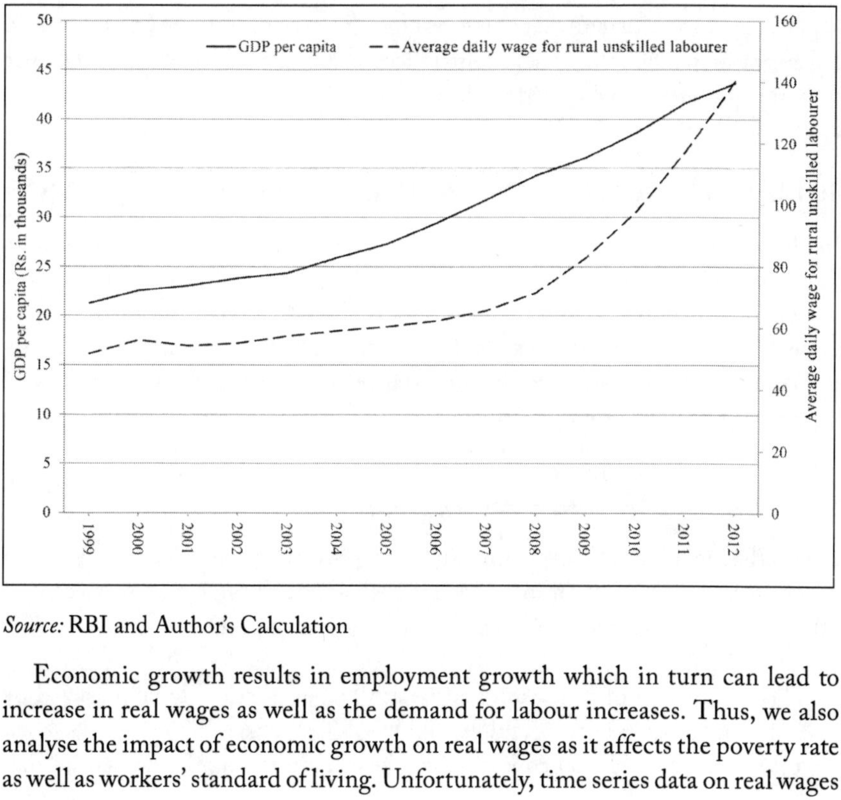

*Source:* RBI and Author's Calculation

Economic growth results in employment growth which in turn can lead to increase in real wages as well as the demand for labour increases. Thus, we also analyse the impact of economic growth on real wages as it affects the poverty rate as well as workers' standard of living. Unfortunately, time series data on real wages are not readily available for a long period; we could find data only for 1999–2012 for the real average daily wage rate (for rural unskilled workers averaged over all states). Figure 2.4 shows that the relationship between the real average daily wage rate for rural unskilled workers and real GDP per capita. The figure shows a close and long-run association between GDP per capita and the wage rate, which suggests that higher GDP growth rate also leads to higher growth in real wages over time as the demand for labour increases.

We also carried out an econometric analysis of the long run relation between log of real wages (LWAGE) and log of real GDP per capita (LGDPpc) using the ARDL co-integration procedure. The results were as follows (t-statistics of coefficients are given in brackets below them and *, ** denote significance at 5 per cent and 1 per cent levels):

$$LWAGE = 0.41 \ LRGDPpc$$
$$(72.98)^{**}$$

$R^2 = .98; DW = 2.03;$ *Serial correlation* $[\chi^2(1)] = .20;$ *Functional form* $[\chi^2(1)] = 1.81$
*Normality test* $[\chi^2(2)] = 0.71;$ *Heteroskedasticity* $[\chi^2(1)] = 1.35$

The result show that all diagnostic test for a good fit are satisfied and that each 1 per cent increase in GDP per capita is accompanied by an increase of 0.41 per cent in real wages for unskilled workers.

## SOCIAL EXPENDITURE, GROWTH AND POVERTY ALLEVIATION

In this section we examine empirical evidence from India on the impact of increased social expenditure on education, health and welfare on poverty alleviation (Section 4.1), and then consider the role that economic growth plays in enabling increased social expenditure (Section 4.2). The analysis addresses the controversy over the relative importance of economic growth and social expenditure in alleviating poverty.

### Social expenditure and poverty alleviation

One of the important channels through which poverty can be reduced is increased government expenditure on social sectors such as education, health services, and other welfare services for the poor, elderly, widows, etc. (Dreze and Sen 1995; Bhagwati 2001).

The importance of education and health has been strongly emphasized by several economists (see for example, Shultz 1993; Becker 1978 and 1995; Sen 1996). Sen has argued that education and health are among the necessities that give value to human life. Education and health are the basis for work productivity; the capacity to learn; and the capability to grow intellectually, physically, and emotionally. In economic terms, education and health are the two cornerstones of human capital that, as Shultz and Becker have argued, are the basis of an individual's economic productivity.

Education has a clear and comprehensive effect on the quality of life. A society with better quality of education and better access to education for all provides its citizens a better quality of life and better economic opportunities and, at the same time, reduces poverty and inequality (as many from poorer families also get good education and subsequently are able to live productive lives with high incomes). Thus, an improved education level in a country—other factors being equal—should lead to higher labour productivity, increased GDP, and reduced poverty. Improved education, especially of girls and women, improves their health status as well as of their children and family members. At the same time, education alone is not a panacea for all social problems—for example, not everyone has the same ability for higher education, and all the educated ones may not necessarily be absorbed by the labour market, which could de-motivate people from pursuing education. Therefore, rapid growth is also important to create enough jobs.

Table 2.1 reports some education indicators from 1990 to 2011. While most of the developed and emerging economies achieved a literacy rate of close to 100 per cent in 2011, India was way behind at 74 per cent , although 48.5 per cent in 1990. The divide in the case of youth was somewhat smaller, with India being at 81 per cent. In addition to the literacy rate, the average number of years of schooling is an indicator commonly used to measure education attainment. Indians obtained just 4.4 years of schooling on average, which is marginally greater than 3 years in 1990, showing very slow improvement in educating the population. Enrolment rates have significantly improved in elementary education; the gross enrolment ratio (GER) for primary sections grew from 91.2 per cent in 1990 to 111.9 per cent in 2011. The secondary enrolment rate was about 36.8 per cent for India in 1990; it has improved steadily and is now around 63.2 per cent. The tertiary enrolment rate has increased from 6 per cent to 18 per cent over two decades. Nevertheless, by international standards, enrolment at the secondary and tertiary level remains low, particularly the latter. Teaching staff constitutes a vital aspect of education. The pupil–teacher ratio (PTR), a critical indicator and measure of the quality of education, is excessively high at primary and middle level averaging 35.2 and 25.3 respectively in the year 2011 (Table 2.1). Thus, it is imperative to lower the PTR and improve the institutional structure of schools and colleges to enhance the quality of education and to make our human resources globally competitive.

**Table 2.1: Indicators for access to and quality of education in India**

| Indicator | 1990 | 1995 | 2000 | 2005 | 2011 |
|---|---|---|---|---|---|
| Literacy rate, adult total (% of people aged 15 and above) | 48.5 | 54.3 | 61.1 | 67.3 | 74.04 |
| Literacy rate, youth total (% of people ages 15–24) | 61.9 | | 76.4 | 81.1 | 82.8 |
| School enrolment, primary (% gross) | 91.2 | 94.8 | 93.8 | 110.4 | 111.9 |
| School enrolment, secondary (% gross) | 36.8 | 45.05 | 45.3 | 53.8 | 63.2 |
| School enrolment, tertiary (% gross) | 5.8 | 5.5 | 9.4 | 10.8 | 17.9 |
| Pupil-teacher ratio, primary | 43.2 | 44.4 | 39.9 | 40.2 | 35.2 |
| Pupil-teacher ratio, secondary | 38.0 | 37.1 | 33.6 | 32.6 | 25.3 |
| *Average years of schooling* | *3* | *3.3* | *3.6* | *4* | *4.4* |

*Source:* World Development Indicators, 2012

Some economists have also argued that ill-health can lead to poverty (especially for those who are only somewhat above poverty line), and have shown that poor health has a negative impact on households' income and economic growth rate (Barro, 1996; Mayer, 2000; Bhargava, 2001). Poor health would reduce a household's capacity to earn income and accumulate wealth by limiting work, raising medical expenses and reducing savings. Individuals affected by certain diseases, such as tuberculosis and HIV/AIDS, may never develop the capacity to earn enough income to get out of the illness–poverty trap. Moreover, health is increasingly recognized as an attribute of human capital. As such, better health increases the productivity of other forms of capital and contributes to economic growth.

Table 2.2 reports some real indicators of access to health care from 1990 to 2011. The table shows that generally, medical facilities have remained stagnant over the period. For example, the number of beds per 1000 people has increased marginally from 0.8 beds in 1990 to 0.9 beds in 2011. Similarly, number of physicians available per 1000 population has also remained stagnant in recent years, increasing marginally from 0.5 to 0.65 from 1990 to 2011. However, overall life expectancy has increased from 58.4 to 65.5 during the same period; this improvement is supported with corresponding improvement in access to water and sanitation facilities both in rural and urban areas.

When we plot HCR against per capita expenditure on education and health, we can see both the plots (Figure 2.5) exhibit a negative relationship between the two variables, especially since 2004–05, when the government increased the expenditure on both education and health. HCR is highly correlated with the value −0.93 and −0.85 with education and health respectively.

**Table 2.2: Indicators for access to and quality of health in India**

| Indicators | 1990 | 1995 | 2000 | 2005 | 2011 |
|---|---|---|---|---|---|
| Life expectancy at birth, total (years) | 58.4 | 59.8 | 61.6 | 63.4 | 65.5 |
| Hospital beds (per 1,000 people) | 0.8 | 0.7 | 0.7 | 0.9 | 0.9 |
| Physicians (per 1,000 people) | 0.5 | 0.5 | 0.6 | 0.6 | 0.65 |
| Improved Water source (% of population with access) | 70 | 76 | 81.0 | 86 | 91.6 |
| Improved Sanitation facilities (% of population with access) | 18 | 21 | 26.0 | 30 | 35.1 |

*Source:* World Development Indicators, 2012

**Figure 2.5: Education and health expenditure per capita and HCR**

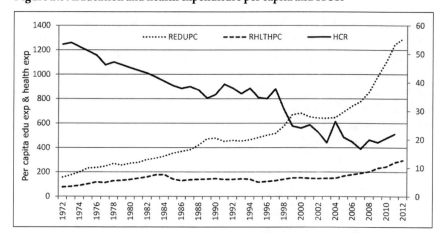

*Source:* EPW Research Foundation and Author's Calculations

To further examine the question whether increased expenditure on social sectors helps to reduce poverty, regression analysis was carried out between the incidence of poverty (*LHCR*) and expenditure on social sectors per capita. Further regressions to check the relative merit of the different types of social expenditure in reducing poverty were also undertaken. One-fifth of the total expenditure on the social sector in India is borne by the central government, and four-fifths by state governments. Therefore, we have included expenditure incurred by both central and state governments in our analysis.

Ideally, we should estimate the relationship between the head count ratio of poverty (HCR) as a function of GDP per capita, Gini co-efficient of inequality and with the per capita social expenditures either total (total social expenditure per capita (TSOCpc)) or its components: education expenditure per capita (EDUpc), health expenditure per capita (HEALTHpc) and other welfare expenditure (WELFAREpc). Thus, using logarithmic functional form (variable names prefixed by L indicate their logarithmic form) the equation to be estimated should be as follows:

$$LHCR = a + b\, LGINI + c LGDPpc + dLEDUpc + e\, LHEALTHpc + f WELFAREpc$$

Poverty rate, HCR, would be expected to increase with increasing inequality, so that the coefficient, b, of the Gini measure of inequality should be positive. On the other hand, HCR should decline with rising GDP per capita, or rising social expenditures on education, health and welfare. Thus the co-efficents of each of these variables, c, d, e, and f are expected to have a negative sign. Unfortunately, we found that there was high co-linearity among these social expenditure and GDPpc variables (because rising GDP is accompanied with increase in each of the social expenditures (Figure 2.6).), The co-linearity problem can lead to estimation problems and unreliable results. Thus unfortunately we were unable to estimate above equation. However, we were able to estimate it one social expenditure variable at a time. This means that while we are unable to determine the individual contribution of each social expenditure, we can at least check that each dos contribute to poverty reduction by including them one at a time. Since the results for the case where only Gini and GDPpc were included in the equation were estimated earlier and the coefficient c found negative (Section 3.2), here we estimate results with gini and each of the social expenditures , one at a time as well as with their sum, namely total social expenditure (LTSOCpc).

The results of the estimation are shown in Table 2.3. The results show that each of the three variables had a negative sign (meaning increase in each social expenditure-reduced poverty), and the coefficients for total social, education and health expenditure turned out significant at the 1 per cent level of significance, although not the coefficient of expenditure on welfare. Overall, the results show that the incidence of poverty declines faster if the government increases its expenditure on social services.

These results show that increased expenditure per capita on social sectors, such as education, health and social welfare, are associated with reduced poverty, and as such are highly desirable. The above results suggest the need for increasing expenditure on social sectors in India, especially on education and health, to help reduce poverty and improve human development.

**Table 2.3: Estimation result for social expenditure**

| | Model 1 | Model 2 | Model 3 | Model 4 |
|---|---|---|---|---|
| Dependent Variable | LHCR | LHCR | LHCR | LHCR |
| LGINI | 0.57 | 0.14 | 0.42 | 1.40** |
| LSOCPC | −1.01*** | | | |
| LEDUPC | | −1.06*** | | |
| LHLTHPC | | | −1.40*** | |
| LWELPC | | | | −0.90 |
| C | 8.68*** | 9.75*** | 9.44*** | 4.040*** |
| R-Squared | 0.86 | 0.85 | 0.85 | 0.86 |
| DW-statistic | 1.91 | 2.22 | 1.75 | 2.56 |
| Serial Correlation | 0.02 | 1.45 | 0.06 | 3.58 |
| Functional Form | 1.05 | 0.15 | 0.01 | 0.74 |
| Normality test | 0.62 | 0.12 | 0.25 | 0.43 |
| Heteroscedasticity | 0.37 | 0.15 | 1.13 | 0.11 |

*Source:* Author's Calculation

Finally, we compare the expenditure on education and health sectors as a percentage of GDP for India and several other transitional and developed countries. These countries comprise East Asian countries (such as Malaysia, South Korea, Indonesia, Thailand and Philippines); the average of Brazil, Russia, China and South Africa (i.e., BRICS countries other than India); and the average of high income countries (as defined by World Bank). The data are shown in Table 2.4.

It is seen that expenditure on education and health as a share of GDP is considerably lower in India than in other emerging and developed economies. Government expenditure on education was just 3.1 per cent of the GDP and on health was 1.2 per cent in 2010–11, much less than 5.3 per cent and 3.7 per cent in the case of other BRICS countries, and far below the 5.2 per cent and 8.7 per cent for the high income countries where we aspire to reach. Similarly, annual health expenditure per capita in 2010–11, with purchasing power parity adjustments, was just $141 dollars in India while it was $432 (about three times) in China, $678 in East Asia, $933 in BRCS countries and a whopping $4680 (about 30 times) in developed countries. The data support the need to increase such expenditure in view of the impact this is likely to make on reducing poverty and promoting human development in India.

**Table 2.4: Public education and health expenditures for selected countries, 2010–11**

| Indicators | India | China | East Asia | BRCS | High Income |
|---|---|---|---|---|---|
| Public expenditure on education, total (% of GDP) | 3.1 | – | 4.3 | 5.3 | 5.2 |
| Health expenditure, public (% of GDP) | 1.2 | 2.9 | 2.2 | 3.7 | 8.7 |
| Health expenditure, public (% of government expenditure) | 8.1 | 12.5 | 9.9 | 11.0 | 18.4 |
| Health expenditure per capita, PPP (constant 2005 international $) | 141.0 | 432.0 | 677.6 | 933.4 | 4679.6 |

*Source:* World Development Indicators

Government revenue and social expenditure

We have seen above the importance of social expenditure in poverty alleviation. Next, we consider the role of growth in enabling higher social expenditure.

**Figure 2.6: India's GDP, government revenue receipts, and government total expenditure in real (2004–05) prices**

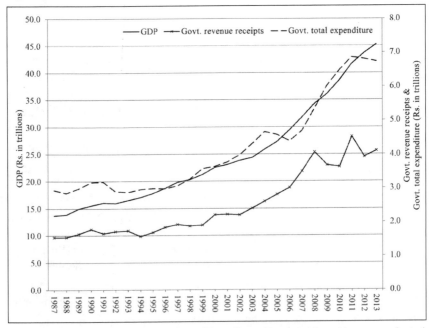

*Source:* EPW Research Foundation's India Time Series Database  http://www.epwrfits.in/

Figure 2.6 plots India's GDP, government revenue receipts and government total expenditure in real (constant 2004–05) prices, and demonstrates that GDP growth leads to higher government revenue which, in turn, allows the government to increase its total expenditure and again, in turn, social expenditure. This is evident from Figure 2.7, which plots the real government total and social expenditure (comprising expenditure on social security and welfare and relief because of natural calamities, education, sports, youth affairs, health and family welfare, water supply and housing, labour and employment). This increased social expenditure on welfare schemes for the poor, subsidized education and health facilities for the poor helps reduce poverty. Thus, the evidence in Figures 2.6 and 2.7 show the importance of higher GDP growth as well as good fiscal policy in providing increased social expenditure, which helps to reduce poverty.

Thus, government policy should always focus on rapid GDP growth. For developing countries like India, this is best achieved with the help of increased expenditure on infrastructure, education and skill formation.

**Figure 2.7: Government total and social expenditure in real (2004–05) prices**

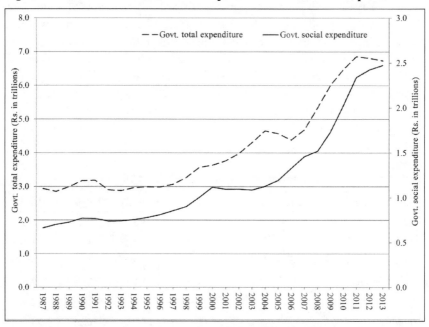

*Source:* EPW Research Foundation's India Time Series Database  http://www.epwrfits.in/

As government revenues rise with rapid GDP growth, a pro-poor government can increase expenditure on social sectors such as education, health services, infrastructure and other welfare services for the poor (Bhagwati 2001). The increased social sector spending enhances the opportunities of human development and promotes poverty alleviation in the long run.

Table 2.5A shows the composition of public spending on the social sectors in India from 1980–81 to 2010–11. When we consider social expenditure as a percentage of GDP, the table shows that the expenditures have remained more or less constant over the last three decades. While the expenditure on education as a percentage of GDP has increased slightly—from 3.1 per cent to 3.6 per cent— expenditure on health has remained in the range of 1 per cent to 1.3 per cent of GDP and on agriculture in the range of 1.6 per cent to 2.2 per cent of GDP. Expenditure on infrastructure declined from 3.9 per cent of GDP in 1980 to 3.5 per cent in 2010. Only the expenditure on anti-poverty programmes increased from 0.9 per cent in 1980 to 2.4 per cent in 2010–11. Overall, the total expenditure on all these social sectors together remained largely constant from 1980 to 2000 at about 11 per cent of GDP. Only in 2010–11, it has shown a significant increase to 13 per cent of GDP.

However, when we look at these expenditures in per capita terms over the same period, a very different picture emerges (see Table 2.5B). Between 1980 and 2010, the per capita expenditure in all the social sectors has increased at least three times. This reflects the increase in real expenditure in these sectors in alignment with the increase in GDP over these three decades. This again demonstrates the magic of growth: even when social expenditures as share of GDP and as share of total government expenditure stagnated (which is the most likely scenario in most countries, given various pressures on the budget from different sectors), more rapid GDP growth has enabled three-fold increases in the per capita social expenditure and helped to improve the condition of the poor.

**Table 2.5A: Government social expenditure as per cent of GDP, 1980–2010**

| Govt Social Expenditure as % of GDP | 1980–81 | 1990–91 | 2000–01 | 2010–11 |
|---|---|---|---|---|
| Education | 3.1 | 3.3 | 3.2 | 3.6 |
| Health | 1.1 | 1.2 | 1.2 | 1.3 |
| Agricultural support services | 2.1 | 2.2 | 1.6 | 2.2 |
| Infrastructure | 3.9 | 3.1 | 3.2 | 3.5 |
| Anti-poverty programmes | 0.9 | 1.2 | 1.4 | 2.4 |
| *Total* | *11.1* | *11* | *10.6* | *13* |

*Source:* EPW Research Foundation's India Time Series Database  http://www.epwrfits.in/

This evidence shows that while Sen's (1996) emphasis on social expenditure, especially on education, as a way of reducing poverty is certainly valid, his de-emphasis on growth is certainly not. Indeed, growth is seen to be crucial to enable the government to increase the social expenditure that Sen advocates.

**Table 2.5B: Government social expenditure per capita, 1980–2010**

| Govt Social Expenditure per capita | 1980–81 | 1990–91 | 2000–01 | 2010–11 |
|---|---|---|---|---|
| Education | 457 | 526 | 737 | 1476 |
| Health | 162 | 199 | 282 | 519 |
| Agricultural support services | 310 | 354 | 356 | 902 |
| Infrastructure | 576 | 505 | 720 | 1418 |
| Anti-poverty programmes | 133 | 193 | 319 | 982 |
| *Total* | *929* | *1079* | *1375* | *2897* |

*Source:* EPW Research Foundation's India Time Series Database http://www.epwrfits.in/

## CONCLUSIONS

Poverty continues to remain a serious problem in India with its consequent toll on human welfare in the form of poor health, low levels of education and a poor quality of life. Unfortunately about 33 per cent of India's population still lives in acute poverty (less than $1.25 per person per day). Thus a careful analysis of the determinants of poverty and of various government policies that can help reduce poverty is very desirable. This is the purpose of this chapter.

Thus, in this study we empirically examines the various factors that affect the poverty level in India and shows that growth is the key to rapid poverty reduction in India. We show that main factors affecting poverty can be decomposed into the growth of income per capita and the distribution of income and then undertakes empirical analysis to show that poverty rate declined with growing of GDP per capita and declining inequality of income distribution. However the impact of growth in GDP per capita (which nearly tripled over the last 20 years) in reducing poverty was much larger than that of reduced expenditure inequality (which declined by about 10 per cent over the same period)

We show that growth reduced poverty by leading to increased employment and higher real wages. Further, both government revenue and expenditure increased considerably in real per capita terms, even while not changing much as per cent of GDP – this demonstrates the magic of growth. Government revenue, which has tripled since 1993 was used partly to increase expenditure on education, health and welfare measures. This increased social expenditure has helped reduce poverty as Sen (1996) had argued. However the increase in the real social expenditure per capita was made possible by the rising government revenues due to the rapid growth. In fact, the social expenditure as per cent of GDP or as per cent of government revenue has not increased significantly over the last 20 years. So that in the absence of growth, even a very well-meaning government would not have been able to achieve much in terms of increasing social services or reducing poverty.

Our analysis shows that growth is indeed the most crucial element in the fight against poverty by creating increased output and government revenues, increased employment and higher wages. Government's social expenditure on education, health and welfare etc. also helps in reducing poverty, but even a well-meaning and pro-poor government can increase social expenditure only with the help of increased tax revenue generated by the high growth rates. Thus, in the final analysis, growth should be the paramount concern of the governments. India's experience of last 5 years under the Congress Party led UPA government which focused on populist welfare measures leading to high inflation and slowing growth followed by a disastrous election loss is a lesson that other governments will do well to learn.

Another insight that emerges from our analysis is that given that raising per capita income (or output) is the most crucial factor in reducing poverty, controlling population growth also has a significant role to play in the fight against poverty, at least in a surplus labour economy like India where the marginal contribution of labour to output in close to zero. The government should, therefore, actively promote smaller family norms and try to move towards a zero population growth target for the country at the earliest. Thus, near abandonment of promoting smaller family norms by the government over the last decade is highly regrettable and needs to be changed.

## REFERENCES

Aghion, P., E. Caroli, and C. Garcia-Penalosa. 1999. 'Inequality and Economic Growth: The Perspective of the New Growth Theories'. CEPREMAP Discussion Paper: 9908, June 87.

Barro, R. J. 1996. 'Determinants of Economic Growth: A Cross-country Empirical Study', WP No. w5698, *National Bureau of Economic Research*.

Benabou, R. 1996. 'Inequality and Growth'. CEPR Discussion Papers: 1450.

Becker, G. 1978. 'The Effects of the State on Family'. Centre for Study of Economy and State, University of Chicago.

———1995. 'Human Capital and Economic Growth', Prague-Economic Papers, September 1995 4(3): 223–28.

Besley, T. and R. Burgess. 2000. 'Land Reform, Poverty Reduction, and Growth: Evidence from India'. *The Quarterly Journal of Economics*, 115(2), 389–430.

Bhagwati, J. 2001. 'Growth, Poverty and Reforms'. *Economic and Political Weekly*, 11 March, Mumbai.

Bhargava, A. 2001. 'Nutrition, Health, and Economic Development: Some Policy Priorities'. *Food & Nutrition Bulletin*, 22(2): 173–77.

Binswanger, H.-P., and R.S. Khandker. 1995. 'The Impact of Formal Finance on the Rural Economy of India'. *Journal of Development Studies*, 32(2): 234–62.

Datt, G., and M. Ravallion. 1998. 'Farm Productivity and Rural Poverty in India'. *The Journal of Development Studies*, 34(4): 62–85.

Datt, G., and M. Ravallion. 2002. 'Is India's Economic Growth Living the Poor Behind'. Mimeo, Washington DC: World Bank.

Deaton, A., and J. Dreze. 2001. 'Poverty and Inequality in India: A Reexamination'. *Economic and Political Weekly*, 7 September, Mumbai, 3729–48.

——— 2002. 'Poverty and Inequality in India: A Re-examination'. *Economic and Political Weekly*, 3729–48.

Dollar, D., and A. Kraay. 2002. 'Growth is Good for the Poor'. *The Journal of Economic Growth* 7(3): 195–205.

Dreze, J., and A. Sen. 1995. *India: Economic Development and Social Opportunity*. New Delhi: Oxford University Press.

Johansen, S., and K. Juselius. 1990. 'Maximum Likelihood Estimation and Inference on Cointegration—with Applications to the Demand for Money'. *Oxford Bulletin of Economics and Statistics*, 52(2): 169–210.

Kraay, A. 2004. 'When is Growth Pro-poor?' *Cross-country evidence*. International Monetary Fund.

Myrdal, G. 1968. *Asian Drama: An Inquiry into the Poverty of Nations*. New York: Pantheon.

Patnaik, P. 2008. 'The Accumulation Process in the Period of Globalisation'. *Economic and Political Weekly*, 108–13.

Pesaran, M., and Y. Shin. 1999. *An Autoregressive Distributed Lag Modeling Approach to Cointegration Analysis'* in S. Strom, ed. *Econometrics and Economic Theory in the 20th*

Pesaran, M.H., Y. Shin, and R.J. Smith. 2001. 'Bounds Testing Approaches to the Analysis of Level Relationships'. *Journal of Applied Econometrics*, 16(3): 289–326.

Ravallion, M., and G. Datt. 1996. 'India's Checkered History in Fight Against Poverty: Are There Lessons for the Future?' *Economic and Political Weekly*, September 2479–85.

Ravallion, M., and G. Datt. 1996. 'How Important to India's Poor is the Sectoral Composition of Economic Growth?' *World-Bank-Economic-Review* 10(1): 1–25.

Schultz, T. P. 1993. 'Returns to Women's Education'. In *Women's Education in Developing Countries: Barriers, Benefits, and Policies*, edited by Elizabeth M. King and Anne M. Hill. Baltimore and London: Johns Hopkins University Press for the World Bank, 51–99.

Sen,-A. 1996. *Consumption Externalities and the Financing of Social Services: Comment.* In *Individual and social responsibility: Child care, education, medical care, and long-term care in America,* edited by Fuchs, Victor R. National Bureau of Economic

Research Conference Report series. Chicago and London: University of Chicago Press 190–94

Sen, A., and Himanshu. 2004. 'Poverty and Inequality in India: II: Widening Disparities during the 1990s'. *Economic and Political Weekly*, 4361–75.

Sundaram, K., and S.D. Tendulkar. 2003. 'Poverty in India in the 1990s: An Analysis of Changes in 15 Major States'. *Economic and Political Weekly*, 1385–93.

Tendulkar, S.D. 1998. *'Indian Economic Policy Reforms and Poverty: An Assessment'*. In Ahluwalia, Isher Judge. *India's Economic Reforms and Development: Essays for Manmohan Singh*, edited by Little, I. M. D. Delhi, Oxford and New York: Oxford University Press 280–309.

World Bank. 1993. *The East Asian Miracle*. Washington DC: Oxford Press for the World Bank.

World Bank. 1997. *India, Achievements and Challenges in Reducing Poverty*. Washington DC.

# APPENDIX

## A.1 Poverty measurement issues

Measurement of poverty and inequality are based on the distribution of household's expenditure from various Consumer Expenditure Surveys by National Sample Survey Organization (NSSO) and base poverty line. The poverty line specified by the Indian Government has been fixed at monthly per capita expenditure (MPCE) of ₹ 49 for rural areas and ₹ 57 for urban areas in 1973–74 prices. These lines meet the recommended per capita daily intake of 2400 calories for rural areas and 2100 calories for urban areas as per observed NSSO consumption pattern for 1973–74.

Ravalion and Datt (1998) of the World Bank have estimated poverty in India using data from various NSSO rounds for the period 1951 to 1997. In this study, we have updated these estimations up to the latest NSSO survey of 2009–10 following the World bank methodology using the POVCAL software of the World Bank. The updating of the poverty line is carried out using adjusted consumer price index for agricultural laborers for rural poverty line and for industrial workers for urban poverty line with appropriate weights that reflect consumption pattern of people around the poverty line. Three alternative measures of poverty can be calculated : (a) the head count ratio (HCR) which measures the percentage of population which is below the poverty line, (b) poverty gap (PG) which measures how far below the poverty line is the average expenditure of the poor in the country and square of the poverty gap (SPG) or poverty severity index which gives more weight for the poorest and thus can be used to examine how the poorest of the poor are doing over time or across districts, states, etc.

The exact formulas for these (Foster-Greer-Thorbeke) measures can be expressed as:

$$P_k = \frac{1}{n}\sum_{i=1}^{q}\left(z - yi / z\right)^k$$

where z is the poverty line, $y_i$ is the income of various individuals below the poverty line (income gap $z - y_i$ is taken as zero for those above the poverty line), q is the total number of people below the poverty line, n is the total population and k takes the values 0 1 and 2. The measure $P_k$ reduces to the head count ratio (q/n) when k = 0, to the poverty gap when k = 1 and to the poverty severity index when k = 2.

Official estimates of the extent of poverty, i.e., the head count ratio below the official poverty line, have been the subject of much debate. One commonly cited recent problem relates to the comparability of consumption expenditure estimates over time, especially given the problems with the 1999–2000 survey. The NSSO used a 30-day recall period for expenditure information from its inception in the early 1950s until 1993–94. In 1999–2000 (55th round) survey NSSO collected consumption data on food items using two different recall periods of 7 days and 30 days from the same households. Critics pointed out that the respondents in the survey overestimated food consumption due to the mix-up of the recall periods. Alternative estimates made by Deaton and Dreze (2002) and Sundaram and Tendulkar (2003) show that poverty reduced during 1990s but by a lower extent of 5–7 per cent points than 10 per cent points by official estimates. Sen and Himanshu (2004) make a critical and comprehensive examination of the comparability of the 55th round data with various adjustment procedures and argue that comparable reduction in HCR was lower by about 3 percentage points at the most, they also do not rule out possibility of no reduction.

However, concerns have also been expressed with the determination of the poverty line itself (Patnaik 2005, 2008). The line and method of estimation, determined in 1973, by Lakadwala Committee, has been extended for subsequent years based on the consumer price indices for agricultural labourers in rural areas and for industrial workers in urban areas. Several criticisms can be directed against such a method: that it does not take into account the changing consumption basket of explicit and implicit necessities, including health care costs and energy costs; and therefore the weights assigned to these commodities, that it no longer bears any relation to actual calorie intake, which was the basis for deriving the original line; that it does not even always ensure that households at or above the poverty line can purchase sufficient food to meet the calorie requirements at prevailing prices.

Since the 1973–74 poverty lines were adjusted over time to reflect inflation using different inflation indices, they moved indifferent ways because of different rates of measured inflation in urban and rural areas. For 2004–05, the rural poverty lines appeared much lower than the urban poverty lines. While the All-India rural poverty line was 87 per cent of the All-India urban poverty line in 1973–74, it had come to be only 66 per cent in 2004–05 using the present (Lakdawala) methodology.

In a GoI report published in November 2009, the Tendulkar Committee used a new methodology to show that the actual ratio in 2004–05 was around 76 per cent, and recommended that the rural poverty line should be recomputed to reflect the money value in rural areas of the same basket of consumption associated with the existing urban poverty ratio. Using this methodology, rural poverty is significantly higher than by the Lakdawala methodology (followed in the World Bank calculations and our extension of the same to 2009–10). Given that the official measures of poverty based on the Tendulkar committee methodology is available only for 2009–10, we have used the Lakdawala methodology throughout the 1951–2009 period to get comparable series over the years. Further, it is worth noting that both measures give essentially the same trend in poverty changes. Hence, the difference is not important in understanding the various factors determining poverty reduction.

## A.2 The econometric estimation procedure (ARDL)

In this study, we estimate the drivers of incidence of poverty using the long run equation derived from ARDL co-integration procedure proposed by Pesaran et al. (2001). The ARDL model is valid for non-stationary variables as well as for a mixture of I(0) and I(1) variables. Further, we have a small sample size of about 40 annual observations, which is not sufficient for a Johansson and Juselius (1990)–type vector error correction procedure. Thus, the ARDL estimation procedure is appropriate in our case for determining the long-run relation for HCR, Gini, MPCE and social expenditure.

The augmented ARDL model can be written as follows:

$$\alpha(L)y_t = \mu_0 + \sum_{i=1}^{k} \beta_i(L)x_{it} + u_t \tag{1}$$

where $\alpha(L) = \alpha_0 + \alpha_1 L + \alpha_2 L^2 + ... + \alpha_t L^t$; $\beta(L) = \beta_0 + \beta_1 L + \beta_2 L^2 + ....$ $+ \beta_t L^t$; $\mu_0$ is a constant; is the dependent variable; $L$ is the lag operator such that $L^i x_t = x_{t-i}$. In the long-run equilibrium $y_t = y_{t-1} = y_{t-2} = ... y_0$ and $x_{it} = x_{it-1} = x_{it-2} = ... x_{i0}$.

Solving for y, we get the following long-run relation:

$$y = \alpha + \sum b_i x_i + \gamma_t \tag{2}$$

where $\quad a = \dfrac{\mu_0}{\alpha_0 + \alpha_1 + \ldots \alpha_t}$ ; $b_i = \dfrac{\beta_{i0} + \beta_{i1} + \beta_{i2} + \ldots \beta_{it}}{\alpha_0 + \alpha_1 + \alpha_2 + \ldots \alpha_t}$ and

$$\gamma_t = \dfrac{u_t}{\alpha_0 + \alpha_1 + \alpha_2 + \ldots \alpha_n}$$

In this procedure, the existence of the long-run relationship is confirmed with the help of an F-test that tests if the coefficients of all explanatory variables are jointly different from zero. Pesaran and Shin (1999) have provided upper and lower critical bound values for an F-test when all or some of the variables are I(1).

The error correction (EC) representation of the ARDL method can be written as follows:

$$\Delta y_t = \Delta \breve{\alpha}_0 - \sum_{j=2}^{p} \breve{\alpha}_j \, \Delta y_{t-j} + \sum_{i=1}^{k} \breve{\beta}_{i0} \Delta x_{it} -$$

$$- \sum_{i=1}^{k} \sum_{j=2}^{q} \beta_{i,t-j} \Delta x_{i,t-j} - \alpha \left( 1, p \right) ECM_{t-1} + \mu_t \tag{3}$$

where $ECM_t = y_t - \breve{\alpha} - \displaystyle\sum_{i=1}^{k} \breve{\beta}_{i0} \Delta x_{it}$ ; $\Delta$ is the first difference operator; $\alpha_j, _{t-j}$

and $\beta_{ij}, _{t-j}$ are the coefficients estimated from Eq. 1; and $\alpha(1, p)$ measures the

speed of adjustment.

# Section 2
# Reviving growth of industry and exports

# 3

# Sustaining a High Rate of Industrial Growth in India in the Next 10 Years

Bishwanath Goldar

## INTRODUCTION

India's new *National Manufacturing Policy* (announced in 2011) aims at raising the share of manufacturing in aggregate Gross Domestic Product (GDP ) from about 15 per cent at present to about 25 per cent by 2022 (or thereabout), and creating in that process an additional 100 million jobs.[1] Achievement of this goal requires the real output of India's manufacturing to grow at the average rate of about 15 per cent per annum in the next 10 years if one assumes that the aggregate GDP will grow at the rate of 10 per cent per annum in that period. The required growth rate in real output of India's manufacturing is about 13 per cent per year if the growth rate in aggregate GDP in the next 10 years is taken to be lower at about 8 per cent per annum.[2] During the period 1999–2000 to 2011–12, the trend growth rate

---

[1]  It is somewhat unclear when the targets of raising manufacturing share in GDP to 25 per cent and creating 100 million additional jobs are to be achieved. A document available in the website of the Press Information Bureau dated November 2011 mentions that these targets are to be achieved within a decade. A recent document placed in the website of the DIPP (Department of Industrial Policy and Promotion, Ministry of Commerce and Industry, Government of India) dated March 2013 (*National Manufacturing Policy: Guidelines for establishment of National Investment & Manufacturing Zones*) mentions that these targets are to be achieved within a decade. Taking the target date as 2022 or thereabout, therefore, seems appropriate.

[2]  The target growth rate for manufacturing in the Twelfth Five Year Plan is 9.8 to 11.5 per cent per annum (corresponding to the overall growth target of 9 or 9.5 per cent per annum). The medium term growth target for manufacturing is 12 to 14 per cent per annum. Going by (a) the growth targets of the Twelfth Five Year Plan, (b) the growth rate of the economy achieved in 2012–13 (4.5 per cent) and (c) the advanced estimates of growth rate of the economy in 2013–14 (4.9 per cent), a growth projection of aggregate GDP in the range of 8 to 10 per cent per year in the next decade appeared reasonable at the time of writing this chapter. The situation has changed now - GDP growth rate might be lower.

in aggregate GDP was 7.7 per cent per annum and that in manufacturing GDP was slightly higher at 8.3 per cent per year. According to first revised estimates of national income released by the Central Statistical Office (CSO) (Press note dated 31 January 2014) and advanced estimates of national income released by the CSO (press note 7 February 2012), the growth rate in real GDP in manufacturing in 2012–13 over the previous year was 1.1 per cent, and that in 2013–14 is expected to be −0.2 per cent. Thus, the average growth rate in manufacturing GDP during the period 1999–2000 to 2012–13 was less than 8 per cent per year, which holds true also for the period 1999–2000 to 2013–14. Evidently, a huge increase in the growth rate in manufacturing real output (by 5 per cent or more) would be required if the target of enhancing the share of manufacturing in aggregate GDP to 25 per cent within a decade is to be achieved. Is such an increase in the growth rate of manufacturing real GDP possible and sustainable, and if so, what does it entail? This chapter focuses on these questions. In particular, it examines the investment requirements for a high rate of growth of 13 to 15 per cent per annum in output of Indian manufacturing and the required rate of productivity growth. It also looks into the employment implications of such a high rate of growth in Indian manufacturing.

The chapter is organized as follows. The second section is devoted to an analysis of trends in growth in output and employment in manufacturing, segregated into the organized and unorganized manufacturing sectors.[3] The third section presents an analysis of trends in capital stock and investment in manufacturing. An attempt is made to relate investment in manufacturing to the overall investment rate in the economy. The fourth section analyses trends in total factor productivity (TFP) growth in organized and unorganized manufacturing. In addition, it goes into the question, what is the required TFP growth in manufacturing if the average output growth rate in manufacturing has to be stepped up by about 5 per cent in the next 10 years. The fifth section is devoted to a discussion on factors determining TFP growth in Indian manufacturing. It tries to provide some indication of the interventions or policy measures needed to attain a significantly faster growth rate in TFP in manufacturing. The sixth section examines the employment implications of a rapid manufacturing growth. The seventh section is devoted to a brief discussion on policy measures that are required to boost the rate of investment in Indian manufacturing. Finally, the eighth section summarizes and concludes the chapter.

---

[3] Organized manufacturing covers manufacturing units registered as factories under Indian Factories Act, 1948. Such units have 10 or more workers with the use of power or 20 or more workers without the use of power. The rest of the manufacturing units are included in the unorganized sector.

## TRENDS IN OUTPUT AND EMPLOYMENT GROWTH IN MANUFACTURING

### Output growth

Analysis of trends in output growth in organized and unorganized manufacturing is based on data on GDP at 2004–05 prices (real gross value added) reported in the National Accounts Statistics (NAS) (Central Statistical Office, Government of India). The period covered for the analysis is 1975–76 to 2011–12.

Figure 3.1 shows the growth rates in real GDP in total manufacturing and its two components, organized and unorganized manufacturing, in various years from 1976–77 to 2011–12. It is evident that there have been wide year-to-year variations in the growth rate in real GDP in manufacturing. It is seen from the figure that there is considerable similarity in the growth rate of real GDP in organized manufacturing and that at the total manufacturing level. Since the organized sector accounts for a dominant part of manufacturing in terms of output, this is expected. The correlation coefficient between the growth rate in real GDP of organized manufacturing and that of total manufacturing is 0.94. In contrast, the correlation coefficient between the growth rates in real GDP of the organized and unorganized manufacturing sectors is lower at about 0.6.

**Figure 3.1: Growth rates in real GDP in manufacturing**

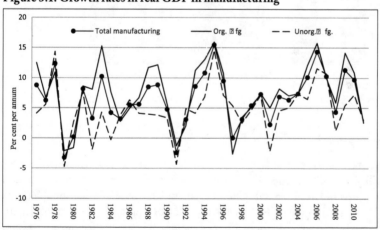

*Source*: Author's computations based on *National Accounts Statistics* (CSO).

The trend growth rate in real GDP in organized manufacturing during the period 1975–76 to 2011–12 was about 7.3 per cent per annum, and that in unorganized manufacturing was about 4.5 per cent per annum. The corresponding figure for total manufacturing is 6.2 per cent per annum. The share of unorganized manufacturing in real GDP of total manufacturing has, therefore, fallen over time. It declined from about 52 per cent in 1975–76 to about 30 per cent in 2011–12.

Considering the growth trends in real GDP in manufacturing, three periods of relatively high growth can be identified: (a) 1976–77 through 1978–79, (b) 1993–94 through 1996–97 and (c) 2004–05 through 2007–08. The average annual growth rates achieved in these three periods were 9.1, 11.1 and 10.5 per cent, respectively (see Figure 3.2). Interestingly, in each of these episodes, the growth rate of the unorganized manufacturing sector was high, over 8 per cent per year as against a trend growth rate of 4.5 per cent per year during the period 1975–76 to 2011–12. It seems, therefore, that if the growth rate of manufacturing has to reach a level of 13 to 15 per cent per annum, the unorganized sector output has to grow at a rate of over 8 per cent per annum.

**Figure 3.2: Growth rates in real GDP in manufacturing**

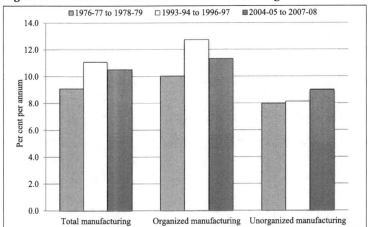

*Source*: Author's computations based on *National Accounts Statistics* (CSO).

### Employment growth

Unlike the real GDP series, an employment series for the manufacturing sector is not readily available. Hence, employment in manufacturing has been estimated from the results of Employment–Unemployment surveys of the National Sample Survey (NSS). Employment data for the major NSS employment–unemployment survey rounds have been used for making employment estimates for those years and then these have been interpolated/ extrapolated to construct an employment series for manufacturing for the period 1975–76 to 2011–12. Availability of employment data is better for the organized manufacturing, since one can use the Annual Survey of Industries (ASI), Central Statistical Office, Government of India. Using this data source, the employment series for organized manufacturing has been formed for the years 1975–76 through 2011–12. Having obtained employment series for total manufacturing and organized manufacturing, an employment series for unorganized manufacturing has been formed by subtracting the estimate for organized manufacturing from the estimate for total manufacturing.[4]

Analysis of the employment series reveals that the trend growth rate in employment in total manufacturing during the period 1975–76 to 2011–12 was 2.3 per cent per annum. Corresponding growth rates for the organized and unorganized manufacturing sectors were 1.7 and 2.4 per cent per annum, respectively. Evidently, the growth rate of employment was significantly lower than that in real value added (real GDP). The gap is particularly marked for organized manufacturing. While the trend growth rate in real GDP in organized manufacturing during 1975–76 to 2011–12 were 7.3 per cent per annum that in employment was only 1.7 per cent per annum. This implies that labour productivity in organized manufacturing grew at the trend rate of over 5 per cent per annum. By contrast, labour productivity in unorganized manufacturing grew at the trend rate of about 2 per cent per annum.

It is interesting to note that employment growth in organized manufacturing in recent years has been much faster than that in the past. The average annual growth rate in employment in organized manufacturing during 1976–77 to 2004–05 was about 1.4 per cent per annum, and much higher at about 6.9 per cent per annum during 2005–06 to 2011–12 (see Figure 3.3).

**Figure 3.3: Growth rate in employment in manufacturing**

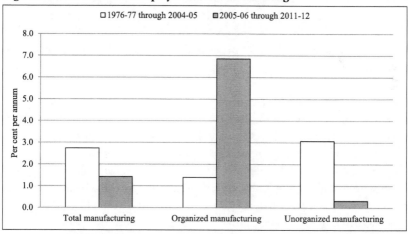

*Source*: Author's computations based on ASI and NSS Employment–Unemployment Survey Results.

---

4   This indirect method of deriving an estimate of employment in unorganized manufacturing suffers from a limitation that the conceptual basis of employment estimate for organized manufacturing (based on ASI) differs from that for aggregate manufacturing (based on NSS employment–unemployment surveys).

While organized manufacturing has experienced marked acceleration in the growth rate of employment after 2004–05, the experience of unorganized manufacturing has been quite different (see Figure 3.3). The growth rate of employment in unorganized manufacturing has decelerated in the period after 2004–05. The average annual growth rate in employment in unorganized manufacturing was about 3.1 per cent per annum during 1976–77 to 2004–05 and it was only 0.3 per cent per annum during 2005–06 to 2011–12. It would be noticed from Table 3.3 that the growth rate in employment in aggregate manufacturing in the period 2005–06 through 2011–12 was substantially lower than that during the period 1976–77 through 2004–05: the fall in the growth rate is by over 1 per cent per annum. The explanation lies in the marked fall that took place in the growth rate in employment in unorganized manufacturing.

The deceleration in the growth rate in employment in unorganized manufacturing in the period after 2004–05 is perhaps exaggerated in the estimates shown in Figure 3.3, which may have been caused by the indirect method applied to make an estimate of employment in unorganized manufacturing. But, there is other evidence to indicate that there was very little growth, if not a decline, in employment in unorganized manufacturing in the recent period. The Reports on the NSS 62nd and 67th round survey results provide estimates of employment for the unorganized manufacturing sector for 2005–06 and 2010–11. A comparison of these estimates reveals that employment in unorganized manufacturing fell from about 36.4 million in 2005–06 to about 34.9 million in 2010–11. The annual rate of fall in employment was about 0.9 per cent. A more detailed examination of NSS 62nd and 67th round survey results reveals that the fall in employment has occurred in own account enterprises and not in establishments.[5] Between 2005–06 and 2010–11, employment in establishments grew at the rate of 1.9 per cent per annum, while employment in own account enterprises fell by 2.5 per cent per annum. This signifies a restructuring taking place in India's unorganized manufacturing, away from own account enterprises and towards establishments that are relatively bigger in size and have relatively higher productivity. This is probably the reason why a trend growth in real GDP in unorganized manufacturing could be maintained at about 6.4 per cent per annum during 2000–01 to 2010–11 even though there was a downward trend, or a sluggish growth, in employment in this period.

Attention may be drawn here to the fact that in the period 1975–76 to 2000–01, labour productivity growth rate in organized manufacturing far exceeded that in unorganized manufacturing. The trend growth rates in labour productivity in the two sectors were 5.5 and 1.3 per cent per annum respectively. In the period

---

[5] Own account enterprises are relatively small in size. These enterprises do not have any hired workers.

after 2000–01, this has reversed. The trend growth rates in labour productivity in organized and unorganized manufacturing in the period 2000–01 to 2011–12 were 4.4 and 4.8 per cent, respectively. Thus, in the recent period, unorganized manufacturing has attained a faster growth rate in labour productivity than organized manufacturing. The hike in the growth rate of labour productivity in unorganized manufacturing in the recent period is probably a result of a structural change that is taking place within unorganized manufacturing, as mentioned above.

The following two points emerge from the discussion above: (a) The trend growth rate in real GDP in organized manufacturing has been much higher than that in unorganized manufacturing. But, it appears that for attainting a sustained growth rate of 13 to 15 per cent per annum in real GDP in aggregate manufacturing in the next 10 years, the growth rate in unorganized manufacturing should be at least 8 per cent per annum. This may not be easy to achieve because the trend growth rate in unorganized manufacturing output was only about 4.5 per cent per year during the period 1975–76 to 2011–12; (b) Growth rate in manufacturing employment has been quite low in low in relation to the growth rate in real GDP. In the period since 2005–06, the growth rate in employment in organized manufacturing has significantly accelerated and that in unorganized manufacturing has significantly decelerated. Since unorganized manufacturing accounts for the dominant part of employment in manufacturing, the marked deceleration in employment growth in unorganized manufacturing has caused the rate of employment growth in aggregate manufacturing to come down substantially.

## TRENDS IN CAPITAL STOCK AND INVESTMENT

During the period 1975–76 to 2011–12, the trend growth rate in Net Fixed Capital Stock (NFCS) in manufacturing was 7.8 per cent per annum, higher than the trend growth rate in real GDP at 6.2 per cent per annum (both capital stock and GDP are at 2004–05 prices, taken from the NAS). The same is true for organized and unorganized manufacturing sectors. In organized manufacturing, the trend growth rate in net fixed capital stock during the period 1975–76 to 2011–12 was 7.7 per cent per annum while the trend growth rate in real GDP was 7.3 per cent per annum. Similarly, in unorganized manufacturing, the trend growth rates in net fixed capital stock and real GDP during the period 1975–76 to 2011–12 were 8.5 and 4.5 per cent per annum, respectively.

In the more recent period, the gap between the growth rates in manufacturing GDP and fixed capital stock in manufacturing was narrow. During the period 2000–01 to 2011–12, the trend growth rates in real GDP in manufacturing was 8.6 per cent per annum, while the growth rate in the value of net fixed capital stock at constant prices was 8.8 per cent per annum. The corresponding figures for organized manufacturing were 9.8 and 9.1 per cent per annum, respectively, and those for unorganized manufacturing were 6.3 and 7.9 per cent per annum, respectively. Thus, in organized manufacturing, GDP growth rate exceeded that in fixed capital stock implying improvement in capital productivity, whereas in unorganized manufacturing, GDP growth rate lagged behind the growth rate in capital stock.

Considering the pattern of growth in GDP and capital stock in manufacturing during the period 2000–01 to 2011–12, it appears that if the growth rate in real GDP in manufacturing has to accelerate to somewhere in the range of 13 to 15 per cent per annum in the next 10 years (from 8.6 per cent during 2000–01 to 2011–12), there should be a similar increase in growth rate of capital stock. In other words, the growth rate in capital stock in manufacturing should increase to 13 per cent per year or higher. However, from the long-term trends in the growth rate of fixed capital stock in manufacturing, it seems that such an increase may not take place. This is depicted in Figure 3.4 which shows the growth rate in real net fixed capital stock in manufacturing for the period 1976–77 to 2011–12. Taking the time series on capital stock growth rates for the period 1990–91 to 2011–12 and extending it forward based on a linear trend, it is found that the rate of growth in capital stock would remain below 9.5 per cent in the period 2011–12 to 2022–23. Clearly, for the growth rate in capital stock to reach above 13 per cent per year, it has to deviate significantly from the past trend.

**Figure 3.4: Growth rate in fixed capital stock in manufacturing and the investment rate in the economy, 1976–77 to 2011–12**

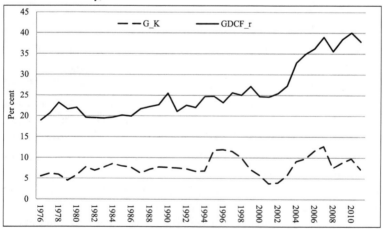

*Note*: G_K = growth rate in net fixed capital stock in manufacturing; GDCF_r = the gross domestic capital formation rate of the economy.

*Source*: Author's computations based on *National Accounts Statistics* (CSO).

Figure 3.4 also shows, for the period 1976–77 to 2011–12, the gross domestic capital formation (GDCF) rate in the economy. It is evident that there was an upward trend in the investment (GDCF) rate in the economy, particularly from the early 2000s. In contrast, there is no clear upward trend in the growth rate of fixed capital stock in manufacturing. Yet, there are indications that, in certain periods, hikes in the overall investment rate in the economy have been associated with similar hikes in the growth rate of fixed capital stock in manufacturing. Between 2002–03 and 2011–12, for instance, the investment (GDCF) rate in the economy went up from 24 per cent to 38 per cent. Between these 2 years, the growth rate in fixed capital stock in manufacturing increased substantially from 3.9 to 7.2 per cent per annum. This is suggestive of a positive relationship between the investment rate in the economy and the growth rate in fixed capital stock in manufacturing. A similar positive relationship seems to be prevailing between the investment rate of the economy and the investment rate in manufacturing (measured by the ratio of gross fixed investment to gross value added, both at 2004–05 prices). This is depicted in Figure 3.5.

**Figure 3.5: Rate of investment in manufacturing and in the economy**

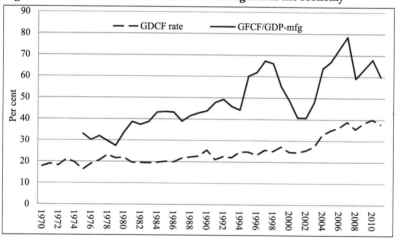

*Note*: GFCF/GDP-mfg = ratio of gross fixed capital formation to GDP in manufacturing; GDCF rate = the gross domestic capital formation rate of the economy.

*Source*: Author's computations based on *National Accounts Statistics* (CSO).

To investigate the impact of the overall investment rate of the economy on the investment rate in manufacturing, a regression analysis has been undertaken. The fixed investment rate (ratio of gross fixed capital formation to GDP) in manufacturing is taken as the dependent variable. The overall investment (GDCF) rate in the economy is taken as the explanatory variable. The Dickey-Fuller and

Augmented Dickey-Fuller tests have been applied to examine the properties of the time series. The test results indicate that the series on the overall investment rate in the economy and the ratio of fixed capital formation to GDP in manufacturing are both integrated of order one. The test results are shown in Annexure A. The econometric model has been estimated by taking the two abovementioned variables in first difference form and adding the lagged value of the dependent variable as an additional regressor. The regression results are reported in Table 3.1.

Table 3.1: Regression results, explaining increase in fixed capital stock in manufacturing

| Explanatory variable | Estimated coefficients: Dependent variable: ΔInvestment rate in manufacturing (Fixed investment/GDP) |
|---|---|
| ΔGross domestic capital formation rate in the economy | 1.227 (2.49) [P = 0.018] |
| Lagged value of dependent variable (Investment rate in manufacturing, Fixed investment/GDP) | −0.119 (1.52) [P = 0.122] |
| Constant | 5.789 (1.52) [P = 0.137] |
| R-squared | 0.22 |
| DW statistic | 1.75 |
| Period | 1976–77 to 2011–12 |

*Note*: Figures in parentheses are t-ratio. Probability is shown in square brackets.

*Source*: Author's computations based on data taken from the *National Accounts Statistics* (CSO).

The estimated regression equation indicates that the investment rate in the economy has a significant positive impact on the investment rate in manufacturing. This probably means that as the rate of savings increases in the economy and more investible resources become available, greater amount of investment will be done in various sectors of the economy including manufacturing.

There has been a significant upward trend in the investment rate in the economy in the period since the early 2000s (see Figures 3.4 and 3.5), and this might continue in the near future. Thus, as the overall investment rate in the economy goes up further, the rate of investment in manufacturing will increase, and accordingly there should be a hike in the growth rate in capital input in manufacturing. However, the crucial question is whether the increase in the growth rate of capital input in manufacturing that is likely to take place in the coming years will be sufficient to accelerate the growth rate of manufacturing

GDP by 5 per cent or so, which is the hike in growth rate required to ensure that manufacturing GDP reaches 25 per cent of aggregate GDP in a decade. This seems quite unlikely. It would be noticed from Table 3.1 that the coefficient of GDCF rate is 1.23 and the coefficient of the lagged dependent variable is −0.12, which is statistically insignificant. If the lagged dependent variable is dropped from the equation, the coefficient of GDCF rate increases to 1.27. It may be inferred, therefore, that even if the overall investment rate goes up by 10 per cent (so that it reaches about 50 per cent), the investment rate in manufacturing will increase by about 12 to 13 per cent, which will in turn cause the growth rate of capital stock in manufacturing to go up only by 2 per cent or thereabout (since the ratio of net fixed capital stock to GDP in manufacturing is in the range of 5:1 to 6:1). This is not sufficient to raise the growth rate of real GDP in manufacturing by 5 per cent. One implication of this finding is that the productivity growth rate needs to go up substantially, if the growth rate of output of Indian manufacturing has to be hiked by 5 per cent. An analysis of productivity growth, therefore, becomes very important. This is taken up in the next section.

## TREND IN TOTAL FACTOR PRODUCTIVITY GROWTH

### *Aggregate level analysis*

The computation of TFP growth has been done by using a two-input framework (gross value added taken as the output, and labour and capital taken as the two inputs) and applying the Translog index of TFP.[6] TFP growth rates for different years have been computed for organized and unorganized manufacturing sectors and also for total manufacturing. Real GDP at 2004–05 prices (obtained from the NAS) is taken as the measure of output. Net fixed capital stock at 2004–05 prices (obtained from the NAS) has been taken as the measure of capital input. Number of persons employed is taken as the measure of labour input. The source of employment data and the methodology applied to construct a time series have been explained in the previous section. The computation of the Translog index of TFP also needs the labour income share in gross value added. This has been computed from the data on factor incomes given in the NAS.[7]

---

[6]  The Translog index of total factor productivity is described in Christensen, Cummings and Jorgenson (1980), among others.

[7]  One problem encountered in computing labour income share in gross value added in unorganized manufacturing is that in the NAS data the income of the self-employed persons has not been split into labour income and capital income components. Rather, in the NAS, this is shown as mixed income. It has been assumed here that 60 per cent of mixed income

Table 3.2 shows average annual growth rates in TFP in organized manufacturing, unorganized manufacturing and total manufacturing for the periods 1975–76 to 1999–2000 and 1999–2000 to 2011–12, and for the entire period 1975–76 to 2011–12.[8] It also shows decomposition of output growth into the contributions of labour input, capital input and TFP. This is shown separately for organized manufacturing, unorganized manufacturing and total manufacturing for different sub-periods.

Table 3.2: Sources of output growth, Indian manufacturing, by sub-periods

| Sector/period | Contribution of capital input growth to output growth | Contribution of labour input growth to output growth | TFP Growth | Real gross value added growth |
|---|---|---|---|---|
| **Organized manufacturing** | | | | |
| 1975–76 to 1999–2000 | 4.65 | 0.54 | 1.43 | 6.62 |
| 1999–2000 to 2011–12 | 5.98 | 0.90 | 1.57 | 8.45 |
| 1975–76 to 2011–12 | 5.09 | 0.66 | 1.48 | 7.23 |
| **Unorganized manufacturing** | | | | |
| 1975–76 to 1999–2000 | 2.99 | 1.60 | −0.48 | 4.11 |
| 1999–2000 to 2011–12 | 2.67 | 1.56 | 1.18 | 5.41 |
| 1975–76 to 2011–12 | 2.88 | 1.58 | 0.08 | 4.54 |
| **Total manufacturing** | | | | |
| 1975–76 to 1999–2000 | 4.00 | 1.06 | 0.53 | 5.59 |

*Table 3.2 Continued*

is labour income and the remaining 40 per cent is capital income. The figure of 60 per cent used for splitting mixed income has been chosen on the following consideration. According to NSS survey results for unorganized manufacturing for 2000–01, 2005–06 and 2010–11, the ratio of wage rate of hired workers to gross value added per worker in establishments was about 0.6, which may be treated as labour income share in establishments. When 60 per cent of mixed income is treated as labour income, the share labour income in gross value added computed for the unorganized manufacturing tallies with the computed labour income share for establishments obtained from the NSS survey results for unorganized manufacturing.

[8] The rationale for the periodization is as follows. A comparison is made between the long term growth rate and the growth rate achieved in the recent past. The estimate for the period 1975 to 1999 provides the long term growth rate over a 25 year period, and the estimate for the period 1999 to 2011 provides the growth rate achieved in the recent past. The year 1999–2000 is taken as the cut-off because it was a normal year, one used by the CSO as a benchmark year for the *National Accounts Statistics*.

*Table 3.2 Continued*

| | | | | |
|---|---|---|---|---|
| 1999–2000 to 2011–12 | 4.89 | 1.07 | 1.44 | 7.40 |
| 1975–76 to 2011–12 | 4.30 | 1.07 | 0.82 | 6.19 |

*Source*: Author's computations based on data taken from NAS, ASI and NSS Employment–Unemployment Surveys.

It is observed from Table 3.2 that the rate of TFP growth in Indian manufacturing in the period 1999–2000 to 2011–12 was higher than that in the period 1975–76 to 1999–2000. This hike is mostly contributed by improved TFP growth performance in the unorganized sector. The growth rate in TFP in unorganized manufacturing was –0.48 per cent per annum during 1975–76 to 1999–2000, which rose to 1.18 per cent per annum during 1999–2000 to 2011–12. This is probably a consequence of the restructuring within the unorganized manufacturing sector (previously mentioned) that has taken place in the 2000s.

Capital accumulation is the dominant source of output growth in Indian manufacturing at the aggregate level. Growth in capital inputs accounted for more than two-thirds of the output growth during 1975–76 to 2011–12. This is true also for the sub-periods, 1975–76 to 1999–2000 and 1999–2000 to 2011–12.

In organized manufacturing, the acceleration in the growth rate of output in the period 1999–2000 to 2011–12 in comparison with the period 1975–76 to 1999–2000 is mostly attributable to increased contribution of capital accumulation. But, this is not true for the unorganized manufacturing sector. In this case, the acceleration in output growth in the period 1999–2000 to 2011–12 as compared to the period 1975–76 to 1999–2000 is entirely attributable to improvement in the rate of TFP growth; capital accumulation does not explain the observed hike in the rate of output growth.

The rate of TFP growth in organized manufacturing in the period 1999–2000 to 2011–12 has been only marginally higher than that in the period 1975–76 to 1999–2000 (1.57 per cent per annum as against 1.43 per cent per annum). The latter period includes a phase of rapid industrial growth: the years 2004–05 through 2007–08 during which the average growth rate of output was over 11 per cent per annum. A close examination of the data reveals that the average annual growth rate in TFP in organized manufacturing during the period 1999–2000 to 2007–08 was 2.5 per cent as against the growth rate of 1.4 per cent per year during 1975–76 to 1999–2000.

To provide further insight into the inter-temporal changes in the rates of TFP growth, average annual growth rate in TFP has been computed for the periods: 1975–76 to 1993–94, 1993–94 to 2004–05 and 2004–05 to 2011–12. The computed growth rates are shown in Table 3.3. Trend growth rates in TFP obtained by fitting an exponential trend equation are shown in the table for comparison.

**Table 3.3: Average annual growth rates in TFP, Indian manufacturing, by sub-periods**

| Period | Organized manufacturing | Unorganized manufacturing | Total manufacturing |
|---|---|---|---|
| 1975–76 to 1993–94 | 1.9 (2.1) | –1.5 (–2.0) | 0.4 (0.2) |
| 1993–94 to 2004–05 | 1.5 (0.7) | 0.3 (–0.7) | 0.7 (–0.4) |
| 2004–05 to 2011–12 | 0.3 (0.3) | 3.8 (3.6) | 2.1 (1.9) |
| 1975–76 to 2011–12 | 1.5 (1.5) | 0.1 (0.0) | 0.8 (0.7) |

*Source*: Author's computations based on data taken from NAS, ASI and NSS Employment–Unemployment Surveys. Figures in parentheses are the trend growth rates obtained by fitting an exponential trend equation.

It is interesting to observe from Table 3.3 that the rate of TFP growth in aggregate manufacturing in the period 2004–05 to 2011–12 was significantly higher than that during 1975–76 to 1993–94 as well as that during 1993–94 to 2004–05. The growth rate in TFP in organized manufacturing came down between the first (1975–76 to 1993–94) and the second (1993–94 to 2004–05) period, and fell further in the third period (2004–05 to 2011–12). The opposite pattern was there for unorganized manufacturing. The rate of TFP improved in the second period compared to the first, and improved further in the third period. Indeed, the growth in TFP in Indian manufacturing at the aggregate level during the period 2004–05 to 2011–12 is mostly attributable to the productivity advance that took place in unorganized manufacturing.

The explanation for the excellent productivity growth performance of India's unorganized manufacturing in the period since 2004–05 requires detailed investigation, which is not attempted in this chapter. However, it appears that it may have a lot to do with the structural changes that have taken in unorganized manufacturing in the recent period.

### *Industry-level analysis*

Industry-level analysis of TFP growth has been undertaken for the organized manufacturing sector. This is done at two-digit industries level.[9] The period considered is 1980–81 to 2007–08. Time series on real gross value added,[10] net

---

[9]  The two-digit industry groups included in the study are NIC 15 to 36 which constitute manufacturing. While ASI data for more recent years have become available, the analysis is confined to the period up to 2007–08 because the industrial classification in ASI has undergone a major change from 2008–09 making it difficult to construct comparable time-series data at disaggregate level beyond 2007–08.

[10]  For each two-digit industry, the best available price index has been taken from the official wholesale price indices series as the deflator or the output price index.

fixed capital stock at constant prices,[11] number of employees and wage share in value added have been constructed from the ASI.

Table 3.4 shows the trend growth rates in TFP in various two-digit industries during the periods 1980–81 to 1999–2000 and 1999–2000 to 2007–08. The trend growth rates have been estimated by the kinked-exponential model, which makes it possible to test whether the TFP growth rates in the two periods are significantly different from each other. The difference in the trend growth rates between the two periods and whether the difference is statistically significant is shown in the last column of the table.

**Table 3.4: Growth rate in TFP in organized manufacturing industries, two-digit**

| NIC code | Trend growth rates, two periods | | |
|---|---|---|---|
| | 1980–81 to 1999–2000 | 1999–2000 to 2007–08 | Difference in growth rate |
| 15 | 2.7 | –0.7 | –3.4 |
| 16 | 1.6 | –2.3 | –3.9 |
| 17 | 2.4 | 2.2 | –0.2 |
| 18 | 2.4 | –8.7 | –11.1* |
| 19 | 0.8 | 0.8 | 0.0 |
| 20 | –3.5 | 2.1 | 5.6 |
| 21 | 0.8 | 4.3 | 3.5 |
| 22 | –1.0 | –0.6 | 0.4 |
| 23 | 1.6 | –0.1 | –1.7 |
| 24 | 3.8 | –0.4 | –4.2* |
| 25 | 2.2 | 1.6 | –0.6 |
| 26 | 1.2 | 5.1 | 3.9* |
| 27 | 2.2 | 6.3 | 4.1* |
| 28 | 1.6 | 6.4 | 4.8* |

*Table 3.4 Continued*

---

[11] Net fixed capital stock at constant prices is taken as the measure of capital input. This series has been formed by the perpetual inventory method for the period 1973–74 to 2007–08. The net fixed capital stock (at 1999–2000 prices) in registered manufacturing reported in the NAS for March 1974 has been used to make the benchmark estimates of net fixed capital stock in each of the two-digit industries. The NAS estimate has been distributed among two-digit industries in proportion to the book value of fixed capital in these industries in 1973–74 reported in ASI. To the benchmark estimate (for 1973–74), gross investment (computed from ASI data) at 1999–2000 prices has been added and adjustment has been made for depreciation to yield the net fixed capital stock series. The rate of depreciation has been taken as 5 per cent.

*Table 3.4 Continued*

| | | | |
|---|---|---|---|
| 29 | 1.6 | 3.8 | 2.2 |
| 30 | 6.7 | 4.0 | −2.7 |
| 31 | 3.3 | 6.1 | 2.8 |
| 32 | 6.4 | 7.5 | 1.1 |
| 33 | 3.1 | 11.2 | 8.1* |
| 34 | 1.3 | 6.1 | 4.8* |
| 35 | 4.8 | 9.3 | 4.5* |
| 36 | 7.0 | −4.9 | −11.9 |
| All manufacturing industries | 2.4 | 3.8 | 1.4 |

*Note*: Trend growth rates for sub-periods have been estimated by the kinked exponential model (Boyce, 1986)

* Statistically significant at 5 per cent level.

*Source*: Author's computations based on data taken from ASI

Industry codes and description

15 Manufacture of Food Products and Beverages

16 Manufacture of Tobacco Products

17 Manufacture of Textiles

18 Manufacture of Wearing Apparel Dressing and Dyeing of Fur

19 Tanning and Dressing of Leather Manufacture of Luggage, Handbags, Saddlery, Harness and Footwear

20 Manufacture of Wood and Products of Wood and Cork, Except Furniture, Manufacture of Articles of Straw and Plating Materials

21 Manufacture of Paper and Paper Products

22 Publishing, Printing and Reproduction of Recorded Media

23 Manufacture of Coke, Refined Petroleum Products and Nuclear Fuel

24 Manufacture of Chemicals and Products

25 Manufacture of Rubber and Plastic Products

26 Manufacture of Other Non-Metallic Mineral Products

27 Manufacture of Basic Metals

28 Manufacture of Fabricated Metal Products, Except Machinery and Equipment

29 Manufacture of Machinery and Equipment N.E.C

30 Manufacture of Office, Accounting and Computing Machinery

31 Manufacture of Electrical Machinery and Apparatus N.E.C.

32 Manufacture of Radio, Television and Communication Equipment and Apparatus

33 Manufacture of Medical, Precision and Optical Instruments, Watches and Clocks

34 Manufacture of Motor Vehicles, Trailers and Semi-Trailers

35 Manufacture of Other Transport Equipment

36 Manufacture of Furniture; Manufacturing N.E.C.

For aggregate manufacturing, the estimated TFP growth rate is 2.4 per cent per annum for the period 1980–81 to 1999–2000, and 3.8 per cent per annum for the period 1999–2000 to 2007–08. These growth rates are higher than the TFP growth rates for organized manufacturing shown in Table 3.2 above. The gap is a little over 1 per cent. A closer examination of the data reveals that the growth rates in net fixed capital stock computed from the ASI data do not tally with those for organized manufacturing obtained from the NAS. The estimate of fixed capital formation in organized manufacturing given in the NAS is much higher than the estimate of fixed capital formation in organized manufacturing obtained from the ASI. No attempt is made here to reconcile the two estimates. But, it is important to draw attention to this gap because it explains the discrepancy in the estimates of TFP growth presented in Tables 3.2 and 3.4.

It may be mentioned in this context that Hashim et al. (2009) and Virmani and Hashim (2011) have found a much higher growth rate in TFP in organized manufacturing in the period 2002–03 to 2007–08 as compared to the periods 1992–93 to 1997–98 and 1998–99 to 2001–02, which is consistent with the estimates presented in Table 3.4.[12] They called attention to a possible 'J curve of liberalization and productivity' and find support for their hypothesis in their estimates of TFP growth for organized manufacturing. According to them, the structural transformation arising from a large trade reform would cause a slowdown in productivity growth initially, which will pick up later. This, in their opinion, is largely explained by two factors: (a) obsolescence of product lines and capital used to produce it which would still be a part of measured capital and (b) the gradual adoption and spread of new technology and the diversion of human resource for learning.[13] The acceleration in TFP growth in organized manufacturing since 2002 is, therefore, attributable to delayed effects of economic reforms.

---

[12] A similar pattern is observed by Goldar (2014) who has found a significant increase in the growth rate in TFP in India's organized manufacturing in the period 2001–02 to 2007–08 (3.1 per cent per annum) as compared to the period 1995–96 to 2001–02 (–0.6 per cent per annum).

[13] This argument is similar to the basic argument underlying a growing body of literature on innovation led growth and transitional dynamics. A paradigm shift in technology causes information asymmetry among new and existing firms due to transitional phase of the economy. The existing firms are compelled to spend on research and development, and assimilation of the new technology before actual gains are realized. The assets created by this process are intangible as they do not contribute to the conventionally measured output. This tends to lower productivity which increases later. Seen against this background, economic reforms may be equated to a technology paradigm shift since it vastly increases access to new technology by liberalizing imports of intermediate goods, capital goods and technology.

Turning now to individual industries, it is seen from Table 3.4 that in most industries, there was an increase in the rate of TFP in the period 1999–2000 to 2007–08 as compared to the period 1980–81 to 1999–2000. In six cases, the difference in the rate of TFP growth is found to be significantly positive. This is in agreement with the trends observed at the aggregate level. Interestingly, in two cases, there has been a significant decrease in the rate of TFP growth in the latter period. These two industries are: (a) Manufacture of Wearing Apparel, and Dressing and Dyeing of Fur (industry 18) and (b) Manufacture of Chemicals and Products (industry 24).

From the examination of the TFP growth estimates presented in Table 3.4, it may be surmised that although at the aggregate level there has not been any statistically significant increase in the rate of TFP growth in organized manufacturing in the 2000s, there are industries which experienced an acceleration in TFP growth (e.g., metal and metal products) that was nullified by the poor productivity growth performance of some other industries (e.g., wearing apparel and chemicals). It is important to investigate the reasons for poor productivity growth in the latter group of industries and take remedial measures. That will help in enhancing the rate of productivity growth in Indian manufacturing.

### Required rate of TFP growth in Indian manufacturing

It has been noted in the third section above that the time series on the growth rate in fixed capital stock in manufacturing covering the period since 1975–76 does not show an upward trend. Hence, if the series for the period 1976–77 to 2011–12 is extended forward up to 2022–23 based on a linear trend, the projected growth rate in fixed capital in manufacturing remains below 9.5 per cent. This is not much higher than the average growth rate in fixed capital stock achieved in the last two or three decades. An important question here is, what conditions will lead to a faster growth in fixed capital stock in manufacturing, and how high can the rate of growth be.

Analysis presented in the third section above indicated that there is a positive relationship between the rate of investment in manufacturing and the overall investment rate in the economy. Hence, if the investment rate in the economy goes up, the investment rate in manufacturing will also go up, and this is expected to raise the growth rate in capital stock in manufacturing. The size of the impact will depend on two factors: (a) the expected increase in the overall investment rate in the Indian economy and (b) the expected share of manufacturing in the investments flows in the Indian economy.

There has been a clear upward trend in the overall investment rate in the Indian economy particularly from the early 2000s, and one would expect the investment rate to go up further in the coming years. But, the moot question is, how large an increase in the overall investment rate can take place in India. One should not be too optimistic on this point. Figure 3.6 shows the rate of gross investment in eight developing countries including India during the period 1980 to 2011. In most of these cases, the gross investment rate in the 2000s has been by and large in the range of 20 to 30 per cent. China and India are exceptions. In 2011, the gross investment rate in China was 48 per cent and that in India was 35 per cent. Given that the investment rate of most major developing countries is less than 30 per cent, it seems unlikely that the investment rate in India will continue to rise sharply and reach somewhere around 60 per cent or beyond. Even the prospects of the investment rate in India exceeding that in China do not seem very bright. It, therefore, seems reasonable to assume that while there will some increase in the gross investment rate in India in the next 10 years, the increase is unlikely to exceed 10 per cent. It will probably be less.

**Figure 3.6: Gross capital formation (per cent of GDP)**

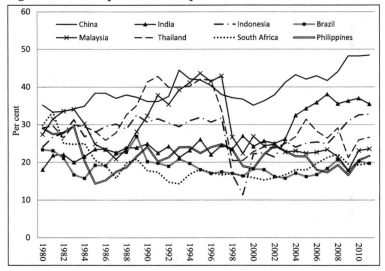

*Source*: Prepared by the author using gross investment rates given in World Economic Indicators database of the World Bank.

As regard the share of manufacturing in aggregate investment in India, there is no clear trend. The ratio in question increased between 2001–02 and 2007–08. But, since then, there has been a fall. This may be seen from Figure 3.7 that shows the share of manufacturing in aggregate gross fixed capital formation in India in various years during 1975–76 to 2011–12. Taking the entire period 1975–76 to 2011–12 into consideration, there is an upward trend in the share of manufacturing in aggregate gross fixed capital formation in India, and one may use this trend line to forecast the future values of this ratio. According to this forecast, the share of manufacturing in aggregate fixed capital formation in India will increase over time to about 36 per cent in 2022–23, which is close to the peak level reached in 2007–08 (see Figure 3.7).

**Figure 3.7: Share of manufacturing in aggregate gross fixed capital formation in the economy (per cent)**

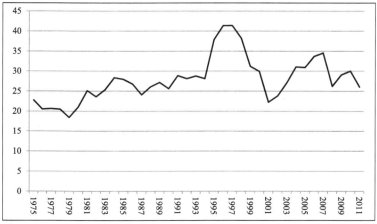

*Source*: Author's computations based on *National Accounts Statistics* (CSO).

Keeping in mind the points made above, an estimate of the likely growth rate in fixed capital stock in Indian manufacturing in the period 2013–14 to 2022–23 has been made under the following assumptions: (a) the aggregate fixed investment rate in the economy will go up by 1 per cent each year till 2022–23, (b) India's real GDP will grow at the rate of 10 per cent per year till 2022–23 and (c) the share of manufacturing in aggregate fixed capital formation will increase steadily over time so as to reach 36 per cent by 2022–23.[14] The fixed capital series for manufacturing constructed under these assumptions has an average growth rate of 12.6 per cent per annum during the period 2013–14 to 2022–23. This hike in the growth rate of capital input will raise the annual growth rate of real GDP of manufacturing by about 2.5 to 3 per cent.[15] This is an appreciable gain, but not enough to reach the target of 25 per cent of aggregate GDP in a decade, which needs the annual growth rate in manufacturing output to go up by 5 per cent. It

[14] These are somewhat optimistic assumptions and it is difficult to provide a solid basis for the assumptions. Yet, some reasons for making these assumptions may be provided. The assumed growth rate in GDP of 10 per cent per annum is based on the target of the Twelfth Five Year Plan. The assumption about the about the share of manufacturing in aggregate fixed capital formation is based on the long term trend observed for the period 1975–76 to 2011–12. The assumption about the aggregate investment rate in the economy is based on the upward trend in India's investment rate observed in Figure 3.6 and the hope that India will be able to reach over the next 10 years the current level of investment rate in China.

[15] This is computed as the increase in the growth rate of capital stock multiplied by the income share of capital input in value added.

follows that if the annual growth rate in manufacturing real GDP has to go up by 5 per cent, the annual rate of growth in TFP in manufacturing needs to increase by 2 to 2.5 per cent, and if there is not much improvement in the growth rate of TFP in unorganized manufacturing, which seems reasonable to assume, the annual rate of TFP growth in organized manufacturing needs to increase by about 3 per cent. The average annual growth rate in TFP in organized manufacturing in the period 1999–2000 to 2011–12 was about 1.6 per cent. The growth rate in TFP in organized manufacturing needed in the next decade is about 4.5 per cent per year. The required growth rate in TFP in organized manufacturing is high and not easy to achieve, but not altogether unattainable.[16] It requires appropriate policy action. A discussion on the impact of policy on TFP growth is taken up in the next section.

## FACTORS DETERMINING TFP GROWTH IN INDIAN MANUFACTURING

There have been a large number of studies on productivity growth in Indian manufacturing (for a review of studies, see Balakrishnan and Pushpangadan, 1998; Goldar and Mitra, 2002; Krishna, 2007; and Goldar, 2014). Many of these studies have looked into the determinants of the level of productivity or the growth rate in productivity. The effect of economic reforms on productivity has been one of the major issues studied. Since this literature is reviewed elsewhere, only three points have been taken up for a brief discussion here. These points relate to: (a) the effect of trade, (b) the effect of investment climate and (c) the effect of human capital formation. These are discussed below in that order.

### Effect of trade

A number of studies have found that trade liberalization had a favourable effect on industrial productivity in India. These include Krishna and Mitra (1998), Chand and Sen (2002), Kambhampati (2003), Goldar and Kumari (2003), Topalova (2004), Das (2006), Sivadasan (2006, 2009) and Mitra and Ural (2008). In a recent study, Topalova and Khandelwal (2011) find that both lowering of tariff on final goods and improved access to imported intermediate inputs due to lowering of tariff on intermediate inputs have increased firm-level productivity in India.

---

[16] During 1993–04, the rate of TFP growth in the industry sector in China was 6.1 per cent per annum in China, while that in India was 1.1 per cent per annum (Bosworth and Collins, 2008). This shows that a high rate of TFP growth in manufacturing in excess of 5 per cent per annum sustained over a decade is not impossible.

They point out that while the pro-competitive effects of the lowering of tariffs led firms to become more efficient, the larger impact probably came from increased access to imported intermediate inputs.

While there is a good deal of empirical evidence on the favourable effect of import liberalization on industrial productivity in India, there is not much empirical evidence to indicate that there was a productivity enhancing effect of increased export orientation of Indian industries. Siddharthan and Lal (2004), Banga and Goldar (2007) and Nallari and Bayraktar (2010) are among the studies undertaken for Indian industries that failed to find a positive effect of export intensity on industrial productivity. There have been several studies on Indian industrial firms which tested the learning-by-exporting and self-selection hypotheses. These include Sharma and Mishra (2009), Mukim (2011), Ranjan and Raychaudhuri (2011) and Haidar (2012). The body of empirical evidence emerging from these studies provides support to the self-selection hypothesis, but only limited support to the learning by exporting hypothesis. Thus, these studies do not provide sufficient empirical support to the view or hypothesis that greater export orientation would increase productivity in Indian industries.

## *Effect of investment climate*

Investment climate is expected to exert a significant influence on productivity of industrial firms. This includes the effect of infrastructure as well as the effects of policies and institutions, particularly the labour market conditions. Several studies undertaken for Indian manufacturing have shown that the investment climate has a significant effect on productivity. Veeramani and Goldar (2005), for instance, found a significant effect of investment climate (IC) on TFP. A study undertaken by the CII and the World Bank (Goswami et al., 2002) found that in comparison with medium IC states, the best IC states have about 3 per cent higher TFP, and the poor IC states have about 13 per cent lower TFP. This is in agreement with the findings of Veeramani and Goldar (2005).

A number of studies have found that infrastructure has a significant influence on industrial productivity. Using data on Indian manufacturing industries for the period 1994 to 2008, Mitra et al. (2012) have found that core infrastructure has a significant positive impact on TFP and TE (Technical efficiency) in Indian manufacturing. The findings of Mukherjee and Majumdar (2007) are similar. They find a positive correlation between infrastructure (physical, financial and social) and Technical efficiency (TE) in Indian manufacturing, especially in the latter half of the 1990s.

Another dimension of the investment climate that has drawn a good deal of attention of the researchers is the labour market regulations. Aghion and

Burgess (2003), Veeramani and Goldar (2005) and Mitra and Ural (2008) found that labour market regulation (measured by the Bisley-Burgess index) has significant adverse effect on TFP in manufacturing. Goldar (2014) uses a different index of labour market reforms and finds a positive correlation between labour market reforms and TFP growth in Indian manufacturing.

A related aspect is the exit policy. The research on inter-firm dispersion in productivity conducted for Indian industries has shown that there is considerable dispersion in productivity among Indian industrial firms, and the dispersion has not declined over time. This is important because a reduction in inter-firm dispersion in productivity would have led to an improvement in the average level of productivity among Indian industrial firms. The barrier to exit is claimed to be an important reason why the inter-firm dispersion in productivity has not declined and the level of technical efficiency has not improved (see, for example, Mahambare and Balasubramanyam, 2005).

### Effect of human capital formation

The review chapters by Isaksson (2007) and Isaksson and Ng (2006) dealing with the literature on the determinants of productivity have observed that education or human capital formation is an important determinant of TFP growth. Several cross-country studies have concluded that education is an important determinant of productivity (see for example, Kumar and Chen, 2013). There are individual country studies reaching the same conclusion. For instance, analysing data for Malaysian manufacturing industries, Kim and Shafi'i (2009) have found that skill and quality of workers were the most important determinants of technical efficiency. Also, labour quality was found to be one of the important factors determining technical progress.

This aspect, i.e., the effect of education on productivity has not received sufficient attention in the productivity studies done for Indian manufacturing. Only two chapters could be found in which this issue has been investigated. Kathuria et al. (2010b) and Babu and Natarajan (2013) have undertaken econometric analysis of determinants of productivity in Indian manufacturing, and have found literacy to be a significant determinant of productivity, with a positive effect.

### Supplementary econometric evidence

To supplement the findings of earlier studies done on the determinants of productivity in Indian manufacturing, an econometric exercise has been undertaken, primarily directed at assessing the effect of export intensity of industries on the rate of productivity growth attained by them. The findings of this exercise are reported below.[17]

The model used for the econometric exercise aims at explaining the inter-industry variation in the rate of TFP growth in the period 1999–2000 to 2007–08. Underlying the model is a relationship between output growth rate and productivity growth rate, known as Verdroon's law, which is well established empirically and has a good theoretical basis. The implication is that ceteris paribus an industry that achieves a greater acceleration in output growth should also achieve a larger increase in the rate of productivity growth. Also, there are grounds to believe that export orientation of an industry will create conditions conducive to productivity advance and will, therefore, have a favourable effect on the growth rate in productivity. Combining these two relationships, it may be argued that acceleration in output growth will have a bigger impact on productivity growth for an industry that has high export orientation than a similar industry which is not export oriented. Accordingly, in the regression equation estimated, the inter-industry variation in TFP growth during the period 1999–2000 to 2007–08 (see Table 3.4) is taken as the dependent variable and this has been regressed on the following variables: (a) TFP growth during 1980–81 to 1999–2000, (b) change in the growth rate of output between the periods 1980–81 to 1999–2000 and 1999–2000 to 2007–08 and (c) export intensity of industries in 2006–07 (derived from the input-output table for 2006–07). An interaction term involving export intensity and output growth acceleration has also been included among the explanatory variables.

The estimated regression equation is shown in Table 3.5 below. The finding of a significant positive coefficient of the output growth acceleration variable is consistent with the Verdroon's law. The results clearly indicate a positive effect of export orientation on TFP growth in Indian manufacturing. This is indicated by the estimated coefficient of the export intensity variable. The positive effect of export orientation of TFP growth is indicated also by the significant positive coefficient of the interaction term between export intensity and change in the rate of output growth. It appears from the estimated coefficients, that a 10 per cent hike in export intensity of Indian manufacturing will raise the rate of annual TFP growth by about 0.7 to 0.8 per cent.

---

[17] It should be pointed out that the exercise is based on ASI data and, therefore, relates to organized manufacturing. Data on unorganized manufacturing are not available on regular basis. Such data are available for only certain years. In addition, there are some problems of comparability. Hence, an analysis based on unorganized sector data or combined organized and unorganized sector data has not been done.

**Table 3.5: Regression results: Explaining inter-industry variation in TFP growth**
**Dependent variable: TFP growth rate (1999–2000 to 2007–08)**

| Explanatory variable | Regression-1 | Regression-2 |
|---|---|---|
| TFP growth rate in the previous period (1980–81 to 1999–2000) | 0.79* (1.74) | 0.66 (1.34) |
| Output growth acceleration (Difference in the trend growth rate in output between the periods 1980–81 to 1999–2000 and 1999–2000 to 2007–08) | 0.75*** (8.32) | 0.57*** (3.83) |
| Export intensity | 0.07 (1.67) | 0.08** (2.50) |
| Interaction term: Export intensity multiplied by the change in growth rate in output | | 0.007* (1.77) |
| Constant | 0.31 | 0.63 |
| R-squared | 0.67 | 0.69 |
| No. of observation | 21 | 21 |

*Source* and *Note*: Author's computations. Export intensity is based on input-output table for 2006–07. The TFP growth rates are based on ASI data and, hence, relate to the organized sector. The t-ratios are based on robust standard errors. These are shown in parentheses.
*, **, *** statistically significant at 10, 5 and 1 per cent level respectively.

## EMPLOYMENT IMPLICATIONS OF A RAPID MANUFACTURING SECTOR GROWTH

In the next 10 years, about 70 to 80 million youth will enter the Indian labour market. If the trends in the past 10 years continue, the organized manufacturing sector will create about ten million new jobs in the next 10 years. In case the employment elasticity observed in the past 10 years[18] continues, but the growth rate of manufacturing output accelerates significantly, the increase in new employment opportunities will be much more than ten million. As regards unorganized manufacturing, it is difficult to judge how much additional employment opportunities will be created in this sector because there has been a downward trend (or at best a sluggish growth) in employment in unorganized manufacturing

---

[18] This measures the impact of output growth on employment: What percentage increase in employment will be there if output grows by 1 per cent. Ideally, this parameter should be estimated with the help of an econometric model. However, a crude measure is commonly used; it is computed by taking the ratio of employment growth rate to output growth rate.

in the 2000s (in contrast to an upward trend in the previous three decades), and it is unclear if the current trends will continue. The current trends in employment in unorganized manufacturing (a downward trend or sluggish growth) will probably not continue and some increase in employment will probably take place. If the employment growth rate in unorganized manufacturing returns to about 2 per cent per annum, which is the trend growth rate in employment in unorganized manufacturing in the period 1983–84 to 2011–12, then an additional eleven million jobs will be created. It appears that, within unorganized manufacturing, a large part of this increase in employment will take place in establishments rather than in own account household enterprises.

At the aggregate manufacturing level, the trend growth rate in employment in the period 1990–91 to 2011–12 was 2.2 per cent per year. In this period, the growth rate in real GDP of manufacturing was 7.2 per cent per year. The employment elasticity, therefore, comes to 0.30. Assuming that the employment elasticity does not change and the growth rate in real GDP of manufacturing increases to 13 per cent per year for the next 10 years, the additional employment opportunities created will be about 30 million.[19] This is only a little over one third of the number of young persons who will enter the Indian labour market in the next 10 years.

It is important to draw attention to the fact that the educational requirements of workers in organized services is much higher than that in organized manufacturing (Figure 3.8). The level of educational attainment of a typical youth entering labour market does not match up to the educational requirements of both organized manufacturing and organized services. However, if the structure of the economy shifts towards manufacturing away from services, the uneducated and low educated youth would have a better chance of finding job opportunities in the organized sector.[20]

---

[19] It has been mentioned earlier that the official policy documents connected with the *National Manufacturing Policy* projects creation of 100 million new jobs. From the policy document and the commentaries on the policy that have appeared in the media, it is not clear whether the additional 100 million jobs are to be created entirely or mostly in manufacturing, or will it take place elsewhere. The estimate of 30 million jobs made here, associated with a rapid growth in manufacturing output at the rate of 13 per cent per annum in the next 10 years, falls far short the figure of 100 million. Perhaps, a large part of the aforesaid additional 100 million jobs are expected to be created in activities connected with manufacturing (e.g., transport, storage and financial services) rather than in manufacturing itself.

[20] I thank Prof Suresh Chand Aggarwal for providing estimates of educational attainments of the youth and educational profile of workers in manufacturing and services on which Figures 3.8, 3.9 and 3.10 are based.

**Figure 3.8: Mismatch between education profile of the youth (15-24) and requirement of organized sector, 2009-10**

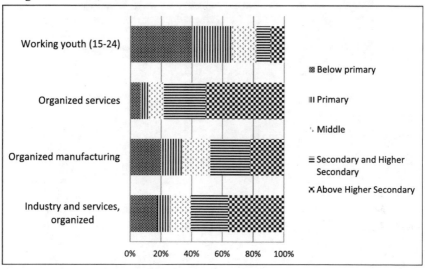

*Source*: Author's computations based on NSS Employment–Unemployment Survey, 2009–10

There has been a significant increase in the ratio of students to populations in recent years because of which the growth of workforce has been slow in the second half of the 2000s (see, among others, Thomas, 2012). The ratio of students to population increased from 20.5 per cent in 1993–94 to 24.3 per cent in 2004–05 and further to 26.6 per cent in 2009–10. Also, the level of educational attainment among the youth has been on the rise (see Figure 3.9). Yet in terms of technical qualifications, there remains a serious deficiency. Data on technical qualification of individuals surveyed by the NSSO for 2009–10 reveal that only 1.7 per cent of the youth of age 15–24 years had technical education, whereas in a majority of manufacturing industries at least 5 per cent of the workers had technical education (see Figure 3.10). There are several industries (constituting about one-fifth of all three-digit manufacturing industries) in which more than 30 per cent of the workers had technical education. Clearly, low educated youth with no technical education will find it difficult to get a job in such industries.

**Figure 3.9: Education profile of the youth (age 15-24), 1999 and 2009**

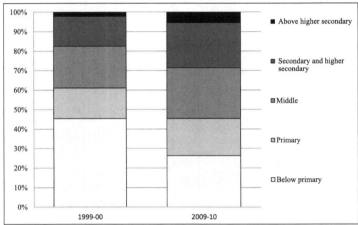

*Source*: Author's computations based on NSS Employment–Unemployment Survey, 1999–2000 and 2009–10

**Figure 3.10: Distribution of 3-digit manufacturing industries (organized sector) according to proportion of workers with technical education, 2009-10**

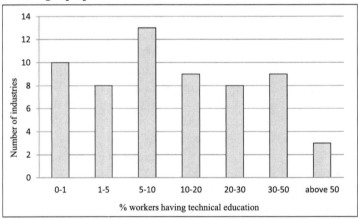

*Source*: Author's computations based on NSS Employment–Unemployment Survey, 2009–10

The analyses of the previous sections have given an indication of the required rates of capital accumulation and productivity growth if the rate of output growth of Indian manufacturing has to be substantially raised. It needs to be recognized that even if sufficient investible resources could be mobilized and appropriate policy environment could be created for efficiency utilization of resources, the attainment of a high rate of output growth in manufacturing may face a serious challenge posed by the shortage of skilled workers. Investment in education and skill development, therefore, must find a prime place in any plan to boost the rate of industrial growth in India.

## MEASURES FOR BOOSTING INVESTMENT IN MANUFACTURING

The analysis presented above has brought out clearly that for attaining the goals of the National Manufacturing Policy, it is important that the rate of investment in manufacturing go up substantially from the levels achieved in the past. The annual growth rate of capital stock needs to go up by about 5 per cent or more. Currently, as discussed below, there are major hurdles to boosting the investment rate in manufacturing, and these hurdles have to be overcome by appropriate policy measures.

A major problem that the Indian industry faces today is lack of business confidence. This has been going down in the recent times, as indicated by various business confidence indices. The NCAER-Master Card Index of business confidence has declined from 156.8 in April 2010 to 114.1 in May 2013. The index had an all-time high of 162.1 in October 2010. Similarly, the business confidence index based on the surveys undertaken by Business Today and Cfore had registered a fall from 74.8 in January-March 2011 to 52.3 in October-December 2011 and to 49.3 in April-June 2012. It was 48.7 in April-June 2013, lower than the index value in the corresponding period 1 year ago. The business confidence index of Confederation of Indian Industries was 51.30 in the second quarter of 2013 as against an average of 60.14 during 2005–12. The index had peak of 71.80 in March 2007. While the abovementioned indices reflect the views of domestic entrepreneurs, which are getting increasingly pessimistic over time, the views of global players are not much different either. The foreign direct investment confidence index (which is based on survey of global executives by A.T. Kearney) shows that India's rank has fallen from no. 2 in 2012 to no. 5 in 2013.

It is needless to say that an accelerated rate of investment in Indian manufacturing cannot be achieved without reviving investor confidence, and the revival of investor confidence in turn requires substantial economic reforms. For certain reasons, the pace of economic reforms had slowed down considerably in India in the last few years and restoring the pace of reforms is essential for growth. The government has recently indicated that it will urgently pay attention to coal and iron ore, and try to ease the bottlenecks these sectors are facing. But, there is need for reforms in many other areas, particularly labour reforms and streamlining of the system of approvals. According to 'Doing Business 2012', a report of the

World Bank, India ranked 132 out of 183 countries compared in term of the ease of doing business. Brazil ranked 126, Russia ranked 120 and China ranked 91. In terms of individual components of business environment, India's ranks were as follows: starting a business (166), dealing with construction permits (181), getting electricity (98), registering property (97), paying taxes (147), trading across borders (109), enforcing contracts (182) and resolving insolvency (128). India ranked relatively better in getting credit (rank 40) and protecting investors (rank 46). This brings out that India will have to do huge policy reforms to create a business friendly environment comparable to the best in the world. Clearly, such reforms need to be initiated soon and this will have a favourable effect on industrial investment and growth.

A related issue is infrastructure. It is well known that inadequate infrastructure facilities has been a major constraint on Indian industry, and investment in infrastructure needs a boost to revive the rate of industrial growth. What is holding back the infrastructure sector is a moot question. Goel (2012) argues that the real cause for the slowdown in infrastructure in India is the failure of the official apparatus to gear up to provide various clearances for infrastructure proposals that came up during the boom phase. As a solution to the problem she suggests that there is a need to simplify administrative procedures to make them more responsive, yet robust. She feels that while a National Investment Board will help, it is the ground-level improvements that are really needed.

The Approach Paper to the Twelfth Plan and the report of steering committee on manufacturing list a host of measures that need to be taken for accelerating the pace of manufacturing growth. The listed strategies/measures include: (a) Integrating into global networks; (b) Developing technology and depth; enhancement of human capital, R&D, etc.; (c) Establishing business regulatory framework; (d) Development of a national land use policy; (e) Clustering and aggregation and (f) Boosting manufacturing exports. It will be noticed that some components of the strategy aim at augmenting industrial growth from the supply side (e.g., national land use policy) while some other components aim at augmenting industrial growth from the demand side (e.g., integrating into global networks). Obviously, if these measures identified by the Planning Commission are fully implemented, a right environment will be created for investment in manufacturing. It may be possible to deviate significantly from the past trend, and thus, bring the growth rate of manufacturing to a high level, not achieved in the past.

The upshot of the above discussion is that there is scope for enhancing substantially the investment rate in manufacturing, but to realize a much higher rate of investment, a considerably better business environment has to be created through appropriate policy action.

## CONCLUSIONS

The National Manufacturing Policy (announced in 2011) aims at raising the share of manufacturing in aggregate GDP from about 15 per cent at present to about 25 per cent by 2022 (or thereabout). For attaining this objective, the rate in real output growth of the manufacturing sector should be about 13 to 15 per cent per annum in the next 10 years, which is much higher than the trend growth rate in manufacturing real output during the period 1999–2000 to 2011–12 (8.3 per cent per year). Thus, the annual growth rate in real output growth of the manufacturing sector needs to increase by about 5 per cent.

The overall investment rate of the Indian economy had a clear upward trend since the early 2000s. One may expect the overall investment rate in Indian economy to go up by about 10 per cent in the next 10 years. The share of manufacturing in investment flows in India had a downward trend in the recent period. However, the long-term trend in this ratio is an upward one. Thus, there are reasons to believe that this ratio will increase in the years to come. In 10 years' time it may again reach the peak it reached in 2007–08 (36 per cent). The fixed capital series for manufacturing constructed under these assumptions has a growth rate of 12.6 per cent during the period 2013–14 to 2022–23. This hike in the growth rate of capital input will raise the annual growth rate of real GDP of manufacturing by about 2.5 to 3 per cent. If the annual growth rate in manufacturing real GDP has to go up by 5 per cent, then the annual rate of growth in TFP in manufacturing needs to increase by 2 to 2.5 per cent. Much of this increase has to take place in organized manufacturing. Thus, the rate of TFP growth in organized manufacturing needs to increase from about 1.6 per cent in the period 1999–2000 to 2011–12 to about 4.5 per cent per year in the coming 10 years. This is high, but not unachievable. With appropriate policy action, it might be possible to raise the rate of TFP growth in organized manufacturing to 4.5 per cent per year.

Greater export orientation of the Indian manufacturing firms, substantial improvements in the investment climate, particularly labour market reforms, sizeable investment in infrastructure, and large investments in human capital formation can go a long way in raising the rate of TFP growth in India's organized manufacturing sector. This will also create a favourable environment for investment in manufacturing, and thus, contribute further to growth. However, a mismatch between skilled labour requirements of manufacturing firms and the availability of skilled workers among the youth who would be entering the Indian labour market in the next 10 year may pose a serious obstacle to growth of Indian manufacturing. While 1.7 per cent of the youth of age 15–24 years have technical education (in 2009), in a majority of manufacturing industries at least 5 per cent of the workers have technical education. There are several industries (constituting about one-fifth of all three-digit manufacturing industries) in which more than 30 per cent of the workers have technical education. Evidently, only a very small proportion of the youth have the skill levels required by organized manufacturing industry. This is a major problem that needs to be solved.

## REFERENCES

Aghion, P., and R. Burgess. 2003. 'Liberalisation and Industrial Performance: Evidence from India and the UK', Mimeo, London School of Economics, www.ycsg.yale.edu/ activities/files/Aghion-Burgess_Paper.pdf, accessed on 24 September 2010.

Babu, S.M., and R. R. S Natarajan. 2013. 'Growth and Spread of Manufacturing Productivity Across Regions In India'. Springerplus, 2: 53, http://www.springerplus. com/content/2/1/53.

Balakrishnan, P., and K. Pushpangadan. 1998. 'What Do We Know about Productivity Growth in Indian Industry?', *Economic and Political Weekly*, 33 (33/34): 2241–46.

Banga, R., and B. Goldar. 2007. 'Contribution of Services to Output Growth and Productivity in Indian Manufacturing: Pre- and Post-Reforms', *Economic and Political Weekly*, 42(26): 2769–77.

Bosworth, B., and S. M. Collins. 2008. 'Accounting for Growth: Comparing China and India', *Journal of Economic Perspectives*, 22(1): 45–66, Winter.

Boyce, J. K. 1986. 'Kinked Exponential Models for Growth-Rate Estimation,' *Oxford Bulletin of Economics and Statistics*, 48(4): 385–91.

Chand, S., and K. Sen. 2002. 'Trade Liberalisation and Productivity Growth: Evidence From Indian Manufacturing', *Review of Development Economics*, 6 (1): 120–32.

Christensen, L.R., D. Cummings and D. Jorgenson. 1980. 'Economic Growth, 1947–73: An International Comparison,' in John W. Kendrick and Beatrice N. Vaccara (eds.), *New Developments in Productivity Measurement and Analysis*, NBER.

Das, D. K. 2006. 'Improving Industrial Productivity: Does Trade Liberalisation Matter? Evidence from Indian Capital and Intermediate Goods Sectors'. In *India: Industrialisation in a Reforming Economy: Essays for K.L. Krishna*, edited by S. Tendulkar, Arup Mitra, K. Narayanan and Deb Kusum Das, 321–48, New Delhi: Academic Foundation.

Goel, A. 2012. 'Explaining the Infrastructure Slowdown,' *Business Line*, October 12, 2012.

Goldar, B. 2014. 'Productivity in Indian Manufacturing in the Post-Reform Period: A Review of Studies.' In *Productivity in Indian Manufacturing*, edited by Vinish Kathuria, Rajesh Raj S N and Kunal Sen, 75-105, New Delhi: Routledge.

Goldar, B., and A. Kumari. 2003. 'Import Liberalisation and Productivity Growth in Indian Manufacturing Industries in the 1990s', *Developing Economies*, 41(4): 436–60.

Goldar, B., and A. Mitra. 2002. 'Total factor Productivity Growth in Indian Industry: A Review of Studies.' In *National Income Accounts and Data Systems*, edited by B.S. Minhas, 218–37, New Delhi: Oxford University Press.

Goswami, O., A. K. Arun, S. Gantakolla, V. More, A. Mookherjee, D. Dollar, T. Mengistae, M. Hallward-Driemier, and Giuseppe Iarossi. 2002. *Competitiveness of Indian Manufacturing: Results from a Firm Level Survey*, Confederation of Indian Industry and the World Bank.

Haidar, J. I. 2012. 'Trade and Productivity: Self-selection or Learning-by-Exporting in India', *Economic Modelling*, 29(5): 1766–73.

Hashim, D. A., A. Kumar, and A. Virmani. 2009. 'Impact of Major Liberalisation on Productivity: The J Curve Hypothesis', Working Paper no. 5/2009-DEA, Ministry of Finance, Government of India.

Isaksson, A. 2007. '*Determinants of Total Factor Productivity: A Literature Review*,' Staff working Paper 02/2007, Research and Statistics Branch, United Nations Industrial Development Organization, Vienna.

Isaksson, A., and T.H. Ng. 2006. '*Determinants of Productivity: Cross-Country Analysis and Country Case Studies*', Staff working Paper 01/2006, Research and Statistics Branch, United Nations Industrial Development Organization, Vienna.

Kambhampati, U.S. 2003. 'Trade Reforms and the Efficiency of Firms in India', *Oxford Development Studies*, 31(2): 219–33.

Kathuria, V., S. N. R. Raj and K. Sen. 2010a. '*Rain, Rain, Go Away? The Investment Climate, State Business Relations and Firm Performance in India*', MPRA Paper no. 20316, Munich Personal RePEc Archive, http://mpra.ub.uni-muenchen.de/20316/, accessed on 30 December 2011.

Kathuria, V., S. N. R. Raj and K. Sen. 2010b. '*Human Capital and Manufacturing Productivity Growth in India*', Paper presented at *International Conference on: Science, Technology and Economy Human Capital and Development (Annual Conference of IASSI & Knowledge Forum Hosted by IIT Bombay during Nov. 11–12, 2010)*.

Kim, S., and M. Shafi'i. 2009. 'Factor Determinants of Total Factor Productivity Growth in Malaysian Manufacturing Industries: A Decomposition Analysis', *Asian-Pacific Economic Literature*, 23(1): 48–65, May.

Krishna, K.L. 2007. 'What do we know about the Sources of Economic Growth in India?'. In *Institutions and markets in India's development: Essays for K.N. Raj* edited by A. Vaidyanathan and K.L. Krishna, 45–69, New Delhi: Oxford University Press.

Krishna, P., and D. Mitra. 1998. 'Trade Liberalisation, Market Discipline and Productivity Growth: New Evidence from India', *Journal of Development Economics* 56: 447–62.

Kumar, A., and W. Chen. 2013. 'Education, Health and the Dynamics of Cross-Country Productivity Differences,' Department of Economics, University of Victoria, Victoria, British Columbia, Canada, February.

Mahambare, V., and V.N. Balasubramanyam. 2005. 'Trade Liberalisation and India's Manufacturing Sector', Working Paper. Centre for Forecasting, Management School, Lancaster University, Lancaster, http://ideas.repec.org/p/wpa/wuwpdc/0505010.html, accessed on 1 March 2011.

Mitra, A., C. Sharma, and M.-A. Veganzones-Varoudakis. 2012. 'Estimating Impact of Infrastructure on Productivity and Efficiency of Indian Manufacturing', *Applied Economic Letters*, 19: 779–83.

Mitra, D., and B. P. Ural. 2008. 'Indian Manufacturing: A Slow Sector in A Rapidly Growing Economy', *Journal of International Trade and Economic Development*, 17(4): 525–59.

Mukherjee, D., and R. Majumdar. 2007. 'Efficiency, Technological Progress and Regional Comparative Advantage: A Study of Organised Manufacturing Sector in India', *Asia Pacific Development Journal*, 14(2): 23–54.

Mukim, M., 2011. 'Does Exporting Increase Productivity? Evidence from India', Working Paper, Department of International Development, London School of Economics, *siteresources.worldbank.org/INTRANETTRADE/.../mukim.pdf,* accessed on 17 December 2012.

Nallari, R., and N. Bayraktar. 2010. 'Micro Efficiency and Macro Growth', Policy Research Working Paper no. 5267, Growth and Crisis Unit, World Bank Institute, World Bank.

Ranjan, P., and J. Raychaudhuri. 2011. 'Self-Selection vs. Learning: Evidence from Indian Exporting Firms', *Indian Growth and Development Review*, 4(1): 22–37.

Sharma, C., and R. K. Mistra. 2009. 'Does Export and Productivity Growth Linkage Exist? Evidence from the Indian Manufacturing Industry'. Paper presented at the Fifth International Conference on Economic Growth and *Development, Indian Statistical Institute, Delhi, December 16–18, 2009.*

Siddharthan, N.S., and K. Lal, 2004. 'Liberalisation, MNE and Productivity of Indian Enterprises', *Economic and Political Weekly, 34(5): 448–53.*

Sivadasan, J. 2006. 'Productivity Consequences of Product Market Liberalisation: Micro-evidence from Indian Manufacturing Sector Reforms', Working chapter no. 1062, Stephen M. Ross School of Business, University of Michigan.

Sivadasan, J. 2009. 'Barriers to Competition and Productivity: Evidence from India'. *The B.E. Journal of Economic Analysis & Policy* (electronic journal), 9(1), Article no. 42.

Thomas, J.J. 2012. 'India's Labour Market during the 2000s', *Economic and Political Weekly*, 47(51): 39–51.

Topalova, P. 2004. 'Trade Liberalisation and Firm Productivity: the Case of India', IMF Working Paper no. WP/04/28, International Monetary Fund.

Topalova, P., and A. Khandelwal. 2011. 'Trade Liberalisation and Firm Productivity: the Case of India', *Review of Economics and Statistics*, 93(3): 995–1009.

Veeramani, C., and B. Goldar. 2005. 'Manufacturing Productivity in Indian States: Does Investment Climate Matter?', *Economic and Political Weekly*, 40(24): 2413–20.

Virmani, A., and D. A. Hashim. 2011. 'J-Curve of Productivity and Growth: Indian Manufacturing Post-Liberalisation', IMF Working Paper no. WP/11/163, International Monetary Fund.

**Annexure A: Unit root tests, investment rate series, 1975–76 to 2011–12**

| Series | Type of test | Version | Test statistic | Critical value at 5% level of significance | Result: Null hypothesis (presence of unit root) is rejected or not |
|---|---|---|---|---|---|
| Gross domestic capital formation rate in the economy | DF | Intercept, no trend | −0.29 | −2.95 | Not rejected |
| | DF | Intercept and trend | −1.87 | −3.54 | Not rejected |
| | ADF (1) | Intercept, no trend | 0.10 | −2.95 | Not rejected |
| | ADF (1) | Intercept and trend | −1.44 | −3.54 | Not rejected |
| ΔGross domestic capital formation rate in the economy | DF | Intercept, no trend | −6.95 | −2.95 | Rejected |
| | DF | Intercept and trend | −7.13 | −3.55 | Rejected |
| | ADF (3) | Intercept, no trend | −3.83 | −2.95 | Rejected |
| | ADF (2) | Intercept and trend | −4.65 | −3.55 | Rejected |
| Investment rate in manufacturing, Fixed investment/ GDP | DF | Intercept, no trend | −1.79 | −2.96 | Not rejected |
| | DF | Intercept and trend | −2.47 | −3.57 | Not rejected |
| | ADF (5) | Intercept, no trend | −0.27 | −2.96 | Not rejected |
| | ADF (3) | Intercept and trend | −5.31* | −3.57 | Rejected* |
| ΔInvestment rate in manufacturing, Fixed investment/ GDP | DF | Intercept, no trend | −4.58 | −2.97 | Rejected |
| | DF | Intercept and trend | −4.50 | −3.57 | Rejected |
| | ADF (4) | Intercept, no trend | −4.64 | −2.97 | Rejected |
| | ADF (4) | Intercept and trend | −4.54 | −3.57 | Rejected |

*Note*: DF = Dickey-Fuller, ADF = Augmented Dickey-Fuller. Figures in brackets are the leg length used for the ADF test, which has been chosen on the basis of Akaike information criterion.

* For lag lengths 1, 2, 4 and 5, the test statistic is less than the critical value at 5 per cent level of significance, and thus, the null hypothesis is not rejected.

# 4

# Growth Drivers: ICT and Inclusive Innovations

## Ashima Goyal

## INTRODUCTION

Innovations are essential to raise productivity and sustain growth. Inclusion is also important to sustain growth, since it prevents possible political unrest, raises average productivity and expands the market size. Innovations using Internet and mobile communication technologies (ICT), especially, suit inclusion, and therefore, sustain inclusive growth, which is a major Indian objective. Inclusion and growth can go together if inclusion is of the type that facilitates growth. 'Active inclusion,' defined as creating conditions for the many to contribute to and participate in growth (Goyal, 2012), is of this type.

An inclusive innovation is one that creates products that can be accessed by all classes, improving their productivity, and are not restricted to the elite. This chapter develops a simple analytical framework that clarifies the conditions that foster inclusive innovation in Emerging and Developing Economies (EDEs).[1] It brings out two ways of facilitating inclusion through innovation: first, to induce more technical change in products consumed by the less well off, thus, lowering costs for them and second, to make more resources available for them or reduce their transaction costs so that they can afford better products. Alternative ways of doing this are through income transfers or through better systems or public provision of the relevant infrastructure. The latter are suited to active inclusion.

The analytical framework shows that large market size stimulates innovation to profit from it, since adoption and further adaptation of technology responds to economic incentives. Increasing the market size creates broader incentives for

---

[1]  This chapter is a revised version of IGIDR working paper no. WP-2013-018.

innovation and reduces the need for direct government inputs that have been difficult to provide. Since market size strengthens private incentives for inclusive innovation, it is likely to improve outcomes.[2]

Next, the chapter assesses India's telecommunication policy (2012) and policy changes towards mobile banking to examine the extent to which they have improved relevant infrastructure such as broadband, or taken steps to increase the market size. Policy statements have normally emphasized inclusion but implementation has been lacking. A case study comparing mobile banking regulations and outcomes in India with Pakistan shows flexibilities in Pakistani policies encouraged market size, while India paid inadequate attention to user convenience, thus, limiting the potential market size and innovation. Comparison with Pakistan is particularly apt since they are a neighbouring country, which India generally outperforms on most economic criteria. Both introduced mobile banking in 2008 but Pakistan has far overtaken India in this area.

The mobile is an example of a technology product whose falling costs made it accessible to all income classes. Mobile telephony has been one of India's success stories demonstrating ICT for inclusion. The growth of the Indian communication sector was in double digits after 2000 and its annual contribution to Gross Domestic Product (GDP) growth around 10 per cent. According to the regulator, India moved from just 5 million telephone subscribers in 1991 to 37 million in 2001 and 898.02 million in 2013. Mobile cellular subscriptions per 100 at 72 in 2011 compared well with the US figure of 95. But still the mobile's contribution has fallen far short of potential in terms of availability of mobile enabled services. Many other EDEs had greater success with mobile banking.

For new technologies to create greater domestic inclusion, policies have to be appropriate. But assessing Indian technology policies on these yardsticks shows they have fallen far short. Better coordination mechanisms and incentives envisaged in recent policies may finally aid implementation, since the use of such technologies may have reached a critical threshold. Further innovation in an enabling environment can make substantial contributions to Indian growth, bringing more of the marginalized into the mainstream in productive ways.

Gorden (2012) divides innovations in advanced economies such as US and UK into three periods. While 1750 to 1830 was the period of steam and railroads; from 1870 to 1900 electricity, motors, plumbing, water supply, telephone, chemicals,

---

[2]  Manoj Pant pointed out Governments can rarely be relied on to achieve results. But although government failures are frequent so are market failures. That is why policies that work through improving private incentives could to be more effective.

and petroleum contributed; and 1960 onwards is the period of ICT. We label the three technology regimes Mark I, Mark II and Mark III, respectively. He argues Mark II was the most important and was the major contributor to rapid twentieth century productivity growth. In his view, ICT created only a short growth burst between 1996 and 2004 and is unlikely to create further growth.

In India even the spin-offs from Mark II inventions such as urbanization, good transport, water on tap, sanitation, and the release of household time are far from complete. Many of these have to come in the form of better public services. While the well-off can compensate for failures in the latter, the less well-off cannot.

This was the reason ICT largely created opportunities for skilled elites, even while helping India catch the outsourcing wave. Poor governance and delivery of public services such as health, education and infrastructure handicap the less well-off who cannot afford private substitutes for these services. But ICT can itself reduce the cost of some of these public services. E-delivery can improve transparency and governance as it reduces discretion and corruption. A technology-based strategy of inclusion is uniquely suited to Indian catch-up growth and youthful demographics, since it increases rewards to work, while redistributive strategies suit persistent poverty.

If public services that more widely apply Mark II technology, expand the size of the middle class and induce more innovation in technology, Mark III itself can create more inclusion. While private innovation generally favours the better-off, ICT has more potential for innovation for the middle-and lower middle classes. Thus, improving public services can trigger more innovation in ICT, generating cumulative inclusive growth.

Technology imports play a major role in catch-up growth. In past such episodes, technology was biased towards using capital: for example, in the US catch-up years of the early to mid-nineteenth century and for the early period of Japanese industrialization. The capital-output ratio rose and the contribution of Total factor productivity (TFP) to growth in labour productivity was less than that of the growth in capital-labour ratio. The Kuznets's stylized fact of capital-output ratios that fell as TFP rose emerged only after 1890 when maturity was reached (Hayami, 1998). This was so even in Asia where labour was naturally more abundant, perhaps because the Western technology imitated was capital intensive. TFP's contribution to labour productivity growth in the Asian economies was less than half its contribution in developed economies. It is possible that ICT based innovations in populous EDEs, currently in the catch-up phase, can have a medium- rather than a high-skill or capital-bias after they reach a critical threshold if supported by appropriate policy action. The analysis helps identify some of the latter.

But it is widely perceived that ICT has the opposite effect. It is regarded as only helping those with skills, leading to a 'winner takes all' outcome. The best drives out the average. Technology companies such as Microsoft, Facebook and Google become globally dominant and earn huge amounts. In advanced economies (AEs) inequality rose with higher rewards to exceptional skills. Cecchini and Scott (2003) show how, in the EDE context, more technical progress (TP) tends to occur at the higher end and widens the digital divide. In 2009 Indian finance, insurance and real estate sectors had the highest labour productivity but employed less than 2 per cent of the labour force (Hasan et. al., 2012).

Nevertheless, Mark III technologies reduce inequalities between nations, by creating a virtual labour market and making information more easily available. Subramanian (2013) points out that post 2000 (the Mark III period), cross-country inequality reduced since about 80 EDEs grew faster than AEs. Pre-2000, only about 20 EDEs managed this feat. The potential contribution of ICT to development was recognized early. The World Bank has many reports on this topic. Avgerou (1998) offers an early analysis. Jorgensen (2001) and OECD (2001) assess ICT's contribution to productivity improvement in AEs, which should also happen in EDEs.

Goyal (2005, 2007, 2011) analyses some of the associated virtuous cycles. ICT that substitutes electronic for physical transactions reduces transaction costs and speed of market access, thus, compensating for other constraints. It lowers the cost of entry for a new firm, and raises productivity. Finally, it encourages cumulative improvements in technology and skills, inducing more labour-using TP.

Employment and wages to intermediate skills rise when new technologies, which make it possible to employ distant labour, allow an AE with high and medium-skilled labour to interact with an EDE with medium and low-skilled labour. If the elasticity of substitution between labour inputs is high, expansion in labour supply induces medium-skill biased technical change, which raises the demand for such labour. As a result, inequalities tend to fall in the AE, skill premiums rise marginally in the EDE, but equality improves because labour employed in the low-skilled sector shrinks, and average wages also rise.

A concept of household production technology shows why ICT has the potential to increase the equity and efficiency of female participation in the labour force. It helps restore flexibility in female external labour supply since it facilitates distance work, flexi-time and location activity, making it easier to match skill to jobs, and to maintain and upgrade skills. But complementary policies and changes in entrenched social structures and perceptions are also required.

The endogenous growth literature has explored different kinds of mechanisms that escape diminishing returns to capital and allow growth to sustain. The mechanism this chapter explores is innovation induced through market size. It is well understood how endogenous productivity improvements sustain growth. What this chapter focuses on is how this type of growth can also be inclusive.

The structure of the chapter is as follows: The second section presents the analytical framework, which is used to assess ICT and technology policy in the third section. The fourth section similarly analyses mobile banking before the fifth section concludes.

## AN ANALYTICAL FRAMEWORK

We give an example that shows how the market size for an intermediate, rather than an expensive high-end technology can rise. Consider an economy whose ICT sector has three techniques, and their convex combinations, available at any period of time. The first A is more skill and capital intensive, B is intermediate, and C can be produced with low skills.[3] These generate the segmented production isoquant $P_1$ in Figure 4.1 in the H and O input space. H denotes high quality inputs including skills and capital, while O denotes 'ordinary' or low skilled labour inputs. The economy also has two groups of consumers, the well-off (W) whose endowment has more capital compared to labour, so that the budget set facing them has slope WW, and the less well-off (L) with more labour compared to capital and a trade-off between the two inputs given by the slope of LL.[4] The W group chooses technique A while L can only afford technique C.

**Figure 4.1: Captial biased technical change**

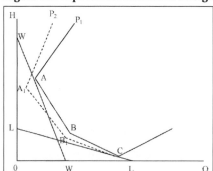

*Source*: Author's Illustrations

---

[3] In the context of ploughing in agriculture the three can be thought of as a tractor, a bullock cart, and a spade.

[4] The endowment inequality is severe enough so that trade between the agents cannot reduce inequality. Thus, the market imperfection is persistent to possible resolution from market action. I thank Uday Bhanu Sinha for this point.

In period 2, technology improves, thus, the isoquant shifts downwards. There is no improvement in the low level technology C. Indeed, development requires moving away from the use of C. In Figure 4.1 both B and A improve to $B_1$ and $A_1$. Since the W group can shift to a lower budget line and improve welfare by using technology $A_1$ compared to $B_1$, they prefer to use $A_1$. Technique A becomes obsolete. As long as the slope of $B_1C$ exceeds that of LL, C continues to be the welfare maximizing or expenditure minimizing technology for the L group, since the rate at which group L can substitute H for O to reach $B_1$, given their budget constraint, is lower than that required in the technology of production: the marginal rate of substitution is less than the marginal rate of transformation. In the new equilibria, the welfare of group W improves and that of group L is unchanged. The digital divide, or distance between the W and L groups, widens. The economy remains in a low level trap.[5]

In Figure 4.2, techniques A and B improve to $A_2$ and $B_2$ respectively, but the improvement is relatively more now in the intermediate technology. If the slope $B_2C$ is equal to or less than LL, the L group shifts from using technique C to using $B_2$. If slope $B_2A_2$ exceeds WW the group W can also raise welfare by shifting to technique $B_2$ from technique A, since the marginal rate of substitution in technology exceeds that on their budget line.

**Figure 4.2: Intermediate technology biased technical change**

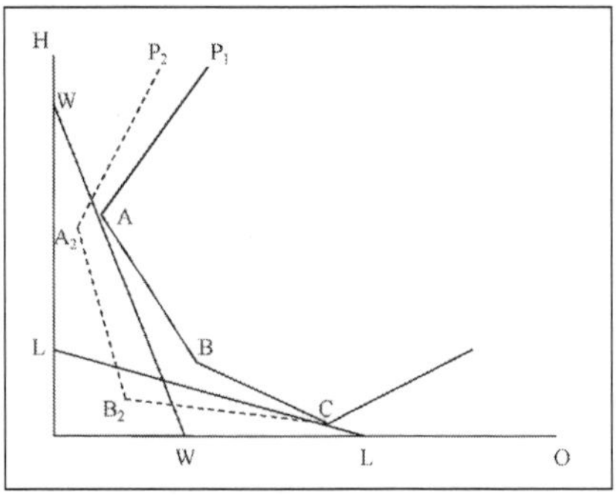

*Source*: Author's Illustrations

This is a simplified example. In reality there will be product differentiation even among intermediate techniques with the W group choosing higher-end and more feature rich products.

Even so, the example has interesting implications for policy. There are two ways to shift group L to the better technology B, thus, improving their prospects. One

---

5    Cecchini and Scott (2003) use this framework to show how technology can favour the elite, and widen disparities.

is to induce more technical change in B, thus, lowering its costs for the group L and making it accessible. The second is to make more of capital available to group L or reduce their transaction costs, thus, steepening the slope of their budget line. This could be done through income transfers or through better public provision of the relevant infrastructure, since group L finds it more difficult to compensate privately for poor public infrastructure. For example, poor business services favour big business since small business is more dependent on public services.

What affects the rate of technological change? In order to answer this question we develop a more formal model, without an arbitrary restriction on the number of techniques, in which to explore the drivers of technological change. If increasing the scale of use of the intermediate technology induces TP, then the second way to shift L would support the first also, as it induces inclusive TP.

### A formal model

Consider an economy in which aggregate output is produced by a combination of two worker-types: first with high ($H$) and second with intermediate or low skills ($O$).[6] A large number of techniques allow smooth substitution between the two inputs, so the aggregate production function can be written in the constant elasticity of substitution (CES) form, where $\rho \leq 1$. The $A$ terms denote factor augmenting technology.

$$Y(t) = \left[ \left( A_0(t)O(t) \right)^\rho + \left( A_h(t)H(t) \right)^\rho \right]^{1/\rho} \tag{1}$$

The intermediate-skilled, $O(t)$, and high-skilled, $H(t)$ workers are risk neutral and maximize the discounted present value of labour income in competitive labour markets. The elasticity of substitution between the two inputs is $\sigma \equiv 1/(1-\rho)$. The two-worker types are gross substitutes if $\sigma > 1$ (that is, $\rho > 0$). Empirical estimates for the elasticity of substitution between more and less educated labour give a range between 1 and 2 [Freeman (1986), pp. 366].[7]

The simplest interpretation, without loss of generality, for the aggregate production function (1) is that of a two-good economy, with each good produced by one type of worker and aggregated by consumer preferences over the two goods.[8] Dropping time subscripts, the production functions for the two goods are:

---

[6]   This section adapts part of the model in Goyal (2007).

[7]   Goyal (2007) shows, with a high elasticity of substitution, a rise in $A_o$ relative to $A_h$ will increase demand for intermediate-skilled workers.

[8]   It can also be interpreted as the production function for a multi-good economy where different sectors employ both O and H worker types and produce goods that are imperfect substitutes.

$$Y_b = A_b H \tag{2}$$

$$Y_O = A_o O.$$

The consumers' utility function is defined over the two goods as:

$$\left[ Y_o^\rho + Y_b^\rho \right]^{1/\rho} \tag{3}$$

### Endogenous technical change

We assume firms in the two sectors choose between specialized ICT machines or processes, which raise the productivity of $H$ or $O$ worker-types, on the basis of relative profitability.

For a simple analysis of endogenous choice of technique, let $N_h$ and $N_O$ be the number of specialized machines for high and intermediate-skilled workers, respectively. The sectoral production functions then become $Y_b = N_b H$ and $Y_O = N_O O$, where $A_b = N_b$ and $A_o = N_o$, so that the production functions are equivalent to (2).[9]

Under competitive conditions, consumers' maximization of utility (3), subject to a budget constraint, results in a standard relative demand function for the two goods. Inverting this demand function, and substituting the production functions in it, gives the relative price of the skill intensive good:

$$p = \frac{p_b}{p_o} = \left[ \frac{N_b H}{N_o O} \right]^{\rho - 1} \tag{4}$$

The marginal willingness to pay for an additional machine is the marginal increase in profit due to a new machine. In each sector, this is the derivative of $p_b Y_b$ and $p_o Y_o$ with respect to $N_b$ and $N_o$, i.e., $p_b H$ and $p_o O$, respectively.

Schmookler (1966) and the endogenous growth literature have analysed how demand-pull and market size is important for the development of technology since the latter responds to profit motives. For example, as long as horses were commonly used, there was a high rate of innovation in horseshoes. Technology is exogenous in the sense that basic research and major technical inventions occur before they are really used, but adoption and further adaptation respond to economic incentives. So,

---

[9] Our simple linear technology can be derived, as is common in the endogenous growth literature, from a more complex model with a continuum of firms and machines. At the firm level, the technology parameter A depends on the continuum of machines adopted. Decreasing returns for each firm gives a tractable solution to the firm's problem, even with constant returns at the aggregate sectoral level. Decreasing returns to R&D effort for each sector can also be considered as in Acemoglu (1998).

advances in basic science may be independent of profit motives, but 'micro inventions', or applications that follow, are often not so independent (Acemoglu, 2002, pp. 31–38). Diamond (1997) also emphasizes relative economic advantage of new technology over existing technology as a strong influence on acceptance of innovations. Social factors such as the prestige of a new technology, the ease with which its advantages can be observed, and its compatibility with vested interests also play a role.

Now introduce innovators that create the machines. To bring out the basic issue in the simplest possible manner we assume $C$, measured in units of final output $Y$, is the fixed cost of creating a new machine. The marginal cost of producing a machine once it is created is zero. The creation of new machines continues for both sectors until the marginal increase in profit equals the fixed cost of innovation.[10] It follows that in equilibrium:

$$p_h H = p_o O \tag{5}$$

Thus, two effects that stimulate the creation of new technologies are the price and market size effects. The price of the good using a more expensive factor will be higher from equation 4. But the market size effect encourages innovation for the more abundant factor, since a larger scale of use would generate profits. The rise in the market size for techniques adapted to intermediate-skills, and used by a larger customer base, would be expected to stimulate more of such adaptations.

Given endowments of $H$ and $O$, relative price has to adjust to satisfy equation 5. From equation 4 relative price can change only if $N_h/N_o$ changes. Therefore, the relative skill bias of technology has to adjust to clear the technology market. Equations 4 and 5 together give this equilibrium skill bias:

$$\frac{N_h}{N_o} = \frac{A_h}{A_o} = \left[\frac{H}{O}\right]^{\rho/(1-\rho)} \tag{6}$$

Equation 6 implies that when $\rho > 0$, (or $\sigma > 1$) so the goods are gross substitutes, $N_o$ rises with $O$. So the market size effect dominates the price effect. It follows a larger relative size of intermediate-skills, and markets for the products of such skills, will create more intermediate-skill biased technologies, as technology or organization of production responds to profit opportunities.

The size effect stimulates the creation of more intermediate technologies. But if the higher priced skilled factor is more productive, high-end innovation may still be more profitable. To see this, suppose there are diminishing returns to innovation in $O$ but $H$ has constant returns. For the market size effect to

---

[10] If C is not the same in the two sectors, the condition (5) would include the cost difference. Equilibrium profits in the sector with the more expensive machines would have to exceed those in the sector with the less expensive machines by the cost difference. The general results would not change. I thank Prabal Roy Chowdhury for raising this issue.

dominate, $O$ must be sufficiently larger than $H$ to compensate for the latter's greater productivity. If there are decreasing returns in the $O$ sector, then $Yo = No$ $O^\alpha$, where $\alpha < 1$. The equilibrium condition (6) becomes $p_b H = p_o O^\alpha$. For more intermediate technologies to be created, $O$ must exceed $H$ by a multiple given by $1/\alpha$, that is $O > ((p_b/p_o) H)^{1/\alpha}$. Then there exists a threshold in the market size of B below which innovation will be high skill intensive and further the digital divide, and above which it will be inclusive.[11]

A virtuous cycle[12] can occur if – the number of consumers of the intermediate technique B and the revenues from selling it rise, more TP takes place in B (Figure 4.2). Policies to increase use of B are a possible trigger for such a virtuous cycle. Large firms are normally capital and skill intensive and so develop high end products such as A. But mobile technology is naturally more inclusive. The insights of this section are used to assess how well Indian telecom (third section) and mobile banking policy (fourth section) have aimed to and succeeded in triggering such innovation. The methodology is to compare policy objectives with outcomes, using data on broadband coverage and rural and urban teledensity over time, and a case study on mobile banking in India and Pakistan. There is special emphasis on regulatory design and features that could induce better outcomes.

## TELECOM POLICY

There was dynamism in a policy driven shift from fixed line to mobile telephony, with better incentives for private entry. This encouraged the development of intermediate technologies such as B. The National Telecom Policy was announced in 1994, followed by the New Telecom Policy of March 1999[13] and the recent National Telecom Policy (NTP) 2012 (GOI, 2012). The policies had similar themes, uniformly emphasizing the potential contribution of new technologies, inclusive innovation, competition, universal service, quality, India's security and its development as an export and manufacturing hub.

The 1994 policy focused on the funds required and saw privatization as a means of realizing these, but fell far short of its targets. In 1992 private operators

---

[11] Acemoglu, Gancia, and Zilibotti (2012) derive a similar result more formally in an endogenous growth model of offshoring. TP increases inequality in the beginning but reduces it later.

[12] An example of tech driven virtuous cycles arises in a model of matching ICT to labour (Goyal, 2005) with endogenous choice of training and technology. Multiple equilibria are possible. Investment in training and technology can be at less than socially optimal levels, and policy intervention can lead to a shift towards better equilibria.

[13] See respectively: http://www.trai.gov.in/Content/telecom_policy_1994.aspx, http://www.trai.gov.in/Content/ntp_1999.aspx.

were allowed in mobile telephony, with foreign partners to bring in the latest technology. Licenses were granted over 1994–95. Licenses were allotted to more than one provider in a circle to make sure there was competition.

The new policy of 1999 was a response to market players' concerns about poor revenue realization. The sector really took off after a move from a fixed fee to a revenue sharing model, since lower start-up costs enabled the development of and realization of profits from a large potential market. The Telecom Regulatory Authority of India, set up in 1997 and reconstituted in 2000, separated the regulatory function from policy-making, and aided the process. The non-Congress government then in power lowered license fees. Competitive entry led to many new businesses that did very well, even as one of the world's lowest tariffs ensured that millions of poor could use the services.

The riches created, however, led to private corruption and public extortion that harmed the industry. In 2008 minister A. Raja, in the Congress coalition government allocated more 2G mobile licenses on a first come first served basis. The government auditor CAG alleged a large revenue loss to the government. The figure gained credibility from the INR 1062 billion the government earned from 3G and 4G licenses allotted through auctions in 2010. So, in 2012, the Supreme Court (SC) cancelled the old allocation and ordered new 2G auctions. But when they were held in November 2012, only 94 billion were raised against the 400 billion expected, casting doubt on the CAG figure that had triggered a series of corruption allegations. Subsequent auctions that kept high reserve prices also failed.

The SC then clarified, in response to a Presidential query, resource allocation was a policy decision and, therefore, a prerogative of the executive. So the executive had flexibility in designing policy. An auction was not essential, but if the allocation was not in the 'common good', and did not satisfy the criteria of 'fairness and non-arbitrariness', as in the case of Raja's allocations, the SC could intervene.

Industry will always lobby to reduce taxes. But high imposts are passed on to consumers, and reduce investment. Falling industry growth rates reduce future revenue to the government, and the welfare of the subscriber. Auctions have the desirable property of removing the government's discretion in allotting natural resources, which can be a major source of corruption. A single-step auction based allocation, with a low reserve price, and part of the payment to come from future royalties, could avoid both discretion in allocation and large upfront costs that reduce subsequent development. The 2G auctions held in 2014 had these features and so were successful. Apart from the contract, adequate competition can ensure prices remain low, and service quality improves, so the major gain from their natural resources, such as spectrum, goes to citizens.

NTP internalized these lessons by taking the position that the entry fee regime will be made flexible even as spectrum is made available at a price determined through market related processes. Pricing and competition are major factors affecting incentives. Affordable prices increase the customer base with reasonable returns for companies. Easier entry and revenue or profit sharing worked in the past.

Although easier private entry increased market size, policy failed to provide the requisite infrastructure. This meant intermediate technologies such as B remained out of reach of a large chunk of the population who remain stuck in low level technologies such as C. This limited spillovers from ICT that could compensate for failures in the spread of technologies Mark II, and help steepen the budget line for the less well-off.

The failure is puzzling despite telecom receiving sustained policy attention, the contribution of ICT to the expansion of domestic labour service exports,[14] and given its potential to contribute to inclusive growth that is often stated as an objective of the Indian government. Table 4.1, focusing on infrastructure relevant to telecom, shows that although a couple of states have done well, the average broadband coverage of Village panchayats (VPs) and rural teledensity remain below 50 per cent. Unambitious short-term targets are set and even those are not achieved, let alone the universal access promised in every policy. Table 4.2 shows that although rural penetration has increased in recent periods, it still remains below urban. Rural areas accounted for about 40 per cent of total connections in 2013.

**Table 4.1: Per cent broadband coverage of village panchayats under Bharat Nirman-II and rural teledensity**

| State /UTs | Broad-band covered (March 2011) | % of 2010–11 target achieved | 2010–11 target as a % of uncovered panchayats | % rural teledensity (end Feb 2011) |
|---|---|---|---|---|
| Andhra Pradesh | 58 | 70 | 26 | 35.1 |
| Assam | 25 | 50 | 21 | 25.4 |
| Bihar | 50 | 105 | 55 | 29.0 |
| Chhattisgarh | 22 | 0 | 19 | 2.8 |
| Gujarat | 53 | 39 | 22 | 48.2 |
| Haryana | 84 | 74 | 202 | 53.0 |
| Himachal Pradesh | 51 | 47 | 41 | 71.8 |
| Jammu & Kashmir | 21 | 0 | 36 | 29.6 |
| Jharkhand | 56 | 158 | 78 | 2.3 |
| Karnataka | 61 | 65 | 67 | 36.7 |
| Kerala | 100 | 80 | 500 | 54.5 |
| Madhya Pradesh | 18 | 20 | 38 | 31.8 |

*Table 4.1 Continued*

---

[14] In 2011, at USD 84 billion, ICT exports exceeded any other Indian export item (World Bank database).

*Table 4.1 Continued*

| | | | | |
|---|---|---|---|---|
| Maharashtra | 37 | 15 | 35 | 47.5 |
| Nagaland | 88 | 0 | 100 | 8.2* |
| Orissa | 34 | 51 | 34 | 29.9 |
| Punjab | 81 | 50 | 62 | 58.8 |
| Rajasthan | 32 | 25 | 33 | 39.3 |
| Tamil Nadu | 62 | 21 | 31 | 50.2 |
| Uttar Pradesh | 47 | 102 | 51 | 29.0 |
| West Bengal | 47 | 38 | 44 | 38.1** |
| **Total** | **45** | **59** | **39** | **35.2** |
| **Average** | **50** | **44** | **51** | **34.8** |

*Notes:* * Arunachal Pradesh, Manipur and Nagaland ; ** West Bengal including Sikkim

*Source:* Calculated from March 2011 report to DU PMO available at http://www.dot.gov.in/

**Table 4.2: Rural urban differences in teledensity**

| | Total wireless subscribers (in million) | Rural share (%) | Teledensity | Urban teledensity | Rural teledensity |
|---|---|---|---|---|---|
| March 2013 | 867.8 | 39.5 | 70.9 | 140.7 | 40.2 |
| June 2012 | 934.1 | 36.0 | 77.0 | 162.5 | 39.8 |
| June 2009 | 427.3 | 29.5 | 36.6 | 87.2 | 15.4 |

*Source:* http://www.trai.gov.in/Content/PerformanceIndicatorsReports.aspx?ID=1&qid=1

Expansion of broadband remained inadequate even in cities.[15] Only 10 per cent of the population had access to the Internet. In the financial capital Mumbai, in 2013, the best available broadband was much below the standard in an average US city, and yet was six times more expensive. Table 4.3 shows continuing gaps, compared to best practices in key parameters. This hinders the development of a supporting ecosystem and potential markets.[16]

---

[15] It was only in 2004 that the Broadband Policy defined connectivity as 'An always-on data connection that is able to support interactive services including Internet access and has the capability of the minimum download speed of 256 kilobits per second (kbps) to an individual subscriber from the Point of Presence (POP) of the service provider', as compared to the 128 kbps that was earlier considered as broadband. India was far behind other Asian countries (see http://www.trai.gov.in/Content/broadband_policy.aspx).

[16] Broader yet relevant policy frameworks such as the Science, Technology and Innovation Policy (STIP) 2013, and its precursors also suffer from similar drawbacks in emphasizing R&D expenditure rather than factors that induce R&D. STIP aims to increase spending on R&D from the current 0.8 per cent in GDP to 2 per cent in the next 5 years. Mani (2013)

Table 4.3: Comparing ICT and mobile use in India and Pakistan

| | Fixed broadband internet subscribers (per 100 people) | | Internet users (per 100 people) | | Mobile cellular subscriptions (per 100 people) | |
|---|---|---|---|---|---|---|
| | India | Pakistan | India | Pakistan | India | Pakistan |
| 1991 | | | | | | 0.007 |
| 1992 | | | | | | 0.011 |
| 1993 | | | | | | 0.013 |
| 1994 | | | 0.001 | | | 0.020 |
| 1995 | | | 0.026 | | 0.008 | 0.032 |
| 1996 | | | 0.046 | 0.003 | 0.033 | 0.052 |
| 1997 | | | 0.071 | 0.028 | 0.088 | 0.101 |
| 1998 | | | 0.139 | 0.044 | 0.117 | 0.142 |
| 1999 | | | 0.273 | 0.055 | 0.182 | 0.188 |
| 2000 | | | 0.528 | | 0.339 | 0.212 |
| 2001 | 0.005 | | 0.660 | 1.319 | 0.610 | 0.503 |
| 2002 | 0.008 | | 1.538 | 2.577 | 1.194 | 1.129 |
| 2003 | 0.013 | | 1.686 | 5.041 | 3.046 | 1.570 |
| 2004 | 0.021 | | 1.976 | 6.164 | 4.650 | 3.223 |
| 2005 | 0.118 | 0.009 | 2.388 | 6.332 | 7.907 | 8.050 |
| 2006 | 0.199 | 0.016 | 2.805 | 6.500 | 14.35 | 21.37 |
| 2007 | 0.267 | 0.027 | 3.950 | 6.800 | 19.90 | 38.22 |
| 2008 | 0.443 | 0.089 | 4.380 | 7.000 | 29.13 | 52.57 |
| 2009 | 0.641 | 0.178 | 5.120 | 7.500 | 43.48 | 55.33 |
| 2010 | 0.897 | 0.306 | 7.500 | 8.000 | 61.42 | 57.14 |
| 2011 | 1.075 (27) | 0.417 | 10.07 (78) | 9.000 | 71.99 (95) | 61.61 |
| 2012 | 1.137 (28) | 0.515 | 12.58 (81) | 9.964 | 68.72 (98) | 66.77 |

*Note*: Figures in brackets are for the US

*Source*: International Telecommunication Union, World Telecommunication/ICT Development Report and Database, and World Bank estimates.

NTP recognized the potential of the mobile to be 'an instrument of empowerment' facilitating citizen-centric participative electronic service delivery

---

writes this requires the share of private sector R&D to rise from the current 30 per cent to almost 50 per cent. The tax regime is already very generous—200 per cent super corporate income tax deduction for R&D. But private R&D investment tends to be concentrated in pharmaceuticals, chemicals and automotive industries, and is dominated by MNCs whose quick patenting reduces spillovers. More attention is required on increasing the demand-side of innovations using competition (Mani, 2013) and wider innovation in society (Abrol, 2013)—our market size effect.

in key neglected Mark II areas such as health, education, agriculture,[17] skill development, employment as well as in governance, and in secure financial transactions without constraints from the skill and literacy barrier. The recognition is not new, but technological developments in convergence, together with NTP's promise of a simpler and more enabling policy regime, better incentives and coordination improve the chances of improving infrastructure.

The evolution from analog to digital technology has facilitated the conversion of voice, data and video to the digital form. This implies future convergence in networks, services and devices, in turn requiring convergence of licensing, registration and regulatory mechanisms in these areas. Such regulatory convergence will enable flexible public-private partnership (PPP) participation to create the missing last mile connectivity. But good infrastructure is a pre-requisite. Broadband is the key driver for network connectivity of mobile technology and availability of spectrum. NTP aims to provide affordable and reliable broadband-on-demand by the year 2015 at minimum 2 Mbps download speed with higher speeds of at least 100 Mbps on demand; increase rural teledensity to 70 by the year 2017 and 100 by 2020; provide broadband coverage to all VPs by 2014 and all villages and habitations by 2020. It will also work towards a 'Right to broadband'.

Optical fibre network is planned to be laid in all villages and habitations using the Universal Service Obligation Fund (USOF), providing non-discriminatory and technology neutral access. The methodology for utilizing USOF is to be periodically reviewed and benchmarked against best practices in other countries. Even as rural expansion is incentivized, the aim is to optimally utilize existing infrastructure. To facilitate this, telecom is to be recognized as an infrastructure sector.

The licensing framework is to be simplified by creating one national license, full mobile number portability, and free nationwide roaming. Fixed-mobile convergence is expected to release spectrum for other wireless services. Delinking of the licensing of networks from service delivery to end users is expected to enable optimal and efficient utilization of networks and spectrum as operators share active and passive infrastructure even as adequate competition is ensured through resale at the service level. Content neutral carriage charges, based on bandwidth utilization, are expected to also encourage non value added services, such as provision of data and information, on mobiles, even as competitive provision of value added services grows. These changes will themselves enhance infrastructure and allow it to be used more flexibly. Enforcing the VOIP facility will enhance affordability.

---

[17] A specific example is the use of new service formats such as Machine-to-Machine communications for remote operation of irrigation pumps and smart grids, thus, reducing current waste of water.

Infrastructure is used and created if there is a demand for the services it can provide. NTP aims to coordinate closely with all stakeholders, including other government entities to ensure last mile access and local content creation in regional languages, thus, developing an eco-system for broadband. Absence of coordination, even within the government, is a major reason for past failures.

The themes echo past policies but NTP adds value in emphasizing better governance and incentive structures. In addition to using price and competition based incentives, NTP also aims to improve regulation. Institutional, legal, and regulatory frameworks are to be strengthened, processes re-engineered, there is to be regular audit of spectrum usage, and better grievance redressal mechanisms for consumers.

NTP seeks to facilitate the active role of both private sector and different tiers of Government in expanding telecom infrastructure by smoothing the coordination. For example, by establishing an appropriate institutional framework and by simplifying the right of way policy for tower installation and laying of cable network. It also aims to promote synergies between broadband roll-out and other related Government programs. Taxes, duties and levies on the sector are to be rationalized even as a stable fiscal regime stimulates investments and lowers costs.

All telecom policies have sought, unsuccessfully, to boost domestic production and exports of telecommunication equipment and products. But NTP breaks new ground by creating better incentives. It promotes an ecosystem to meet Indian telecom sector demand and provides fiscal and financial incentives and specific guidelines for giving preference to domestic manufactures. Telecom service providers are to be asked to commit to purchase indigenous products that are comparable in price and performance to imported products, participate in trials of new indigenous products, and place pilot orders for them. Indian IPRs are to be incorporated in global standards, and open platform standards mobile phones encouraged to make India a global hub for value added services.

Better incentives will help but appropriate and timely decisions are also to be made. NTP lays down underlying principles to balance the interests of consumers, service providers and government revenue. But although competition is a stated principle, a duopoly in undersea cables raises costs of Internet connectivity. Although consumer interest is a stated principle, the Government continues to attempt to maximize revenues. Although convergence and flexibility is a stated principle, Bharati was not allowed to share 3G spectrum. Reliance brought a case against Bharati to prevent them from such sharing. Inaction is harming a major potential for inclusive innovation.

The analytical framework developed in the second section suggests improved implementation and a better local ecosystem has the potential to change the slopes of the budget line of the less well-off, as better infrastructure substitutes for their scarce private capital. Then they shift to intermediate technologies such as B, which develop in a virtuous cycle of induced innovation, as market size increases. This section shows despite some success in developing intermediate techniques such as mobiles, failures in supporting infrastructure continued to limit market size. The section below shows how, despite the growth in mobile use, absence of a focus on market size in banking policy limited the growth of mobile banking, thus, limiting further innovations in this area.

### Harnessing mobile telecom in payment systems

A major potential inclusive application of mobile technology is in mobile banking. About 60 per cent of the Indian population remains unbanked. Although new technologies offer many opportunities, banks seem to be slow in making use of these. But rapid growth in mobile usage, their wide penetration, competition and dynamism in designing new products, suggests mobile financial services could enable rapid strides in financial inclusion. Delays and transaction costs could fall for users.

But the Reserve Bank of India's (RBI's) preference is that banks use the services of business correspondents (BCs), with the definition expanded to include large corporates and small shops as BCs, to further inclusion. In mobile banking, remittances have to be from bank account to bank account. It wanted to give banks the opportunity to leverage new technology and extended agent network. Although payment gateways for e-commerce are also regulated by the RBI, and electronic payments are regarded as very secure with modern payment legislation, it was reluctant to allow person-to-person transactions and deposit holding by non-banks because of potential risks to deposit holders. Concerns also remain on sources of funds since it is difficult to implement Know Your Customer (KYC) with mobile service providers (MSPs). Their prepaid customer identification processes are lax as such customers pose a low financial risk for them. Given the large potential numbers of such cards, it is difficult to contain risks of anonymity, elusiveness and poor oversight.

Moreover, the belief was pure MSP transfers may not be so useful, since the use of electronic money was not yet widespread. RBI mandated charges and subsidy for banks issue cost of biometric access/smart cards, and make account-to-account fund transfers the cheapest mode of remittance. A bank-to-bank fund transfer of INR 1 lakh using NEFT would cost only INR 5/- for the customers. In contrast, a fund transfer of 1,000 Ksh (Kenyan Shilling) in M-PESA, the Kenyan MSP, costs the remitter 30 Ksh and the recipient between 25 Ksh to 75 Ksh. Failure of bank transactions are expected to be lower as compared to SMS based transactions. Failure to process transactions, or confirmation not received due to peak congestion, are major sources of M-PESA customer dissatisfaction. Resolution of complaints takes a long time because of the high volume of such calls.

In a smart card based technology, an agent is required for initiation of all transactions. Account details and the transaction data are stored on the smart card. The RBI is open, however, to mobile banking that links payment gateways and MSPs to banks. BCs are then required for enrolment, cash deposit and cash withdrawal, since all transaction data are held on the mobile phone. Mobile-based products could make customers independent of agents. Because the overarching goal is to expand financial services to unbanked population, permitted points of service for small value transactions are being expanded, for example, by allowing MSPs to function as BCs. MSPs are permitted to issue mobile wallets, but cash withdrawal is not yet allowed.

The provision of additional banking services, increasing access to credit, and raising the level of savings, for those currently excluded from the formal financial sector is the additional advantage of bank involvement. India has about 100 million migrant workers from central India who need to send remittances home. In Africa remittances sent across borders are known as 'taxi money', because of the taxis that routinely carry it (Maimbo et. al., 2010). A cost of transfer much below informal transfer methods, encouraged its entry into the formal financial sector. M-PESA provides a virtual prepaid payment product, used widely for remittances. The MSP is allowed to retain the prepaid amount and make person-to-person payments. M-PESA model also uses a National-ID scheme, which is yet to come up in India.

Wizzit Bank in South Africa and G-Cash in Philippines are successful models of partnership between banks and MSPs. The Central bank in the Philippines worked with mobile operators to provide branchless banking. Brazil also has 10 years of experience. Wizzit provides bank accounts on mobile phones with MSPs support. Services like person-to-person payments, transfers and prepaid purchases, and the use of a Maestro card for cash withdrawal are provided.

ICT and telecom developed similarly in India and Pakistan (Table 4.3) with India ahead on most parameters by 2011. The regulatory structure for mobile banking was set out in 2008 in both the countries. Better Indian payment systems allowed greater functionality in mobile banking.[18] Yet even 4 years after the approval for mobile banking transaction, Indian volumes remained low although there was some growth. Mobile banking transactions doubled to 5.6 million in January 2013 as compared to 2.8 million in the previous year.[19] But

---

[18] See the comparison in http://www.sbp.org.pk/Saarc/Publications/Matrix/PSMatrix.pdf

[19] See news report at http://www.business-standard.com/article/finance/mobile-banking-transactions-double-payments-rise-threefold-113041100353_1.html

this was small, given the large mobile subscriber base. Pakistan, with a much smaller population, already had double this number at 10.4 million transactions in September 2012 (SBP, 2012). So, it is helpful to compare the regulations in India with those in Pakistan, using our analytical framework, to identify the crucial differences.

### Regulatory requirements for Internet and mobile banking

The regulatory perspective in this rapidly changing area follows concerns first enunciated in the RBI guidelines for Internet banking. Mobile banking transactions were defined as undertaking banking transactions using mobile phones by bank customers that involve credit/debit to their account. The guidelines for Mobile Banking Transactions initially set out in October 2008, mandated that all transactions have to originate from one bank account and terminate in another bank account.

Initial regulatory clarifications related especially to:

(a)  Technology and security issues: Logical access control techniques and technological up gradation ensure secure Internet banking. Sensitive data like passwords are encrypted in transition. Periodic checks, tests and back-ups are prescribed, and every breach or failure of security systems is to be reported to RBI. Banks have to put in place appropriate risk mitigation measures like transaction limit (per transaction, daily, weekly, and monthly), transaction velocity limit, fraud checks, etc. Validation through a two-factor authentication, one of which is mPIN or any higher standard, with end-to-end encryption, was initially required at all stages of transaction processing irrespective of value limit. The mPIN was not to be in clear text anywhere in the network.

Standardized message formats like ISO 8583 are to be adopted for inter-operability between banks, and between their mobile banking service providers. Until the creation of a 24×7 robust national clearing and settlement infrastructure, banks are allowed to enter into bilateral or multilateral arrangement for inter-bank settlements, ensuring inter-operability.

(b)  Legal: Bilateral contracts are to be drawn up between the payee and the payee's bank, the participating banks and service provider that clearly define the rights and obligations of each party. Banks must make mandatory disclosures of risks, responsibilities and liabilities of the customers. They must be aware of customer rights, the extent to which they can be satisfied in the new environment, and how to protect themselves from new threats such as hacking. Customer complaints and grievance mechanism were laid down.

(c)  Sources of funds: Absence of full capital account convertibility implies restrictions for Internet banking also. Only banks licensed and supervised in India, and with a physical presence in India, are permitted to offer Internet banking products to residents of India. The products are restricted only to account holders and to local currency products. Existing exceptions for limited purposes, under the Foreign Exchange Management Act, such as where resident Indians maintain accounts with overseas banks, are permitted. Overseas branches of Indian banks can offer Internet banking services to overseas customers, but must satisfy both the host and the home supervisor. Guidelines on KYC, anti-money laundering, combating the financing of terrorism and filing suspicious transaction report to Financial Intelligence Unit–India are applicable to mobile based banking services also. These necessitate mandatory physical presence for registration of customers. Document-based registration is also required before starting the mobile banking service.

Banks were to seek one-time prior approval of the Reserve Bank of India for starting mobile services after obtaining their respective Board's approval. Such services could also be offered through the BCs.

An initial daily transaction limit prescribed was INR 5,000 per customer for funds transfer and INR 10,000 per customer for transactions involving purchase of goods or services. But these were successively relaxed. On 24 December 2009, the daily cap transaction limits for funds transfer and for purchase of goods and services was raised to INR 50,000. Transactions up to INR 1,000 were allowed without end to end encryption of messages. Cash-outs to the recipients were permitted through ATMs or BCs subject to a cap of INR 5,000 per transaction and a maximum of INR 25,000 per month per customer. On 4 May 2011 the transaction limit without end to end encryption was raised to INR 5,000. On 22 December 2011 the transaction cap of INR 50,000 per customer per day was removed. Banks were allowed to place their own limits based on their risk perception with the approval of their Board. The ceiling on cash-outs to the recipients through ATMs or BCs was raised to INR 10,000 per transaction subject to the existing cap of INR 25,000 per month (Khan, 2012). The RBI lowered reporting requirements on the reasoning that small amounts cannot be used for terrorist financing. It also permitted non-bank entities to issue mobile-based prepaid payment instruments, based on representation from MSPs. But the response was poor.

These changes responded to demands. Banks found end-to-end encryption costly, and wanted to avoid it for low value transactions. They wanted limits to be revised upwards to permit transactions like air-ticket purchases. They found entering into partnerships with MSPs difficult, with conflicts over each party's value creation. For example, MSP's think banking is only a value addition since they provide their mobile customer base. But banks think mobiles provide only an additional access channel, similar to the Internet, for their customer base. MSPs may be interested in the financial float. But RBI regards this as equivalent to deposit taking, which it is not willing to allow non-banks, because of problems in extending deposit insurance to non-banks.

Pakistan also started in 2008 with a bank led model that was expected to continue until the players and stakeholders gained some maturity. It was also not restricted to MSPs but could be offered through fuel distribution companies, Pakistan post and chain stores. Like India, customer account relationship had to reside with some financial institution (FI) and each transaction had to be through the customer account with no actual monetary value stored on the mobile-phone or server.

Permissible activities included opening and maintaining a branchless bank (BB) account, account-to-account fund transfer, person-to-person fund transfers, cash-in and cash-out, bill payments, merchant payments, loan disbursement or repayment, and remittances.

BB accounts were categorized in three levels. Level 1 BB accounts are for individuals only, level 2 accounts can be opened by individuals as well as by firms, entities, trusts, not-for-profit organizations, legal persons, etc., and level 3 BB accounts are for businesses only. Different KYC norms for these levels were laid down by SPB, subject also to the FIs policies.

The maximum balance for Level 1 was 60,000, and for level 2 and 3 it was set by the FI. The limit on debit/credit for Level 1 was 10,000 per day, 20,000 per month and 1,20,000 per year, for level 2 and 3 it was set by the FI. FIs had to make sure that customers did not breach their limits, sending them alerts when they were close to their limit, and they had to identify suspicious transactions.

Amendments in 2011 included introducing a level '0' to encourage involvement and learning by low income segments. The transaction and maximum balance limits on Level '0' accounts were ₹15,000 daily limit, ₹25,000 monthly limit, ₹1,20,000 annual limit and ₹1,00,000 maximum balance limit. The biometric fingerprint scans requirement for account opening that had discouraged participation, was removed. Accounts could now be opened electronically with a digital image. Physical presence was no longer essential. The transaction and maximum balance limits applicable to Level '1' Accounts were increased as follows: daily Limit ₹25,000 (previous limit was ₹10,000), monthly Limit ₹60,000 (previous limit was ₹20,000) and annual Limit ₹5,00, 000 (previous limit was

₹1,20,000). The maximum balance limit was removed. Account-to-person and person-to-person fund transfers facilities were introduced and payment of utility bills was excluded from normal transaction limits (SBP 2008, 2011 and 2012).

*Comparison:* So, Pakistan also insisted on a key role for FIs and data records to ensure security and stability. But the differences were higher initial levels and limits, more income categories, a wider universe of BCs, more flexibilities and functions for FIs, and reduction of transaction costs. These features brought in both the more and the less well off, increased creativity in use, linking it more closely to customer needs. As in Figure 4.2, the mobile banking intermediate technique B became the choice of both classes. Thus, it increased market size and sustained cumulative use. Bill payments and P2P transaction accounted for more than 80 per cent of Pakistani mobile transactions (SBP, 2012).

Mobile payment systems and wireless broadband are preconditions for mobile banking to succeed. They are in place in both countries, although improvements are possible and are on-going. For example, Bhandari and Kale (2010) argue that after the Payment Act India has the most advanced regulation in the world in this area. It is MSPs' provision of value added services that is inadequate. Transaction costs are probably higher because of security concerns. As UID is implemented KYC will become easier. Standardized simplified procedures are required that can work even for very basic mobiles (Rajan, 2014). Together with the UID Authority of India, the National Payments Council of India is working on a National Automated Clearing House or switch for mobile to mobile payments, called India Pay Mobile Switch, which will enable UID to UID micropayments. A UID would be linked to a mobile number and a bank account in a central database. Any bank or mobile phone enabled BC can then initiate a payment, which will be credited to the beneficiary's bank account linked to her UID.

The cost of smart phones is also expected to fall from INR 25,000 to INR 5,000, and together with cheaper cloud computing, enable a jump in Internet usage. Business opportunities for service providers will also expand with rapid growth planned in electronic government transfer payments. Thus, the market size of intermediate technologies is reaching the critical threshold. In responding to the opportunity, policy must identify measures that raise market size. Careful system design to keep transaction costs at a minimum and improve flexibility is essential.

## CONCLUSIONS

In a country in transition to higher per capita income levels, much of the growth comes from transferring population from low to high productivity activities. In ICT intermediate techniques such as mobiles can confer large rise in productivity, especially if induced innovation further improves affordability. Productive inclusion is also important in order to prevent the political economy problems that can otherwise reduce growth. Growth models have explored the contribution of endogenous technical change to sustaining growth. In this chapter, we focused on how this can also improve productive inclusion, and thus, help drive catch-up growth. The methodology is to derive the conditions under which more innovation occurs in intermediate technologies, which are widely affordable, and then to examine if Indian telecom policies satisfied those conditions.

The analysis shows that in order to shift the excluded to higher productivity intermediate techniques, policy can either lower the cost of the technique through innovation or make more capital available to the less well off, thus, improving the rate at which they can substitute low for high skills. This could be done through credit subsidies, income transfers, reducing technology and transaction costs, or through better public provision of the relevant infrastructure since it is more difficult for the less well-off to compensate privately for poor public infrastructure.

A large market size turns out to induce more innovation if goods of different quality are gross substitutes. The price effect, which favours high quality products, is overcome after the market size for intermediate technology crosses a threshold determined by relative prices, productivity and quantity. Productivity improving measures in the second policy set can help cross this threshold. They are to be preferred since they induce innovation in a decentralized manner, with less scope for policy errors, or requirement of large government funding. A virtuous cycle can occur if the number of consumers of and the revenues from selling intermediate technologies rise, then more innovations take place in such technologies.

Of the second policy set, infrastructure is to be preferred to income transfers since it directly increases productivity harnessing the fruits of the Mark II technological revolution, even as the Mark III, ICT, improves inclusion as well as spreads Mark II. Better infrastructure also suits the needs of India's demography as large numbers of young enter the workplace. Transfers suit the shrinking set of the persistent poor. Despite inclusive growth being the Indian policy objective, how to trigger the potential of ICT for inclusion is not well understood.

Although mobiles, which met a customer need, spread rapidly in India as freer private entry reduced costs, there were failures in the provision of complementary infrastructure such as broadband. Clarity regarding the importance of easier entry was lost. This reduced technology spillovers and the markets size for applications. Comparison of India's mobile banking policy with that of Pakistan illustrates measures limiting market size was partly responsible for India's relative failure.

The 2012 telecom policy internalizes some of these lessons and promises change on multiple fronts. More flexibilities, coordination, better incentives and governance may address weaknesses in implementation, last mile connectivity and the required ecosystem. But policy clarity is necessary to ensure decisive action. A focus on market size would generate more innovations that sustain inclusive growth. The analysis can be extended in a number of different directions. The analytical results can be derived in a more fully specified general equilibrium model. Across-country panel data can be built and used to test effect of market size on inclusive innovation. Further case studies of specific EDEs can also be undertaken.

## REFERENCES

Abrol, D. 2013. 'New Science, Technology and Innovation: A Critical Assessment'. *Economic and Political Weekly*, 48(9): 10–12. March 2.

Acemoglu, D., G. Gancia, and F. Zilibotti. 2012. 'Offshoring and Directed Technical Change'. *NBER working paper no. 18595*. Available at http://www.nber.org/papers/w18595.

Acemoglu, D. 2002. 'Technical Change, Inequality, and The Labour Market'. *Journal of Economic Literature* 40, 7–72.

Avgerou, C. 1998. 'How Can it Enable Economic Growth in Developing Countries?' [online] *London: LSE Research Online*. Available at http://eprints.lse.ac.uk/2581/

———— 1998. 'Why do New Technologies Complement Skills? Directed Technical Change and Wage Inequality'. *The Quarterly Journal of Economics* 113 (4): 1055–1089.

Bhandari, L., and S. Kale. 2010. 'Financial Inclusion via Universal Access to Electronic Payments, in India on The Growth Turnpike'. *Essays in Honour of Vijay L. Kelkar.* Sameer Kochhar (ed.). New Delhi: Academic Foundation.

Chakrabarty, K. C. 2010. *Mobile commerce, mobile banking: the emerging paradigm* http://www.rbi.org.in/Scripts/BS_ViewBulletin.aspx?Id=10854

Cecchini, S., and C. Scott. 2003. 'Can Information and Communications Technology Applications Contribute to Poverty Reduction? Lessons From Rural India'. *Information Technology for Development*, 10, 73–84.

Diamond, J. 1997. *Guns, Germs, and Steel: The Fates of Human Societies.* New York: W.W. Norton and Co.

Freeman, R. 1986. 'Demand for Education'. In *Handbook of Labour Economics,* edited by O. Ashenfelter and R. Layard. Vol. I. North Holland: Elsevier.

GOI (Government of India). 2012. *National Telecom Policy-2012*, Department of Telecommunications, June 2012, accessed from http://www.dot.gov.in/ in January 2013.

Goyal, A. 2005. 'New Technology and Labour Markets: Entrants, Outsourcing, and Matching'. *The Indian Journal of Labour Economics*, 48(4): 853–68. October–December.

———— 2007. 'Distant Labour Supply, Skills and Induced Technical Change'. *Information Analysis and Policy*, 19(2): 133–50. June.

———— 2011. 'Developing Women: Why Technology Can Help'. *Journal of Information Technology for Development*, 17(2): 112–32, April.

———— 2012. *'An Appraisal of Five Year Plans and the Future'*. *Yojana*, special issue on 'An Approach to 12th Five Year Plan – Issues and Challenges'. January.

Hasan, R., D. Mitra, and A. Sundaram. 2012. 'What Explains the High Capital Intensity of Indian Manufacturing?' *Indian Growth and Development Review*.

Hayami, Y. 1998. 'Toward an East Asian Model of Economic Development'. In *The Institutional Foundation of East Asian Economic Development*, edited by Y. Hayami and M. Aoki. *IEA Conference*, 127, 3–35. New York: Macmillan.

Jones, R. W., and H. Kierzkowski. 2005. 'International Trade and Agglomeration: An Alternative Framework'. *Journal of Economics*, Supplement 10, 1–16.

Jorgenson, D. 2001. 'Information Technology and the US Economy', *American Economic Review*, 91(1): 1–32.

Khan, H. 2012. 'Customizing Mobile Banking in India: Issues and Challenges'. *Address Delivered by Deputy Governor, Reserve Bank of India*, at the FICCI-IBA (FIBAC) Conference, September 5 Mumbai, accessed from http://rbidocs.rbi.org.in/rdocs/Speeches/PDFs/CMBI060912SC.pdf on January, 2012.

Kapoor, R., 2010. 'Financial Inclusion: Game Changer for Urban Renewal'. *The Economic Times* Mumbai, 20 September.

Maimbo, S., T. Saranga, and N. Strychacz. 2010. 'Facilitating Cross-border Mobile Banking in Southern Africa'. *The WB Economic Premise*, No. 26.August.

Mani, S. 2013. 'The Science, Technology and Innovation Policy 2013: An Evaluation'. *Economic and Political Weekly*, 48(10): 16–8. March 9.

Mani, S. 2007. 'Revolution in India's Telecommunications Industry', *Economic and Political Weekly*, 42 (7): 578–80. February 17.

OECD. 2002. Measuring the Information Economy, *OECD*, Paris.

Rajan, R. 2014. 'Financial Inclusion: Technology, Institutions and Policies'. *Keynote address by Governor, Reserve Bank of India, at the NASSCOM India Leadership Forum in Mumbai*, February 12.

Schmookler. J., 1966. *Invention and Economic Growth*. Harvard University Press: MA.

SBP (State Bank of Pakistan). 2008. 'Branchless Banking Regulations for Financial Institutions Desirous to Undertake Branchless Banking'. *Banking Policy and Regulations Department*, March 31, http://www.sbp.org.pk/bprd/2008/Annex_C2.pdf

———— 2011. 'State Bank Revises Branchless Banking Regulations to Bring Low Income Segment of Society into Financial Loop'. June 20, http://www.sbp.org.pk/press/2011/Regulations-20-Jun-11.pdf

———— 2012. 'Branchless Banking Newsletter: Leveraging Technologies and Partnerships to Promote Financial Inclusion'. Issue 5, July–September. Available at http://www.sbp.org.pk/publications/acd/BranchlessBanking-Jul-Sep-2012.pdf

Subramanian, A. 2013. 'This is a Golden Age of Global Growth (yes, you read that right)'. *Financial Times*, April 7. Available at http://www.ft.com/intl/cms/s/0/d69ec792-9e08-11e2-9ccc-00144feabdc0.html#axzz2Pw8fxvmR

# 5

# Determinants of India's Service Exports

Pravakar Sahoo
Ranjan Kumar Dash
Prabhu Prasad Mishra

## INTRODUCTION

Exports facilitate better resource allocation, efficient management style, economies of scale, and efficiency of production—and thereby favourably impact economic growth. This has been well established in the literature (Kruger, 1975; Balassa, 1978; Bhagwati, 1982; Srinivasan, 1985; Williamson, 1978; Awokuse, 2003). Further, exports enable imports of essential raw materials and capital goods—thus, increasing investment in the economy and thereby output (Rana & Dowling, 1990). Following the export-oriented growth argument, many developing countries—particularly East Asian countries—changed their development strategy from import substitution to export promotion during the 1970s. Consequently, East Asian countries have experienced a sustained increase in exports as well as economic growth[1] over the past three decades. Several studies have established the effectiveness of export-promotion strategies in promoting higher economic growth in East Asian countries (Krugman, 1986; Bhagwati, 1988; Dornbusch, 1992; Kruger, 1998).

Similar to East Asia, India also followed the export-led growth strategy in the 1990s as a part of its economic reforms[2] (comprising liberalization, privatization, and open economy policy). Empirical evidence also suggests that the export led growth strategy has been successful in India (Dhavan and Biswal, 1999; Parida and Sahoo, 2007). While export was contributing only around 7 per cent of Gross Domestic Product (GDP) until 1990–91, it has increased substantially over the past

---

[1]    Except the few years following the East Asian currency crisis.

[2]    However, the emphasis on the trade liberalization and export orientation started much before after recommendation of Alexander committee Report, 1978.

two decades and reached 24.64 per cent in 2011–12. At the same time, the share of service exports in the GDP has risen from a mere 1.39 per cent in 1990–91 to 7.73 per cent of GDP in 2011–12 (Figure 5.1).

**Figure 5.1: Exports as per cent of GDP**

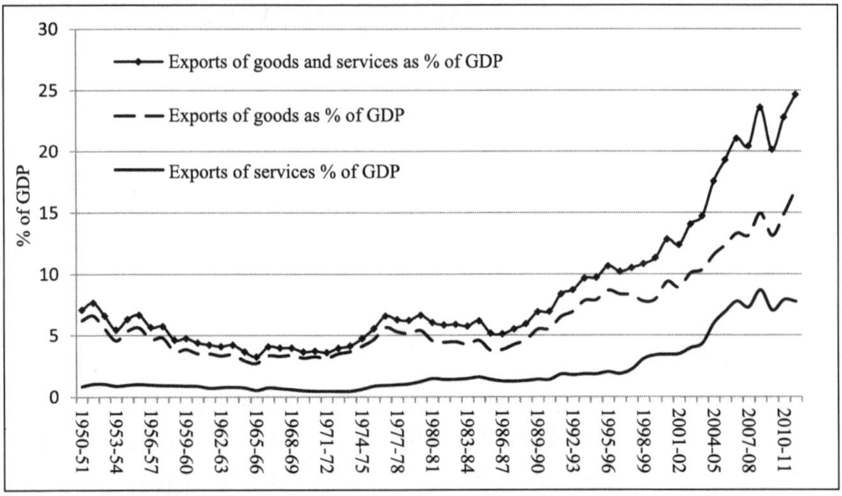

*Source*: Hand Book of Statistics on Indian Economy, 2011–12, RBI

Further, the growth of India's service exports has been substantial; for example, the growth rate between 2000–01 and 2011–12 was nearly 881 per cent in current prices, which is far higher than the 140 per cent absolute increase in world total export in services during the same period (Table 5.1). This is in line with the Indian economy's changing growth pattern, largely supported by the contribution of the services sector. The share of the service sector to the GDP increased from 50 per cent in 1990–91 to 66 per cent in 2011–12. The growth of the services sector in India has also been dependent on India's services exports. The importance of services export is enhanced due to the gap created by the deficit in goods exports. Given the high trade and transaction costs in India because of poor physical infrastructure, India has been increasingly depending on services exports for maintaining its external stability and growth. In this context, an attempt has been made to analyse India's exports over the past three decades and empirically examine the determinants of services exports. Although many studies analyse the factors of total exports and manufacturing exports, hardly any study comprehensively analyses the growth and determinants of service exports in India. It is hoped that this study would be useful to both scholars and policy makers in this area.

**Table 5.1: Absolute increase in world total service export (at current prices)**

| Category number | Category type | % increase from 2000 to 2010 |
|---|---|---|
| 1 | Transportation | 128 |
| 2 | Travel | 77 |
| 3 | Communication | 72 |
| 4 | Construction | 191 |
| 5 | Insurance | 222 |
| 6 | Financial | 198 |
| 7 | Computer and information | 460 |
| 8 | Royalties and fees | 198 |
| 9 | Other business services | 203 |
| 10 | Personal, cultural and recreational services | 96 |
| 11 | Government n.i.e. | 91 |
| (1 to 11) | Total service export | 140 |
| (3 to 11) | Other Services of IMF's BoP | 197 |

*Source*: UN Service Trade Data, http://unstats.un.org/unsd/servicetrade/default.aspx

## TRENDS, PATTERN AND COMPOSITION OF SERVICES EXPORTS: INDIA AND WORLD

The export trends show that the shares of total exports and of goods exports in GDP rose from the middle of the 1980s, while the share of services exports began increasing only in the early 1990s. The shares of total exports and of goods exports rose steeply during the 1980s and the 1990s while the share of service exports increased relatively faster in the 2000s (Figure 5.1). Growth in the exports of goods and services was stronger in the 1990s and 2000s than in the 1980s. During the 2000s, goods exports grew at 14 per cent on average while services exports increased at 17 per cent on average (Table 5.2).

**Table 5.2: India's export growth (decadal average)**

| Year | Total export growth | Goods export growth | Service export growth |
|---|---|---|---|
| 1950–59 | −0.85 | −1.63 | 3.40 |
| 1960–69 | 1.89 | 2.50 | −1.11 |
| 1970–79 | 8.73 | 7.80 | 14.34 |
| 1980–89 | 4.13 | 4.61 | 2.54 |
| 1990–99 | 11.94 | 10.72 | 15.71 |
| 2000–12 | 14.99 | 13.84 | 17.56 |

*Source*: Hand Book of Statistics on Indian Economy, 2011–12, RBI

The share of exports of miscellaneous services—software, business, financial, and communication services—has grown markedly over the past three decades and more so in the past decade (Table 5.3), from 27.04 per cent during 1950–60 to around 72 per cent of the total services exports during 2001–11. Far-reaching reforms during the 1990s in telecommunications, information technology (IT), and the financial sector brought about this spectacular growth. Except goods not included elsewhere (G.n.i.e), all components of services exports experienced higher growth in the past decade. The growth rate of exports of miscellaneous services was the highest (Table 5.4) during the past two decades, leading to a decrease in the share of other components in the total services exports.

**Table 5.3: Components of services export as share of total service export (decadal average)**

| Period | Travel | Transportation | Insurance | G.n.i.e receipts | Miscellaneous receipts |
|--------|--------|----------------|-----------|------------------|------------------------|
| 1950–60 | 8.69 | 32.60 | 7.47 | 24.21 | 27.04 |
| 1961–70 | 11.11 | 36.79 | 5.27 | 27.87 | 18.96 |
| 1971–80 | 28.15 | 33.89 | 4.41 | 9.77 | 23.77 |
| 1981–90 | 34.76 | 17.58 | 2.37 | 2.77 | 42.51 |
| 1991–2000 | 33.46 | 20.52 | 2.30 | 1.90 | 41.81 |
| 2001–11 | 14.01 | 11.49 | 1.70 | 0.82 | 71.99 |

G.n.i.e implies Goods Not Included Elsewhere which basically includes government expenditure on administrative machinery and foreign services outside the country.

*Source*: Hand Book of Statistics on Indian Economy, 2011–12, RBI

**Table 5.4: Decadal average growth rate of component of service exports**

| Year | Total service export | Travel | Transportation | Insurance | G.n.i.e. | Miscellneous |
|------|----------------------|--------|----------------|-----------|----------|--------------|
| 1950–59 | 3.40 | 8.69 | 3.10 | −0.95 | 5.63 | 0.94 |
| 1960–69 | −1.11 | 1.56 | 2.82 | 0.47 | −7.67 | −2.63 |
| 1970–79 | 14.34 | 28.72 | 3.12 | 4.07 | 4.66 | 24.22 |
| 1980–89 | 2.54 | 0.84 | 6.88 | 3.17 | −11.53 | 3.44 |
| 1990–99 | 15.71 | 8.56 | 9.97 | 10.95 | 51.75 | 21.80 |
| 2000–12 | 17.56 | 11.47 | 16.71 | 16.92 | −5.05 | 19.57 |

*Source*: Hand Book of Statistics on Indian Economy, 2011–12, RBI

The disaggregated data for these components are available for only a few years.[3] The share of miscellaneous service exports in total service exports has been growing; the most important component of miscellaneous service exports is software services exports, its share has been about 60 per cent in recent years (Table 5.5). Business services too has been showing growth potential—its share in miscellaneous service has increased from 9 per cent in 2000–01 to 25 per cent in 2011–12. Although the share of financial services looks miniscule, it is expected that financial services shall become a strong contributing factor to India's growth in services exports in future given its shares in the world services exports.

**Table 5.5: Miscellaneous service export and its component (as per cent of total)**

| Year | Misc service export as % of total service export | Software service export as % of total misc service export | Business service export as % of total misc service export | Financial service export as % of total misc service export | Communication service export as % of total misc service export | Other services exports as % of total misc service export |
|------|------|------|------|------|------|------|
| 2000–01 | 60.23 | 64.6 | 9.5 | 0.9 | 2.6 | 22.4 |
| 2001–02 | 64.35 | 68.5 | 12.4 | 1.2 | 3.3 | 14.5 |
| 2002–03 | 68.68 | 67.3 | 14.4 | 1.4 | 3.9 | 13.0 |
| 2003–04 | 66.88 | 71.4 | 18.4 | 1.8 | 4.9 | 3.5 |
| 2004–05 | 70.79 | 57.9 | 16.8 | 1.7 | 4.5 | 19.1 |
| 2005–06 | 73.02 | 56.0 | 22.2 | 2.9 | 3.7 | 15.2 |
| 2006–07 | 74.87 | 56.7 | 26.4 | 5.6 | 4.1 | 7.2 |
| 2007–08 | 74.21 | 60.1 | 25.0 | 4.8 | 3.6 | 6.5 |
| 2008–09 | 77.34 | 56.2 | 22.7 | 5.4 | 2.8 | 12.9 |
| 2009–10 | 73.84 | 70.3 | 16.1 | 5.3 | 1.8 | 6.6 |
| 2010–11 | 75.89 | 55.0 | 23.9 | 6.5 | 1.5 | 13.1 |
| 2011–12 | 71.98 | 60.7 | 25.3 | 5.8 | 1.6 | 6.6 |

*Source*: Hand Book of Statistics on Indian Economy, 2011–12, RBI

*Note*: For business service, financial service and communication service data for the period 2000–01 to 2003–04 has been extrapolated from the subsequent data.

---

[3] RBI provides data for software services export since 2000–01, and for other components since 2004–05. Therefore, it is not possible to analyse the trends of sub-sectors miscellaneous category before 2001.

**Table 5.6: World export of services (three main components) in US$ billion**

| Year | Transportation | Travel | Other services of IMF's BoP | Total service export |
|------|---------------|--------|------------------------------|----------------------|
| 2000 | 341 | 556 | 679 | 1,577 |
| 2001 | 337 | 536 | 694 | 1,567 |
| 2002 | 362 | 572 | 771 | 1,705 |
| 2003 | 409 | 644 | 911 | 1,964 |
| 2004 | 510 | 730 | 1,134 | 2,374 |
| 2005 | 579 | 769 | 1,250 | 2,598 |
| 2006 | 645 | 847 | 1,475 | 2,966 |
| 2007 | 769 | 974 | 1,809 | 3,553 |
| 2008 | 895 | 1,060 | 2,019 | 3,974 |
| 2009 | 688 | 934 | 1,930 | 3,551 |
| 2010 | 778 | 982 | 2,021 | 3,781 |

*Source*: UN Service Trade Data, http://unstats.un.org/unsd/servicetrade/default.aspx

### *World service trade*

To analyse India's position in service trade vis-á-vis the world, we used the UN Service Trade data, which is available from 2000 to 2011[4] (see Appendix A1 for details). Three main components of the IMF's traditional BoP data in services—transport, travel, and other services—consistently increased in absolute terms from 2000 to 2008 in current value. They slumped a little in 2009 due to the recession in the world economy, but recovered in 2010 (Table 5.6). The value of transportation export was US$ 341 billion during 2000, US$ 895 billion in 2008, and US$ 778 billion in 2010, after recovering from the recession in 2009. Likewise, the total value of travel export was US$ 556 billion during 2000, US$ 1,060 billion in 2008, and US$ 982 billion in 2010. Importantly, the other service category (which includes categories 3–11 in UN's EBOPS) increased threefold from US$ 679 billion in 2000 to US$ 2019 billion during 2008 and stood at US$ 2,021 billion in 2010 after the recovery. The sub-sectors that fuelled this increase are computer and information services, insurance, other business services, financial services, and royalties and fees. Although the volume of computer and information services increased 460 per cent, the biggest impact was from other

[4] Since for the year 2011, large number of countries including India has not reported the data yet our period of analysis would be 2000–10.

business services: it constitutes almost half of other services exports (item 3 to 11), i.e., US$ 920 billion out of US$ 2,021 billion (2010). As a percentage of total service exports, three items formed the lion's share during 2010: transport (20.6 per cent), travel (26 per cent), and other business services (24.3 per cent). The other eight sub-sectors of EBOPS shared the other 29 per cent (Table 5.7).

We also use Herfindahl-Hirschman index to measure market concentration of world services exports (see Appendix A.2). The concentration in total services exports has reduced from 0.059 in 2000 to 0.0 41 in 2010 (Table 5.8). While the pattern of concentration is not uniform across sectors, there is a declining trend in HHI in travel and royalties and fees export over the past decade. Concentration is generally lower than 0.1 in most sectors except insurance services, financial services, computer and information services, royalties, and license fees. In these highly concentrated services exports markets, there are variations in concentration over the decade. The concentration in the insurance and financial services exports market rose steeply in and around 2003 and fell soon after. There was a decline in travel, transport, and communication services exports concentration since 2000, but the concentration in transportation and communication and in other business services and personal, cultural, and recreational services rose towards the end of the decade. There was a steep rise in HHI in computer and information service from 2009 to 2010, possibly due to India's increasing influence. The case with construction is also the same with a rise since 2007, which may be because China displaced Japan as the largest exporter in this segment. Overall, concentration is not very high except in a few sectors such as licence, fees, computer, and information service, which are technology-intensive sectors. There is much scope for India in sectors such as other business services, which is less concentrated, and a high growth sector. Likewise, there is scope in financial services, royalties, and licence fees where dominant players are losing their place to newly emerging exporting countries.

The analysis of the composition, trend, and patterns show that India is doing better in certain services exports category but there is potential in many other sectors such as financial, communication and business services. The next step is to empirically analyse the factors that affect the services exports of India.

Table 5.7: Share of different category of world services export over the year

| Year | Transportation | Travel | Communication | Construction | Insurance | Financial | Computer and information | Royalties and fees | Other business services | Personal, cultural and recreational services | Government n.i.e. |
|------|------|------|------|------|------|------|------|------|------|------|------|
| 2000 | 21.6 | 35.3 | 3.7 | 1.8 | 2.0 | 5.7 | 2.4 | 5.3 | 19.3 | 0.8 | 2.1 |
| 2001 | 21.5 | 34.2 | 3.2 | 1.9 | 2.3 | 5.5 | 2.9 | 5.2 | 20.5 | 0.7 | 2.1 |
| 2002 | 21.2 | 33.5 | 2.8 | 2.0 | 3.0 | 5.5 | 3.1 | 5.3 | 20.7 | 0.7 | 2.2 |
| 2003 | 20.8 | 32.8 | 2.4 | 2.0 | 3.1 | 5.7 | 3.5 | 5.4 | 21.5 | 0.7 | 2.2 |
| 2004 | 21.5 | 30.8 | 2.4 | 1.9 | 4.3 | 6.0 | 3.8 | 5.7 | 20.8 | 0.7 | 2.1 |
| 2005 | 22.3 | 29.6 | 2.5 | 2.1 | 2.4 | 6.6 | 3.9 | 5.9 | 21.8 | 0.7 | 2.2 |
| 2006 | 21.7 | 28.5 | 2.7 | 2.2 | 2.2 | 7.3 | 4.3 | 5.7 | 22.5 | 0.7 | 2.1 |
| 2007 | 21.7 | 27.4 | 2.6 | 2.3 | 2.3 | 8.2 | 4.5 | 5.6 | 22.9 | 0.6 | 1.9 |
| 2008 | 22.5 | 26.7 | 2.7 | 2.7 | 2.3 | 7.4 | 5.1 | 5.6 | 22.8 | 0.6 | 1.7 |
| 2009 | 19.4 | 26.3 | 2.8 | 2.8 | 2.9 | 7.2 | 5.5 | 6.4 | 24.2 | 0.6 | 1.8 |
| 2010 | 20.6 | 26.0 | 2.7 | 2.2 | 2.7 | 7.1 | 5.6 | 6.6 | 24.3 | 0.6 | 1.7 |

*Source:* UN Service Trade Data, http://unstats.un.org/unsd/servicetrade/default.aspx

Table 5.8: Normalized Herfindahl index of concentration in world service export market

| Year | Total services export | Transportation | Travel | Communications services | Construction services | Insurance services | Financial services | Computer and information services | Royalties and license fees | Other business services | Personal, cultural, and recreational services | Government services, n.i.e. |
|---|---|---|---|---|---|---|---|---|---|---|---|---|
| 2000 | 0.059 | 0.042 | 0.071 | 0.057 | 0.084 | 0.101 | 0.140 | 0.105 | 0.404 | 0.056 | 0.092 | 0.091 |
| 2001 | 0.055 | 0.039 | 0.065 | 0.053 | 0.069 | 0.107 | 0.145 | 0.112 | 0.390 | 0.058 | 0.070 | 0.074 |
| 2002 | 0.051 | 0.036 | 0.060 | 0.049 | 0.061 | 0.110 | 0.139 | 0.106 | 0.383 | 0.056 | 0.070 | 0.064 |
| 2003 | 0.046 | 0.033 | 0.056 | 0.045 | 0.064 | 0.094 | 0.148 | 0.106 | 0.319 | 0.052 | 0.083 | 0.066 |
| 2004 | 0.044 | 0.033 | 0.046 | 0.043 | 0.060 | 0.266 | 0.154 | 0.108 | 0.270 | 0.052 | 0.084 | 0.073 |
| 2005 | 0.042 | 0.032 | 0.041 | 0.041 | 0.069 | 0.132 | 0.144 | 0.110 | 0.259 | 0.049 | 0.078 | 0.074 |
| 2006 | 0.041 | 0.031 | 0.043 | 0.040 | 0.071 | 0.084 | 0.136 | 0.106 | 0.267 | 0.045 | 0.060 | 0.088 |
| 2007 | 0.040 | 0.031 | 0.041 | 0.039 | 0.065 | 0.081 | 0.138 | 0.109 | 0.266 | 0.044 | 0.050 | 0.088 |
| 2008 | 0.038 | 0.031 | 0.040 | 0.037 | 0.068 | 0.076 | 0.134 | 0.106 | 0.238 | 0.042 | 0.051 | 0.068 |
| 2009 | 0.041 | 0.031 | 0.041 | 0.040 | 0.074 | 0.100 | 0.138 | 0.102 | 0.214 | 0.045 | 0.055 | 0.087 |
| 2010 | 0.041 | 0.032 | 0.039 | 0.040 | 0.081 | 0.098 | 0.135 | 0.117 | 0.213 | 0.045 | 0.063 | 0.077 |

*Source:* UN Service Trade Data, http://unstats.un.org/unsd/servicetrade/default.aspx

## LITERATURE REVIEW

Although there exists a vast literature on the determinants of goods exports, the literature on the determinants of service exports is limited and a recent phenomenon. Therefore, the types of policies that can help support services export growth are not widely known. Increasing tradability of services allows the cross-border exchange of services such as professional services that previously required the close proximity of providers and consumers (World Bank, 2010).

Barcenilla and Molero (2003) estimate the determinants of services export flows for 15 European countries for the years 1976–2000. Using the traditional demand function, the study finds that foreign income is one of the important variables, with the coefficient being more than 1 for 11 countries out of 15 countries. In addition to foreign income, price and exchange rate are important variables in explaining services exports. Grunfeld and Moxnes (2003) identified the determinants of service trade and foreign affiliate sales in a gravity model using bilateral data for the 22 OECD countries and their trading partners over 1999–2000. The study finds that trade barriers and corruption in the importing country have a strong negative impact on service trade and foreign affiliate sales. In addition, distance has a considerable negative impact on exports and foreign affiliate sales. Kimura and Lee (2006) assessed the impact of various factors on bilateral services trade relative to that on bilateral goods trade, using the standard gravity model from 10 OECD member countries to other economies (including OECD and non-OECD member countries) for the period 1999 to 2000. The results show that the gravity equation is applicable for services trade, and it is observed that there are some differences between services and goods trade with regard to the elasticities with respect to the explanatory variables. Among others, the study found that geographical distance, cost of transport and general economic liberalization are important for services trade.

Using the standard gravity model, Shepherd and Marel (2010) explore the determinants of services trade for APEC member countries during 1995–2008. The study finds that market size, members in regional trade agreement, distance, restrictive regulation, and common language are major determinants of service trade. Based on the empirical evidence, the chapter suggests that measures designed to reduce transport costs and improve infrastructure and network connectivity are likely to boost trade in services as well as in goods. Similarly, using a gravity model, Shingal (2010) analyses various determinants of trade in services, including market size, trade in goods, the presence of an English-speaking workforce, quality of infrastructure, the openness of the trade policy regime toward the various modes of services delivery, cost of human capital, and common laws/legal systems for 25 exporting and 53 importing countries for 5 years over 1999–2003. Shingal's main findings are that human capital, teledensity, and trade restrictiveness variables have the biggest impact on bilateral services trade, and thus, should be the policy focus if the objective is to promote services trade.

Nyahoho (2010) examines the importance of factor intensity as a determinant of trade in disaggregated services. Human capital is clearly related to exports of computer and information services. Construction services and public works, royalties and licence fees, and computer and information services are positively linked to research and development intensity. Marel (2011) examines the determinants of comparative advantage in explaining services trade. Using a country sample of 23 OECD countries and panel fixed effects model, the study finds that factor endowments such as skilled labour force and Internet and mobile communication technologies (ICT)-related capital stock, institutions, and better regulatory framework are the major sources of comparative advantage in services trade. Kaur (2012) has examined the export potential in the US service sector with its Asian trade partners (Japan, China, India, Singapore, South Korea, and Hong Kong) by using the gravity model over the period 2000–08. Based on panel data analysis, the study finds that the US has export potential in services for India and Japan. Further, the US had convergence in services exports with three Asian countries (Hong Kong, India, and Korea) and divergence with three Asian countries (Japan, China, and Singapore) in total services exports.[5] Eichengreen and Gupta (2012) examined the determinants of the services export performance of 60 developing countries, including India, over the period 1980–2008. The study finds that, among other factors, per capita income of exporter country, size of the market, world demand of services exports, infrastructure development, FDI, goods export and human capital are important factors that explain services exports. Nasir and Kalirajan (2013) examine the determinants of modern export performance of South Asian and East Asian countries over 2002–08. Estimation results show that the performance of emerging economies in South Asia and the ASEAN region in terms of the realization of export potential is considerably lower than that of North America and Europe. The results also show that the number of graduates and the ICT infrastructure in emerging countries are among key factors for modern services exports.

Most of these studies are cross country studies, which may not be applicable to an emerging country such as India that has been doing better in services exports. The present study tries to fill this gap by carrying out an India-specific study.

---

[5]   The Speed of convergence is defined as average growth rate of potential trade divided by average growth rate of actual trade between the years of observations. There is a convergence if growth rate of potential is lower than that of actual exports and the computed speed of convergence is negative. There is a divergence in the opposite case.

## POSSIBLE DETERMINANTS OF SERVICES EXPORTS

Based on the above empirical studies, we find that service sector performance critically depends on human capital, world demand, exchange rate behaviour, the quality of the telecommunications network, infrastructure stocks, the quality of institutions, and inflows of FDI. In this section, we briefly discuss these factors and other potential factors.

### *World demand/income (SIMP/WY)*

There exists a vast literature estimating demand/income elasticities for exports of goods but very few studies estimate the demand/income elasticity for export of services, especially for developing economies. The services export demand is also influenced by the condition prevailing in the world market. The demand for services exports increases in response to the income of the rest of the world, i.e., higher the level of foreign real income, larger would be the demand for nations services export, ceteris paribus. Empirical results suggest that the average long-run income elasticities are found to be approximately more than 1, but there is a wide diversity of experiences (Pain and van Welsum, 2004). The highest income elasticity of exports to the world is found to be for travel services, which is consistent with other studies (Huang and Viana, 1995; Deardorff et al., 2000). The measurement of world demand variable has often varied across studies. Generally, three income measures are used in the literature: GNP or GDP, industrial production, and world demand for real imports of services. In this study, we consider both world demand for Services Imports (SIMP) and World income (WY), net of exporting country.

### *Real exchange rate*

The impact of relative price movements on exports of services depends on the size of the price elasticity. The second major factor that affects export supply capacity is the real exchange rate, which can be an important element in determining export growth, diversification, and the international competitiveness of goods produced in a country (UNCTAD, 2005). A stable real exchange rate is conducive to export expansion (Mouna and Reza, 2001). While an overvalued currency can undermine export competitiveness through a direct loss of price competitiveness for exporting firms, undervaluation of the currency can bolster export competitiveness (Biggs, 2007), enhance the incentives for export activities, and lead to diversification of exports (Mouna and Reza, 2001). The appreciation of the Real effective exchange rate (REER) decreases the competitiveness of domestic exports in foreign markets, resulting in decreased demand for exports (Joshi & Little, 1994; Edwards and Alves, 2005). Hence, we expect a negative link between the appreciation of REER and export demand, and vice versa. International studies typically conclude that price elasticities for services are smaller than those found for merchandise trade. The overall price elasticity for services exports is typically around −0.2 to −0.4, with travel-related services being more elastic and business services relatively inelastic (Pain and van Welsum, 2004).

## Manufacturing Exports

It is argued that an increase in manufacturing exports leads to a higher demand of services, due to the network effect. Further, the exports of services are linked closely with and arise due to the export of goods since services like transport, travelling, communication and business services are used as inputs (Lodefalk, 2012; Eichengreen and Gupta, 2012). The use of knowledge intensive business and of financial, transport, and communication services in manufacturing production has been found to be positively correlated with productivity and the source of comparative advantage in international trade (Hoekmanand Mattoo, 2008; Francois and Hoekman, 2010). Therefore, a rise in manufacturing exports is expected to boost services exports.

## Human Capital

Poor human capital in the service-exporting country hinders technology transfer and learning and has been shown to hamper export growth and diversification in low-income countries (Hausmann, Hwang and Rodrik, 2006; Biggs, Shah and Srivastava, 1996). The empirical literature confirms that service sector performance critically depends on human capital, the quality of the telecommunications network, and the quality of institutions (Shingal, 2010). A country's level of human development indicators is an important and useful barometer of how much it is likely to benefit from international trade in services. A healthier and more skilled and educated workforce is likely to contribute to productivity, competitiveness, and higher exports, particularly services exports. Therefore, high human capital stock is positively related to the export capacity of the domestic economy.

## Financial development

Financial sector development is another important factor of export supply; for example, firms that can access finance at reasonable cost find it easier and cheaper to finance working capital needs (including trade financing) and investments in technical upgrading and new innovative activities and can, therefore, export or export more (Biggs, 2007; Aghion and Griffith, 2005). If financial markets are underdeveloped and risks not diversified, firms' supply response is affected adversely. Therefore, it is expected that financial development is positively associated with services exports. In this study, the financial development index[6] is based on the studies by Bandiera et al. (2000) and King and Levine (1993) and developed through principal component analysis. It includes bank branches per million population, bank credit as percentage of GDP, and M2 by GDP ratio. Alternatively, we also consider domestic bank credit.

## Infrastructure development

One of the major factors of services exports supply capacity is domestic infrastructure, particularly telecom and communication infrastructure. To sustain the rapid growth of services exports, it is necessary to have a well-functioning infrastructure, including electric power, road and rail connectivity, telecommunications, air transport, and efficient ports (UNCTAD, 2005). Infrastructure can refer to the financial system that facilitates and supports trade or the education and training system that produces skilled labour. Poor infrastructure facilities characterize most South Asian countries and impede their trade, competitiveness, and sustainable development (Jones, 2006; Sahoo and Dash, 2010). Empirical studies also support the positive relationship between infrastructure development and services export performance (Eichengreen and Gupta, 2012; Shingal, 2010). Therefore, we expect positive relationship between infrastructure stock and services exports performance. Here, we develop a infrastructure development index by taking important infrastructure variables such as air freight transport (million tons per km), electric power consumption (kWh per capita), rail density (per 1,000 population), rail density (per 1,000 population), energy use (kg of oil equivalent per capita), and total telephones lines (main line plus cellular phones) per 1,000 population.

## Institutions

The quality of institutions and policies decisively determines if countries can benefit from globalization (UNCTAD, 2008; Mattoo et al., 2008). In low-income countries, weak and missing institutions have been shown to limit the ability of

---

[6] The first factor or principal component has an eigenvalue larger than one and explains over two-thirds of the total variance. There is a large difference between eigenvalues and variance explained by the first principal component and the next. Hence, we choose the first principal component for making a composite index of the combined variance of the different aspects of financial development captured by the three variables.

firms to take advantage of new trading opportunities (Stiglitz and Charlton, 2006; Biggs, 2007). It has also been shown that institutional quality is highly correlated with trade (Francois and Manchin, 2006). In this regard, Francois and Manchin (2006) show that export performance and the propensity to take part in the trading system depends on institutional quality. In addition to the direct effect, institutions may also indirectly affect trade through their impact on other variables of trade flows, such as investment and productivity (Méon and Sekkat, 2006). Kimura and Lee (2006) suggest that trade in services is positively influenced by the quality of institutions as measured by the degree of corruption, complexity of export procedures, and rigidity in employment law (Lennon, 2006) or by the economic freedom index (). Therefore, we expect this variable to have a positive sign. In our case, we use an index of economic freedom in the world (scaled 0–10) from the Cato Institute.

### Foreign direct investment

Foreign direct investment influences supply-side determinants of services exports, reflecting to some extent the quality of physical capital as well as worker skills and market penetration potential (De Gregorio, 1992). There is consensus among development economists that FDI inflows are likely to play an important role in explaining the growth of recipient countries (De Mello, 1999). However, the World Bank (1993) notes that the role of FDI in export promotion depends crucially on its motive: FDI may contribute to export growth if it is aimed at tapping export markets by exploiting a country's comparative advantage but not if it is aimed at capturing the domestic market (tariff-jumping type of investment). Thus, whether FDI contributes to export growth or not depends on the nature of the policy regime (Sharma, 2000). Like the theoretical views, the existing empirical studies of the role of FDI in export performance also report mixed findings. In contrast, others indicate that FDI have a positive effect on the export performance of host countries (UNCTAD, 2005; Eichengreen and Gupta, 2012).

### Services trade barriers (STB)

The service sector encompasses a largely heterogeneous selection of activities, and operates differently. This heterogeneity gives rise to a range of barriers to services trade. As noted in the introduction, these barriers tend to be qualitative or non-tariff barriers (NTBs), such as legal or regulatory restrictions on the import of services. The types of restrictions imposed vary between service sectors and modes of supply that are relevant in each (Walsh, 2006). Hoekman and Braga (1997) summarize four major barriers to services trade and explain that quantity-based restrictions impose quotas or other types of quantity limitations. Findlay and Warren (2000) show the importance of non-discriminatory barriers, i.e., barriers that restrict the supply of services by domestic and foreign producers equally. More importantly, barriers to trade in services are difficult to measure compared to tariffs and non-tariff barriers to trade in goods. In the empirical literature, various studies have used different measures: for example, Grünfeld and Moxnes (2003) use the Services trade restrictiveness index (STRI) developed by Findlay and Warren (2000), Kimura and Lee (2006) use the Economic Freedom of the World (EFW) index, and Nasir and Kalirajan (2013) use regional/multilateral trade agreement that covers goods and services. In our case, we use the cumulative number of regional/multilateral trade agreements that help reduce the barriers to services exports. We expect a positive relation between reduction in trade barriers because of trade agreements and services export demand.

## METHODOLOGY, DATA SOURCES AND RESULTS

We finally estimate services export function considering all possible determinants based on both theoretical and empirical literature. The total services export function is given below:

$$\text{TSER}_t = \alpha_0 + \beta_0 \, \text{SIMP}_t + \beta_1 \text{RER}_t + \beta_2 \, (\text{INFRA/TEL})_t$$

$$+ \beta_3 \, (\text{GSER/SCH})_t + \beta_4 \, (\text{FIN/DBC})_t + \beta_5 \text{MNEXP}_t$$

$$+ \beta_6 \text{FDIY}_t + \beta_7 \text{INST}_t + \beta_8 \, \text{TA} + \text{u}_t \qquad (1)$$

As the services exports are broadly divided into modern (MSER) and traditional services exports (TRSER),

The expected sign of $(\beta_0, \beta_2, \beta_3, \beta_4, \beta_5, \beta_6, \beta_7, \beta_8 > 0)$ and $(\beta_1 < 0)$

The definition of the variables along with sample period and data sources is given below.

| Variables | Definition | Sample period | Sources |
|-----------|------------|---------------|---------|
| TSER | Total services exports as ratio of GDP | 1980–2011 | RBI |
| MSER | Modern services (software, business, financial, insurance and communication) exports as ratio of GDP | 1980–2011 | RBI |
| TRSER | Traditional services (transportation and travelling) exports as ratio of GDP | 1980–2011 | RBI |

*Continued*

*Continued*

| LSIMP | Log of world demand for services imports | 1980–2011 | WDI |
|---|---|---|---|
| WY | Real world GDP net of India | 1980–2011 | WDI |
| RER | Real exchange rate | 1980–2011 | WDI |
| INFRA | Infrastructure index | 1980–2011 | WDI |
| GSER | Gross secondary enrollment ratio proxy for human development | 1980–2011 | WDI |
| FINDEV | Financial development index | 1980–2011 | WDI and RBI |
| MNEXP | Manufacturing exports as ratio of GDP | 1980–2011 | WDI |
| FDIY | FDI inflows as ratio of GDP | 1980–2011 | WIR |
| EF | Index of economic freedom in the world | 1980–2011 | Cato Institute |
| TA | Cumulative number of free trade agreements | 1980–2011 | Ministry of Commerce |
| DBC | Domestic credit provided by banks as ratio of GDP | 1980–2011 | WDI |
| SCH | Average years of school | 1980–2011 | UNDP |
| LQL | Labour force adjusted for average years of school | 1980–2011 | UNDP, WDI |
| TEL | Telecom density | 1980–2011 | WDI |

*Source*: Authors' compilation

### Data sources

Annual data on aggregate and disaggregate services exports and bank branches have been collected from the Reserve Bank of India (RBI). Data on world demand for Services Imports (SIMP) manufacturing exports (MNEXP), World income (WY), gross enrolment ratio (GER), exchange rate (RER), consumer price index of India and USA, broad money ratio (M2Y), and domestic credit by banking sector (DBC) are collected from the World Development Indicators (WDI) of the World Bank. The index of economic freedom in the world is collected from the Cato Institute.[7] Infrastructure variables considered in this study are air freight transport (million tons per km), electric power consumption (kWh per capita), rail

---

[7] The index consists of five major areas: Size of Government; Legal System and Property Rights; Sound Money; Freedom to Trade Internationally; and Regulation. Within the five major areas, there are 24 components in this year's index. Many of those components are themselves made up of several sub-components. In total, the index comprises 42 distinct variables. Each component and sub-component is placed on a scale from 0 to 10. For more on this index see http://www.cato.org/economic-freedom-world.

density (per 1000 population), rail density (per 1000 population), energy use (kg of oil equivalent per capita), and total telephone lines (main line plus cellular phones) per 1000 population are taken from various years of the World Development Indicators (see appendix 3A). The financial development index used in this study is developed through principal component analysis, like the infrastructure index, and includes bank branches per million population, bank credit as percentage of GDP, and M2 by GDP ratio (See Appendix 4A).

### Analysis of results

We test for unit roots in each series before estimating a model, as it involves time series data. The stationary property of each series is tested by using the Augmented Dickey-Fuller (ADF) unit root test. First, we test unit root by assuming there is no trend but only intercept. Then, we test stationarity by assuming time trend in the variable. Since regressions have been run for aggregate exports as well as for sector-specific exports, we have undertaken tests separately. The results[8] of ADF unit root test show that we have a combination of I(1) and I(0) variables and given that we have only 32 observations, we use Auto-Regressive Distributed Lag (ARDL)for cointegration analysis and Dynamic OLS technique for estimating long-run coefficients. All the variables are non-stationary at level but stationary at first difference except the log value of real world income and FDI as ratio of GDP. Therefore, ADF unit root test results suggest that we have a mixture of I (1) and I(0) variables. Therefore, the next step in empirical analysis includes the establishment of a long-run equilibrium relationship between various services exports and their determinants.

We use an ARDL method developed by Pesaran et al. (2001) to find out the long-run relationship among the relevant variables.[9] The ARDL bound test is based on the Wald-test (F-statistic). The asymptotic distribution of the Wald-test is non-standard under the null hypothesis of no cointegration among the variables. Two critical values are given by Pesaran et al. (2001) for the cointegration test. The lower critical bound assumes all the variables are I(0), meaning that there is no cointegration relationship between the examined variables. The upper bound assumes that all the variables are I(1), meaning that there is cointegration among the variables. When the computed F-statistic is greater than the upper bound critical value, then the H0 is rejected (the variables are cointegrated). The result

---

[8]  Unit root results are available on request.

[9]  ARDL model is not only suitable for small sample size but also takes care the problem of endogeneity (Narayan, 2004).

of the ARDL co-integration test is presented in Table 5.9. There is a long-run relationship or co-integration among the variables when services exports (total, modern, and traditional) are the dependent variables because their F-statistic exceeds the upper bound critical value (3.50) at the 5 per cent levels (Table 5.9). Given that we have only 32 observations, we have considered maximum 2 lags and the lags are selected on the basis of AIC. Thus, the null of non-existence of stable long-run relationship is rejected in favour of long-run stable relation. These results also warrant proceeding to the next stage of estimation.

**Table 5.9: ARDL Co integration test (1980–2011)**

| Dependent variable | F-stat | 5% Critical value# | Result |
|---|---|---|---|
| TSER | 7.87* | 3.50 | Rejection of null of no co-integration |
| MSER | 6.72* | 3.50 | Rejection of null of no co-integration |
| TRSER | 6.96* | 3.50 | Rejection of null of no co-integration |

*Notes:* The order of ARDL is selected on the basis of Akaike Information Criteria (AIC). # denotes upper bound critical values with seven independent variables. * denotes Rejection of null hypothesis of no-co-integration in favour of co-integration.

*Source:* Author's Computation

### *The Dynamic OLS (or DOLS) procedure*

This procedure, developed by Saikonnen (1991) and Stock and Watson (1993), has the advantage that the endogeneity of any of the regressors has no effect, asymptotically, on the robustness of the estimates. Further, statistical inference on the parameters of the co-integrating vector is facilitated by the fact that the *t*-statistics of the estimated co-efficient have asymptotic normal distribution, even with endogenous regressors (Stock and Watson, 1993). This procedure also allows for direct estimation of a mixture of I (1) and I (0) variables. The DOLS procedure incorporates the lags and leads of the first differences of the I (1) variables. Thus, estimation of the long run relation between $Y$ and $X$ is carried out with a regression of the type:

$$Y = \lambda^{d'} X + \Sigma\text{-n}^n a_i \Delta X_{t-i} \tag{7}$$

where $\lambda^d$ denotes the vector of long run coefficients of $X$ using the DOLS procedure. The inclusion of $\Delta X_{t+j}$ terms take care of the possibility of endogeneity of $X$, i.e., feedback from $Y$ to future values of $X$ (see Stock and Watson, 1993).

## Determinants of services exports

Having found the long-run relationship between services exports and other variables (Table 5.9), we estimate determinants of services exports by using the DOLS procedure to counter the problem of endogeneity and small sample bias. The results are presented in Tables 5.10—5.12, respectively. Diagnostic test indicates that the serial correlation, ARCH effect and heteroscedasticity are not a problem. Further, the Ramsey test also suggests there is no misspecification problem for the model. Adjusted $R^2$ is high, indicating the model fits the data very well.

## Determinants of total services exports

The long-run estimates of total services exports estimated by both DOLS are presented in Table 5.10. The results show that, as expected, demand for services exports has a positive significant effect on real services exports of India. The coefficient of real world demand is greater than 1, indicating that a 1 per cent increase in world GDP leads to a more-than-1 per cent increase in India's services exports to the world. As the world demand for services imports is directly and positively related to world income, it reflects that India's services exports depends on the growth of the world economy. This is in line with previous empirical studies on goods exports (Deardorff et al., 2000; Pain and van Welsum, 2004; Eichengreen and Gupta, 2012). Therefore, exports from India are more likely to be affected by external shocks, such as any changes in economic activity in major export destination markets. The coefficient of real exchange rate (RER) is found to have a negative impact on real exports as appreciation of domestic currency adversely affects exports. The appreciation of the real exchange rate (RER) reduces export (Joshi & Little, 1994; Srinivasan, 1998; Sharma, 2003); hence, a negative link between the appreciation of RER and export demand is expected. However, compared to demand effect, the price effect is much smaller. In addition, the impact of manufacturing exports on services export is positive and significant, indicating the spillover impact of manufacturing impact on services exports in India, as countries that export more goods also export more services. This is because exports of traditional services are linked closely with the export of goods and arise from it and also because of network effects (Eichengreen and Gupta, 2012). The coefficient of manufacturing exports is less than one, indicating that a one unit increase in manufacturing exports would lead to a less-than-one-unit increase in total services exports.

Supply side or endowment factors (infrastructure stock, telecom density, human capital, financial development, and FDI) have expected signs. The coefficients of infrastructure stocks have a positive impact on services exports as better infrastructure stocks such as telecom, transport, and power reduce the cost of trade and increase competitiveness in international markets. Infrastructure facilitates improvement in the education and training system that produces skilled labour, thereby inducing services exports. Services such as communications, transportation, and construction are physical capital-intensive and, therefore, the availability of better infrastructure increases the exports of these services (Urata and Kiyota, 2003). Alternatively, telecom density or penetration rate has a positive impact on services exports. Since the mid-1990s, when reform began and the telecom sector in India was opened to private investment, there has been a teledensity revolution. Low cost tele-services are a major reason for services exports, particularly modern services exports.

**Table 5.10: Estimated result of total services (TSER)**

| Variables | DOLS | | | |
|---|---|---|---|---|
| Constant | −13.75 (−0.89) | −9.01* (0.78) | −9.50** (−1.25) | −151.22* (−2.05) |
| LSIMP | 2.59* (2.90) | 2.10** (3.18) | 2.23* (2.80) | 1.86* (2.89) |
| RER | −0.18* (−2.27) | −0.14** (−3.86) | −0.13** (−2.37) | −.08* (−2.06) |
| INFRA | 1.84* (2.67) | | 1.44* (2.65) | − |
| TEL | | 0.26** (3.45) | − | 0.18** (3.46) |
| DBC | 0.16* (2.03) | 0.24** (3.74) | − | |
| FINDEX | | | 0.78* (2.15) | 0.66* (2.58) |
| GSER | 0.14** (2.37) | 0.14* (2.07) | 0.09* (1.99) | − |
| SCH | | | | 1.04** (3.12) |
| MNFEX | 0.89** (7.20) | 0.88* (2.67) | 0.97** (6.57) | 0.66* (3.16) |
| INST | | | 0.21 (1.27) | 0.70* (2.43) |
| | Adj. $R^2$ = 0.96, S.E = 0.14 DW = 2.43 LM = 1.09 ARCH = 0.38 Reset - 1.5 | Adj. $R^2$ = 0.98, S.E = 0.18 DW = 1.78 LM = 1.51 ARCH = 1.46 Reset - 2.3 | Adj. $R^2$ = 0.97, S.E = 0.43 DW = 1.76, LM = 1.74 ARCH = 0.89 Reset - 2.1 | Adj. $R^2$ = 0.97, S.E = 0.34 DW = 2.4, LM = 0.6, ARCH = 1.5 7 Reset - 1.4 |

*Notes*: *** and ** denotes Significant at 1 per cent, 5 per cent and 10 per cent level, respectively. Figures in the parentheses are *t*-ratio.

*Source*: Author's Computation

As measured by domestic credit by banking sector, financial development has a positive impact on services exports in India because, as in the case of goods exports, it reduces the variable costs of exporting services (i.e., freight and transportation costs), thereby increasing the competitiveness of services exports (Beck, 2003). When we replace domestic credit by financial development index, which includes variables such as bank branches per million population and bank credit as percentage of GDP and M2 by GDP ratio, similar results are also found. Therefore, access to financial institutions and finance at reasonable cost can be important for services exports of India. Availability of human capital, proxied by gross secondary enrollment ratio and average years of schooling, is vital for services exports; the results support this. The coefficient of human capital-GSER and SCH-is positive and significant across specifications. Therefore, we find that success in India's service exports is attributed to the large pool of high-quality, low-cost human capital.

Similarly, the coefficient of index of economic freedom, which is the proxy for institution quality, is positive and significant. Overall, we find that the major determinants of total services exports are real world income, real exchange rate, manufacturing exports, and relative endowment factors (infrastructure stock, human capital, and financial development).

### Determinants of modern services

Having analysed the determinants of aggregate services exports, we next estimate the determinants of modern services exports.[10] Like total exports, modern services exports are influenced by real world demand, real exchange rate, manufacturing exports, and relative endowments (infrastructure stocks, human capital development, financial development, and FDI) (Table 5.11). The coefficient of world demand for services exports is greater than one, which indicates that a rise in world income will boost modern services exports from India. On the other hand, rupee appreciation will reduce exports as real exchange rate reduces the competitiveness of India's services exports.

The stock of physical infrastructure boosts modern services as infrastructure (telecom, transport, power, etc.) help in developing human capital. Poor infrastructure facilities characterize India and impedes services trade, competitiveness, and sustainable development (Jones, 2006; Sahoo and Dash,

---

[10] Diagnostic test indicates that the serial correlation, ARCH effect, and heteroscedasticity are not a problem. Further, Ramsey test also suggest there is no mis-specification problem for the model. Adjusted $R^2$ is also very high indicating the model fits the data very well.

**Table 5.11: Estimated results of modern services (MSER)**

| Variables | DOLS | | | |
|---|---|---|---|---|
| Constant | 22.24*<br>(2.21) | 12.01<br>(1.78) | 33.12*<br>(2.03) | −3.22<br>(−1.05) |
| LSIMP | 2.81*<br>(2.10) | 1.67*<br>(2.49) | 2.43*<br>(2.77) | 1.84*<br>(2.25) |
| RER | −0.12**<br>(−4.87) | −0.10**<br>(−4.26) | −0.17**<br>(−3.01) | −0.09**<br>(−4.09) |
| INFRA | 1.46*<br>(2.20) | | 1.41*<br>(2.24) | |
| TEL | | 0.17*<br>(2.17) | - | 0.24*<br>(2.34) |
| DBC | 0.14**<br>(4.03) | 0.12*<br>(2.78) | - | |
| FINDEX | | | 0.62**<br>(3.56) | 0.48**<br>(3.58) |
| GSER | 0.16* (2.07) | 0.13*<br>(2.18) | 0.14*<br>(2.22) | - |
| SCH | | | | 2.12*<br>(2.42) |
| MNFEX | 0.88**<br>(6.06) | 0.73*<br>(4.88) | 0.96**<br>(5. 79) | 0.56*<br>(2.43) |
| FDIY | | 0.14*<br>(2.56) | - | - |
| INST | - | - | - | 0.41*<br>(2.24) |
| | Adj. R2 = 0.96,<br>S.E = 0.76<br>DW = 2.07<br>LM = 1.39<br>ARCH = 18<br>Reset - 1.45 | Adj. R2 = 0.98,<br>S.E = 0.47<br>DW = 2.32<br>LM = 0.65<br>ARCH = 1.06<br>Reset - 1.87 | Adj. $R^2$ = 0.98,<br>S.E = 0.68<br>DW = 2.45, LM<br>= 0.98<br>ARCH = 1.3<br>Reset - 1.66 | Adj. R2 = 0.95,<br>S.E = 0.14<br>DW = 2.12,<br>LM = 0.7,<br>ARCH = 1.2<br>Reset - 1.12 |

*Notes*: *** and ** denotes Significant at 1 per cent, 5 per cent and 10 per cent level respectively. Figures in the parentheses are *t*-ratio.

*Source*: Author's Computation

2010). Similarly, the availability of skilled, low-cost labour in India improves her exports of modern services. As expected, telecom density or penetration rate has a positive impact on modern services exports as telecom is the lifeline of ICT, financial services, and communication. Foreign direct investment has positive impact on modern services as it promotes exports by augmenting export capacity, increasing physical capital, worker skills, and market penetration potential (De Gregorio, 1992). In addition, the index of economic freedom (which is the proxy for better institutional quality) has a positive influence on modern services since better institutions improve the confidence of importers of services. The literature suggests that the quality of institutions positively influences trade in services (Lennon, 2006; Kimura and Lee, 2006).

### Determinants of traditional services exports

Finally, we estimate the long-run coefficients of traditional services exports. The results indicate that although the world demand effect is positive and significant, the magnitude of the coefficient is smaller than total and modern services. Similarly, the coefficient of real exchange rate is negative as in the case of total and modern services. However, the coefficient of real exchange rate is smaller compared to total and modern services. In addition real exchange rate is now significant at 5 per cent level only.

Like total and modern services, better infrastructure stock boosts traditional services such as transport and travel services. Similarly, human capital development in terms of higher skills also improves traditional services as in other cases. The coefficient of manufacturing services also boosts traditional services but its impact is less than its impact on aggregate and modern services. Other important variables like financial development, FDI, index of economic freedom, and telecom penetration do not have significant impact on traditional services. These variables are dropped from the final estimation of traditional services exports.

**Table 5.12: Estimated results of traditional services (TRSER)**

| Variables | DOLS | |
|-----------|------|------|
| Constant | −12.33** | −16.67** |
| | (−4.36) | (−3.98) |
| LSIMP | 2.03** | 2.32** |
| | (4.77) | (4.22) |
| RER | −0.07* | −0.04** |
| | (−2.61) | (−2.15) |

*Table 5.12 Continued*

*Table 5.12 Continued*

| | | |
|---|---|---|
| INFRA | 1.12* (2.87) | 1.24* (2.07) |
| GSER | 0.06** (3.25) | - |
| SCH | - | 0.52* (2.64) |
| MNFEX | 0.26** (4.26) | 0.12* (2.88) |
| | Adj. R² = 0.94, S.E = 0.05, DW = 2.13 LM = 0.52 ARCH = 0.06 Reset - 1.24 | Adj. R² = 0.96, S.E = 0.26, DW = 2.24 LM = 0.57 ARCH = 0.28 Reset - 1.91 |

*Notes:* *** and ** denotes Significant at 1 per cent, 5 per cent and 10 per cent level respectively. Figures in the parentheses are *t*-ratio.

*Source*: Author's Computation

## CONCLUSIONS

In sum, based on the above analysis, we find that India's aggregate services are determined by world demand, exchange rate, manufacturing exports, endowment factors (human capital and physical infrastructure stock), and financial development. Similarly, the performance of modern services exports is determined by traditional factors and, additionally, institutions and FDI inflows. In comparison to modern services, traditional services exports are dependent on limited factors (world demand income, exchange rate, and manufacturing exports) and endowment factors (human capital and infrastructure stocks). The impact of FDI, institutions, and financial development is not significant.

In the past few years, the pace of growth of the world economy has been moderate; this might limit the growth of India's manufacturing and services exports. Therefore, India needs to focus on supply-side factors (development of human capital, infrastructure, financial sector, and broadband teledensity. The effort to improve the competitiveness of the manufacturing sector and manufacturing exports will also help services exports through the networking effect. Infrastructure development (energy availability, transportation, and communication) reduces trade and transaction costs, and India must focus on these sectors to make manufacturing and services exports competitive. In addition, further trade and financial liberalization and removal of FDI caps in areas like health, education, and financial sectors is required to achieve sustained export growth in services. India's software exports are concentrated to a few developed countries, which are expected to grow at a moderate rate in the coming decades. Therefore, India needs to diversify software exports by targeting developing countries.

## REFERENCES

Aghion, P., and R. Griffith. 2005. 'Competition and Growth: Reconciling Theory and Evidence'. Cambridge, MA: MIT Press.

Aitken, B., G.H. Hanson, and A.E. Harrison. 1997. 'Spillovers, Foreign Investment, and Export Behavior'. *Journal of International Economics* 43(1): 103–32.

Awokuse, T.O. 2003. 'Is the export-led growth hypothesis valid for Canada?'. *Canadian Journal of Economics/Revue canadienne d'économique* 36(1): 126–36.

Balassa, B. 1978. 'Exports and Economic Growth: Further Evidence.' *Journal of Development Economics* 5(2): 181–89.

Barcenilla, S., and J. Molero. 2003. 'Service Export Flows: Empirical Evidence for European Project' SETI PROJECT.

———. 2002. 'Financial Development and International Trade: Is there a link?' *Journal of International Economics* 57, 107–31.

Beck, T. 2003. 'Financial Dependence and International Trade'. *Review of International Economics*, 11(2): 296–316.

Bhagwati, J.N. 1982. Introduction to 'Import Competition and Response'. In *Import Competition and Response*, University of Chicago Press, 1–8.

———. 1988. 'Export-promoting Trade Strategy: Issues and Evidence'. *The World Bank Research Observer*, 27–7.

Biggs, T. 2007. 'Export Promotion and Diversification: What Do We Learn from the DTISs in Low-Income Countries?' World Bank, unpublished.

Biggs, T., M. Shah, and P. Srivastava. 1996. Technological Capability and Learning in African Firms. Regional Program for Enterprise Development, Technical Paper, World Bank, Washington, D.C.

De Gregorio, J. 1992. 'Economic Growth in Latin America'. *Journal of Development Economics*, 39, 58–84.

De Mello, L.R. 1997. 'Foreign Direct Investment in Developing Countries and Growth: A Selective Survey'. *The Journal of Development Studies*, 34(1): 1–34.

Dhawan, U., and B. Biswal. 1999. 'Re-examining Export-led Growth Hypothesis: A Multivariate Cointegration Analysis for India'. *Applied Economics*, 31(4): 525–30.

Deardorff, Alan, S. Hymans, R.M. Stern, and C. Xiang. 2000. 'Forecasting U.S. Trade in Services'. Mimeo, University of Michigan.

Dornbusch, R. 1992. 'The Case for Trade Liberalization in Developing Countries'. *The Journal of Economic Perspectives*, 6(1): 69–85.

Edwards, S. 1998. 'Capital Flows, Real Exchange Rates and Capital Controls: Some Latin American Experiences'. NBER Working Paper 6000. Also in author's web page: http://www.anderson.ucla.edu/faculty/sebastian.edwards/

Edwards, L., and P. Alves. 2006. 'South Africa's Export Performance: Determinants of Export Supply'. *South African Journal of Economics*, 74(3): 473–500.

Eichengreen, B., and P. Gupta. 2013. 'Exports of Services: Indian Experience in Perspective'. *Indian Growth and Development Review*, 6(1): 35–60.

Findlay, C., and Warren, T. eds. 2000. *Impediments to Trade in Services: Measurements and Policy Implications*. Routledge. Francois, J., and B. Hoekman. 2010. Services Trade and Policy. *Journal of Economic Literature*, 642–92.

Francois, J., and M. Manchin. 2006. *Institutional Quality, Infrastructure, and the Propensity to Export*. Unpublished, January, World Bank, Washington, DC. Available at http://siteresources. worldbank. org/INTTRADECOSTAND FACILITATION.

Goldstein, M., and M. Khan. 1985. 'Income and Price Effects in Foreign Trade'. In *Handbook of International Economics 2*, edited by R. Jones and P. Kenen, Amsterdam: Elsevier.

Grünfeld, L.A., and A. Moxnes. 2003. *The Intangible Globalization: Explaining the Patterns of International Trade in Services*. Norwegian Institute for International Affairs. Discussion paper no. 657.

Hausmann, R., J. Hwang, and D. Rodrik. 2007. 'What You Export Matters'. *Journal of Economic Growth*, 12(1): 1–25.

Helpman E., M.J. Melitz, and S.R. Yeaple. 2003. 'Export versus FDI with Heterogeneous Firms'. *American Economic Review*, forthcoming.

Hoekman, B., and C.A.P. Braga. 1997. 'Protection and Trade in Services: A Survey'. *Open Economies Review*, 8(3): 285–308.

Hoekman, B., and A. Mattoo. 2008. Services Trade and Growth. In *Opening Markets for Trade in Services: Countries and Sectors in Bilateral and WTO Negotiations*, 21–58.

Huang, J.H., and S. Viana, 1995, 'Modelling US Services Trade Flows: A Cointegration ECM Approach', Federal Reserve Bank of New York Research Paper, No. 9518.

Jones, S. 2006. 'Infrastructure Challenges in East and South Asia'. *IDS Bulletin*, 37(3): 28–44.

Joshi, V., and I.M.D. Little. 1994. *India: Macroeconomics and Political Economy 1964–1991*. Washington DC: The World Bank.

Kimura, F., and H.H. Lee. 2006. 'The Gravity Equation in International Trade in Services'. *Review of World Economics*, 142(1): 92–121.

Krueger, A. 1998. 'Why trade liberalisation is good for growth?' *The Economic Journal*, 108(450): 1513–22.

Krueger, A.O. 1975. *Foreign Trade Regimes and Economic Development: Turkey*. New York: National Bureau of Economic Research, 271–339.

Krugman. P.R. ed. 1986. 'Strategic Trade Policy and the New International Economics'. Cambridge, MA: MIT Press.

Lennon, C. 2006. *Trade in Services and Trade in Goods: Differences and Complimentarities*. Paper presented at Eighth Annual Conferences of the European Trade Study Group, Vienna, Austria, 7–9 September.

Lodefalk, M. 2012. Servicification of Manufacturing: Evidence from Sweden. *International Journal of Economics and Business Research*.

Van der Marel, E. 2011. Determinants of Comparative Advantage in Services. Working Paper Groupe d'Economie Mondiale (GEM), Sciences Po.

Mattoo, A., I.C. Neagu, and Ç. Özden. 2008. 'Brain waste? Educated Immigrants in the US Labor Market'. *Journal of Development Economics*, 87(2): 255–69.

Méon, P.G., and K. Sekkat. 2008. 'Institutional Quality and Trade: Which institutions? Which trade?' *Economic Inquiry*, 46(2): 227–40.

Mouna, C., and J. Reza. 2001. *Trade Liberalization, Real Exchange Rate, and Export Diversification in Selected North African Economies*. Nasir, S., and K. Kalirajan. 2013. Export Performance of South and East Asia in Modern Services. ASARC Working Paper 2013/07.

Nyahoho, E. 2010. 'Determinants of Comparative Advantage in the International Trade of Services: An Empirical Study of the Hecksher-Ohlin Approach'. *Global Economy Journal*, 10(1).

Pain, N., and D. Van Welsum. 2004. *International Production Relocation and Exports of Services*. National Institute of Economic and Social Research.

Parida, P.C., and P. Sahoo. 2007. 'Export-led Growth in South Asia: A Panel Cointegration Analysis'. *International Economic Journal*, 21(2): 155–75.

Pesaran, M.H., Y. Shin, and R.J. Smith. 2001. 'Bounds Testing Approaches to the Analysis of Level Relationships'. *Journal of Applied Econometrics*, 16, 289–326.

Pesaran, M. H., and Y. Shin. 1998. 'An Autoregressive Distributed-Lag Modelling Approach to Cointegration Analysis'. *Econometric Society Monographs*, 31, 371–413.

Rana, P.B., and J.M. Dowling. 1990. 'Foreign Capital and Asian Economic Growth'. *Asian Development Review*, 8(2): 77–102.

Sahoo, P., and R.K. Dash. 2009. 'Infrastructure Development and Economic Growth in India'. *Journal of the Asia Pacific Economy*, 14, 351–65.

Saikonnen, P. 1991. 'Asymptotically Efficient Estimation of Cointegration Regressions'. *Econometric Theory*, 7, 1–21.

Sharma, K. 2000. *Export Growth in India: Has FDI played a role?* Economic Growth Center, Yale University.

———. 2003. 'Factors Determining India's Export Performance'. *Journal of Asian Economics*, 14, 435–46.

Shepherd, B., and E. Van Der Marel. 2010. *Trade in Services in the APEC Region: Patterns, Determinants, and Policy Implications*. APEC Policy Support Unit.

Shingal, A. 2010. *How much do agreements matter for services trade?* Available at SSRN 1586839.

Srinivasan, T.N. 1998. 'India's Export Performance: A Comparative Analysis'. In *India's Economic Reforms and Development Essay for Manmohan Singh*, edited by I.J. Ahluwalia and I.M.D. Little. New Delhi: Oxford University Press.

Stiglitz, J., and A. Charlton. 2006. *Fair Trade for All*. New Delhi: Oxford University Press.

Stock, J.H., and M.W. Watson. 1993. 'A Simple Estimator of Cointegrating Vectors in Higher Order Integrated Systems'. *Econometrica*, 61, 783–820.

UNCTAD. 2005. *World Investment Report*. Geneva: United Nations Conference on Trade and Development.

———. 2008. *World Investment Report*. TNCs and the Infrastructural Challenge.

Urata, S., and K. Kiyota. 2003. Services Trade in East Asia. In *Trade in Services in the Asia Pacific Region*, NBER East Asia Seminar on Economics (EASE), 11, 379–428. University of Chicago Press.

World Bank. 1993. *World Development Report 1993*. New York: Oxford University Press for the World Bank.

Young, L.W. 1995. 'Free Trade or Fair Trade? NAFTA and Agricultural Labor'. *Latin American Perspectives*, 22(1): 49–58.

# APPENDIX

### Data for world services exports analysis

For the analysis of India's service trade, we use data sets provided by RBI. The concepts classification and compilation procedure used for the trade in services is as per the standards set out in IMF's prescriptions (BPM/EBOPS). While the aggregate data provided by IMF's balance of payment data from 1976 to 2012 gives three categories of services that is transport, travel, and others (OCS). The other commercial services in this IMF BOP data is too broad and includes components such as financial, legal, computer, etc. This aggregate data is not amenable to the mode of services in GATS. In comparison, RBI data is more disaggregated and since 2001–02, this also gives disaggregation of miscellaneous category of services into Software, business services, financial services and communication services. This is more in tune with fifth edition of balance of payments manual ($BPM_5$). The standards components of ($BPM_5$) corresponds to the four modes of services of WTO, while RBI data gives 5 categories where misc is further divided into 4 categories of data. UN service trade data is in consonance with $BPM_5$ and this gives service data at 11 broad category levels that are further disaggregated at various levels. At this stage we will use only these 11 broad categories to get more general picture.

| RBI service data | UN service data |
| --- | --- |
| Travel ((1950–2011) | 1. Transportation (2000–10) |
| Transport (1950–2011) | 2. Travel (2000–10) |
| Insurance (1950–2011) | 3. Communication services (2000–10) |
| G.n.i.e (1950–2011) | 4. Construction services (2000–10) |
| Miscellaneous (1950–2011) (Construction and license fees, personal, cultural and recreational services, etc.) Of which Software service (2001–11) Business service (2004–11) Communication services(2004–11) Financial services (2004–11) | 5. Insurance services (2000–10) |
| | 6.Financial services (2000–10) |
| | 7.Computer and information services (2000–10) |
| | 8. Royalties and license fees (2000–10) |
| | 9. Other business services (2000–10) |
| | 10. Personal, cultural and recreational service (2000–10) |
| | 11. Government services n.i.e. (2000–10) |
| | Also given are: (2000–10) (2000–10) |
| | Compensation of employees (2000–10) |
| | Workers' remittances (2000–10) |
| | Migrant's transfers (2000–10) |
| | Direct investment (2000–10) |

## Herfindahl index of service export concentration

While Herfindahl-Hirschman index is generally used to measure market concentration of firms in any industry, here HHI is used as a measure of concentration in service export market of various service sector.

HHI = Sum of square of shares of all exporting countries in Total export of that sector

$1/N <= HHI <= 1$ where N = number of exporting countries

Normalized HHI or $HHI^* = (HHI-1/N)/(1-1/N)$

$0 <= HHI^* <= 1$ (Here normalized Herfindahl index is used as it is easier for comparison over time and across sectors. A low Herfindahl index is considered as less concentrated and more competitive market where as a higher $HHI^*$ or nearer to 1 means more concentrated or monopolized export market. Though the HHI is quite easy to calculate, its geographic scope and inability to define the scope of the markets are criticized in the literature.

## Infrastructure development index

The Infrastructure index has been made by using the Principal Component Analysis. We include major infrastructure indicators as follows:

(a) Per capita electricity power consumption
(b) Per capita energy use (kg of oil equivalent)
(c) Telephone line (both fixed and mobiles) per 1,000 population
(d) Rail Density per 1,000 population
(e) Air Transport, freight million tons per kilometre
(f) Road density per 1,000 population.

The first factor or principal component[11] has an Eigen value larger than one and explains over two thirds of the total variance. There is a large difference between the Eigen values and variance explained by the first and the next principal component. Hence, we choose the first principal component for making a composite index representing the combined variance of different aspects of infrastructure captured by the six variables.

The financial development index has been made by using principal component analysis. Three major financial development indicators included as:

(a) Bank Branches per million people
(b) Bank Credit provided to domestic sector (per cent GDP);
(c) M2 by GDP ratio

The first factor or principal component[12] has an Eigen value larger than one and explains over two-thirds of the total variance. There is a large difference between the Eigen values and variance explained by the first and the next principal component. Hence, we choose the first principal component for making a composite index representing the combined variance of different aspects of financial development captured by the three variables.

---

[11] The Eigen values and factor loadings are available on request.
[12] The Eigen values and factor loadings are available on request.

# Section 3
# The dampeners to growth: Controlling inflation

# 6

# Macroeconomic Effects of Monetary Policy in India

Sushanta K. Mallick

## INTRODUCTION

Despite the structural differences between advanced and emerging market economies, cyclical fluctuations seem to have been more synchronized in the last decade, although it has been accompanied by pro-cyclical macroeconomic policies in the latter group of countries in the 1990s,[1] partly due to the existence of large negative output gaps and structural inflation in these economies. In this chapter, we investigate the interaction of business cycles in India (as a key small open emerging market economy) and its macroeconomic policy, as understanding the macroeconomic dynamics has become important during the post-reform period. The mechanism by which monetary policy is transmitted to the real economy remains a crucial question to assess the relative importance of the interest rate or exchange rate channels in the context of India. The monetary authority in India adopts a multiple indicators approach to signal the central bank's assessment of the economy. Changes in the policy environment since the later half of the 1990s have brought in alternative monetary policy instruments in transmitting policy signals to the financial markets (see Bhattacharyya and Sensarma, 2008). Further, given the openness of the Indian economy, particularly since the mid-1990s, the monetary and financial system can no longer be immune to external shocks (Bhattacharya et al., 2008). This chapter, therefore, examines the monetary policy transmission mechanism over this post-reform period along with understanding the influence of the exchange rate as the central bank [Reserve Bank of India (RBI)] used to be a

---

[1] See Lane (2003) about the inappropriateness of these policies. Also, see Mallick and Sousa (2012).

net-buyer of foreign exchange in the FX market (see Figure 6.1). Figure 6.1 clearly shows a regular net purchase of foreign exchange, while the net sale is resorted to only occasionally in times of crisis. This regular intervention explains why the real effective exchange rate remains stable while the nominal effective exchange (NEER) rate shows a depreciating trend (see Figure 6.2), in an attempt to boost export competitiveness. However, the accumulated inflation differential of India over its trading partners contributed to the recent collapse of the rupee in 2013.

**Figure 6.1: Central Bank intervention**

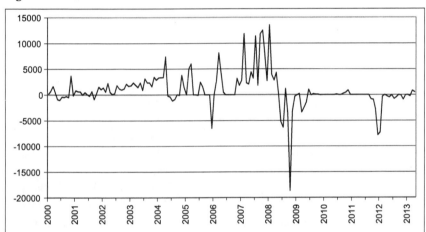

*Source*: Reserve Bank of India

This chapter, therefore, considers all the macroeconomic linkages including both short-term and long-term interest rates since private sector demand can be affected if funds are channelled to long-term government bond market following changes in short-term policy rates. As the central bank can monitor aggregate demand via controlling short-term interest rates, the transmission channel to the economy can be affected via consequent change in the long-term rate. In India, banks tend to change their demand for government securities following a change in the policy rate as they prefer to invest more than the required proportion of their assets in government bonds and, hence, the change in policy rate can have little impact on credit allocation to the private sector. The monetary policy could work through the long-term government bond market as banks prefer to park their excess liquidity in safe and liquid government securities rather than making illiquid loans to the private sector.

**Figure 6.2: Nominal and real effective exchange rates**

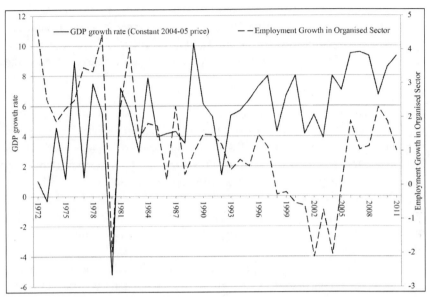

*Source*: Thomson Reuters Datastream

Thus, we need to consider the long rate along with the policy rate to examine the impact of monetary policy on the Indian economy. If the term premium is high, whatever be the policy stance, banks will prefer to hold government securities, which will make monetary policy ineffective via the bank-lending channel as demand could respond less to shocks in short-term interest rates. It appears that monetary policy is accommodating changes in government expenditure being financed via the long-term debt market. So, we consider fiscal deficit [as a per cent of Gross Domestic Product (GDP)] to understand the impact of monetary impulses as the government could be finding it easier to finance its deficit via the long-term government bond market. This is the transmission channel of monetary policy in India, which is characterized in this chapter as the fiscal channel of monetary transmission. Additionally, inflation may persist when the government resorts to deficit financing to meet its expenditure targets. There is no clear and agreed-upon channel on how monetary shocks are transmitted to the real sector in India. This chapter, therefore, makes a new attempt to understand the channels influencing macroeconomic dynamics in India.

According to the RBI, India's exchange rate policy in recent years has been guided by the broad principles of careful monitoring and management of exchange rates with flexibility, without a fixed target or a pre-announced target or a band, coupled with the ability to intervene if and when necessary, while allowing the underlying demand and supply conditions to determine the exchange rate movements over a period in an orderly way (Mohan, 2008). On the other hand, there is some argument that India is adopting a *de facto* fixed exchange rate policy (Shah and Patnaik, 2007), with evidence in support of the hypothesis that India's central bank intervenes in the foreign exchange market to prevent currency appreciation (Ramachandran and Srinivasan, 2007). It has been quite apparent that the RBI uses reserves to intervene energetically to avoid excess volatility of the nominal exchange rate. However, there is some evidence in case of major markets that intervention increases spot exchange rate volatility (see, for example, Baillie and Osterberg, 1997). There is also mixed empirical evidence on the degree of effectiveness of intervention in advanced countries.[2] However, given the practice of regular intervention by the RBI to prevent currency appreciation in India, the exchange rate channel also needs to be considered in the central bank's interest rate rule. Further, the higher degree of openness in India since the early 1990s exposes the economy to large exchange rate shocks that can have a significant influence on short-run inflation.

In many developing and emerging market economies, official intervention in foreign exchange markets is frequently used to influence currency values other than conventional fiscal and monetary policy measures to effectively manage the exchange rate (Hutchison, 2003). Although the extent of existing deregulation seems to have led to near-integration of domestic rates with the international interest rates, asset prices are not fully market-determined and an exogenous UIP (uncovered interest rate parity) shock may not move nominal exchange rate due to frequent intervention by the monetary authority. Besides, an exogenous term premium shock due to changes in inflation expectations and government's financing requirement can move the long rate and can, therefore, create volatility in both output and inflation. Besides, while explaining price formation in a developing economy, one cannot ignore the well-established finding that several structural or cost-push factors have been crucial in predicting inflation. At the same time, the exchange rate policy adopted by India, which results in massive expansion of the central bank's balance sheet and broad money supply,

---

[2] For an extensive review on this and on the determinants of intervention, see Sarno and Taylor (2001).

can generate inflationary pressure. In the absence of a commensurate increase in money demand, it can spill over into excess demand for goods and services, putting pressures on overall inflation. Thus, it makes sense to include exchange rate in this exercise as the central bank continues to intervene to prevent the exchange rate from appreciating in the face of surge in capital inflows, which could have tamed inflation. To some extent, the easy liquidity created by the influx of foreign capital, especially in the form of portfolio investments in government securities and bonds, might be contributing to lowering the higher floor of the interest rate in a developing country like India compared to that in rich countries with surplus capital.

During the second half of the last century, many traditional large structural macroeconometric models were estimated for India using annual data, but those models suffer from model mis-specification due to the problem of spurious correlation, which is already a common knowledge in the modern time series literature.[3] As there is little modelling effort using high-frequency data for short-term policy analysis for India, the present chapter builds a short-term macroeconometric model for India using quarterly time series data, including aggregate output, over the period 1996–2013, to undertake a shock analysis within a structural VAR setting to analyse interactions between monetary policy and business cycles in India by evaluating the role of different shocks, namely exchange rate, demand, supply, monetary policy, term premium and fiscal shocks, and then showing the relative importance of these innovations in explaining inflation and output growth, while investigating the extent to which the exchange rate is a source of shocks due to intervention. There is a huge SVAR literature using short-run zero restrictions to identify structural shocks in the context of advanced countries with aggregate demand–aggregate supply models (see, for example, Cover et al., 2006). Using the benchmark recursive identification, we show that monetary policy is seen to have stabilizing effect in response to demand shocks in this sample period, showing a significant positive response to demand shocks, while exchange rate shocks have a negative short-run impact on monetary policy. The response for short-term interest rate suggests that the RBI conducts a counter-cyclical monetary policy to a shock in output as opposed to inflation, which implies that the sources of inflation are not demand-led rather they are primarily supply-driven and imported inflationary shocks, which in turn lead to a rise in interest rate, whereas monetary policy shocks do not significantly influence inflation in

---

[3] For an exhaustive critical review of those traditional macro models and for a small macroeconomic policy model for India following the contemporary time series modelling literature, see Mallick (1999).

the medium term, suggesting an accommodative nature of monetary policy in stabilizing output via fiscal channel, which explains a high level of trend inflation of at least 5 per cent when one decomposes inflation into its trend and cyclical components.

As the central bank regularly intervenes in the foreign exchange market to minimize volatility, we need to jointly identify monetary policy and exchange rate shocks. Therefore, we carry out further estimation by imposing a set of restrictions in a sign-restriction-based VAR (Uhlig, 2005) to jointly identify two shocks (exchange rate shock and monetary policy shock). Although sign-restricted VAR has been applied mostly to identify different shocks in the developed economies, there has been little attempt in the literature to identify macroeconomic shocks in the case of emerging market economies, except Ho and Yeh (2010), who identify monetary policy shocks in the case of Taiwan using sign-restricted VAR. In our chapter, by identifying both shocks jointly within a sign-VAR setting, the impact of exchange rate shock on output is positive in the short run and negative in the medium term, whereas the effect of monetary shock on output is negative, inflation declines when interest rate increases, but exchange rate shows an appreciation in the long run. Here, the restrictions are only imposed for two quarters to identify shocks and, then, we look at the long-run response. This exchange rate appreciation should occur if the central bank does not intervene given the excess supply of foreign exchange. However, the regular intervention by the RBI keeps the rupee at a depreciated rate, thereby generating some inflation, over and above the structural supply-driven inflation on the back of endemic rise in food prices. Thus, both price stability and exchange rate stability are incompatible objectives, and effectively there is no proper anchor to stabilize inflationary expectations in India.

Monetary policy is found to be counter-cyclical and has a stabilizing effect on output growth rather than stabilizing inflation. Given the growing fiscal imbalance (deficit), monetary policy appears accommodative in helping finance the fiscal deficit. How can a central bank reduce interest rate when there is a growing demand for funds in the market, that is, by the government? The RBI is able to do so, on the back of accumulation of massive external liquidity that increases overall money supply leading to decline in the cost of borrowing. The exchange rate management strategy that helps the RBI to accumulate reserves and adopt expansionary monetary policy, thus, partly contributes to higher inflation. The remainder of the chapter is organized as follows. The second section contains a description of the monetary policy environment in India as well as an analytical model to derive a monetary policy rule, providing a foundation for the VAR exercise. The third section discusses the data and estimation results. A summary and discussion of implications of the findings are provided in the fourth section.

## A THEORETICAL SETTING FOR EXCHANGE RATE AND MONETARY SHOCKS

The framework is in line with a New Keynesian model consisting of an open economy Phillips curve on the supply side and an IS curve for the demand side, which is derived from a two-period optimizing model with money. As the surge in capital flows is putting upward pressure on exchange rate, the intervention by the RBI in the FX market is making exchange rate as a source of shocks. If the central bank follows a policy of preventing the currency from appreciating, this may help in currency stability and in making the intervention profitable for the central bank.[4] However, a policy of currency depreciation could imply higher inflation expectations and, thus, rising interest rates, but that will make financing fiscal deficit difficult for the government and, hence, monetary policy could remain accommodative to meet government's borrowing requirements by keeping interest rates low. It is, therefore, important to identify both exchange rate and monetary policy shocks, alongside other structural shocks.

To begin with, we formulate a theoretical framework in an open economy setting to show to what extent monetary policy reacts to changes in exchange rate. An output growth equation is derived via a two-period optimizing model with money for the optimal consumption problem to show the relationship between output and monetary policy with exchange rate introduced via Purchasing power parity (PPP) assumption that the exchange rate equalizes purchasing power in two countries. The consumer begins the first period with resource endowment of $M_1$ (say 'bank balances') and income of $y_1$. Once the consumer has reached the last period of life, he will consume all available resources, $M_2$, including $y_2$. Now, suppose that the consumer's utility is time-separable so that

$$\underset{\{C_1,C_2\}}{Max} \quad u\left(C_1,\frac{M_1}{P_1}\right)+\theta\ u\left(C_2,\frac{M_2}{P_2}\right)$$

where $\theta$ is a discount factor $[\theta \in (0,1)]$. If $\theta = \frac{1}{1+\rho}$ , then $\rho > 0$ is the rate of time preference that specifies how the consumer trades off utility in period 1 against utility in period 2.

$$P_t C_t + M_{t+1} = P_t y_t + M_t \Rightarrow C_1 = y_1 - \frac{M_2 - M_1}{eP^f} \quad \text{where } P_1 = eP^f$$

$$P_{t+1}C_{t+1} = P_{t+1}y_{t+1} + M_{t+1} \Rightarrow C_2 = y_2 + \frac{M_2}{P_2}$$

---

[4] Szakmary and Mathur (1997) argue that central bank intervention introduces noticeable trends in the evolution of exchange rates which in turn create profit opportunities in the FX market.

Assuming equilibrium on the money market:

$$\frac{M_2}{P_2} = \varphi\, y_2 - \tau\, i_t^l \Rightarrow C_2 = \left(1+\varphi\right) y_2 - \tau\, i_t^l$$

where the left-hand side is the real money supply and the right-hand side is money demand which depends positively on the level of output and negatively on the interest rate on bonds, $i^l$ is the long-term nominal interest rate, $e$ is the nominal exchange rate (the domestic currency price of a unit of foreign currency), foreign currency price is denoted as $P^f$ and the domestic-currency price is $P$. Assuming money market equilibrium, the real money balances equal money demand, which depends on real income and opportunity cost ($i^s$) of holding money. The income elasticity of money holdings is $\varphi$ and $\tau$ is interest elasticity of money demand.

Substituting the above equations, the Lagrangian can be formulated as follows:

$$L = u\left(C_1, \frac{M_1}{P_1}\right) + \theta\, u\left(C_2, \frac{M_2}{P_2}\right) + \lambda\left(y_1 - \frac{\Delta M}{eP^f} - C_1\right) + \mu\left(\left(1+\varphi\right)y_2 - \tau i^l - C\right)$$

The first order conditions are as follows:

[1] $\quad \dfrac{\partial L}{\partial C_1} = u'_{C_1} - \lambda = 0 \Rightarrow u'_{C_1} = \lambda$

[2] $\quad \dfrac{\partial L}{\partial C_2} = \theta u'_{C_2} - \mu = 0 \Rightarrow u'_{C_2} = \dfrac{\mu}{\theta}$

[3] $\quad \dfrac{\partial L}{\partial \lambda} = y_1 - \dfrac{\Delta M}{eP^f} - C_1 = 0 \Rightarrow y_1 = \dfrac{\Delta M}{eP^f} + C_1$

[4] $\quad \dfrac{\partial L}{\partial \mu} = \left(1+\varphi\right)y_2 - \tau i^l - C_2 = 0 \Rightarrow y_2 = \dfrac{\tau}{\left(1+\varphi\right)}i^l + \dfrac{1}{\left(1+\varphi\right)}C_2$

Assuming a specific functional form[5] with separable utility as:

$$u = \log C_1 + \log C_2 + \log \frac{M}{P}$$

[5] $\quad u'_{C_1} = \dfrac{1}{C_1}$ and $u'_{C_2} = \dfrac{1}{C_2}$

Substituting [5] in [1] and [2], we get:

---

[5]  This utility function is of the constant relative risk aversion type, given by $u(C_t) = \left(1-\phi\right)^{-1} C_t^{1-\phi}$, where $u'(C) = C^{-\phi}$; $\phi$ is the coefficient of relative risk aversion and $1/\phi$ is the inter-temporal substitution elasticity between consumption in any two periods, i.e., it measures the willingness to substitute consumption between different periods. If $\phi = 1$, we can write $u(C) = \log(C)$.

[6] $\quad C_1 = \dfrac{1}{\lambda} \quad \text{and} \quad C_2 = \dfrac{\theta}{\mu}$

Substituting [6] in [3] and [4] and subtracting [3] from [4], we can write:

[7] $\quad y_2 - y_1 = \Delta y = \dfrac{\tau}{(1+\varphi)} i^{\prime\prime} - \dfrac{\Delta M}{eP^f} + \left( \dfrac{\theta}{\mu(1+\varphi)} - \dfrac{1}{\lambda} \right)$

Considering the following life-time resource constraint and substituting $C_1$ and $C_2$ from [6], we get:

$$C_1 + \dfrac{C_2}{1+i^{\prime}} = M_1 + \dfrac{M_2}{1+i^{\prime}}$$

$$\Rightarrow M_2 - M_1 = \Delta M = \dfrac{1+i^{\prime}}{\lambda} + \dfrac{\theta}{\mu} - \left( 2 + i^{\prime} \right) M_1$$

Assuming zero initial endowment and substituting $\Delta M$ in equation 7 (with foreign price level being normalized to one and $1 + i^{\prime} \approx 1$), we can rewrite equation 7 as:

[8] $\quad \Delta y_t = \dfrac{\tau}{(1+\varphi)} i_t^{\prime} - \left( \dfrac{\theta}{\mu} + \dfrac{1}{\lambda} \right) \dfrac{1}{e_t} + \left( \dfrac{\theta}{\mu(1+\varphi)} - \dfrac{1}{\lambda} \right)$

As $\tau < 0$ and $\varphi > 0$, a rise in interest rate will have a negative impact on output growth, whereas exchange rate depreciation will have a positive impact on output growth, as both $C_2$ ($\theta/\mu$) and $C_1$ ($1/\lambda$) are positive and $\theta$, $\mu$ and $\lambda$ are all greater than zero. Further, an aggregate demand shock ($\varepsilon_d$) could be added to equation 8, along with interest rate and exchange rate as key variables.

As India's monetary authority continues to intervene in the foreign exchange market by buying foreign exchange more often (see Figure 6.1) and sterilize the flows, this can create more domestic money in the system leading to exchange rate depreciation. Such regular intervention can hinder the credibility of monetary policy because the economic agents will expect that stabilizing the exchange rate takes precedence over promoting price stability as a policy objective (see Mishkin, 2000). Regardless of nominal exchange rate strategies, it has been argued that the real exchange rate always floats: if not through nominal exchange rate adjustment, then through price change (Gylfason, 2002). Further, because prices and wages tend to be sticky, the adjustment of real exchange rates towards long-run equilibrium takes time. Although theoretically there is no need for a central bank to monitor changes in the exchange rates, the central bank intervention suggests a desired level of exchange rate, which we consider as a random walk process:

[9] $\quad e_t^d = e_{t-1} + \varepsilon_e$

where $\varepsilon_e$ is an exchange rate shock.

Now, we consider an aggregate supply curve (AS) – the Phillips curve equation – which assumes that inflation depends on its past level, real output, exchange rate and an exogenous supply shock.

[10] $\quad \pi_t^d = \pi_{t-1} + \beta\Delta y_t + \delta e_t + \varepsilon_\pi$ $\qquad\qquad$ AS-curve

where $\pi$ is inflation, $\gamma$ is real output and $\varepsilon_\pi$ is a supply shock.

The long-term nominal interest rate($i^l$) can be hypothesized to equal a risk premium over the short rate ($i^s$), along with being negatively influenced by the level of fiscal balance. A fiscal deficit will lead to more issuance of long-term debt which can put downward pressure on the long-term rate; however, if there is lack of monetary liquidity in the market, the new issuance will create demand for market borrowing and, hence, long rate will edge upwards:

In the literature on Indian inflation, the importance of sectoral aspects of inflation has been strongly emphasized, (see Balakrishnan, 1991; Sen and Vaidya, 1995; Dutta-Roy and Darbha, 2000; Callen, 2001; Nachane and Lakshmi, 2002; Mallick, 2004) indicating the importance of accounting for supply shocks in explaining inflation in India. One of the well-established findings in this line of literature on Indian inflation is that cost-push factors have a greater predictive power than demand-pull factors. Further, inflation is also driven by many supply side factors like the effect of monsoon on agriculture, where monetary policy action may have little role. Therefore, in many emerging market economies, central banks tend to be particularly concerned about food price inflation. In an economy as large as that of India, with continued existence of market imperfections in factor and product markets between regions, the focus of monetary policy in India continues to be managing inflation expectations.[6] While the Fisher relation suggests that high inflation goes with high-interest rates, the contractionary monetary policy raising interest rates is likely to make future inflation lower, thereby influencing the term structure of interest rates.

[11] $\qquad i_t^l = i_t^s - \alpha f_b + \varepsilon_p$ $\qquad\qquad$ Term premium

where $f_b$ is the level of fiscal balance (as a per cent of GDP), and $\varepsilon_p$ is a term premium shock. The ownership of public debt in India suggests that banks hold big part of the government domestic debt relative to non-banks. Any increased debt issuances on the back of growing fiscal deficit could lead to increase in bank

---

[6] The indicators of inflationary expectations that the RBI implicitly monitors are output growth, capacity utilization, inventory, corporate performance, industrial/investment expectations and other indicators of aggregate demand. Thus, we include output growth in the model estimated here.

holdings of debt, making new issues of debt held by banks as a substitute for lending to the private sector if there is a change in monetary policy.

Given the openness of the Indian economy, any change in the exchange rate has a direct effect on prices. In the recent literature, the importance of supply-side channel (or the so-called 'cost channel') for the transmission of monetary policy has been emphasized.[7] By following the same logic, when the central bank aims at keeping its currency at a depreciated level, it makes imported goods expensive and, thus, affects firms' marginal cost and their pricing decisions, which in turn can cause inflation and thereby changes in nominal interest rates. As it transpires, the monetary authority tries to minimize deviations from a low single-digit level of desired inflation and a depreciated level of desired exchange rate, formally represented by the loss function ($L$).

[12]  $L = (\pi - \pi^d)^2 + (e - e^d)^2$ with $\pi > \pi^d$ and $e > e^d$.

If actual inflation is less than its desired level, there is no policy problem, the loss will be minimized. Because the monetary authority does not want $e$ to be lower than its desired level (a more depreciated level), this can act as a constraint on its objective to lower inflation to a desired level. With this policy objective in mind, we will determine an interest rate reaction function. We would like to examine the reaction of the interest rate in response to currency appreciation. If we do not see an appropriate response, it might lead to higher inflation. Substituting [8–11] in [12], we minimize the loss function with respect to exchange rate because the central bank aims at maintaining exchange rate stability. The following expression can, therefore, be obtained from the first order condition with respect to the exchange rate:

$$\frac{\partial L}{\partial e} = -\delta\left(\frac{\theta}{\mu} + \frac{1}{\lambda}\right)\frac{1}{e_t^2}\left(\pi_t - \pi_{t-1} - \beta\left\{\frac{\tau}{(1+\varphi)}\left(i_t^s - \alpha f_b + \varepsilon_p\right) - \left(\frac{\theta}{\mu} + \frac{1}{\lambda}\right)\frac{1}{e_t}\right.\right.$$

$$\left.\left. + \left(\frac{\theta}{\mu(1+\varphi)} - \frac{1}{\lambda}\right) + \varepsilon_d\right\} - \delta e_t - \varepsilon_\pi\right) + \left(e_t - \left(e_{t-1} + \varepsilon_e\right)\right) = 0$$

Assuming that the monetary authority maintains exchange rate stability, we can solve the above expression for the corresponding interest rate policy. Assuming $e = e^d$, the monetary policy reaction function or the interest rate rule can be derived from the above expression as follows:

---

[7]  See, Batini et al. (2010) for a discussion on these issues. Aizenman et al. (2011) find that both inflation and real exchange rates are important determinants of policy interest rates in many emerging markets. Also, see Mohanty and Klau (2005) who emphasize the importance of exchange rate in policy rules in emerging markets.

$$[13] \quad i_t^s = \left(\frac{1+\varphi}{\lambda\tau} - \frac{\theta}{\mu\tau}\right) + \frac{(1+\varphi)}{\beta\tau}\left(\pi_t - \pi_{t-1}\right) + \frac{1+\varphi}{\tau}\left(\frac{\theta}{\mu} + \frac{1}{\lambda}\right)\frac{1}{e_t}$$

$$-\frac{\delta(1+\varphi)}{\beta\tau}e_t + \alpha\,f_b - \left(\frac{1+\varphi}{\tau}\varepsilon_d + \frac{1+\varphi}{\beta\tau}\varepsilon_\pi + \varepsilon_p\right)$$

This equation represents a monetary policy rule, which includes inflation, exchange rate, fiscal balance and four unexpected shocks. This reduced form optimal reaction function first suggests that higher interest rate can bring down inflation, and any depreciation in the exchange rate will lead to a higher interest rate, but fiscal deficit will require lowering short-term interest rates to inject extra liquidity into the market as we have experienced in the recent years in India. Because the RBI prefers depreciation of the domestic currency over appreciation, the loss function is asymmetric and the interest rate rule is non-linear in exchange rate. The model, however, needs to be estimated to know the response of interest rate to unexpected shocks to prove whether the current monetary policy stance of the central bank is geared towards exchange rate stability or price stability. In addition to the four shocks in the reaction function, the impact of the monetary and fiscal policy shocks will also be examined in a SVAR setting. These additional shocks can capture the effect of monetary and fiscal disequilibrium.

It is well-known in the literature that inflation is driven by excess money creation as the high level of money supply growth in the past 10 years, averaging 17 per cent per annum, has far exceeded the real output growth in the economy, on average, of around 7 per cent, assuming a constant velocity of money. One can expect money demand to increase in line with the rate of growth of the economy. Thus, the excess money supply is manifesting itself as high inflation. As our aim is to look at the impact of inflation or exchange rate shocks on interest rate, the monetary policy (MP) rule suggests that the central bank is more likely to change interest rate depending on inflation $(\pi)$ in the economy driven by aggregate demand; cutting the rate when there is low inflation and raising it when there is high inflation.[8] In the recent years in many emerging market economies, inflation targeting has proved to be an attractive element in the monetary policy; however, in the context of India, it has been observed that the short-term interest rate, which is the principal tool used to affect inflation, does not have significant impact on the rate of inflation (see Jha, 2008). Further, as exchange rate stabilization is one of the objectives of many emerging market

---

[8]    See Romer (2000) for the rationale underlying an upward sloping MP curve, which captures the actions of a central bank more realistically.

central banks, identifying exchange rate shocks in a monetary policy rule is important as suggested in Taylor (2001).[9] Thus, we use different methodologies to empirically identify the key macroeconomic shocks in the context of India as a major emerging market economy. The following propositions summarize the main theoretical predictions:

Proposition 1: Central bank intervention could lead to higher currency depreciation, which in turn can increase output in the short run but cause higher inflation. With PPP, the volatility of inflation and exchange rate can be similar. If inflationary shocks are supply-driven, currency depreciation could be slower than what relative PPP would predict.

Proposition 2: As government deficit has been accepted as a norm, higher fiscal deficit can lead to higher term premium. However, monetary policy becomes more accommodative to meet government financing needs. On impact, both short and long rate decline to meet higher government financing needs, which becomes a channel for monetary policy transmission.

Proposition 3: Monetary policy can have counter-cyclical impact even in a rapidly growing economy. While contractionary monetary shocks should lead to currency appreciation, fiscal imbalances (deficit) could result in higher inflation, leading to currency depreciation.

## DATA AND EMPIRICAL RESULTS: IMPULSE RESPONSE FUNCTIONS

Quarterly observations from 1996:2 to 2013:1 are used to estimate the model. Real GDP (at constant market prices), GDP deflator as a general index for consumer prices, short-term interest rate (91-day T-bills), long-term treasury bond yield (10-year government security), and nominal effective exchange rate (NEER), fiscal balance as a per cent of GDP have been gathered from Datastream (see Figure 6.3). The GDP data have been seasonally adjusted using the US Census Bureau's X12 seasonal adjustment method.[10] Although the RBI uses both repo and reverse repo rates as short-term interest rates, given the limited sample on this rate, we use the 3-month T-bill yield as a proxy for domestic interest rate. Nominal interest rates are considered here as central banks in any equilibrium model control nominal, not real, interest rates. The NEER is used because it captures imported inflationary pressures and changes in competitiveness more comprehensively than a bilateral exchange rate. Further,

---

[9] Also, see Granville and Mallick (2010), who emphasize the influence of exchange rate shocks in a transition economy.

[10] The X-12 filter was applied to GDP data as it shows significant seasonal behaviour.

**Figure 6.3: Plot of variables used in the VAR**

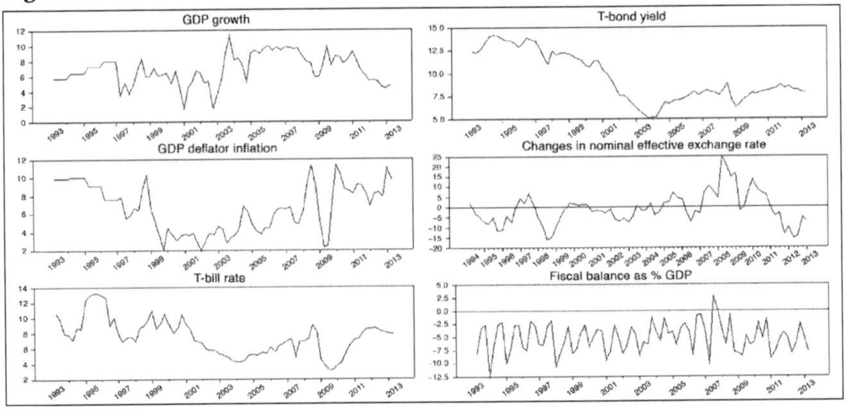

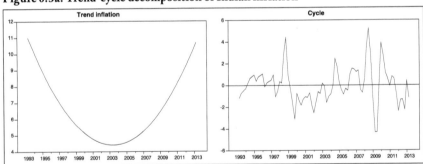

*Source*: Computed using data from Reserve Bank of India, and Datastream

when central banks intervene in the FX market, they tend to influence nominal exchange rates, not real currency values.[11] Therefore, we consider nominal interest rates and nominal effective exchange rates. A Trend-Cycle decomposition of Indian inflation suggests a persistent trend rate of inflation of at least 5 per cent (see Figure 6.3a).

**Figure 6.3a: Trend-cycle decomposition of Indian inflation**

*Source*: Computed using data from Reserve Bank of India, and Datastream

The VAR model is estimated with two lags as the optimal lag length of the VAR system using several lag selection criteria. The impulse-response functions are then derived, describing the response of a variable to a one-time shock to one of

---

11 Scholl and Uhlig (2008) use exchange rate in nominal terms. It is possible that the nominal and the real exchange rates may respond in a very similar way to monetary policy shocks in the case of advanced economies. However, in emerging markets, one may find a different pattern due to a relatively higher level of inflation in these countries.

the elements of $\varepsilon_t$, using a Cholesky decomposition to identify the orthogonalized disturbances, $\varepsilon_t$. The recursive Cholesky decomposition of the variance-covariance matrix of the model residuals considers the causal ordering of the variables.[12] Shocks are extracted by applying a recursive identification structure and formulating the VAR with the following ordering: Changes in NEER, output growth, inflation rate, short-term nominal interest rate, long-term treasury bond yield, and fiscal balance as the benchmark ordering.[13] The ordering of the variables reveals the following relations among them:

(a) Exchange rates do not respond contemporaneously to the shock from any other endogenous variable of the model, given that its movement is being monitored by the central bank followed by intervention whenever there is high volatility.

(b) Real output does not respond contemporaneously to inflation, interest rates and fiscal shocks, while it is contemporaneously affected only by the exchange rate shock. With quarterly data, it seems reasonable to assume that output does not respond contemporaneously to other real shocks due to 3-months lag in the publication of output data in India.

(c) Inflation does not respond contemporaneously to interest rates and fiscal shocks, while it is contemporaneously affected by the exchange rate and demand (real output) shocks. The inflation rate is assumed to respond contemporaneously to output and exchange rate innovations, but not to short-term and long-term interest rates, and fiscal shocks.

(d) Interest rate can react very quickly to output, inflation and exchange rate shocks. Finally, the variable that is ordered last, that is, fiscal balance, is contemporaneously affected by the shocks from all of the endogenous variables of the model.

Given the high fiscal deficits in India, a six-variable system with both monetary and fiscal shocks and by using a causal ordering with NEER being ordered first can be an appropriate identification strategy as the central bank intervenes regularly to stabilize the exchange rate, which can influence output, inflation, interest rate, fiscal balance in that sequential order. The recursive VAR results are presented in Figures 6.4–6.9.

We find that exchange rate appreciation shocks have insignificant effect on output on impact, but following subsequent decline in inflation, interest rates

---

[12] See, for example, Cover and Mallick (2012) for more details on the SVAR methodology and the recursive identifying restrictions. They are not discussed here to save space.

[13] We have performed unit-root tests for all the variables, generally not rejecting the hypothesis of non-stationarity (the null of unit root in levels); thus, the variables are measured in first differences, except interest rates. All the estimations in this chapter have been carried out using RATS econometric software.

appear to decline and, hence, a positive effect on output in the medium term before the impact dies out in the long run (see Figure 6.4). Demand shocks, on the other hand, do not have significant impact on the changes in exchange rate, although demand shocks positively influence inflation (see Figure 6.5). As discussed earlier, inflation in India is found to be driven more significantly by supply shocks than exchange rate and demand shocks (see Figures 6.4-6.7). This is in line with the fact that many developing countries do have large negative output gaps and high structural inflation. Goyal and Pujari (2005) identify a supply curve using data on inflation and industrial output growth and find that supply shocks have a large impact on inflation, whereas demand has large and persistent effect on output. Our results remain consistent with this earlier finding in the literature.[14]

### Figure 6.4: IRFs for exchange rate shock

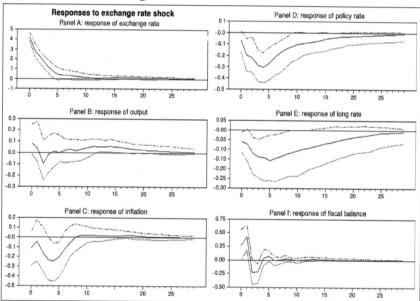

*Source*: Author's own estimates

---

[14] In a more recent paper, Patra and Ray (2010) emphasize that although inflationary pressures emanating from higher food prices may limit the scope for monetary policy action, eventually the monetary authority has to respond to this even if it is an inflationary supply shock. From our impulse responses, it is noted that monetary policy does significantly respond to this type of inflationary supply shock.

**Figure 6.5: IRFs for real GDP shock**

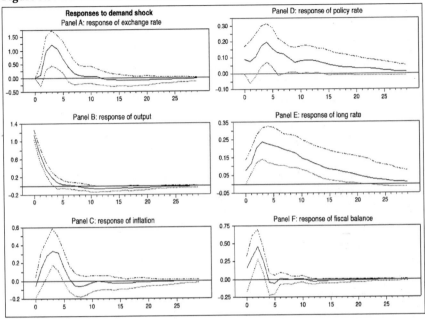

*Source*: Author's own estimates

**Figure 6.6: IRFs for inflation shock**

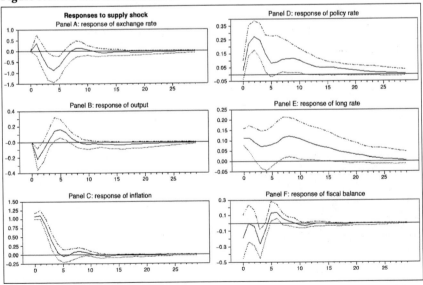

*Source*: Author's own estimates

**Figure 6.7: IRFs for short-term interest rate shocks**

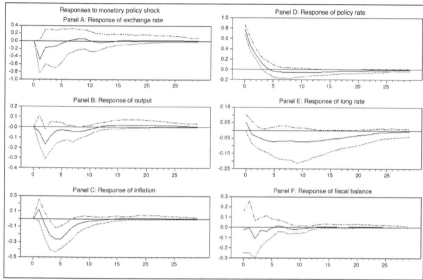

*Source*: Author's own estimates

**Figure 6.8: IRFs for long-term interest rate shock**

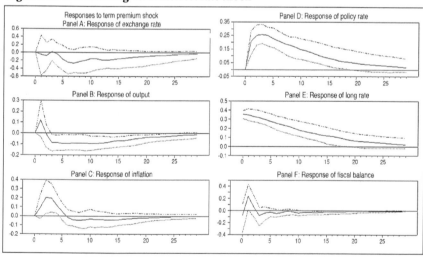

*Source*: Author's own estimates

We find that contractionary monetary policy shocks in the form of increases in interest rates have negative effects on real output in the short run, with no significant impact on the changes in exchange rate (see Figure 6.7). Contractionary

**Figure 6.9: IRFs for fiscal shock**

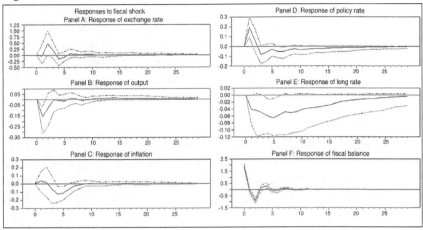

*Source*: Author's own estimates

**Figure 6.10: Derived structural shocks**

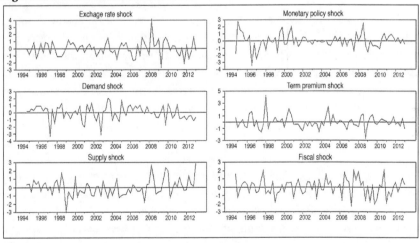

*Source*: Author's own estimates

monetary policy shocks do help stabilize output (not inflation as it is structural to a large extent led by supply shocks), but they create fiscal deficit in the short run due to high-borrowing cost for the government. Term-premium shocks do reflect that the cost of borrowing has a negative impact on output in the long-run (see Figure 6.8). Fiscal shocks on the other hand show that the long-term rates have been coming down to provide cheaper finance for the government's perennial fiscal deficit (see Figure 6.9), which in turn has a positive impact on output in the long-run.[15] Finally, except its innovations, exchange rates do not seem to be significantly influenced by any other shocks except supply shocks (see Figure 6.6), thus providing evidence for intervention by the RBI in maintaining exchange rate stability at a depreciated level and promoting export competitiveness, but it contributes to inflation persistence. The derived structural shocks are shown in Figure 6.10. Estimated structural shocks do tend to capture the turning points.

Checking robustness

Even if one undertakes the above exercise by excluding fiscal variable, the results remain broadly similar for the reduced version of the model. We also altered the ordering by putting fiscal shock first and exchange rate shock last, but the results still remain robust. As it is commonly believed that money supply in India is expanding much faster than the demand for real money balances that is spilling over to the goods market and, thus, fuelling inflation, we may need to include a monetary aggregate in the VAR as opposed to the cost of money. The stock of money being endogenous has been evidenced for India (see Luintel, 2002) showing that money stocks (M1 and M2), consumer price index (CPI) and real GDP are cointegrated and causally related. So, we include the broad money growth in the VAR as a robustness check and most responses remain similar except the responses for monetary shocks.[16] While, in the basic VAR, innovations in the short-term interest rate (contractionary shock) do not increase prices (no price puzzle) and monetary disturbances do contribute to output fluctuations in the short-run, in this reformulated VAR with monetary aggregate, expansionary shocks to the money growth do increase long-term interest rates (liquidity puzzle), but they do play a role in increasing inflation in the medium run, thereby reducing output, which is in part due to rise in inflation expectations as reflected in the response of the long rate. Thus, we conclude that interest rate is playing an important role in monetary policy as opposed to monetary aggregate in the post-reform period in India.

　To further validate the basic SVAR results, we adopt an over-identified SVAR strategy following Sims-Zha within the same 6-variable VAR ordering by imposing the following non-recursive restrictions. Denoting the structural errors as $\varepsilon_t$ and the reduced form disturbances as $u_t$, the SVAR model is written as follows.

---

[15] It is worth noting here that the magnitude of the short-run impact on output could vary depending on whether crowding-in or crowding-out effect dominates (for recent evidence, see Mitra, 2006).

[16] These six sets of responses are available upon request from the author. To save space, they are currently excluded.

## Figure 6.11: Over-identified SVAR (Sims-Zha)

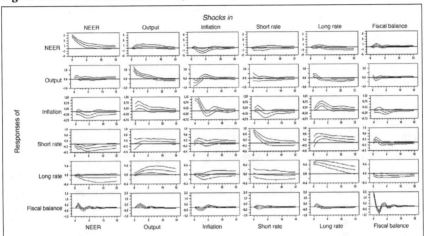

*Source*: Author's own estimates

$$\begin{bmatrix} u_e \\ u_y \\ u_\pi \\ u_i \\ u_p \\ u_f \end{bmatrix} = \begin{bmatrix} 1 & 0 & 0 & 0 & 0 & 0 \\ a_{21} & 1 & a_{23} & a_{24} & a_{25} & a_{26} \\ a_{31} & a_{32} & 1 & 0 & 0 & a_{36} \\ a_{41} & a_{42} & a_{43} & 1 & a_{45} & a_{46} \\ 0 & 0 & 0 & a_{54} & 1 & a_{56} \\ 0 & 0 & 0 & 0 & 0 & 1 \end{bmatrix} \begin{bmatrix} \varepsilon_e \\ \varepsilon_y \\ \varepsilon_\pi \\ \varepsilon_i \\ \varepsilon_p \\ \varepsilon_f \end{bmatrix}$$

$u_e$ is from the exchange rate equation, $u_y$ is the residual from the output growth equation, $u_p$ from the inflation equation, $u_i$ from the interest rate equation, $u_p$ from the term-premium equation, and $u_f$ from the fiscal balance equation. As $u_t$ is the vector of VAR residuals, $\varepsilon_t$ is the vector of corresponding structural shocks. The technique draws a set of posterior samples from the VAR coefficients and computes impulse responses for each sample. These samples are, then, summarized to compute MC-based estimates of the responses using the error band methods in Sims and Zha (1999). The impulse responses are similar to those obtained with the recursive model. The responses further help pinpoint the effects of different shocks, consistent with the results from recursive VARs. While a supply shock shows a declining level of interest rate, a demand shock makes firms more optimistic, boosting aggregate demand and, thus, a rise in interest rates (see Figure 6.11). As the exchange rate shock (increase is appreciation) leads to lowering inflation (see Figure 6.11), it suggests that a market determined exchange rate (without central bank intervention) would more likely stem the inflationary pressure on the back of currency appreciation due to surge in foreign exchange inflows and, thus, help economic activity. However, as the central bank intervention gives rise to a depreciating NEER and higher inflation in the long-run, persistent inflation at high single digit levels in India could be the by-product of RBI intervention, although such a policy strategy helps boost external demand for Indian goods.

## A sign-restriction approach

Besides the above recursive and non-recursive traditional identification strategy, to further validate the results, we adopt a more recent sign restriction method (Uhlig, 2005, and Mountford and Uhlig, 2009) which is robust to non-stationarity of series including breaks.[17] Also, the zero long-run restrictions may appear very stringent as they are based on statistical properties of the data rather than serious theoretical consideration. Within this framework, we identify two types of underlying disturbances, namely an exchange rate, monetary policy and fiscal shocks. We apply identifying sign restrictions to the above VAR with six variables. Having obtained the parameter estimates of the reduced form VAR, we impose three sign restrictions to identify monetary shock and two sign restrictions to identify exchange rate shock, and further two restrictions to identify a fiscal shock (deficit spending) as a robustness check. The restrictions are shown in Table 6.1. We jointly identify a fiscal shock alongside a monetary shock to check any inter-linkage between these two policies.

**Table 6.1: Identifying sign restrictions**

|  | Exchange rate | GDP | Inflation | Short-term rate | Long-term rate | Fiscal balance |
|---|---|---|---|---|---|---|
| Monetary policy shock (tightening) | ? | ? | − | + | + | ? |
| Exchange rate shock (depreciation) | − | ? | + | − | ? | ? |
| Fiscal shock | ? | ? | + | ? | ? | − |

*Source*: Author's own assumptions

In the case of monetary policy shock, no restriction is placed on the nominal exchange rate as we want it to be determined by the model because external factors may influence the exchange rate in an open economy context. Also, we do not determine *a priori* the effect on output, as we wish the impact to be determined by the model. Monetary policy shock is identified as an increase in interest rate (short rate) that will lead to an increase in the long rate and, thus, a decline in

---

[17] Also see Dedola and Neri (2007), and Rafiq and Mallick (2008) for more details.

inflation. To identify exchange rate shock, we impose three restrictions that the RBI attempts not to allow exchange rate to appreciate, and consequently interest rate will decline and inflation will increase.

These restrictions seem reasonable in the light of the observed pattern in the data. As the domestic currency depreciates, inflation could increase; while exported goods become cheaper relative to imported goods, thus, increasing demand for domestic goods and higher output. However, we do not pre-judge this outcome as we would like this to be revealed from the impulse response functions. Also, exchange rate changes can either exhibit depreciation or appreciation. The restrictions imposed can help derive respective impulse vectors, which are defined as innovations to the VAR system in response to a unit shock in each disturbance. We keep those impulse vectors whose impulse response functions satisfy the sign restrictions and discard the others.

**Figure 6.12: Responses to a monetary shock (B > 0, Q > 0, DP < 0) (Exchange rate shock identified first and then monetary shock)**

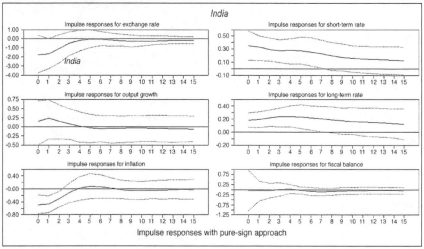

*Source*: Author's own estimates

The responses do satisfy the sign restrictions even in the long run (see Figures 6.12–6.15), although they are required to satisfy the sign restrictions for $k = 2$ quarters. The error bands are illustrated as the dotted lines above and below the response line (the thick line), which are composed of the 16th, 84th and median percentiles of the impulse responses for each shock, from a sample of 1,000 draws from the posterior. The dotted lines also indicate the slope of the posterior distribution of the impulse responses. With exchange rate being restricted not to appreciate (increase), which is likely to occur as a result of exchange rate targeting, we would expect inflation to rise, whereas in case of the monetary policy shock, inflation can be expected to decline. When monetary policy calls for an increase in interest rate, the central bank also at the same time is not allowing the exchange rate to appreciate.

**Figure 6.13: Responses to an exchange rate shock (DE < 0, DP > 0) (Exchange rate shock identified first and then monetary shock)**

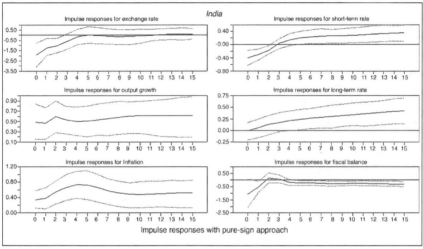

*Source*: Author's own estimates

**Figure 6.14: Responses to monetary policy shock (Fiscal shock identified first and then monetary shock)**

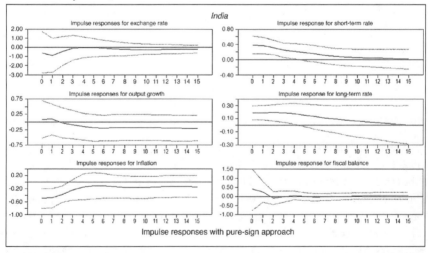

*Source*: Author's own estimates

**Figure 6.15: Responses to fiscal shock (FIS < 0, DP > 0) (Fiscal shock identified first and then monetary policy shock)**

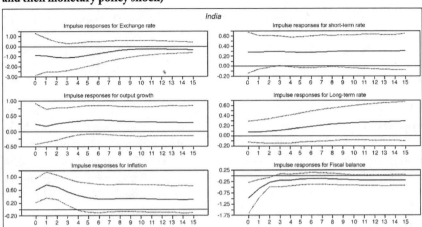

We undertake the exercise for two shocks jointly as the RBI seems to be trying to achieve two objectives at the same time, price and exchange rate stability. In Figure 6.12, in response to a monetary shock, we find that exchange rate depreciates initially, but it tends to appreciate in the long-run, although the contractionary monetary shock has a negative impact on output and inflation. An exchange rate shock (depreciation) on the other hand has a positive impact on inflation initially and then rupee tends to appreciate in the long run, which reduces inflation. The exchange rate shock does not obey the restriction in the long run, and it starts to appreciate immediately after the first quarter albeit gradually (see Figure 6.13). This clearly suggests that the RBI has been following exchange rate targeting to keep it depreciated which makes inflation persistent. Overall, the exchange rate management does appear to be fuelling inflation in India.

To show further robustness of our results, we jointly solve monetary and fiscal shocks. We still find that monetary shock has a negative impact on output growth (see Figure 6.14) and exchange rate tends to depreciate reflecting the pattern in the original data as in Figure 6.2, whereas a fiscal shock (deficit spending) tends to show a positive impact on output growth (exceeding the shock's impact on inflation) and, hence, the exchange rate appreciates (see Figure 6.15). We also carry out forecast error variance decomposition (FEVD) of the monetary and exchange rate shocks identified on the basis of sign restrictions to find the percentage variation in each variable explained by each shock. The FEVD suggests that both monetary and exchange rate shocks explain inflation more than their impact on output fluctuations. This suggests relatively limited importance of demand shocks in a developing economy. The historical decomposition results validate the stabilizing properties of monetary shocks by picking up the turning points accurately. These results are excluded to save space.

## CONCLUSIONS

This chapter provides empirically the interrelated dynamics of macroeconomic variables to throw light on the effect of monetary and exchange rate shocks in India, alongside fiscal shocks, given the government control over monetary policy historically. Over a 17 years (68 quarters) time horizon during the post-reform period, the impulse response exercise in this chapter shows that monetary shocks have little permanent effect on real GDP or inflation, while the impact effect of an exchange rate shock (depreciation) is positive on output growth, but it fuels inflation, thus, transmitting a neutral effect on output in the long run. Even if one changes the ordering in the SVAR exercise, the same results still hold.

The main message of this chapter is that given the exchange rate adjustment either via central bank intervention as in the past years or due to accumulated inflation differential with the key trading partners leading to drastic currency depreciation as happened during 2013, if the monetary authority tries to introduce a contractionary monetary policy shock, such policy has little counter-cyclical impact on output nor it helps stabilize inflation as inflation is largely supply-driven and any currency depreciation further fuels inflationary pressure. This suggests that the central bank intervention in the foreign exchange market to stabilize exchange rate shocks may not be effective as inflation differential plays a big role in driving currency valuation. Monetary transmission appears to be working through the fiscal channel as shown in this chapter rather than the interest rate channel. Therefore, the central bank's recent monetary tightening to stabilize inflation via the interest rate channel is unlikely to be effective in the Indian context because of the modest impact of monetary policy shocks on inflation as the source of inflation continues to be through supply shocks, namely food inflation and surge in global commodity prices.

## REFERENCES

Aizenman, J., M. Hutchison and I. Noy. 2011. 'Inflation Targeting and Real Exchange Rates in Emerging Markets'. *World Development* 39(5): 712–24.

Balakrishnan, P. 1991. 'Industrial Price Behaviour in India: An "Error-correction" model'. *Journal of Development Economics* 37(1–2): 309–26.

Baillie, R. T. and W. P. Osterberg. 1997. 'Why Do Central Banks Intervene'? *Journal of International Money and Finance* 16(6): 909–19.

Batini, N., P. Levine and J. Pearlman. 2010. *Monetary Rules in Emerging Economies with Financial Market Imperfections* in J. Galí and M. Gertler, eds. *International Dimensions of Monetary Policy* NBER Conference Volume, Chapter 5. The University of Chicago Press, 251–311.

Bhattacharya, B. B., N. R. Bhanumurthy and H. Mallick. 2008. 'Modeling Interest Rate Cycles in India'. *Journal of Policy Modeling* 30(5): 899–915.

Bhattacharyya, I. and R. Sensarma. 2008. 'How effective are monetary policy signals in India'? *Journal of Policy Modeling* 30(1): 169–83.

Callen, T. 2001. *Modeling and Forecasting Inflation in India* in Tim Callen, Patricia Reynolds and Christopher Towe, eds. *India at the Crossroads: Sustaining Growth and Reducing Poverty* Washington: International Monetary Fund, 105–21.

Cover, J. P., W. Enders and C. J. Hueng. 2006. Using the Aggregate Demand-aggregate Supply Model to Identify Structural Demand-side and Supply-side Shocks: Results Using a Bivariate VAR'. *Journal of Money, Credit and Banking* 38(3): 777–90.

Cover, J. P. and S. K. Mallick. 2012. 'Identifying Sources of Macroeconomic and Exchange Rate Fluctuations in the UK'. *Journal of International Money and Finance* 31(6): 1627–48.

Dedola, L., and S. Neri. 2007. 'What Does a Technology Shock Do? A VAR Analysis with Model-based Sign Restrictions'. *Journal of Monetary Economics* 54(2): 512–49.

Dutta Roy, S. and G. Darbha. 2000. 'Dynamics of Money, Output and Price Interaction – Some Indian Evidence'. *Economic Modelling* 17(4): 559–88.

Goyal, A., and A. K. Pujari. 2005. 'Identifying Long-run Supply Curve in India'. *Journal of Quantitative Economics, New Series* 3(2): 1–15.

Granville, B. and S. Mallick. 2010. 'Monetary Policy in Russia: Identifying Exchange Rate shocks'. *Economic Modelling* 27(1): 432–44.

Gylfason, T. 2002. 'The Real Exchange Rate Always Floats'. *Australian Economic Papers* 41(4): 369–81.

Ho, Tai-kuang and Kuo-chun Yeh. 2010. 'Measuring Monetary Policy in a Small Open Economy with Managed Exchange Rates: The Case of Taiwan'. *Southern Economic Journal* 76(3): 811–26.

Hutchison, M. M. 2003. 'Intervention and Exchange Rate Stabilization Policy in Developing Countries'. *International Finance* 6(1): 109–27.

Jha, R. 2008. 'Inflation Targeting in India: Issues and Prospects'. *International Review of Applied Economics*, 22(2): 259–70.

Lane, P. 2003. 'Business Cycles and Macroeconomic Policy in Emerging Market Economies'. *International Finance* 6(1): 89–108.

Luintel, K. B. 2002. 'Exogeneity of Money and Its Policy Implications for Price Control: Evidence from South Asia'. *Pacific Economic Review* 7(3): 505–17.

Mallick, S. K. 2004. 'A Dynamic Macroeconometric Model for Short-run Stabilization in India'. *Applied Economics* 36(3): 261–76.

Mallick, S. K. 1999. *Modelling Macroeconomic Adjustment with Growth in Developing Economies: The Case of India*, England: Ashgate.

Mallick, S. K. and R. M. Sousa. 2012. 'Real Effects of Monetary Policy in Large Emerging economies'. *Macroeconomic Dynamics* 16(S2): 190–212.

Mishkin, F. S. 2000. 'Inflation Targeting in Emerging-market Countries'. *American Economic Review* (Papers and Proceedings) 90(2): 105–09.

Mitra, P. 2006. 'Has Government Investment Crowded out Private Investment in India'? *The American Economic Review* (Papers and Proceedings) 96(2): 337–41.

Mohan, R. 2008. 'The Role of Fiscal and Monetary Policies in Sustaining Growth with Stability in India'. *Asian Economic Policy Review* 3(2): 209–36.

Mohanty, M. S. and M. Klau. 2005. *Monetary Policy Rules in Emerging Market Economies: Issues and Evidence* in Langhammer, R. J. and L. V. de Souza, eds. *Monetary Policy and Macroeconomic Stabilization in Latin America* Springer-Verlag, 205–45.

Mountford, A. and Uhlig, H. 2009. ;What Are the Effects of Fiscal Policy Shocks'? *Journal of Applied Econometrics* 24(6): 960–92.

Nachane, D. M., and Lakshmi, R. 2002. 'Dynamics of Inflation in India: A P-star Approach'. *Applied Economics* 34(1), 101–10.

Patra, M. D. and P. Ray. 2010. *Inflation Expectations and Monetary Policy in India: An Empirical Exploration* IMF Working Paper, WP/10/84, Washington DC: IMF.

Rafiq, M. S. and S. K. Mallick. 2008. 'The Effect of Monetary Policy on Output in EMU3: A Sign Restriction Approach'. *Journal of Macroeconomics* 30(4): 1756–91.

Ramachandran, M., and N. Srinivasan. 2007. 'Asymmetric Exchange Rate Intervention and International Reserve Accumulation in India'. *Economics Letters* 94(2): 259–65.

Romer, D. 2000. 'Keynesian Macroeconomics Without the LM Curve'. *Journal of Economic Perspectives* 14, 149–69.

Sarno, L., and M. P. Taylor. 2001. 'Official Intervention in the Foreign Exchange Market: Is It Effective, and if so, How Does It Work'. *Journal of Economic Literature* 39(3): 839–68.

Scholl, A. and H. Uhlig. 2008. 'New Evidence on the Puzzles: Results from Agnostic Identification on Monetary Policy and Exchange Rates'. *Journal of International Economics* 76(1): 1–13.

Sen, K., and R. R. Vaidya. 1995. 'The Determination of Industrial Prices in India: A Post Keynesian Approach'. *Journal of Post Keynesian Economics* 18(1): 29–52.

Shah, A., and I. Patnaik. 2007. *India's Experience with Capital Flows: The Elusive Quest for a Sustainable Current Account Deficit* in S. Edwards, ed. *Capital Controls and Capital Flows in Emerging Economies: Policies, Practices and Consequences* Chapter 13, The University of Chicago Press, 609–43.

Sims, C. A., and T. Zha. 1999. 'Error Bands for Impulse Responses'. *Econometrica* 67(5): 1113–55.

Szakmary, A. C., and I. Mathur. 1997. Central Bank Intervention and Trading Rule Profits in Foreign Exchange Markets'. *Journal of International Money and Finance* 16(4): 513–35.

Taylor, J. B. 2001, The Role of the Exchange Rate in Monetary Policy Rules, *American Economic Review* (Papers and Proceedings) 91(2): 263–67.

Uhlig, H. 2005. 'What Are the Effects of Monetary Policy on Output? Results from an Agnostic Identification Procedure'. *Journal of Monetary Economics* 52(2): 381–419.

# 7

# Role of Monetary Policy in Sustaining High Growth in India
## Lessons from the Recent Dynamics in Determination of Bank Credit

Amaresh Samantaraya

## INTRODUCTION

India's economic performance during the post-reform period has been impressive in the backdrop of low and volatile growth during the first three decades since Independence. Not only the average growth during 1992–2013 at around 7.0 per cent is almost double of that achieved during 1951–80, but the growth performance has also been reasonably stable. Within the post-reform period, achieving a higher growth trajectory of around 9 per cent during 2003–08 and bouncing back from the fallout of global financial crisis during 2009–11 was phenomenal. However, economic slowdown during 2011–13 accompanied by adverse developments such as higher inflationary situation since 2009, fiscal deterioration at the central government level and surging current account deficit has been a matter of great concern. Particularly, economic growth in 2012–13 was at the decadal low of around 4.5 per cent, and the same for the current financial year is not expected to be any better.

While achieving high economic growth is not sufficient to solve all economic woes, it is essential for job creation, and thus, critically important for poverty reduction on an enduring basis. Moreover, sustained higher economic growth for a considerable period of time is generally found to improve various socio-economic indicators. In this perspective, an immediate issue is to what extent we should be concerned about current growth rates of about 5 per cent. A sense of comfort is expressed at certain quarters citing that even at current growth rates, India stands out as one of the world's fastest growing economy. In our view, there is no room for complacency. Given the level of unemployment and poverty existing in India, it has to grow at close to double digit level on a sustained basis so that a sizeable proportion of our population will overcome impoverished conditions every year. Thus, sooner we get back to the growth trajectory of 2003–08, better for us.

Based on the views expressed by several industry leaders, it appears that infrastructural bottlenecks, policy paralysis at the government level coupled with some regressive decisions related to GAAR, retrospective application of some corporate tax laws have dampened current investment climate. It was exacerbated by the reported cases of massive government corruption including 2G scam, coal-gate and mining scam, etc. Some also accuse public agitations and legal complications related to land accusation and environmental clearances as additional roadblocks for infrastructure and industrial growth. Select reform initiatives announced during September 2012 and January–February 2013, while espousing the Government's pro-reform intentions, did not deliver any traction for growth as yet.

Amongst various policy options, there has been a growing demand for monetary policy accommodation to restore the economy back to the higher growth trajectory. The suggestion for interest rate cut has mainly come from industry, government and a section of academia. On the contrary, the Reserve Bank of India (RBI) mostly in last couple of years has been preoccupied itself with fighting its greater devil: inflation by pursuing monetary tightening. This brings to the board the disagreements on whether monetary accommodation through cheap credit policy at the moment is the right thing to do to revive and sustain high economic growth in India. In this backdrop, the present chapter is an attempt to assess to what extent easy monetary policy through reduction in interest rates will be effective. We will look for an answer based on the dynamics in determination of bank credit in India.

In a bank-dominated financial system as in India, bank credit plays a critical role in monetary policy operations. Bank credit is considered to be crucial as it facilitates financing of deficit spenders and has powerful influence on investment and consumption spending. Its relevance is not only confined to demand side analysis, but credit also supports capacity creation through financing long term projects as well as working capital needs of the producers. In a developing country context, its role is further emphasized to uplift the disadvantaged and weaker sections through development financing and financial inclusion.

As regards interlinkages amongst monetary policy, bank credit and economic growth, two issues in the literature are prominently discussed. Firstly, the literature on monetary transmission mechanism established that bank credit channel is fundamentally vital in transmitting monetary policy shocks to the economy (Kashyap et al., 1993, Kashyap and Stein, 1994, Gertler and Gilchrist, 1993, Kim, 1999, Morsink and Bayoumi, 2001). In the Indian context, Mukhopadhyay (1999), Pandit et al. (2006), Nachane et al. (2006) and Samantaraya and Kamaiah (2011) also found evidences supporting the role of bank credit as an effective monetary transmission channel.

Secondly, it is widely observed that bank credit exhibits some tendency of pro-cyclicality, which is further reinforced with adoption of prudential norms of capital adequacy and non-performing assets (NPAs) provisioning (Blum and Hellberg, 1995; Frufine, 2000; Borio et al., 2001; Berger and Udell, 2003; Bikker and Metzemakers, 2004). Amplification of pro-cyclicality of bank credit has important implications for diluting the role of credit channel of monetary policy transmission. Bliss and Kaufmann (2002) have demonstrated with simple arithmetic examples how potency of monetary policy to engineer recovery from economic slowdown is weakened in the face of regulatory capital and reserve requirements. In the Indian context, several studies have attempted to examine the impact of prudential regulations in terms of capital adequacy and NPAs provisioning on bank credit having implication for its pro-cyclicality, since these norms were introduced in the post-reform period (Nachane et al., 2000; Nag and Das, 2002; Ghosh and Nachane, 2003; Ghosh et al., 2003; and Samantaraya, 2009). However, as summarized in Appendix Table 7.1, these studies differ in terms of their inferences for pro-cyclicality.

The above discussion highlights how bank credit is critical for conducting monetary policy and how its role becomes complicated with the introduction of prudential regulatory measures. Therefore, in the perspective of assessing the role of monetary policy to propel the Indian economy back to higher growth trajectory, it is imperative to review the behaviour of bank credit, and how it responds to monetary policy and interest rate decisions. In this backdrop, the present study empirically examines the dynamics in the determination of bank credit in India.

The present study improves upon the previous studies, on several accounts as noted below. Firstly, it develops a simultaneous equations model to explain the credit demand by the public and credit supply by the banks, separately. Improving upon the existing literature, the present study takes into account the endogeneity between bank credit, deposits and lending rate explicitly while estimating the model. On this aspect, it is a fundamental contribution to the empirical literature in this area. Secondly, previous studies ignored stationarity issue in data. We have examined the same using panel unit root tests such as Levin, Lin and Chu test, Augmented Dickey-Fuller (ADF) Fisher Chi-square test and PP Fisher Chi-square test. Thirdly, the period of coverage for the present study is 1996–97 to 2010–11, which covers period of both rapid expansion and slowdown in economic activity as also bank credit in India. It is worth mentioning that business cycles seem to have been relatively pronounced during the period of consideration, which may render this as an interesting case study.

The organization of the study is set out as below. To gain some preliminary idea on the association between bank credit and economic growth, the study begins with a discussion on their interrelationship in the second section. The theoretical model for our empirical analysis on determination of bank credit is developed in the third section, which also covers the related data issues. Based on bank-wise panel data, estimation results for the above model are presented in the fourth section. Policy implications for sustaining high growth in India in general and reviving the economy from current economic slowdown are highlighted in the fifth section. Finally, the sixth section summarizes the study and draws broad conclusions.

## ECONOMIC GROWTH AND BANK CREDIT IN INDIA: PRELIMINARY EVIDENCES

In this section, an attempt has been made to examine the association between economic growth and aggregate bank credit (in terms of non-food credit) in India since 1950s. In the entire study, bank credit is used in real terms adjusted by Wholesale Price Index (WPI). During the first three decades since independence (1951–52 to 1979–80), the average Gross Domestic Product (GDP) growth was lower at around 3.5 per cent. During this period, average growth rate of credit was around 7.8 per cent. Average economic growth moved up to 5.6 per cent in the decade of 1980s (1980–81 to 1989–90), which also witnessed average growth of bank credit accentuating to 9.1 per cent. During the post-reform period (since 1992–93), the average economic growth further increased to 6.9 per cent. During this period, average growth of bank credit moved up to 12.6 per cent, correspondingly. Particularly, with economic growth leaping to the higher growth trajectory of 8.5 per cent during 2003–11, credit growth also concomitantly soared up to 17.4 per cent, during the comparable period.

Figure 7.1 below presents the scatter plot between growth rates in bank credit and GDP for the period 1951–2013. It is apparent from the graph that there is positive association between bank credit and economic growth, although it does not seem to be very strong. The same was also confirmed with the correlation coefficient between growth rates in GDP and bank credit, which was estimated to be 0.3.

**Figure 7.1: Growth in bank credit and GDP**

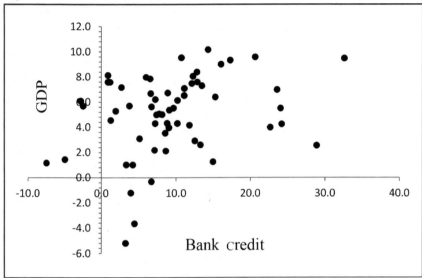

*Source*: *Handbook of Statistics on the Indian Economy 2011–12*, published by the RBI.

**Figure 7.2: Cyclicality of GDP and bank credit**

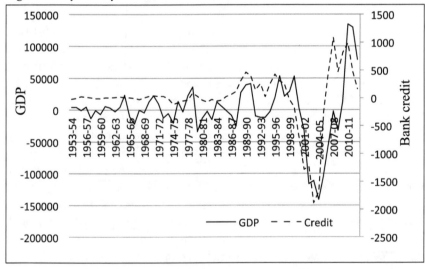

*Source: Handbook of Statistics on the Indian Economy 2011–12*, published by the RBI.

To gain further insight into the association between economic growth and bank credit, let us analyse the pro-cyclicality issue. As a formal tool of pro-cyclicality,

Figure 7.2 depicts cyclical behaviour of GDP and bank credit by applying Hodrick-Prescott (HP)-filter.

As can be observed from Figure 7.2, prior to mid-1980s, cyclical fluctuations in bank credit were very much muted. Since mid-1980s, upward/downward swings in bank credit are largely associated with similar movements in GDP. Moreover, the cyclical movements in both the series became most prominent in last two decades or so.

There are two important facts emerging from the above discussion. Firstly, there are evidences of positive association between growth of the economy and bank credit. Secondly, the pro-cyclicality of bank credit has become prominent in the post-reform period. This reinforces our interest in empirically analysing issues related to determination the of bank credit in India, which is carried out in the following sections.

One possible explanation for the prominence of credit pro-cyclicality in last two decades could be due to the fact that banks gained considerable operational freedom in business decisions departing from the administered regime of the past. Reform initiatives towards greater market orientation in the banking system in India found fuller expression in the second half of the 1990s. These initiatives include freedom to determine lending rates for credit limit of over ₹2 lakh since October 1994 and term deposit rates of maturity over 1 year since July 1996. The SLR and CRR were reduced in a phased manner to rationalize statutory pre-emption of resources of the banks. All these could have facilitated considerable operational autonomy in the banking sector guiding lending decisions on commercial basis, and thus, showing up expected pro-cyclicality vis-à-vis economic activity.

Could introduction of capital adequacy requirements under Basel prudential norms and NPAs provisioning be a contributory factor for this phenomenon? Under this new environment, it will be interesting to examine how credit supply by banks responds to monetary policy decisions and how the banks' customers react to banks' decisions on interest rates on deposits and lending. The model developed in the following section would seek to get answers for these questions. These answers will provide greater insight to draw correct perspectives on the ability of monetary policy to pull the economy out of current economic slowdown.

## ECONOMETRIC MODEL AND DATA ISSUES

In this section, we will develop a small simultaneous equations model to explain the determination of bank credit. The need for a simultaneous model is underscored by the fact that some of the determinants of bank credit such as bank deposits and lending rate are endogenous. Given the supply of credit by the banks and demand for bank credit by public, volume of bank credit and lending rates for respective banks are determined, simultaneously. Secondly, in the process of credit creation in the banking system, volume of deposits is influenced by volume of credit by banks. In this context, deposits which appear in the right hand side of a conventional credit supply equation cannot be treated as exogenous.

In the following, we delineate the specification of the theoretical model to explain the behaviour of bank credit.

Supply of bank credit ($^sL$) is influenced mainly by three sets of factors. Sources of funding are the principal factor contributing to credit flow. There are three major sources of funding namely, (a) deposits ($D$), (b) market funding, and (c) equity. Consolidated balance sheet of Scheduled Commercial Banks in India reveals that deposits constitute close to 80 per cent of total liabilities, and for most of the public sector banks, this proportion is as high as 80 to 90 per cent in the recent period. As the source of funding for influencing bank credit flow, the present study limits to the dominant source of the deposits. Deposits are expected to have positive influence on the bank credit.

Second set of factors influencing bank credit flow are various interest rates. The list may include bank lending rate '$l$' depicting the earning prospects, while return on bank investments '$g$' and call money rate 'CALL' represent the opportunity cost. Bank lending rate is expected to have positive effect on supply of bank lending, while other alternate rates of return are expected to exert negative impact.

Finally, the third set of factors is related to regulatory and prudential measures of bank management. The list may include statutory reserves, capital requirements and provisioning for NPAs. Cash Reserve Ratio (CRR) is used by the Reserve Bank of India (RBI) as an important monetary policy instrument and high CRR is expected to have negative impact on bank credit flow. Banks are also prescribed to maintain minimum capital to risk-weighted assets ratio (CRAR) according to their total risk exposure. During economic downturn, with increasing risk perception and corresponding high risk weights, capital requirements increase which constrains supply of credit to comply with the minimum CRAR. A higher level of current CRAR gives greater comfort for the banks for future contingency, and thus, conducive to expand credit supply. On the other hand, higher non-discretionary provisioning linked to NPAs negatively affects banks' ability to provide credit.

Thus, the supply of bank credit can be mathematically given by:

$$^sL_{it} = a_0 + a_1\,D_{it} + a_2\,l_{it} + a_3\,g_{it} + a_4\,CALL_t + a_5\,NPA_{it} + a_6\,CRR_t + a_7\,CRAR_{it}$$

(1)

$$\quad (+)\qquad (+)\qquad (-)\qquad (-)\qquad (-)\qquad (-)\qquad (+)$$

In the above equation, the subscript '$it$' refers to the value of corresponding variable for $i^{th}$ bank and in $t^{th}$ year.

The demand for bank credit ($^{d}L$) is assumed to be influenced by mainly two factors. Firstly, as a scale factor, higher economic activity augments credit demand. GDP growth ($y$) is used as a proxy for economic activity and is expected to positively impact bank credit. Secondly, bank lending rate '$l$' representing the cost of bank loan negatively affects demand for bank credit.

Thus, the demand for bank credit can be mathematically given by:

$$^{d}L_{it} = \beta_0 + \beta_1\, yt + \beta_2\, l_{it} \qquad (2)$$
$$\quad\quad\quad (+) \qquad (-)$$

The above two equations will determine equilibrium 'bank credit' and 'lending rate' by interaction of demand and supply factors.

However, it may be noted that in Equation (1), bank deposits ($D_{it}$) appear on the right hand side and as discussed above, it is endogenous in the process of credit creation. Keeping this in mind, we need to specify the behavioural equation for bank deposit. We believe that banks largely accept deposits or allow withdrawal of deposits passively as per the amount demanded by the customers. Thus, volume of bank deposits are dominantly determined by demand for deposits by public and supply of bank deposits by the banks largely responds to the demand. So, the present study did not include an equation to explain supply of deposits by banks in the model explicitly and the demand for bank deposits by the public is assumed to be determined as below:

$$D_{it} = \lambda_0 + \lambda_1\, SAV_t + \lambda_2\, r_{it} + \lambda_3\, L_{it} \qquad (3)$$
$$\quad\quad\quad (+) \qquad (+) \qquad (+)$$

In Equation (3), demand for bank deposits by the public is explained by overall domestic savings ($SAV$), interest rate on deposits or deposit rates ($r$) and loans ($L$) of the respective bank. As bank deposits are one form of financial asset among many alternatives, it is believed to be positively influenced by SAV, which is defined as the ratio of gross domestic savings to GDP. Return on deposits in the form of interest earning is considered as an important factor to choose bank deposits among various saving options. Thus, the sign of coefficient of '$r$' is expected to be 'positive'. Finally, in a standard textbook approach, credit creation by the banks entails deposit creation and in the process deposit becomes endogenous. We expect the sign of the coefficient of bank credit in Equation (3) to be 'positive'.

The above three equations constitute the simultaneous equations system used by the present study to analyse the determinants of bank credit in India.

In the above system, other than credit, deposit and lending rate all other variables are considered to be predetermined. Thus, it can be observed that all the three equations are over-identified.

It may also be important to note that we did not include popularly used indicator of 'money stock' to capture the impact of monetary policy in Equation (1).

This is guided by the fact that bank deposits constitute as the dominant part of money stock in India[1]. Using it, on the right-hand side, along with deposits will create high multi-collinearity problem. Monetary policy impacts bank credit through bank deposit under the 'credit channel'. Secondly, CALL is not only the money market interest rate, and hence, a proxy for opportunity cost to lending by a bank, it is also the 'operating target' for current monetary policy operating procedure. Thirdly, CRR is already included as an explanatory variable in Equation (1). Guided by the above, we can infer on the impact of monetary policy on banks' credit supply by summarizing the impact through deposits, CALL and CRR.

### Data issues

For estimation of the model developed in the above, we have obtained bank-wise data for the period 1996–97 to 2010–11. This period witnessed implementation of banking reform measures as per the blue print provided by the Narasimham Committees I and II and adoption of prudential regulatory norms for banking in India. This is the most suitable period to examine the role of regulatory capital requirement and loan loss provisioning for bank credit.

We limit ourselves to the 25 public sector banks (as given in Appendix Table 7.2) which presently contribute to close to three-fourth of bank credit and deposits of scheduled commercial banks in India. Bank-wise credits (advances) and deposits, outstanding as of end-March of a year, are expressed in real terms by deflating with WPI. Both real credit and deposits are used with logarithmic transformations. Bank-wise return on advances, return on investments and cost of deposits are used as lending rate ($l$), rate of return on bank investments ($g$) and deposit rate ($r$), respectively. All these are used in real terms by deducting WPI inflation from the respective nominal rates.

CRR is the weighted average of prevailing CRR during the financial year weighted by number of months/days for which a particular level of CRR remained effective. CRAR is the difference between actual ratio of capital to risk weighted assets of a particular bank in a given year over the minimum ratio prescribed. The RBI had prescribed minimum capital ratio of 8.0 per cent effective from end-March 1996, which was increased to 9.0 per cent effective from end-March 2000. We have used the ratio of gross NPAs to total assets to capture the impact of NPA linked provisioning on banks' loan supply. Growth rate of GDP at factor cost (2004–05 = 100) was used as a proxy for real activity ($y$). As indicated earlier, domestic savings to GDP ratio (SAV) was used as overall savings in the economy.

---

[1]    Bank deposits constitute more than 85 per cent of Broad Money (M3) in recent years.

With data for 25 banks and over 15 years, we have a balanced panel of 375 observations.

All data pertaining to the estimations are obtained from the *Handbook of Statistics on the Indian Economy 2011–12*, various issues of *Report on Trend and Progress of Banking in India* and *Statistical Tables related to Banks in India* , all published by the RBI.

## ESTIMATED RESULTS AND DISCUSSION

Panel data estimation techniques are employed for our empirical analysis. These techniques are discussed in detail in Baltagi (2001). As all the three equations in our model are over-identified, we have used Panel Two Stage GLS (2SLS-GLS) procedure using cross-section weights. Before undertaking estimation of the equations, we have used various Panel Unit Root Tests to examine the stationary property of each of the variables used in the model. The results are reported in Table 7.1.

**Table 7.1: Results of unit root tests**

| Variables | Levin, Lu & Chu t* | ADF – Fisher Chi-Square | PP – Fisher Chi-Square |
|---|---|---|---|
| Bank Credit | 0.69 | 6.96 | 6.81 |
| D (Bank Credit) | −2.48 * | 78.73 * | 155.4 * |
| Bank Deposit | 3.49 | 5.64 | 5.80 |
| D (Bank Deposit) | −4.31 * | 88.30 * | 125.5 * |
| Lending Rate | −9.02 * | 128.8 * | 135.6 * |
| Deposit Rate | −7.65 * | 104.4 * | 223.4 * |
| Return on Investment | −8.23 * | 111.9 * | 92.40 * |
| CRR | −6.12 * | 79.14 * | 157.7 * |
| CRAR | −2.03 ** | 72.65 * | 129.4 * |
| NPAs | −18.20 * | 174.9 * | 314.4 * |
| Call Rate | −5.79 * | 74.45 * | 76.84 * |
| GDP Growth Rate | −4.58 * | 29.98 * | 104.0 * |
| Saving Rate | −2.81 * | 122.5 * | 13.02 |

*Note:* '*' indicates statistical significance at 1 per cent level

*Source*: Author's computation

It can be observed from Table 7.1 that all variables except bank credit and deposits are stationary in levels. Both bank credit and deposits are stationary in first difference. In our panel data estimations, all variables except credit and deposits are used in levels, but credit and deposits are used in first difference of the respective logarithmic form. Thus, all the variables used in our panel estimations are stationary. The first difference of credit and deposits, which are in logarithmic form are meaningful as they approximately represent the growth rates of credit and deposits, respectively. Moreover, bank-wise outstanding credit and deposits which are 'stock' in level, become 'flow' on first differencing.

Under Panel 2SLS-GLS procedure, first we have regressed the three endogenous variables *viz*, bank credit, deposit and lending rate on the pre-determined variables of the system. The fitted values obtained from these reduced form equations are used as instruments for the respective endogenous variables appearing on the right hand side of the structural equations in the second stage of estimation.

Estimation results for Equations 1 to 3 by applying 2SLS-GLS procedure are provided in Tables 7.2 through 7.4. It may be mentioned that for each of the equations, comparing between the pooled regression and the fixed effect models, the latter seems to be better in terms of restricted F test, adjusted $R^2$ and DW statistics. Comparing between fixed *versus* random effects model, the Hausman statistics favoured random effects model over the fixed effect counterparts. For comparative purpose, however, we have placed results of both for each of the equations in Tables 7.2 through 7.4, but our inferences drawn based on random effect models.

The estimated results for credit supply equation reveal that deposit growth and monetary policy action in terms of CRR has statistically significant impact on the credit growth of the respective banks (Table 7.2). One percentage increase in deposit growth leads to around 1.5 per cent increase in bank credit growth by public sector banks in India, keeping everything else constant. Similarly, one percentage hike in CRR may lead to 1.8 per cent fall in bank credit growth. All other variables, including both CRAR and NPAs are statistically not significant to explain growth of credit supply by the banks.

Estimated results of credit demand equations are as per the expectation (Table 7.3). It reveals that keeping all other things constant, 1 per cent increase in economic growth leads to 1 per cent increase in the growth rate of demand for bank credit. On the other hand, 1 per cent increase in bank lending rate dampens the growth rate of demand for bank credit by 0.7 per cent. Both the coefficients are statistically significant, even at 1 per cent level.

**Table 7.2: Estimation results of bank credit supply**

*Dependent variable: D (bank credit)*

| Variables | Fixed effect | Random effect |
|---|---|---|
| Constant | −0.029 | 0.029 |
| | (−0.33) | (0.42) |
| D (bank deposit) | 1.805 | 1.49 |
| | (2.27)** | (2.19)** |
| Lending rate | −0.015 | −0.009 |
| | (−1.38) | (−1.13) |
| Return on investment | 0.009 | 0.006 |
| | (1.54) | (1.38) |
| CRR | −0.014 | −0.018 |
| | (−2.34)* | (2.61)* |
| CRAR | 0.003 | 0.001 |
| | (1.29) | (0.33) |
| NPAs | 0.002 | 0.0004 |
| | (0.25) | (0.06) |
| Call rate | 0.012 | 0.013 |
| | (1.90) | (1.91) |
| *Adjusted R$^2$ =* | *0.10* | *0.11* |
| *DW-statistics =* | *2.00* | *1.99* |
| *Hausman statistic: 1.42 (0.98)* | | |

*Notes:* '*' and '**' indicate statistical significance at 1 per cent and 5 per cent level, respectively. *t*-statistics are in the parenthesis.

*Source*: Author's computation

**Table 7.3: Estimation results of bank credit demand**

*Dependent variable: D (bank credit)*

| Variables | Fixed Effect | Random Effect |
|---|---|---|
| Constant | 0.124 | 0.102 |
| | (7.03)* | (5.00)* |
| GDP growth rate | 0.007 | 0.010 |
| | (3.68)* | (4.28)* |
| Lending rate | −0.008 | −0.007 |
| | (−5.89)* | (−4.58)* |
| *Adjusted R$^2$ =* | *0.14* | *0.13* |
| *DW-statistics =* | *1.56* | *1.45* |
| *Hausman statistic: 1.38 (0.50)* | | |

*Notes:* '*' indicates statistical significance at 1 per cent level. *t*-statistics are in the parenthesis.

*Source*: Author's computation

From the above, it is observed that while credit demand is sensitive to interest rate charged on bank loans, supply of credit by the banks do not seem to be very sensitive to returns on loans.

Table 7.4 presents estimated results for demand for bank deposit. It can be observed that coefficients of interest rate on deposits and bank credit are statistically significant. One percentage increase in interest rate on bank deposits leads to 0.4 per cent increase in bank deposit growth. We also observed that credit creation was associated with deposit creation. One percentage increase in bank credit growth led to 0.36 per cent increase in the growth rate of bank deposits.

**Table 7.4: Estimation results of bank deposits**

*Dependent variable: D (bank deposits)*

| Variables | Fixed effect | Random effect |
|---|---|---|
| Constant | 0.003 | 0.023 |
| | (0.16) | (0.97) |
| Saving rate | 0.003 | 0.001 |
| | (3.09) * | (1.16) |
| Deposit rate | 0.004 | 0.004 |
| | (3.50) * | (3.01)* |
| D (bank credit) | 0.217 | 0.363 |
| | (3.22) * | (4.82)* |
| *Adjusted $R^2$ =* | | 0.28 |
| *DW-statistics =* | | 1.71 |
| *Hausman statistic: 4.62 (0.20)* | | |

*Notes:* "*" indicates statistical significance at 1 per cent level. *t*-statistics are in the parenthesis

*Source*: Author's computation

## POLICY IMPLICATIONS

In this section, drawing from the above empirical analysis, broad policy implications are highlighted to rationalize the role of monetary policy in India is sustaining high and stable economic growth in general, and reviving the economy from the current economic slowdown in particular. Considering the endogeneity aspect on dynamics of determination of bank credit and deposits, the estimated results in the previous section clearly implied asymmetry in the impact of variation of policy rate on bank credit growth. As observed engendering a lower interest rate regime will entail slowdown in deposit expansion as deposit demand responds to lower interest rate on deposits, and through the impact of deposit growth on credit supply, ultimately dilutes credit growth. Thus, monetary policy was observed to have limited potential to revive the economy through adoption of lower interest rate policy. On the contrary, higher interest regime through its adverse impact on credit demand can dampen aggregate demand and be very effective in achieving the objective of price stability.

Drawing from the above, it may be stated that the best contribution that monetary policy can have for sustaining economic growth is through ensuring stable prices as high inflation is believed to be inimical to economic growth. A tentative exercise was undertaken to assess the association between the cyclical components of GDP and WPI in India for the period 1952–2013. The cyclical components of GDP and WPI were constructed by de-trending the respective series (with logarithmic transformation) by using HP-filter and plotted in Figure 7.3. It can be observed from the graph that upward (downward) swings in WPI are largely associated with downward (upward) swings in GDP, indicating some negative association. This was also confirmed by the negative coefficient of correlation between the two cyclical components, which was estimated to be –0.3. Several studies in Indian context have also formally established the adverse consequences of high inflation for economic growth (Samantaraya and Prasad, 2001; RBI, 2002). Thus, if RBI has been placing due emphasis on inflation control, this strategy need not be construed as anti-growth strategy, rather it is due to its conviction that low and stable inflation is conducive to economic growth.

**Figure 7.3: Cyclical GDP & WPI**

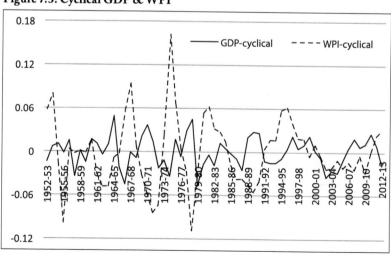

*Source*: *Handbook of Statistics on the Indian Economy 2011–12*, published by the RBI.

Based on recent Indian data we may discuss several channels through which high inflation has been harmful to economic growth.

It has been well documented that acceleration of economic growth in India over the years has been largely associated with similar acceleration in domestic investment, which is predominantly financed by domestic savings (Mohan, 2008). Particularly, household savings has been the main driver of domestic savings in India. Within the household savings, household financial savings enhances the productive capacity of the economy by channelizing savings into investments.

High inflation discourages household financial savings with falling and sometimes negative real return. On the contrary, it makes physical savings and purchase of gold and other precious metals very attractive[2]. This has also been corroborated by available data. As shown in Figure 7.4, share of physical savings in the total household savings has been positively associated with inflation, while the share of financial savings has been inversely related to inflation[3]. High inflation years are associated with falling shares of financial savings. Thus, high inflation generally leads to unproductive savings and discourages financial savings which can easily translate to investments and economic expansion.

**Figure 7.4: Inflation and household savings**

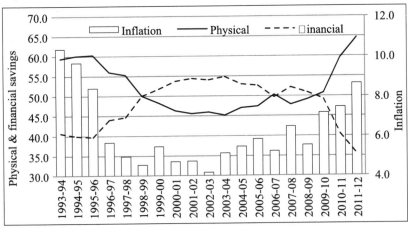

*Source: Handbook of Statistics on the Indian Economy 2011–12*, published by the RBI.

It may be noted that had RBI adopted easy monetary policy, there would have been downward pressure on interest rates, which could have further deteriorated

---

2   There has been growing concern on surging volumes of gold imports to India.
3   In terms of 3-year moving averages of each series to smoothen out the noise in annual figures.

the share of financial savings by the households. As a ratio to GDP, household financial savings declined from 12.0 per cent during 2009–10 to 7.1 per cent during 2012–13. During the comparable period, total household savings to GDP ratio plummeted from 25.2 per cent to 21.9 per cent. This was critical for corresponding drop in the gross investment to GDP ratio in the economy.

In addition to the above, there have been concerns on the serious adverse impact of high inflation on the balance of payments. It is widely believed that inflation makes the imports cheaper and exports become costly having implications for widening of trade deficit. It can be observed from Figure 7.5 that inflation and CAD to GDP ratio are inversely related implying high inflation being associated deterioration in CAD-GDP ratio. As the current account deficit for India has been already high: around 4 per cent of GDP in last couple of years high inflation can make matters worse further.

**Figure 7.5: Inflation and CAD-GDP ratio**

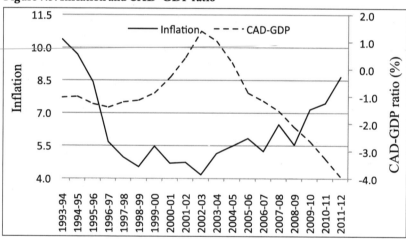

*Source: Handbook of Statistics on the Indian Economy 2011–12,* published by the RBI.

Adverse consequences of high inflation on economic activity by distorting price signal, increasing uncertainty, and adversely affecting credibility of policy authorities are well documented.

Moreover, many leading policy makers in India have underscored the serious adverse implications of high inflation for the poor. People working in unorganized sector and agriculture, which constitutes a vast majority of work force in India, do not receive inflation-adjusted wages. High inflation harshly hurts their standard of living. Many of them live very close to the subsistence level and inflation risks their very livelihood. The general averse to high inflation can be easily sensed by the widespread apprehensions in the event of vegetable/fuel price hikes and a responsible central bank cannot ignore this. In fact, only low inflation environment is conducive to pursue short-run stabilization policies for output and employment by the monetary authority.

Coming to the sectoral distribution of current inflation, there is no second opinion on supply pressures in the form of fuel, food and other commodity prices exacerbating recent inflationary pressure. However, average manufacturing inflation during 2010–13 stands at 6.1 per cent as compared to 4.3 per cent during 2005–10. This confirms that current inflation of manufacturing products with a dominant weight of 64.97 per cent in the entire WPI basket was not muted. It may also be noted that the growth of agricultural sector in GDP in 2010–11 and 2011–12 at 8.6 per cent and 5.0 per cent, respectively, and indicates that the recent inflation is not only a supply side story.

To further assess the policy options for reviving the economy from current economic slowdown, an attempt is made to quickly analyse performance of various sectors in recent period. Available information on estimates of GDP for select sectors/subsectors suggest that sharp deceleration in manufacturing, communication and mining & quarrying predominantly led the overall economic slowdown (Table 7.5). The broad 'services sector', which was main driver of growth since mid-1990s in India witnessed marginal deceleration but not as intense as the select sectors provided in Table 7.5.

**Table 7.5: Growth rates in overall GDP and select sectors**

| Year | GDP | Agriculture | Mining-Quarrying | Manufacturing | Communication |
|------|-----|-------------|------------------|---------------|---------------|
| 2008–09 | 6.7 | 0.1 | 2.1 | 4.3 | 25.1 |
| 2009–10 | 8.6 | 0.8 | 5.9 | 11.3 | 31.5 |
| 2010–11 | 8.9 | 8.6 | 6.5 | 8.9 | 21.8 |
| 2011–12 | 6.7 | 5.0 | 0.1 | 7.4 | 11.2 |
| 2012–13 | 4.5 | 1.4 | −2.2 | 1.1 | 6.5 |

*Source:* Press notes released by Press Information Bureau, Government of India on 31 January 2014

As regards communication and mining, an immediate issue that comes to mind is related to the governance issues. The reported cases of massive corruption in recent period, popularly known as 2G scam and coal-gate definitely could have some adverse implications for investment and expansion activities in these sectors.

Coming to the manufacturing sector, it is widely accepted that investment plays a critical role in manufacturing. Addition of new capital not only facilitates accumulation of the key factor of production, it also significantly contributes to productivity gain as new factories and machines are usually embodied with advanced technology. Gross fixed capital formation (GFCF) as a ratio to GDP has fallen from 32.3 per cent in 2008–09 to 31.8 in 2010–11, and further to 30.4 in 2012–13. The drop is more severe than it appears as there has been deceleration in GDP (the denominator) in last couple of years.

What could be proximate causes for investment slowdown? If anything related to policy on this aspect, policy paralysis/inept handling largely of the central government and to some extent at the state government level are to be on the top of the agenda. Lack of significant progress on public infrastructure particularly power and irrigation facilities, mismanagement on issues related to land acquisition for industrialization process, general public apprehension on reported cases of massive scams can never be conducive to investment initiatives. Ghost of General Anti Avoidance Rules (GAAR) scared away foreign investors juxtaposed with general gloomy global conditions, particularly economic slowdown in the US and crisis in the Euro zone. As discussed by Bhanumurthy (2013), under the conditions in which an economy is facing external and domestic vulnerability as in India, monetary policy and its transmission in such adverse situations are bound to be rather ineffective to support the growth process.

We believe that, under the current depressive business sentiments, only assuming of office by a new stable government at the centre that can provide confidence to the investors through pro-reform and credible policy can boost investments, and overall economic prospects. Monetary policy through adoption of lower interest regime will not be much effective as implied from our empirical analysis. But the observed asymmetry also suggests that monetary policy can be effective for achieving price stability and contribute to economic revival through maintaining price stability.

## CONCLUSIONS

Under the premises of close association between growth of the bank credit and the economy juxtaposed with the fact that credit channel is a powerful channel of monetary transmission mechanism, the present study attempted to examine the determinants of bank credit in India to assess the role of monetary policy to help the economy getting back to the higher growth trajectory from current economic slowdown. It is a matter of fact that the dynamics of determination of bank credit creation is a bit complex involving decisions of several stakeholders including banks, borrowers and the central bank. To understand the overall impact of monetary policy on bank credit, it is imperative to gain insight on how it will influence the behaviour of banks, borrowers and depositors. For this purpose, the present study constructed a small simultaneous equations system taking into account the interplay of demand and supply side factors in the determination of bank credit. Considering the endogeneity of bank deposits in the process of credit creation a separate equation was used for bank deposits, also. The study used bank-wise data pertaining to public sector banks in India for the period 1996–97 to 2010–11. Panel data analysis was employed to estimate a small simultaneous equations model for studying bank credit behaviour, which is perhaps one of the first such attempts.

The estimated results for public's demand for bank credit and deposits were on expected lines. Interest rate offered for bank deposit was found to have positive impact on demand for bank deposits, while interest rate charged on bank credit discouraged public's demand for bank credit. Thus, there are statistically significant evidences that the public's demand for credit and deposit have become sensitive to lending and deposit rates, respectively.

On the other hand, banks' supply of credit was largely influenced by deposit growth and monetary policy considerations. Interest rates charged on loans or return on investment did not influence banks' credit decisions significantly. It is plausible when banks are setting credit targets based on deposit growth and large part of the investments is guided by SLR considerations. As regards the role of prudential norms and reorientation of credit channel of monetary policy, we observed that capital adequacy had a positive impact on bank credit but it was not statistically significant. Similarly, given that NPAs level of the public sector banks were largely within the comfortable limits during the period of our study, we did not find any negative impact of NPAs on bank credit growth. Thus, our results did not support any reinforcing effect of prudential norms in the Indian context for pro-cyclicality of bank credit and related diluting of bank credit channel for monetary policy.

Most importantly, our overall estimated results have significant implications for monetary policy asymmetry as regards monetary policy impact on bank credit. Looking at the estimated results of credit supply equation in isolation, there is a strong support for monetary policy influence on credit supply by banks. To illustrate the point, growth of broad money stock (M3) is predominantly used as an indicator of monetary policy. As M3 consists of largely bank deposits and we found significant influence of bank deposits on bank credit, we can infer on significant influence of monetary policy on credit supply of banks. Furthermore, we also observed significant influence of CRR: a prominent monetary policy instrument on supply of bank credit.

But, we also observed that lower deposit rates discourage demand for deposits by the public. Thus, expansionary monetary policy, which engenders lower interest rates, including interest rate on deposits, dampens deposit creation. Deposits are a major source for bank credit and as observed in the estimated results of credit supply equation, deposit growth has strong positive influence on the credit supply growth.

Combining the above two, we can infer that lower interest regime facilitated by monetary accommodation has an adverse impact on credit supply. It may be noted that lending rates directly did not have statistically significant impact on loan supply. If we ignore the entire process of determination of credit, but limit to credit supply equation alone, we may erroneously infer that monetary expansion boosts up credit flow. Thus, we reiterate that considering the dynamics of credit and deposit creation, empirical evidences based on the present study question the potency of credit channel of monetary policy, during monetary policy accommodation.

On the contrary, the evidences suggest that during monetary tightening, credit channel may still remain relevant. Raising interest rates may become conducive to deposit creation through higher return on deposits, and supportive of augmenting credit supply. But under this regime, higher lending rates will dampen credit demand and may still upset overall credit creation. Moreover, during monetary policy tightening, credit supply will also further be adversely affected if there is hike in CRR, as observed from the credit supply equation.

The above inferences, however, need to be qualified by one observation. If CRR is used as the policy instrument, then monetary policy asymmetry is diluted to some extent. Reduction/hike of CRR unambiguously augments/dampens credit supply as emerged from our estimated results. But as liquidity impact of CRR reduction gets gradually translated to reduction in interest rates in banking, particularly interest rates in deposits, the monetary policy asymmetry again becomes evident. As stated in various policy documents, under the current operating procedure of monetary policy in India, various policy instruments including CRR, OMO, etc., are used by the RBI to calibrate overall liquidity in the system and consequently influencing interest rates and flow of bank credit in the economy.

To summarize, from our empirical analysis, asymmetry of monetary policy becomes evident. It is revealed that while tight monetary policy can effectively dampen credit growth, monetary accommodation may not lead to credit expansion if we consider the process of bank credit determination in entirety. Given the close association between economic growth and bank credit behaviour, this may not be supportive of the current chorus in certain sections for monetary policy accommodation to support economic growth. The monetary authority cannot afford to ignore the much valued sermons of Professor Milton Friedman and should always be aware of what monetary policy can do and cannot do, more emphatically, when inflationary conditions are prevailing. Furthermore, given the adverse impact of high inflation on economic growth, we believe the best contribution the monetary policy can have to sustain high economic growth in general and revive the economy from current slow growth is to achieve and maintain stable prices.

Nevertheless, we admit that there are other channels of monetary policy transmission also. The present study only considered the transmission through 'credit channel' to assess the impact of monetary policy to sustain high growth in India.

## APPENDIX

**Appendix Table 7.1: Summary of findings of previous studies in India**

| Study | Period | Sample | Finding |
|---|---|---|---|
| Nachane, Narain, Ghosh and Sahoo (2000) | 1997–99 (quarterly) | Public sector banks | No conclusive evidence to support a shift from high-risk towards low-risk asset category by banks with adoption of prudential regulations. No evidence for enhancing pro-cyclicality of bank credit. |
| Nag and Das (2002) | 1996–2000 | Public sector banks | Stricter risk management and minimum regulatory capital dampens credit supply. Implies regulatory capital requirements reinforcing pro-cyclicality. |
| Ghosh, Nachane, Narain and Sahoo (2003) | 1997–99 (quarterly) | Public sector banks | Banks adjusted their capital ratios by boosting their capital rather than through systematic substitution away from high-risk loans. Thus, capital requirements do not distort the lending choice of banks. Implies capital requirements not a factor generating pro-cyclicality. |
| Ghosh and Nachane (2003) | 1997–2002 | Public sector banks | Banks tend to postpone provisioning when faced with favourable cyclical and income conditions, until negative conditions set in. Negative association between loan growth and loan loss provisioning and digging into the capital base during cyclical downswings to make provisions provide evidence of reinforcing credit pro-cyclicality. |
| Samantaraya (2009) | 1996–2008 | Public, Indian Private & Foreign banks | Evidences on capital requirements and loan loss provisioning reinforcing pro-cyclicality of bank credit in India since 1990s. |

**Appendix Table 7.2: List of banks included in the sample**

| Sl. No. | Name of the public sector bank |
|---|---|
| 1 | Allahabad Bank |
| 2 | Andhra Bank |
| 3 | Bank of Baroda |
| 4 | Bank of India |
| 5 | Bank of Maharashtra |
| 6 | Canara Bank |
| 7 | Central Bank of India |
| 8 | Corporation Bank |
| 9 | Dena Bank |
| 10 | Indian Bank |
| 11 | Indian Overseas Bank |
| 12 | Oriental Bank of Commerce |
| 13 | Punjab and Sind Bank |
| 14 | Punjab National Bank |
| 15 | State Bank of Bikaner and Jaipur |
| 16 | State Bank of Hyderabad |
| 17 | State Bank of India |
| 18 | State Bank of Mysore |
| 19 | State Bank of Patiala |
| 20 | State Bank of Travancore |
| 21 | Syndicate Bank |
| 22 | UCO Bank |
| 23 | Union Bank of India |
| 24 | United Bank of India |
| 25 | Vijaya Bank |

## REFERENCES

Baltagi, B. H. 2001. *Econometric Analysis of Panel Data*, New York: John Wiley and Sons.

Berger, A. N. and G. F Udell. 2003. 'The Institutional Memory Hypothesis and The Procyclality of Bank Lending Behaviour', BIS Working Papers No. 125. January.

Bhanumurthy, N. R. 2013. 'Misplaced Faith in Interest Rate Cuts', *Mint*, February 18.

Bikker, J.A. and P.A.J. Metzemakers. 2004. 'Bank Provisioning Behaviour and Procyclicality' International Financial Markets, Institutions and Money – available online at www.sciencedirect.com

Bliss, R. R. and Kaufman, G. George. 2002. 'Explaining Bank Credit Crunches and Procyclality', Chicago Fed Letter, Number 179, July, Federal Reserve Bank of Chicago.

Blum, J. and M. Hellwig. 1995. 'The Macroeconomic Implications of Capital Adequacy Requirements for Banks', *European Economic Review*, 39, 739–49.

Borio, C., C. Furfine, and P. Lowe. 2001. 'Procyclicality of the Financial System and Financial Stability: Issues and Policy Options'. *BIS Papers*, 1, 1–57.

Furfine, C. 2000. 'Evidence of Responses of US Banks to Changes in Capital Requirements', BIS Working Papers No. 88.

Gertler, M. and S. Gilchrist. 1993. 'The Role of Credit market Imperfections in the Monetary Transmission Mechanism: Arguments and Evidence', *Scandinavian Journal of Economics*, 95(1): 43–64.

Ghosh, S. and D.M. Nachane. 2003. 'Are Basel Capital Standards Pro-cyclical? Some Empirical Evidences from India'. *Economic and Political Weekly*, February 23, 777–83.

Ghosh, S., D.M. Nachane, N. Aditya, and S. Sahoo. 2003. 'Capital Requirements and Bank Behaviour: An Empirical Analysis of Indian Public Sector Banks'. *Journal of International Development*, 15, 145–56.

Kashyap, A.K., J.C. Stein, and D.W. Wilcox. 1993. 'Monetary Policy and Credit Conditions: Evidence from the Composition of External Finance'. *American Economic Review*, 83(1): March, 78–98.

Kashyap, A.K. and J.C. Stein. 1994. 'The Impact of Monetary Policy on Bank Balance Sheets', NBER Working Paper, No. 4821.

Kim, H. E. 1999. 'Was Credit Channel a Key Monetary Transmission Mechanism Following the Recent Financial Crisis in the Republic of Korea', World Bank Policy Research Working Paper No. 3003.

Mohan, R. 2008. 'Growth Record of the Indian Economy, 1950–2008: A Story of Sustained Savings and Investment'. *Economic and Political Weekly*, Vol. XLIV, May 10, 61–71.

Morsink, J. and T. Bayoumi. 2001. 'A Peep Inside the Black Box: The Monetary Transmission Mechanism in Japan'. *IMF Staff Papers*, 48(1): 22–57.

Mukhopadhyay, H. 1999. 'Monetary Transmission Mechanism: The Credit Channel Hypothesis Revisited'. *International Journal of Development Banking*, 17(2), July, 47–58.

Nachane, D.M., A. Narain, S. Ghosh, and S. Sahoo. 2000. 'Capital Adequacy Requirements and the Behaviour of Commercial Banks in India: An Analytical and Empirical Study', *DRG Study* No. 22, RBI.

Nachane, D.M., S. Ghosh, and P. Ray. 2006. 'Basel II and Bank Lending Behaviour: Some Likely Implications of Monetary Policy'. *Economic and Political Weekly*, March 18, 1053–58.

Nag, A. K. and A. Das. 2002. 'Credit Growth and Response to Capital Requirements: Evidence from Indian Public Sector Banks'. *Economic and Political Weekly*, August 10, 3361–68.

Pandit, B. L., A. Mittal, M. Roy, and S. Ghosh. 2006. 'Transmission of Monetary Policy and the Bank Lending Channel: Analysis and Evidence for India.' *DRG Study* No. 25, RBI, Mumbai.

RBI. 2002. *Report on Currency and Finance, 2001–02*, Mumbai: Reserve Bank of India.

Samantaraya, A. 2009. 'An Empirical Analysis of Pro-cyclicality of Bank Credit in India: Role of Basel Prudential Norms' *RBI Staff Studies* No. SS (DEAP) – 3/2009.

Samantaraya, A. and A. Prasad. 2001. 'Growth and Inflation in India: Detecting the Threshold Level'. *Asian Economic Review*, 43(3): 414–28.

Samantaraya, A. and B. Kamaiah. 2011. 'An Empirical Analysis of Monetary Transmission in India in the Post-reform Period: Relevance of the Banking Channel'. *IUP Journal of Applied Economics*, 10(4): 5–22.

# Section 4
# The supply constraints to growth

# 8

# Sustainability of Indian Agriculture

Nilabja Ghosh

Anita Kumari

Indian agriculture is now at a critical juncture of history, perhaps comparable only to the time when the celebrated green revolution (GR) was launched. On that occasion, the motive force behind the impending change was the urgent need for food security, and its impetus came from a new production technology and its impact was felt on the wide socio-economic-cultural canvas of the Indian nation. Later, experiences were to show that the production pattern that followed from the circumstances had several serious weaknesses and with time the approach to development proved unsustainable.

Interestingly, today the impetus comes from the momentous transformations in society, culture and economy that India accepted as part of a new paradigm. There is no specific and patently clear motive for the present change except to improve the lot of people especially the farmers. The pressure that 'food security cannot wait' is no longer present and India can plan her agriculture much more cautiously than could be done in the earlier instance. All this makes the choice of the path much more flexible but politically and economically more sensitive.

Having learnt many lessons from the past, setting target growth rates and choosing the production paths for achieving them in a sustainable manner appear as a veritable challenge, compounded by the fact that India's domestic economy no longer operates in isolation. Any assessment, methodology, or policy needs to be in tune with the global economic reality. In the face of such confounding decisions, this chapter attempts to reflect rationally on the way forward. This is done by taking the following course: (a) Reviewing and exploring future possibilities for Indian agriculture, (b) identifying the cautions that should guide the path to sustainable growth, and (c) revisiting the observed tendencies in India's production pattern in the perspective of the limitations identified.

The second section reflects on the concept of sustainable growth in agriculture with a futuristic outlook drawing from past experiences, recent events, and international evidences leading to the requisites for sustainable growth listed in third section. The fourth section discusses the directions taken in Indian agriculture, with prospects for the future presented in the fifth section. Finally, concluding comments and policy recommendations are drawn in the sixth section.

## A NEED TO LOOK FORWARD AND A NEED FOR CAUTION

Coined and defined in the document titled *Our Common Future*, also known as the 'Brundtland Report of the UN's World Commission on Environment and Development (WCED)' in 1987, the epithet sustainability is fast becoming an essential component of most development endeavours today. Despite the lack of a universally agreed and practicable specification (Ghosh, 2006, and Gary et al., 2005), the gravity of securing sustainable agricultural development has surfaced repeatedly in the 1990s and thereafter.

Although associated deeply with ecology, in reality the implications of sustainable agrarian development go far beyond that. The GR driven development was based on an unbalanced growth pattern within agriculture, one that drew natural resources more than what could be consistent with endowments and asked for public resources as subsidies greater than the government exchequer could afford without compromising on the interests of other sections and future generations of the country. Above all, it fell out of line with what the market asked for and what nutritional requirements demanded, requiring costly public intervention even as large sections of people suffered malnutrition. Sustainability of growth would depend on the approach taken by the government and its visualization of the development path.

### The globalizing context

Although the Indian economy had two decades of transition under economic reforms and the overtures with the liberalized global market started back in 1995, India remained guarded even years after the WTO treaty. It is only in recent time, that, encouraged by the comfortable production records and the opportunities of disposing stocks, India became more active in her international engagements in agricultural commodity trade.

In this historic phase, Indian agriculture is integrating as a component of global agriculture contributing to global demand and supply. The resources exploited and the environment it occupies is seen as part of global common property with profound externalities debated and negotiated at international forums. India shares data on agricultural attributes such as production, prices and public stocks by her ties with Agricultural Market Information System (AMIS, www.amis-outlook. org/). AMIS is a G20 initiative to strengthen collaboration among main producing, exporting, and importing countries[1] covering around 80–90 per cent of global production, consumption, and trade. Undoubtedly, records and measurements of agricultural performance and growth have to be consistent with international protocols to be comparable across nations for unified decision-making on product quantity and composition.

India is also unifying her internal domestic market and liberating it from restrictive regulations at the sub-national level with the formal encouragement to amend the historic APMC (Agricultural Produce Market Committee) Act in 2003–04. While this gesture is a formal invitation to the private corporate sector to step into agricultural marketing if not into agricultural production, closely following on its heel was the attempt to allow a rush of foreign direct investment (FDI) to flow into the same market, a clear prophesy of an agriculture supported by modern infrastructure and linked more directly than ever before with the wider market. Surely, agricultural growth can be sustainable if it keeps pace with national and global conditions of supply, demand, scientific knowledge base, and environmental outlook.

### Lessons from the past, present, and other countries

The green revolution (GR) was restricted to a narrow ambit and worked almost exclusively on only two of the numerous products that Indian agriculture had the strength to produce. That these crops (wheat and rice) thrived only in certain select pre-conditions practically left out most part of the country from its sway. After adoption of green revolution technology, India achieved self-sufficiency in food production but on reaching the 1990s, ecological damages created by the excessive share of the two resource demanding crops and the emphasis on a few regions in the country began to make further progress difficult. Moreover, the production pattern belied the demands of the consumers showing up in growing public stocks and even leading to uneconomic exports (Ghosh, 2004).

Recent studies on consumer behaviour, culture, and experiences in other countries strongly indicate that the demand for food is gradually shifting from its overarching

---

[1] Apart from G20 members, other participants in AMIS are Spain and seven major producing, consuming, and exporting countries of commodities, wheat, maize, rice, and soybean, covered by AMIS.

anchorage on rice and wheat towards other farm products such as animal-based and horticultural food products. Another ignored product, pulses important as protein food are continually falling deficit, raising unease in the country. The message that came across was that the growth pattern of Indian agriculture in coming times needs to be much more diversified and broad based than so far seen.

Crop yield has been the major indicator of the success of the GR in land scarce India. Received wisdom from experience today also draws attention towards water as a limiting resource besides land, swinging the emphasis to water productivity (Chopra et al., 2003, and Vaidyanathan, 1999). Excessive withdrawal of ground water, land degradation due to canal irrigation practices, saline ingression due to faulty water use and the repercussions on the energy sector translating to inadequacy of power supply and high power subsidies are associated with the production pattern and success of the GR. Any production pattern that characterizes agricultural growth has to be in keeping with the water demands of the crop and the water regime available. Therefore, GR generated production pattern may not be sustainable.

In the years following 1991, the importance of global competitiveness came to be recognized but with trade liberalization. Price movements in the international markets highlighted the continuing significance of national food security as a minimum measure. In the new situation, however, India's commitment to global food security as a 'large country' player is also gaining recognition.

Experiences of similarly placed countries Brazil and China, which are also undergoing institutional restructuring and reorientation, too yield analogous expectations. Shifts in agricultural policies, trade liberalization, and removal of ad hoc price intervention in Brazil had significant impacts on agriculture and agri-business, enhancing the share of the country in exports of chicken meat, maize, and soybean.

In China, the rural reforms initiated in 1978 ended the instability of the pre-reform times and all sub-sectors of agriculture benefited from higher productivity. Thus, as China's agricultural economy moved from a 'grain first' to a 'high value cash crop' economy, China's production capacity became comparable to the world's 'vegetable basket' California. Thus, both the cases of Brazil and China demonstrate the success of reforms in paving the way to a high value and non-grain product-based agriculture, but the success of the grain sector lies at the centre of the revolution.

### The future of Indian agriculture: A vision

The earlier discussion indicates that the green revolution that saved India's population from the pangs of hunger if not starvation was a force of circumstance. Bound by the technology that was available, it clearly failed to imbibe any vision in its evolution. At a time when food insecurity is not an immediate threat at the national level, agricultural growth should be planned with a vision laced with pragmatism and considerable allowance for contingencies. Distributional issues still come in the way of food security at the household and individual levels, leading to legislative measures such as the Food Security Bill, but this shortcoming, associated with equity, only reinforces the need for a cautious approach towards agricultural planning.

The future of Indian agriculture at this point of time can only be envisaged if not imagined but with hard evidence and realistic conjecture as the basis of projections. Although past experience always has a role in projections in this case of string dynamics laced with uncertainty, the support from past is limited. Experiences of a long period in the past have given a few lessons but probably contemporary events are more relevant in lending important insights on how the future may be tackled. Experiences of other countries treading a similar path as India regularly serve as references when information is becoming freer, although such demonstrations can at best serve as cautions and possibilities. Any policy can have differential implications across nations because socio-economic and historical backgrounds vary widely. The vision of India's agriculture in 2040 is portrayed as one marked by small but modern farms, diversified production pattern, strong play of market forces replacing state regulations, efficient water use and market linkage (Kohli and Sood, 2013a and b). This is purely an idealized vision that can be useful but can turn out far different from what reality will unfold. Modelling exercises also project demand being broad-based and less cereal-centric (Binswanger-Mkhize, 2013) but with large food imports being necessitated.

## WHAT CONSTITUTES THE SUSTAINABLE GROWTH PATH FOR INDIAN AGRICULTURE?

The experience of the past in India, the wisdom gained from events in the current times of liberalization and globalization, and evidences filtered from other emerging countries provide a broad understanding of issues that help forming a vision, but nevertheless implicit in the information set are serious trade-offs in gains and losses and political and macro-economic contentions. What comes out from the discourse is not a deterministic outlook but a flexible one that is keenly sensitive to emerging issues and sharply receptive of information.

Therefore, in formulating the path to sustainable agricultural growth, continuous monitoring, evaluation, and reformulation are cornerstones. At each stage, a few major concerns need to be kept in view, namely:

(a) Ensuring food security as a minimal measure, keeping people's habits and nutritional needs in view,

(b) Timely response to global price movements dictated by global demand and supply,
(c) Compatibility with resource endowments at the local and national levels, and keeping with global-level environmental interactions, and
(d) Securing inclusive participation of different sections of farmers who in reality generate the production pattern.

Food security is one of the most important obligations of a stable political system, but it is important to keep in view that food security is neither ensured by large supplies nor is the production of a few specified crops sufficient for its realization. It has been shown that distribution is an important aspect of food security which requires good transportation, thereby facilitating better poverty reduction. Demand for food is shown to be non-static so that there is a continual need for assessment about people's preferences and nutritional needs rather than imposition of planned outcomes on the consumer's decisions. Cereals remain to be important in India and securing their production is shown to have helped agriculture in China and Brazil to diversify (see section two). Nevertheless, there are chances that fruits, vegetables, meat, fish, and food products will find their place in the notion of food security, and diversification up to a level may actually be an integral part of sustainable growth. Also, these crops, often termed as 'high value crops', provide a way for the farmers to earn higher income and ameliorate poverty. These products require special marketing infrastructure that reduces product losses as also improved roads and transport systems. In India, these products are seen as emerging products.

Interestingly, the emerging products, unlike the fruits of the GR, can be raised in different agro-climatic conditions and also provide livelihood to poorer sections of farmers. Processing as well as marketing of food for consumer convenience is likely to become a beacon to the growth path of agriculture as the populace urbanize and grow in affluence. This indication comes from experiences already gained in the country and in other emerging economies. As women's empowerment and participation in economic processes gain strength, there is likely to be increased demand for semi-prepared food consistent with reduced time budget for household chores.

Agriculture in the now globalizing country has also to be in tune with market demands and comparative advantages. There is a vital need for balance between the aims of global competitiveness and domestic food security in the face of India's growing role as a global player. While imports of grains can be viewed as a way to food security, the vision of enlarging import basket is not a comfort, especially for the volatilities witnessed in the global market, not only in the food market but also in other interacting markets like fuel. Thus, a sustainable policy faces the challenge of working out what level of domestic self-sufficiency can be associated with minimal desirable food security while also giving space to agriculture to develop its areas of strength in tune with global demand and supply and to respond to market changes. Processing of products, food safety, and organic production would be important tools in the effort that would bring investment, promote diversification, and integrate agriculture with the national and global economy.

It is critical to ensure that the production pattern that evolves is in tune with resource reality. In particular, the incompatibility with water endowments had been a limitation for the GR and is also inconsistent with the theory of comparative advantage because the export of a water-intensive product is indicative of the virtual export of water. The products promoted and their locational distribution have to be planned in relation with their demand for water and the availability of water. The lack of institutions for water distribution is a serious impediment in this matter. Market forces being poor signals for indicating production pattern in this background, the role of the state is important. A further limiting factor in achieving sustainable growth is the acceptability of the pattern among various classes of farmers. This is of particular relevance in India because over 80 per cent of farmers are small holders with meagre access to resources and limitations in availing technologies and practices that are not scale-neutral in character. Subsidies have been a way to address this malaise in the past, but that solution is also not available under the WTO regime and will be of little help in future. It is believed that small farmers are relatively risk averse, making it difficult for them to diversify from cereals and are more weakly linked with the market, especially when the markets are dominated by stronger players. Without their participation, any production plan is meaningless.

## DIRECTIONS TAKEN BY INDIAN AGRICULTURE

### Production trends

This section takes a look at the tendencies shown by Indian agriculture, to mark any departure from the course taken in the GR years and its consistency with sustainability requisites. The product accounts, from which the output series are taken and further analysed, are created with an eye on international compatibility and deviate from that of India's National Accounts prepared by CSO and conventionally used for the purpose. The method used in this study is in line with those provided by the United Nations System of National Accounts (1993).

The nominal output series for product and sub-product groups in agriculture is first built up for 11 modified categories denoted as Cereals (CER), Millets (MLT), Pulses (PLS), Oilseeds (OLS), Fruits (F), Vegetables (V), Fibres and

Materials (FM), Condiments and Spices (CS), Beverages and Narcotics (BN), Sugarcane (SCN), and Livestocks and Fisheries (LF – elaborated in Appendix 8.A1), with calendar year as the unit of time rather than the financial year. The marketing year of the crops is the reference year depending on the harvest and marketing period rather than the agriculture year. This method ensures that the accounting period is the one when the income accrues to the farm. It is also consistent of international protocols like FAO and USDA. Then to estimate price indices with base year 2005, the Theil-Tornquist method (Appendix 8.A2) was used on each of these modified categories of product groups with calendar year as the unit of time. Finally, we compute the value of real output with reference to the base year 2005 as the ratio of nominal value of output to the estimated price index with the base 2005 in the category. This method implicitly values the products at 2005 prices and, therefore, the series is also called implicit quantity. The main source of data is Ministry of Agriculture (Appendix 8.A3). The sample period considered in this study is 1976 to 2008, covering a span of 33 years and covering the post-green revolution period of Indian agriculture.

Table 8.1 shows the tendencies in the structure of Indian agriculture. Compared to 1976 in the peak of GR, the share of cereals is less at 24.0 per cent in 2008. Sub-groups MLT, PLS, OLS, SCN, and BN in the crop sector have all lost share besides cereals, while the horticultural group F, V and LF gained significant share in the total output at 2005 prices. However, FM and CS also showed some tendency to gain. Interestingly, the LF group has become the largest surpassing cereals from 2001. In the recent decade following 2001, the gainers include only FM, F, and LF, while CS and OLS remained stable; and the groups CER, PLS, MLT, BN, and SCN continued losing share. The share of V increased initially but declined between 2001 and 2008.

The Bray–Curtis index measuring the dissimilarity with 1976 as the reference year (Appendix 8.A2) summarizes the departure of the production structure. Regardless of the momentous shift from a subsistence-driven cereal-based agriculture to a commercially motivated high-value cash-crop-based structure, it is interesting to note that the HI (Herfindahl index – Appendix 8.A2) fails to indicate a diversifying agriculture. Indeed Indian agriculture has become more concentrated although the products of specialization have changed. The excessive concentration in a volatile market may not favour resilience, while timely adjustments of production in responses to market forces and food security imperative could be facilitated by a broad-based system only.

The average annual compound growth rates given in Table 8.2 show a significant contrast between the crop sector and non-crop sector with the

Table 8.1: Shares (per cent) of sub-sectors in value (real) of output at 2005 prices in Agriculture, dissimilarity in composition by Bray–Curtis index (base 1976) and Concentration by Herfindahl index

| Year | CER | MLT | PLS | OLS | FM | CS | F | V | BN | SCN | LF | Dissimilarity | Concentration |
|---|---|---|---|---|---|---|---|---|---|---|---|---|---|
| 1976 | 28.89 | 2.49 | 7.90 | 6.50 | 5.71 | 1.42 | 8.86 | 8.83 | 2.49 | 4.11 | 22.76 | 0.00 | 0.17 |
| 2001 | 26.71 | 1.28 | 3.35 | 5.60 | 4.57 | 1.55 | 9.24 | 11.85 | 1.90 | 3.78 | 30.51 | 2.02 | 0.19 |
| 2008 | 24.04 | 1.05 | 3.06 | 6.01 | 5.99 | 1.73 | 10.25 | 8.49 | 1.67 | 3.57 | 34.45 | 2.45 | 0.20 |

Table 8.2: Average compound annual growth rates (per cent) of real values of output in agricultural sub-groups (2005 based)

| | CER | MLT | PLS | OLS | FM | CS | F | V | BN | SCN | CROPS | LF | All products |
|---|---|---|---|---|---|---|---|---|---|---|---|---|---|
| *Estimates* | | | | | | | | | | | | | |
| 1976–80 | 4.27 | −0.77 | −6.47 | −2.64 | 1.10 | −4.21 | 7.28 | 3.69 | 2.25 | −2.16 | 2.08 | 4.09 | 2.54 |
| 2001–08 | 1.33 | 0.06 | 1.54 | 3.92 | 6.91 | 3.62 | 4.40 | −1.93 | 3.45 | 2.02 | 2.08 | 4.66 | 2.90 |
| 1976–08 | 2.58 | 0.52 | 0.24 | 3.00 | 3.41 | 2.55 | 3.73 | 3.13 | 3.45 | 2.80 | 2.73 | 4.60 | 3.25 |

*Source:* Computed

growth rates being 2.08 per cent and 4.66 per cent, respectively, in the recent period 2001–08. Within the crop sector, growth rates have been poor in cereals (1.33%), millet (0.06%), pulses (1.54%), and sugarcane (2.02%) and are negative for vegetables.

Comparing the growth rates in the two periods 1976–80 and 2001–08, the relatively poor performance of cereals and groups F and V is noticed. The growth rate of the LF group improved mildly, though the rate is largely sustained and robust above 4 per cent even in the period 1976–80 when it was second only to the cereal group.

It is worth noting that the growth rates improved in a number of sub-groups, MLT, PLS, OLS, FM, CS, BN, and SCN. Plotting the growth rates with those based on CSO's financial year data, the result is not much different (Figure 8.A1). The variation in the growth rate of sugarcane measured by the two methods is, however, striking. Sugarcane being a long period perennial crop, the variation appears to be on account of the consideration of the calendar year as the unit of accounting and the marketing year as the reference year in this study.

The growth patterns among the crop groups are shaped not only by market forces within the country, but national policies and various programmes (Appendix 8.A4) for promoting the production of different crops undertaken over the years are also instrumental in the process. Government joining the WTO along with its year-to-year variations in strategy towards market openness based on domestic supply conditions, its political compulsions, and availability of instruments like tariffs, duties, bans on import or export, and phyto-sanitary requirements is also important in influencing the production patterns.

## AGRARIAN EQUITY AND THE FUTURE OF THE FARM

Over the years, land fragmentation triggered by population growth brought average farm size from 1.41 hectare in the year 1995–96 to 1.23 hectare in 2005–06 (MOA, Annual Reports). Over 85 per cent of the Indian farms are small today. A small farm size is associated with resource scarcity and risk aversion which implies the small farmer more comfortable with certain crops than others and finds shifting from subsistence crops costly. Table 8.3 shows that small farms have a claim to over 50 per cent of cereal area as of 2005–06 and their share in V is highest at 60 per cent and for SCN and F, the share is nearly half. Also, the share has increased over time in all cases. About 70 per cent of the area under MLT, PLS, and OLS are cultivated by medium and large holding category. The small farmer's disinterest in the crops may be on account of the low profitability or the risk associated with their farming, but it is interesting to note that PLS and OLS are import crops not demonstrating India's comparative disadvantage in the international market. Millets have lost the consumer interest but chances of these nutritious Cereals (CER) making a comeback in a processed or pre-cooked form or as prepared animal feeds is not unlikely. Estimates of small farmer's production in livestock activities are scarce but evidences suggest equity in the distribution of these assets. Figure 8.1 shows that in the year 2002–03, the small farmers possessed 67 per cent of the cattle, 74 per cent of buffaloes, and 81 per cent of poultry animals in India and their share has increased substantially as compared to 1991–92.

Table 8.3: Share of small farms (per cent) in acreages under different crops

| Crops | 1976–77 | 1985–86 | 1995–96 | 2005–06 |
|---|---|---|---|---|
| Cereals (CER) | 34.0 | 38.1 | 45.3 | 50.2 |
| Millets (MLT) | 20.0 | 21.2 | 28.7 | 28.6 |
| Pulses (PLS) | 19.2 | 26.1 | 32.9 | 36.1 |
| Sugarcane (SCN) | 32.6 | 41.0 | 46.3 | 49.6 |
| Spices and Condiments (SC) | 27.7 | 34.3 | 39.1 | 42.3 |
| Fruits (F) | 39.9 | 53.5 | 47.2 | 48.3 |
| Vegetables (V) | 52.1 | 50.6 | 57.6 | 59.7 |
| Oilseeds (OLS) | 24.7 | 26.8 | 30.2 | 33.3 |
| % Total area | 23.50 | 29.00 | 36.00 | 41.10 |
| % Farms | 72.64 | 76.24 | 80.31 | 83.29 |
| Average farm size (hectare) | 2.00 | 1.69 | 1.41 | 1.23 |

*Source*: Agricultural Census (various)

Figure 8.1: Share of small farmers in livestock population in India

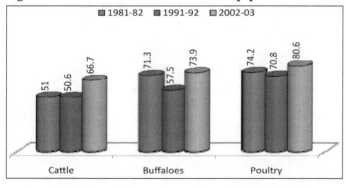

*Source*: GOI (various)

Despite the sharp diminution of farm size in physical area between 1976 and 2005, the scale of operation measured by the implicit quantity of output per farm actually expanded by a factor of 1.6. The average Indian farm though smaller in size than three decades ago, today operates at a larger scale due to higher productivity

(Figure 8.2) which results from reconfiguration of prices, cropping pattern and yield rates along with changing scenario of India's comparative advantage with increasing globalization. Despite being efficient, higher per hectare costs and low absolute returns of small farmers raise questions on risk-bearing capacity and livelihood sustainability (Gaurav and Mishra, 2011).

**Figure 8.2: Average farm size and the average scale of production in Indian farms**

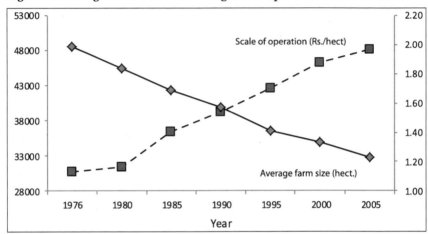

### Water use efficiency and market linkage

Figure 8.3 draws attention to the fact that gaining crop groups, CS and FM, are more irrigation intensive than the slow moving crops OLS, PLS, and MLT. Though the key group, CER, is likely to relieve considerable water resources, V too will require intense water use if they are to be promoted.

**Figure 8.3: Irrigation intensity of different crops in India in the year 2008**

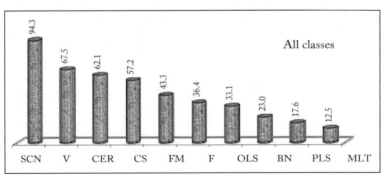

*Source*: Agricultural Census

It is also worth noting that small farms claim 63 per cent of the irrigated area under Vegetables (V – see Figure 8.4). Except for Vegetables (V) and Cereals (CER), their share is, however, less than half in all the other crop groups.

**Figure 8.4: Small farmers' share of irrigated area crop-wise in India in the year 2008**

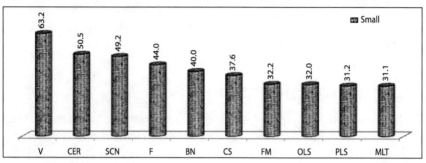

*Source*: Agricultural Census

Water availability to agriculture including livestock is facing increasing competition from other sectors of the economy, domestic, service, and industrial sectors. Per capita water availability has decreased and is expected to decrease by 21 per cent by 2020 (IARI, www.iari.res.in/). This will be further exacerbated by the increasing demand for food and decline in output and water availability as a consequence of climate change. Irrigation, contributing 90 per cent of total withdrawals, is the largest consumptive water use sector in India. Groundwater irrigation, the major source of irrigation in India, will continue to increase which will though increase gross irrigated area will deplete the ground water significantly (Amarasinghe et al., 2008). Therefore, the current pattern of growth though consistent with the demand patterns seems inconsistent with resource endowments.

*Climate change*

Scientists across the world agree that climate changes are unequivocal (IPCC, 2007a and b) as a result of significant warming of earth's atmosphere caused by increased concentration of carbon dioxide and other greenhouse gases. Climate changes will result in gradual changes in temperature and timing and levels of rainfall, increased frequency, and intensity of droughts/floods, pests, and diseases. Though increases in temperature may increase/decrease yields depending on initial conditions, the net impact of climate change is likely to have a detrimental impact on agriculture consisting of crop production, livestock, fisheries, and allied sectors as well as non-agriculture sectors through its linkages. By the year 2030, an expected temperature increase of 2°C is projected to reduce Gross Domestic Product (GDP) by 5 per cent (Ranuzzi and Srivastava, 2012).

The impact of climate change on agriculture in India is expected to pose a serious threat to food security. Indian agriculture is largely dependent on monsoon, likely to be adversely affected by climate change. Around 85 per cent farms are small today, having a high level of subsistence agriculture and less capacity to cope with climate change because of costs associated with mitigating impact of climate changes.

## PROSPECTS FOR THE FUTURE

Table 8.4 shows the per capita production of various commodities in the past and prospects for the future. Population growth rate per annum has been considered to be 1.3 per cent for 2011–15, 1.1 per cent for 2016–20, and 0.9 per cent for 2021–25 as per the projections by Census Commissioner India (NCOP, 2006), and using the same trend pattern, 0.7 per cent growth rate per year is assumed for the period 2026–30. Production growth rates in the future years have been considered to be same as for the period 2001–08 in this study. Projections available for production in other studies are not exactly for the same groups as per the definition in the present study.

Per capita production of cereals in real terms has been found to be declining till 2009. The decline has been more till mid 2000s than after that. However, in the future years, the production per capita of cereals is expected to increase. For pulses and sugarcane also, there has been decline in the per capita production till 2009, but thereafter it has been increasing and is also expected to increase in the future years. Interestingly, for fruits and livestock group, per capita production has been increasing consistently over the years as a result of increase in demand for these products because of rising per capita income and changes in preferences. The per capita production of these products is also expected to increase in the future years but at a rate much more than that for cereals, pulses, and sugarcane. However, in the case of vegetables, though per capita production increased till 2009, but started declining afterwards and is also expected to decline further in the future years. Hence, for all commodities, per capita production in real terms is expected to increase more than population in the future.

Other studies have also found that the country will be able to sustain food security in the future under reasonable scenarios on demand and supply. On the other hand, under different assumptions regarding demand elasticity with respect to income accounting for rapid growth in the livestock sector, a large deficit of cereals is projected by the year 2020 (Ganesh-Kumar et al., 2012, and Jha and Chand, 1999).

**Table 8.4: Outlook on food security in India**

| Year | Population million no | Rupees per capita (2005 price) | | | | | | |
|------|------------|-------|------|-------|------|------|-------|-------------|
| | | CER | PLS | F | V | SCN | LF | All products |
| 1996 | 938 | 1,459 | 236 | 552 | 448 | 220 | 1,575 | 5,525 |
| 2006 | 1,123 | 1,379 | 196 | 652 | 570 | 184 | 1,864 | 5,934 |
| 2009 | 1,183 | 1,367 | 188 | 655 | 578 | 176 | 2,119 | 6,130 |
| 2020 | 1,346 | 1,389 | 196 | 924 | 410 | 193 | 3,074 | 7,379 |
| 2026 | 1,418 | 1,428 | 204 | 1,137 | 346 | 207 | 3,836 | 8,318 |
| 2030 | 1,458 | 1,464 | 211 | 1,313 | 312 | 218 | 4,476 | 9,069 |

*Note*: Figures for 2020, 2026, and 2030 are projections based on population growth rate of 1.1%, 0.9%, and 0.7% per annum and production growth rates same as for the period 2001 to 2008.

Therefore, output will generally be ahead of the population growth assuming current growth rates in the production and population growth rate of 1.4 per cent per annum. However, given the expected substantial increase in production of fruits and livestock products consistent with increase in consumption of these products, likely to increase further because of increase in income and urbanization, as a result of changes in preferences indirect consumption of cereals and pulses is projected to grow more than the current growth rate of these products (Chand, 2009). This may also increase the demand for water substantially (Amarasinghe et al., 2008), causing depletion of resources. Further, these demand and supply projections have not considered net adverse consequences of climate changes posing a serious challenge. Also, sharp diminution of farm size associated with risk aversion and resource scarcity makes further diversification difficult. Therefore, factors like climate changes, compatibility with resource endowments, and national policies along with global price movements dictated by world demand and supply have to be also kept in view for sustainable growth in agriculture.

## POLICY RECOMMENDATIONS AND CONCLUSIONS

India's agriculture has been shifting towards high value products from cereals and other foodgrains. These shifts, though consistent with consumer demand and nutritional merit, have produced a new concentration in the structure of agriculture. These patterns, however, seem to be inconsistent with resource endowments, especially water. Indian farms today are small but more productive. Despite being efficient, higher per hectare costs and low absolute returns of these small farms raise questions on risk-bearing capacity and livelihood sustainability. The study found that output in real terms will generally be ahead of the population growth if current growth rates in the production are sustained and the population grows at officially projected rates in future. However, given the expected substantial increase in the production of livestock products, indirect demand through feed requirement of cereals and oilseeds is projected to grow more than the current growth rate of these products. This will substantially increase the demand of water causing depletion of resources. Output and water availability will also be affected by adverse consequences of climate changes.

Thus, sustaining high growth rates in agriculture is not just about investment and planning for attaining the rate, but it raises the need for a larger perspective encompassing equity, environment, and changing preferences. In other words, production patterns resulting from agricultural planning must be consistent with evolving agronomic structures, availability of water resources, and reality of climate changes and must be finally sensitive to demand situations.

Growth in Indian agriculture, therefore, needs to be planned with care and caution with an eye for not only food security and consumer demands, but environment, resource endowment and economic sustainability also. Further, production also needs to be broad based and diversified, amenable to nuanced shifts in tune with demand and supply conditions in line with the experiences in India and other countries.

**Appendix 8.A1: Sub-groups and crops used for this study**

| Sub-group | Crops |
| --- | --- |
| Cereals (CER) | Rice, wheat, jowar, maize, and barley |
| Millets (MLT) | Bajra, ragi, and small millets |
| Pulses (PLS) | Arhar, gram, moong, urad, masoor, and other pulses |
| Oilseeds (OLS) | Groundnut, rapeseed and mustard, soybean, linseed, sesamum, castor, nigerseed, safflower, and sunflower |
| Fibres and Materials (FM) | Cotton, jute, mesta, sunhemp, rubber, coconut, and guarseed |
| Condiments and Spices (CS) | Cardamom, chillies, black pepper, dry ginger, turmeric, garlic, and coriander |
| Fruits (F) | Banana, cashewnut, apple, mango, orange, grape, papaya, and others (guava, sapota, citrus, pineapple, litchi, mosambi, lemon, etc.) |
| Vegetables (V) | Potato, sweet potato, tapioca, onion, cabbage, cauliflower, tomato and others (brinjal, ladyfinger, peas, mushroom, etc.) |
| Beverages and Narcotics (BN) | Tea, coffee, tobacco and areca nut |
| Sugarcane (SCN) | Sugarcane |
| Livestock and Fisheries (LF) | Milk, meat, egg, and fish |

# APPENDIX 8.A2 METHODOLOGY

## Theil–Tornquist index (TTI)

The Theil–Tornquist index (TTI), because of several useful properties (Prasad et al., 1995), is often preferred over Laspeyere (LI) and the Paasche (PI) or Fisher index (FI). TTI is computed using equation 1 as:

$$TTI_{kj} = \prod_{i=1}^{N} \left( \frac{p_{ij}}{p_{ik}} \right)^{\frac{w_{ij} + w_{ik}}{2}}$$ (1)

Where $w_{ij} = \dfrac{\left( p_{ij} q_{ij} \right)}{\left( \sum_i p_{ij} q_{ij} \right)}$ represents the value of share of $i^{th}$ crop or sub-sector in $j^{th}$ year and $p$ and $q$ represent price and quantity, respectively, and $k$ is the base year.

The National Accounts Statistics (NAS) of Central Statistical Organisation (CSO) on the other hand reports the value of output both at current and constant prices and derives an implicit deflator (ID) for the broad sub-sectors as the ratio of the two values of output instead of using any explicit price index.

## Bray and Curtis index (BCI)

The Bray and Curtis index (BCI) is used popularly in ecology for studying sample resemblance and applied on standardized data (a widely used term in ecology to convert counts into proportions of a total). A number of other indices of the same family have also been suggested in the literature like the Czekanowski index, the Norm of absolute values (NAV), and Modified Lilien index (MLI) to measure dissimilarity (Dietrich, 2009; Stamer, 1998; Michaely, 1962; Stoikov, 1966; and Lilien, 1982) based on certain comparisons across samples.

The BCI index ($d_{ij}$) used as a measure of dissimilarity taking a value between zero and one is computed using equation 2 as:

$$d_{ij} = \frac{\sum_{k=1}^{n} \left| x_{ik} - x_{jk} \right|}{\sum_{k=1}^{n} \left( x_{ik} + x_{jk} \right)}$$ (2)

Where $dij$ is the index of sectoral (sub-sectoral) dissimilarity between two years, $i$ and $j$, $xik$ and $xjk$, are the shares of sub-sectors (crops), $k$ in total value of agricultural output in years $i$ and $j$. In the case of sectoral composition, $k = 1$, 2,......, 11 and within a sub-sector $k = 1, 2,...., m$ where $m$ is the number of crops in the sub-sector.

### Herfindahl index (HI)

Herfindahl index (HI) of concentration is computed using the formula in equation 3. HI has no special emphasis on any particular crop or group like cereals and is different from diversion of production. Lower the concentration in crops or sub-sectors within agriculture (higher the diversity), more balanced is the production pattern.

$$HI = \sum_{k-1}^{n} s_k^2 \tag{3}$$

Where $sk$ is the share of the agricultural sub-sector (or crop within the sub-sector), $k$ is the sub-sector (or crop), and $n$ is the number of sub-sectors and $n = 11$ in this case (or number of crops in the sub-sector).

## APPENDIX 8.A3: SOURCES OF DATA

Production data is mainly taken from the Ministry of Agriculture databases; however, for minor cases where ministry's data is unavailable, we have taken recourse to the national accounts created by the CSO. Production is attributed to the marketing period involved, i.e., the product account is based on income accrual rather than the production period.

Eleven sub-groups of agriculture similar to but not convergent with India's national accounting protocols are considered. For example, rubber and also coconut, which is a raw material for coir (a material used for making mats, beddings, etc.) besides generating cooking oil used by a few communities in the country, are combined with cotton and jute in the sub-group that we titled FM. The sub-group BN includes not only tea and coffee but also areca nut, eaten as a popular intoxicant and LF is presented in one single sub-group of non-crop-based activity and not as two separate ones as in the CSO data. The FV group also includes floriculture. Only a few horticultural crops were conventionally reported by the Ministry of Agriculture, but the National Horticulture Board under the Ministry of Agriculture has started to report production of additional crops only from 1992. To make the data set comparable, an alternative, data reported by the Food and Agricultural Organization (FAOSTAT) on major fruits and vegetables had to be used.

State-level monthly prices are calculated by averaging across the major wholesale markets (*mandis*) for which the Ministry reports and this data is aggregated to the national level using production in the states as weights. Producer prices are estimated as average of monthly prices in the peak marketing season, i.e., three months immediately after harvest. For rice and wheat, the weighted averages of market prices and the MSPs with the shares of sales in the two channels used as weights are the estimates of producer prices. For minor crops and crops where price data is not reported regularly by the Ministry, approximations using current values of crops reported in the National Accounts Statistics deflated by quantities reported by the Ministry has been used with due adjustments for calendar year.

**Appendix 8.A4: Major agricultural programmes**

| Crop group | Major agricultural programmes |
|---|---|
| Cereals | 1. Price support through minimum support prices to guarantee high returns for wheat and rice, and their assured procurement discouraged diversification to the alternative crops having high production and price risks.<br>2. Technology mission on maize in May 1995. Since then, Maize is taken care of under Accelerated Maize Development Programme (AMDP).<br>3. A sub-programme on maize-based cropping system for food security with effect from 1999–2000.<br>4. Integrated Scheme of Oilseeds, Pulses, Oil palm and Maize (ISOPOM) from 2004.<br>5. National Food Security Mission (NFSM), a centrally sponsored scheme launched from 2007–08 to increase the production of rice, wheat, and pulses. |
| Millets | 1. All India coordinated small millets improvement project (1986)<br>2. Millet network of India to promote millets (2007). |
| Pulses | 1. Technology mission on pulses, 1990.<br>2. National Pulses Development Programme (NPDP) 1999–2000.<br>3. Integrated Scheme of Oilseeds, Pulses, Oil palm and Maize (ISOPOM) from 2004.<br>4. NFSM–Pulses–Pulses component of ISOPOM has been merged with the NFSM since 2007–08. |
| OILSEEDS | 1. Technology mission on oilseeds 1986.<br>2. Technology mission on oil palm 1992–93.<br>3. Oil Palm Development Programme (OPDP) during 1992–93.<br>Integrated Scheme of Oilseeds, Pulses, Oil palm and Maize (ISOPOM). |
| Fibres and Materials | 1. The technology mission on cotton was launched in February 2000 to improve cotton production and productivity with internationally competitive fibre quality.<br>2. Approval of commercial cultivation of Bt Cotton in the year 2002. |

*Appendix 8. A4 Continued*

*Appendix 8. A4 Continued*

| | |
|---|---|
| Condiments and Spices | 1. Trade policies |
| Horticultures | 1. Horticulture mission for the north-east, 2001–02 |
| | 2. Extended to Himalayan states 2003–04 |
| | 3. National horticultural mission 2005–06 |
| Sugarcane | 1. Before 2009, pricing mechanism was to recommend statutory minimum support prices based on cost of production |
| | 2. Since 2009, fair and remunerative prices for sugarcane taking into account margins for risk and profit of sugarcane farmers |
| Livestock | 1. Operation flood, 1970–96. |
| | 2. Technology mission on dairy development, 1989–99. |
| | 3. Integrated dairy development programme in non-operational flood, hilly and backward areas launched as a centrally sponsored plan scheme since 1992. |

## APPENDIX 8.A5

**Figure 8.A1: Average compound annual growth rates (per cent) of real values of output in agriculture across sub-groups (2001–08) compared with corresponding rates based on the National Accounts Statistics (NAS).**

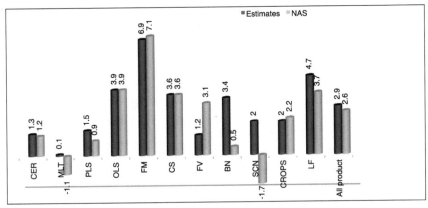

*Notes*:
1. Estimates are based on Theil-Tornquist price indices and refers to calendar years.
2. NAS refers to financial year data reported by CSO(Central Statistical Organisation)

*Source*: Author's calculations

# REFERENCES

Agriculture Market Information System (AMIS). http://www.amis-outlook.org/ amis-about.

Amarasinghe, Upali A., Tushaar Shah, and B. K. Anand. 2008. 'India's Water Supply and Demand from 2025–2050: Business as Usual Scenario and Issues, International Water Management Institute.' New Delhi, India. http://www. iwmi.cgiar.org/ Publications/ Other/PDF/N ... ng-2%20Paper%202.pdf.

Binswanger-Mkhize Hans P. 2013. 'India 1960–2010: Structural Changes, the Rural Non-farm Sector and the Prospects for Agriculture.' In *Transforming Indian Agriculture INDIA 2040 Productivity, Markets, and Institutions*, edited by Marko Ferroni, 17. New Delhi: Sage Publication.

Chand, Ramesh. 2009. 'Demand for Foodgrains During 11th Plan and Towards 2020.' *Policy Brief 28*. New Delhi: National Centre for Agricultural Economics and Policy Research.

Chopra, Kanchan, C. H. Hanumantha Rao, and Ramprasad Sengupta. 2003. 'Water Resources, Sustainable Livelihoods and Eco-System Service.' *Indian Society for Ecological Economics*, Delhi: Institute of Economic Growth.

Dietrich, A. 2009. 'Does Growth Cause Structural Change, or is it the Other Way Round? A Dynamic Panel Data Analysis for Seven OECD Countries.' *Jena Research Papers in Economics*.

Food and Agriculture Organization of the United States (FAO). Available on http:// faostat.fao.org/site/567/default.aspx#ancor.

Ganesh-Kumar, A., R. Mehta, H. Pullabhotia, S. K. Prasad, K. Ganguly, and A. Gulati. 2012. 'Demand and Supply of Cereals in India: 2010–2025.' IFPRI Discussion Paper 01158, January.

Gary W. van Loon, S. G. Patil, and L. B. Hugar. 2005. *Agricultural Sustainability: Strategies for Assessment*. New Delhi: Sage Publications.

Gaurav, Sarthak and Srijit Mishra. 2011. 'Size Class and Returns to Cultivation in India: A Cold Case Reopened.' *Indira Gandhi Institute of Development Research, WP-2011-027*, Mumbai, October.

Ghosh, Nilabja. 2004. 'Impact of Trade Liberalization on Returns from Land: A Regional Study of Indian Agriculture.' In *The WTO Developing Countries and the Doha Development Agenda*, edited by Basudeb Guha-Khasnobis, Studies in Development Economics and Policy Series, United Nations University WIDER, New York: Palgrave Macmillan.

———— 2006. 'Theory and Practice of Agricultural Indicators.' *Economic and Political Weekly* 41(34), August 26.

Government of India. 2004. 'Fruits and Vegetables Sector: An Overview.' *Ministry of Science & Technology*, Department of Scientific and Industrial Research.

————— Various years. *Land and Livestock Holding in India*, National Sample Survey Organisation, Central Statistical Organisation, New Delhi, Ministry of Statistics and Programme Implementation.

IARI. 'A Short Note on Agricultural Policy: Vision 2020 of Planning Commission.' New Delhi: Indian Agricultural Research Institute. www.iari.res.in/.

IPCC. 2007a. *Climate Change 2007: The Physical Science Basis*. Contribution of Working Group I to the Fourth Assessment Report of the Intergovernmental Panel on Climate Change (Solomon, S., Qin, D., Manning, M., Marquis, M., Averyt, K., Tignor, M. B., LeRoy Mil H., eds). Cambridge University Press.

————— *Climate Change 2007: Impacts, Adaptation and Vulnerability*. Contribution of Working Group II to the Fourth Assessment Report of the Intergovernmental Panel on Climate Change (Parry, M. L., Canziani, O. F., Palutikof, J. P., van der Linden, P. J., Hanson, C. E., eds.).Cambridge University Press.

Jha, Dayanatha and Ramesh Chand. 1999. 'Sustainable Food Production, Income Generation and Consumer Protection In India.' www.unescap.org/rural/doc/ GreenFood/NIB-Sept2000_3.PDF.

Kohli, Harinder S. and Anil Sood. 2013a. 'A Vision of Indian Agriculture in 2040.' In *Transforming Indian Agriculture INDIA 2040 Productivity, Markets, and Institutions*. edited by Marko Ferroni, 17. New Delhi: Sage Publication.

————— 2013b. 'Productivity, Markets, and Institutions.' In *Transforming Indian Agriculture INDIA 2040 Productivity, Markets, and Institutions*, edited by Marko Ferroni, 11. New Delhi: Sage Publication.

Lilien, D. M. 1982. 'Sectoral Shifts and Cyclical Unemployment.' *Journal of Political Economy* 90, 777–93.

Michaely, M. 1962. *Concentration in International Trade*, Amsterdam: North Holland.

Ministry of Agriculture. Various years. *Agriculture Census*, Department of Agriculture and Cooperation, New Delhi.

————— Various years. *Agriculture Statistics at a Glance*, Directorate of Economic and Statistics, Department of Agriculture and Cooperation, Government of India.

Ministry of Agriculture, Government of India. Various years. *Agricultural Prices in India*, Directorate of Economics and Statistics.

————— Various years. *Index Number of Whole Sale Price in India*, Directorate of Economics and Statistics.

National Commission on Population (NCOP). 2006. *Population Projections for India and States 2001–2026*, Report of the Technical Group on Population Projections Constituted by The National Commission on Population, Office of The Registrar General and Census Commissioner, Census of India 2001, Delhi.

National Horticulture Board. Various years. *Indian Horticulture Database*, Department of Agriculture and Cooperation, Government of India.

Office of the Registrar General and Census Commissioner. 2006. Population Projections for India and States 2001–2026, Report of the Technical Group on Population Projections Constituted by The National Commission on Population, Census of India, 2001, Delhi.

Prasad P., S. Basu, N. Behera. 1995. A Comparative Account of the Microbiological Characteristics of Soils under Natural Forest, Grassland and Cropfield from Eastern India. Plant Soil 175: 85–91.

Ranuzzi, Anna and Richa Srivastava. 2012. 'Impact of Climate Change on Agriculture and Food Security.' *ICRIER Policy Series No. 16*, May 2012.

Stamer, M. 1998. 'Interrelation between Subsidies, Structural Change and Economic Growth in Germany, A Vector Autoregressive Analysis.' *Konjunkturpolitik*, 44: 3, 231–53.

Stoikov, V. 1966. 'Some Determinants of the Level of Frictional Unemployment: A Comparative Study.' *International Labour Review* 93, 530–49.

Vaidyanathan, A. 1999. *Water Resource Management,* Institutions and Irrigation Development India, Delhi: Oxford University Press.

# 9

# Energy Security for India

Pradeep Agrawal
Shruti Tripathi

## INTRODUCTION

Energy security is crucial for sustaining high economic growth over long periods. With rapid economic growth, petroleum demand has been rising rapidly in India. Crude oil accounts for about 29 per cent of India's energy consumption (IEA, 2013). As India imports most of its crude oil, and there is no alternative to crude oil derivatives such as petrol and diesel for transportation and many other industrial uses, controlling crude oil consumption is difficult, and any rise in its price puts inflationary pressure on the economy. Thus, estimations of demand for crude oil, diesel and projections of likely future demand should be useful to policy makers in making appropriate supply arrangements.

Due to the global recession, crude oil prices have remained relatively stable over the past few years. The Brent crude oil spot price was US$107.97 per barrel in December 2011 and US$109.64 per barrel in December 2012 (Global Economic Monitor, 2013). But demand in the US and Western Europe (which has been roughly constant for the past several years) could start increasing if the recession ends in a few years. Together with rapidly increasing demand from emerging economies such as China and India, this could raise crude oil prices over the long term, unless there are major new oil finds or major technological breakthroughs in alternative energy sources.

If this assessment holds, the Indian economy's growth path could slow down unless well-planned policy responses are adopted. For example, sharp crude oil price increases in 2007–08 and again in 2010–11 led to episodes of high inflation in India that slowed growth because of the tight monetary policy adopted to fight inflation. Therefore, this study empirically analyses the long term demand relations for crude oil and diesel, for which the demand has been rising most rapidly. We then use the long run elasticities to project demand for these products up to 2025 for several scenarios of Gross Domestic Product (GDP) growth and crude oil prices.

The increasingly large subsidy on the price of diesel has also become a controversial issue, especially in view of the large fiscal and current account deficits and the consequent sharp depreciation of the rupee. The food security bill will add considerably to the government's subsidy burden, which makes it mandatory to control other subsidies. Thus, a substantial increase in the price of diesel is inevitable if we are not to destroy our public finances. Therefore, we then use the estimated demand function of diesel to estimate the impact of eliminating the subsidy on diesel (gradually over the next one year or so) and show that doing so will reduce the current account deficit by $7 billion and the fiscal deficit by $12 billion *per year*.

Several previous studies estimate the demand for crude oil and other components. For India, Goldar and Mukhopadhyay (1990) and Ghosh (2009) estimate demand for *imported* crude oil. Several studies estimate demand for crude oil derivatives, e.g., Ramanathan (1999) and Chemin (2012) estimate demand for petrol and Ghosh (2010) estimates demand for diesel. Some studies estimate and forecast future demand for various derivatives of crude oil (Rao and Parikh, 1996; Ghosh, 2006; Parikh et al., 2007; Kumar and Jain, 2010). Adams and Shachmurove (2008) estimated petroleum demand for China; Altinay (2007) for Turkey; and Saad (2009) estimated petroleum demand for Indonesia. An interesting review of previous studies on petroleum demand estimations for various countries is available in Suganthi and Samuel (2012). Several earlier studies on India used the Ordinary Least Square (OLS) method (Goldar and Mukhopadhyay, 1990; Rao and Parikh, 1996; Parikh et al., 2007), which might yield unreliable results since most variables involved are actually non-stationary. Other studies that used co-integration techniques focused on petroleum derivatives (Ramanathan, 1999; Ghosh, 2010; Chemin, 2012) or on demand for imported oil only (Ghosh, 2009). Thus, none of these studies estimates and forecasts the *total* crude oil demand for India.[1] Even the studies that estimate imported crude oil demand (Ghosh, 2009) are dated, with data only until 2005–06. However, since economic growth (and probably also crude oil demand) has been significantly more rapid since 2003 than earlier, it is important to estimate demand using more recent data and provide reliable forecasts. Thus, in this study, we estimate the demand for crude oil and diesel using the Auto-Regressive Distributed Lag (ARDL) co-integration technique and also project their demand up to 2025.

The rest of the chapter is organized as follows. The second section discusses the demand model for crude oil and diesel. The third section presents the empirical

---

[1] Except Ghosh (2006). However, he used data until 2001 only and projected demand until 2011-12. Thus, more up-to-date work is now needed given the critical importance of crude oil in the Indian economy.

results from our estimation. The fourth section provides projections of India's future demand of crude oil and diesel up to 2025. The fifth section presents impact of diesel subsidy withdrawal on India's current account and fiscal deficit and finally the sixth section summarises the main conclusions of the chapter.

## DEMAND MODEL

We follow the traditional demand function for crude oil,[2] where crude oil demand is simply a function of the real prices of crude oil and the real national income, which can be well proxied by real GDP at factor cost. This is appropriate since most industries using crude oil and its derivatives in various forms as the source of energy have no alternative to crude under currently available technologies for a large range of crude oil prices. While one could also estimate this relation using income per capita, given our focus on estimation and projection of India's national demand, we felt it was more convenient and expeditious to estimate the relation in terms of the national income.

This study also separately estimates the demand for diesel whose demand has been rising particularly rapidly in India. We considered the possibility that other variables (such as the number of vehicles of various kinds used in India) may influence diesel demand. However, different types of vehicles consume different amounts of fuel, and consistent time series data on the number vehicles of various types is not available, except for a few years. Moreover, the number of various vehicles in use, etc., is itself determined by the level of economic activity. Therefore, we felt that real GDP—perhaps the single-best measure of the level of economic activity in the country—is a good explanatory variable to use instead of the number of vehicles, etc. We also considered the possibility of including the price of substitutes, such as price of petrol, in the demand for diesel but found it insignificant, probably because a vehicle designed to run on, diesel cannot be run on petrol irrespective of its price and, similarly, petrol vehicles cannot use diesel. Thus, the demand function for diesel is also estimated with real GDP and real price of diesel as explanatory variables.

We tried the linear, log-linear and double log versions and found that the double log model worked best for crude as well as diesel and satisfied all the diagnostic tests, such as the acceptability of functional form, normality of error term, heteroscedasticity, etc. Thus, we used the following double log model to estimate the demand:

$$LogD_{it} = \alpha_i + \beta_i LogP_{it} + \gamma_i LogY_t + u_i \tag{1}$$

---

[2] See, for example, Parikh et al., 2007; Saad, 2009; and Chemin, 2012.

where,

$i$ can take two values: crude and diesel

$D$ and $P$ are the demand and real price, respectively of crude oil/diesel

$Y$ is the real national income proxied here by the real GDP at factor cost,

$\alpha_i$ is constant, $\beta_i$, $\gamma_i$ are the parameters to be estimated reflecting price and income elasticity of crude or diesel and $u$ is the error term;

It is expected that an increase in price, $P$, would reduce demand for crude oil/ diesel, that is long run elasticity with respect to price would be negative ($\beta_i < 0$) whereas an increase in real GDP, $Y$, would imply greater industrial production and increased transportation of goods and people, leading to increasing demand petroleum products ($\gamma_i > 0$). It implies that long run elasticity of demand with respect to income should be positive.

### Data sources

This study is based on annual data for the 1970–2011 period. The data for India's crude oil and diesel consumption (in million tonnes) were collected from the Ministry of Petroleum and Natural Gas, Government of India. The real GDP at factor cost (in 2004–05 prices) is used as a proxy for real national income. The data are collected from the Handbook of Statistics on Indian Economy (Reserve Bank of India, 2012). We collected the annual average international crude oil prices of Brent oil in US$ per barrel from www.indexmundi.com, and converted these into current Indian Rupees using the official exchange rate and then divided these by India's Wholesale Price Index (WPI) (base year 2004–05) to get the real rupee price. The Indian basket oil price is sometimes used in studies on India but that price was available only from 1980 and the two prices are essentially same (correlation co-efficient = 0.999). In the case of diesel, we used the data on their retail prices in Delhi[3] collected from the Ministry of Petroleum and Natural Gas, Government of India. We have used the diesel price in Delhi as a proxy for diesel prices in India because while prices may vary somewhat between states due to differences in local taxes and transportation costs, they are highly correlated with each other. Also, data was not available for all states for the whole sample period. We then converted the nominal price into real price by dividing it with the WPI (base year 2004–05).

---

[3] We can mention the price of diesel in metric tonnes by multiplying by a constant factor (number of litres per metric tonne), but it will make no difference to the estimates of the equation—which work in percentage terms—because the double logform is used. We used the price of diesel because it is better known and understood by most people.

## Econometric methodology

As usual, we began by testing for the stationarity of the variables for the three equations (Table 9.1). All variables were found non-stationary in levels but stationary after first differencing, that is, they are integrated of order 1 [I(1)]. Thus, a co-integration estimation procedure is needed. This study estimates the long run demand for crude oil, petrol, and diesel in India using the ARDL co-integration procedure proposed by Pesaran et al. (2001), generally recognised for reliably estimating the long run relation.

**Table 9.1: Unit root tests using the Augmented Dickey-Fuller (ADF) and PP tests**

| | ADF | | PP | |
|---|---|---|---|---|
| | Levels | 1st difference | Levels | 1st difference |
| $LogD_{crude}$ | −0.93 | −3.45** | −0.51 | −4.49** |
| $LogP_{crude}$ | −1.73 | −3.45** | −1.34 | −5.59** |
| $LogD_{diesel}$ | −1.37 | −2.63** | −2.31 | −5.84** |
| $LogP_{diesel}$ | −0.82 | −3.11** | −0.98 | −6.60** |
| $LogY$ | 3.21 | −2.58** | 4.57 | −5.54** |

Notes: **, * indicates 1 per cent and 5 per cent level of significance respectively

Source: Author's computation

# RESULTS OF EMPIRICAL ESTIMATION

## Demand for crude oil

We estimated the demand for crude oil in India using equation (1) by employing the ARDL co-integration methodology. The results for the long-run demand function are given below:

$$Log\,D_{crude} = -9.09 - 0.41\,LogP_{crude} + 1.00\,LogY \qquad (2)$$

$$(4.86)^{**}(2.37)^* \qquad (9.73)^{**}$$

F-Test Statistics (for testing co-integration) = 3.92**

$R^2 = .99$; $DW = 2.14$; Serial correlation $[\chi^2(1)] = 1.51$; Functional form $[\chi^2(1)] = 2.02$

Normality test $[\chi^2(2)] = 1.00$; Heteroscedasticity $[\chi^2(1)] = 0.003$

Note: Numbers in parenthesis below equation (2) denote the t-statistics of the respective co-efficients. Asterisks * and ** denote significance at the 5 per cent and 1 per cent significance levels.

The F-statistics confirm the co-integration relationship as its values are above the upper bound at the 1 per cent significance level. Further, diagnostic tests show that serial correlation in the error term is not significant, functional form is not rejected, normality of error term is not rejected, and there is no heteroscedasticity in the model. These tests corroborate the validity of the estimated demand function for crude oil. The coefficient of crude oil price is negative and significant at 5 per cent level, indicating that crude oil price significantly influences crude oil demand in India. Further, the coefficient of income is positive as expected and statistically significant at the 1 per cent level. The income elasticity is 1, implying that a 1 per cent increase in real GDP would lead to a 1 per cent increase in the crude oil demand by about 1 per cent in the long run. Thus, India's crude oil demand can be expected to keep increasing rapidly due to rapid economic growth.

The stability of coefficients is essential in estimation for making policy recommendations. Unstable parameters can result from model mis-specification and thus lead to biased results. Since we will use the coefficients of real price and real GDP in this estimation (i.e., the price and income elasticities) for projecting future demand for crude oil, it is particularly important to test the stability of these coefficients. Stability tests like the cumulative sum of recursive residuals (CUSUM) and their square (CUSUMSQ) proposed by Brown et al. (1975) are considered important to analyse stability of the coefficients. In our case, neither the CUSUM nor the CUSUM square test statistics exceed the bounds of 5 per cent levels of significance (Figure 9.1). Thus, the estimated demand relation (Equation 2) for crude oil appears stable and correctly specified.

**Figure 9.1: Plots of CUSUM and CUSUMSQ statistics for crude oil demand estimation**

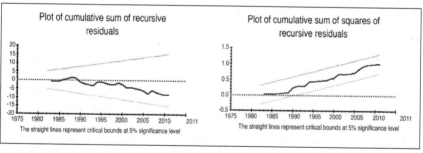

### Demand for diesel

Similar to crude oil demand function, we estimated the diesel demand function. The results for the long run estimated demand function are given below:

$$LogD_{diesel} = -11.89 - 0.56\, LogP_{diesel} + 1.02\, LogY \qquad (3)$$

$$(6.87)^{**} \quad (3.61)^{**} \qquad\qquad (8.62)^{*}$$

$$F\text{-}Test \ for \ Co\text{-}integration = 11.73^{**}$$
$$R^2 = .99, \ DW = 1.50, \ Serial \ Correlation \ [\chi^2(1)] = 2.16; \ Functional \ Form \ [\chi^2(1)]$$
$$= 0.02 \ Normality \ test \ [\chi^2(2)] = 1.77; \ Heteroscedasticity \ [\chi^2(1)] = 0.31$$

*Note: Numbers in parenthesis below equation (3) denote the t-statistics of the respective co-efficients. Asterisks * and ** denote significance at the 5 per cent and 1 per cent significance levels.*

The F-test confirms the long-run relationship between diesel price and real income on diesel consumption in India. As with the crude oil estimation, the diagnostic tests corroborate the validity of the estimated demand function for diesel. Finally, as discussed in the case of crude oil, CUSUM test is undertaken (Figure 9.2) and the demand relation for diesel appeared to be stable. Thus, the estimated demand relation (Equation 3) for diesel appears stable and correctly specified.

**Figure 9.2: Plots of CUSUM and CUSUM square statistics for diesel demand estimation**

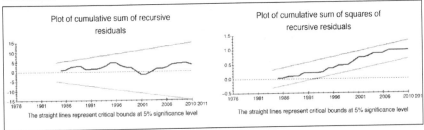

*Source:* Derived for the post modelling estimations

The estimation results for demand for diesel in Equation (3) show that, as expected, the price elasticity is negative and significant at 1 per cent level while the income elasticity is positive and significant at 1 per cent level. The price elasticity for diesel is −0.57, and the income elasticity is +1.02, meaning a 1 per cent increase in real income (i.e., real GDP) leads to an increase in the diesel demand by 1.02 per cent. Thus, the demand for diesel is quite sensitive to its price in the long run. Further, the demand for diesel is quite responsive to changes in real GDP as the coefficient is greater than 1. This could be capturing effects such as an increasing number of motor vehicles for personal travel and increased transportation of goods and services as the real GDP increases.

## PROJECTIONS OF DEMAND FOR CRUDE OIL AND DIESEL

This section projects demand for crude oil and diesel in India until 2025 using the estimated long-run demand elasticities in relations (2) and (3) in the third section.

The growth rate for demand for crude oil and diesel can be obtained using our demand relation (1):

$$LogD_{it} = \alpha_i + \beta_i LogP_{it} + \gamma_i LogY_t + u_i$$

Differentiation of the demand equation with respect to time yields the relation (where a caret (^) over a variable denotes its growth rate.

$$\widehat{D} = \beta_i \widehat{P}_i + \gamma_i \widehat{Y} \tag{5}$$

which can then be used to project future demand starting from a base year, $t_i$:

$$D_{t+1} = D_t + \beta_i P_i + \gamma_i Y \tag{6}$$

Using (6), the future demand for crude oil and diesel can be projected using the likely scenarios for growth rates of real GDP and the real price of crude oil and diesel respectively. Thus, for projecting demand, we need to know the likely future growth rates of real GDP and real prices of crude oil and diesel.

## Likely growth rates of GDP and petroleum prices

The annualized average growth rate of real GDP between 1971 and 2011 was about 5.57 per cent. Following the economic reforms in 1991, it averaged about 6.92 per cent or almost 7 per cent between 1991 and 2011, and about 7.82 per cent or close to 8 per cent over 2001–11. It appears likely that (despite current pessimism) GDP will grow 6–8 per cent annually on average until 2025. Thus, we consider three likely scenarios for average annual GDP growth rate until 2025: (1) a normal scenario of 7 per cent; (2) an optimistic scenario of 8 per cent; and (3) a pessimistic scenario of 6 per cent.

A likely scenario for the probable growth rates of crude oil prices is harder to determine given the high volatility of oil prices. However, between 1970 and 2011, crude oil prices grew at an average rate of 5.62 per cent in real rupee terms (and 4.68 per cent in real dollar terms). Besides, the annualised growth rate of crude oil prices has increased to 6.72 per cent between 1991 and 2011 (4.66 per cent in real dollar terms between 1991 and 2011). Considering these data, we consider three scenarios with oil prices in real rupees, assuming an average growth rate of about 4 per cent, 5.5 per cent, and 7 per cent respectively. Given the current price of crude oil of about $108 per barrel, these growth rates yielded the 2025 crude oil prices of around $187, $229, and $278, respectively.

Similarly, we observed that the average annual growth rate of diesel prices between 1973 and 2011 in real rupee terms was about 2.98 per cent (or almost 3 per cent). These rates are significantly lower than those of crude oil, probably because diesel prices also include refining, transportation, and taxation components that have not risen nearly as rapidly as crude oil prices have. Also, the Government of India regulates diesel prices and at times, subsidies were used to keep diesel prices from increasing in response to increasing crude oil prices. Given these historical growth rates, we consider three different scenarios of growth rate of diesel prices—2 per cent, 3 per cent, and 4 per cent—for projecting diesel demand. Under these scenarios, we expect *real* diesel price (in 2011 price base) to grow from about ₹40.91 in 2011 to around ₹55, ₹65 or ₹75 per litre by 2025.

### Projections for the future demand for crude oil in India

We can project future demand for crude oil in India using Equation (6) and the estimate of the long-run price and income elasticities of demand for crude oil that was obtained in relation (2) above. As discussed in the first section of Chapter 4, we consider three likely scenarios for average annual GDP growth rate at 6 per cent, 7 per cent, and 8 per cent. Regarding real crude oil prices, we also consider three scenarios, with average annual growth rates of 4 per cent, 5.5 per cent, and 7 per cent. These average annual growth rates of crude oil prices and real GDP try to capture the likely long-term scenarios up to 2025 and not the short-term fluctuations (which are extremely difficult to predict). Table 9.2 gives the projections of crude oil consumption in India using the estimated Equation (2) and the above-mentioned scenarios for the likely prices of crude oil and GDP growth rates for 2025.

Table 9.2 and Figure 9.4 show that the projected annual growth rate of crude oil demand would be 3.1–6.34 per cent per annum with a mean of about 4.72 per cent per annum or about 0.7 times the assumed mean of real GDP growth rate of 7 per cent. This will translate into a total compounded increase in crude oil demand between 53 per cent and 136 per cent by 2025. The average of the nine different scenarios in Table 9.1 is 91 per cent for 2011–25. For our normal and most likely case—real GDP growth at 7 per cent and crude oil price growth at 5.5 per cent—the crude oil demand would likely increase from 147 million tonnes in 2011 to 281 million tonnes in 2025, i.e., a growth rate of about 90 per cent from 2011 to 2025. Thus, according to our projections, the most likely increase in crude oil demand over 2011 to 2025 is about 90 per cent (Figure 9.4). It is clear from these calculations that the policy makers in the petroleum ministry must make plans for ensuring availability of supply for dealing with near doubling of demand in the next 15 years.

Table 9.2: Projections of India's crude oil demand for 2012–25 (million tonnes)

| Year | Crude oil demand projection at 6 per cent real GDP growth and at following growth rate of crude oil prices | | | Crude oil demand projection at 7 per cent real GDP growth and at following growth rate of crude oil prices | | | Crude oil demand projection at 8 per cent real GDP growth and at following different growth rate of crude oil prices | | |
|---|---|---|---|---|---|---|---|---|---|
| | 4% | 5.5% | 7% | 4% | 5.5% | 7% | 4% | 5.5% | 7% |
| 2011 | *The actual demand for crude oil in 2011 is about 147.24 million tonnes* | | | | | | | | |
| 2015 | 174.53 | 170.42 | 166.38 | 181.31 | 177.08 | 172.93 | 188.28 | 183.93 | 179.66 |
| 2020 | 215.85 | 204.59 | 193.85 | 235.18 | 223.02 | 211.43 | 256.03 | 242.92 | 230.40 |
| 2025 | 266.96 | 245.61 | 225.85 | 305.06 | 280.88 | 258.50 | 348.16 | 320.82 | 295.48 |
| | *Total increase in projected crude oil demand from 2011 to 2025* | | | | | | | | |
| | 81.31 | 66.81 | 53.39 | 107.19 | 90.77 | 75.56 | 136.46 | 117.89 | 100.68 |
| | *Annualized growth rate of projected crude oil demand over 2011–25* | | | | | | | | |
| | 4.34 | 3.72 | 3.10 | 5.34 | 4.72 | 4.10 | 6.34 | 5.72 | 5.10 |

*Source:* Author's calculations.

**Figure 9.3: Projections of India's crude oil demand for 2012–25**

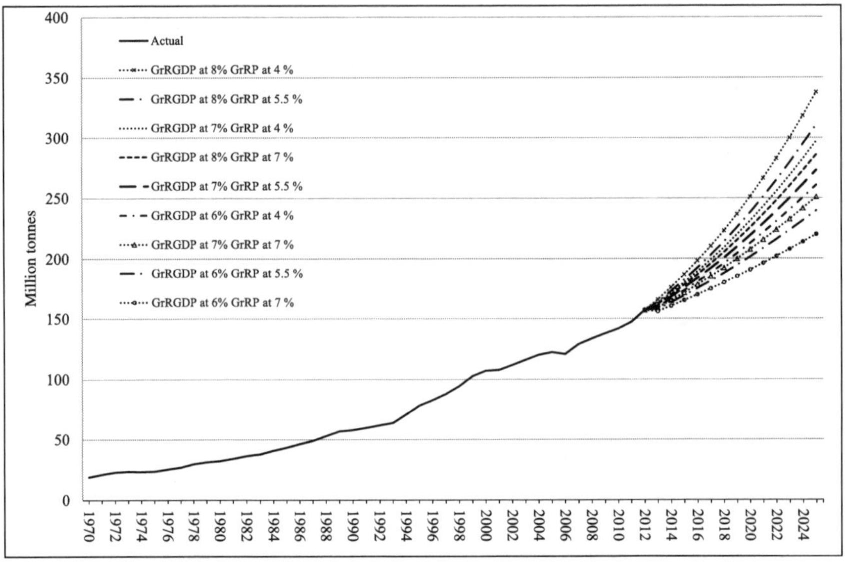

*Source*: Author's calculations

## *Projections for demand for diesel*

Similarly, demand for diesel up to 2025 can be projected using Equation (6) and using income and price elasticities from the estimated Equation (3). As discussed in the first section of Chapter 4, we consider three different scenarios of growth rate of real GDP at 6 per cent, 7 per cent, and 8 per cent. For diesel prices, we consider three scenarios with average annual growth rates of *real* diesel prices in rupees at 2 per cent, 3 per cent, and 4 per cent, respectively. Under these scenarios, we expect *real* diesel price (in 2011 rupees) to grow from about ₹40.91 in 2011 to around ₹55, ₹65, or ₹75 per litre by 2025 (Table 9.3, Figure 9.5). The annual growth rate of projected diesel demand is expected to be 3.84–7.02 per cent, with a mean of 5.43 per cent per annum, or about 0.8 times the assumed mean of real GDP growth rate of 7 per cent. This will translate into a 70–158 per cent total compounded increase in diesel oil demand by 2025. The average of the nine different scenarios is 111 per cent between 2011 and 2025 (Table 9.3, Figure 9.5). If we consider real GDP growth at 7 per cent and diesel price growth of 3 per cent as most likely, demand for diesel would increase from 67 million tonnes in 2011 to 133.56 million tonnes in 2025 or about 110 per cent (Figure 9.5).

**Figure 9.4: Projections for India's diesel demand for 2012–25**

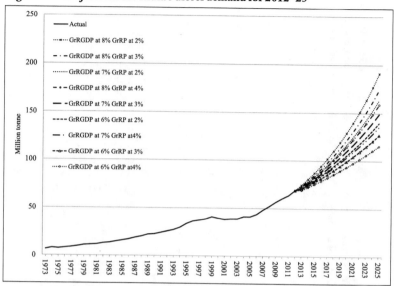

*Source*: Author's calculations.

**Figure 9.5: Total under-recoveries on diesel**

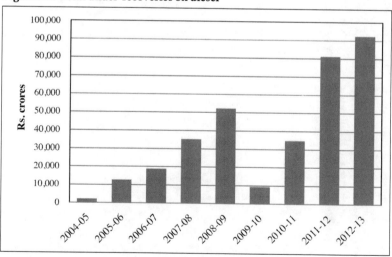

*Source*: PETSTAT, 2013, Ministry of Petroleum and Natural Gas, Government of India

Thus, although there is a large band of projections depending upon actual GDP growth and diesel price increases, it appears likely that diesel demand would increase substantially, probably around 110 per cent or so between 2011 and 2025.

Table 9.3: Projections for India's diesel demand for 2012–25 (million tonnes)

| Year | Diesel demand projection at 6 per cent real GDP growth rate and at following growth rate of diesel prices | | | Diesel demand projection at 7 per cent real GDP growth rate and at following growth rate of diesel prices | | | Diesel demand projection at 8 per cent real GDP growth rate and at following growth rate of diesel prices | | |
|---|---|---|---|---|---|---|---|---|---|
| | 2% | 3% | 4% | 2% | 3% | 4% | 2% | 3% | 4% |
| 2011 | *The actual demand for diesel in 2011 is about 63.70 million tonnes* | | | | | | | | |
| 2015 | 77.37 | 75.71 | 74.07 | 80.42 | 78.71 | 77.02 | 83.57 | 81.80 | 80.06 |
| 2020 | 98.66 | 93.94 | 89.42 | 107.63 | 102.53 | 97.65 | 117.31 | 111.81 | 106.53 |
| 2025 | 125.79 | 116.56 | 107.96 | 144.03 | 133.56 | 123.80 | 164.69 | 152.83 | 141.76 |
| *Total Increase in projected diesel demand from 2011–25* | 97.47 | 82.97 | 69.47 | 126.09 | 109.65 | 94.33 | 158.53 | 139.91 | 122.53 |
| *Annualized growth rate of projected diesel demand over 2011–25* | 4.98 | 4.41 | 3.84 | 6.0 | 5.43 | 4.86 | 7.02 | 6.45 | 5.88 |

*Source:* Author's calculations.

## *Evaluation of the predictive performance of our estimates*

Model selection depends not only on the goodness of fit of a model to the data, but also on the performance of out-of-sample forecasts. In this section, we check our effort by measuring the strength of the ARDL long run estimation model in forecasting the likely future demand for crude oil and diesel. To validate our model, we divide our dataset into two parts. First, from 1970 to 2006, we re-estimate our model based on Equations 2 and 3 and estimate new income and price elasticities of the crude oil and diesel for the above sub-period (Table 9.4). Using these sub-period elasticities, we forecast respective demands for the second sub-period of 2007–11 and then compare the forecast values with the actual values.

**Table 9.4: Long–run elasticities estimated for full and restricted period**

| Demand equation | Price elasticity | Income elasticity |
|---|:---:|:---:|
| | Full period (1970–2011) | |
| Crude oil | –0.41 | 1.00 |
| Diesel | –0.56 | 1.02 |
| | Restricted period (1970–2006) | |
| Crude oil | –0.34 | 1.00 |
| Diesel | –0.58 | 1.03 |

*Source:* Author's calculations.

We compute the predicted values in two ways: (a) predictions based on actual annual growth rate of GDP and prices of crude oil and diesel, respectively; and (b) predictions based on constant growth rate, by assuming normal scenario with annual average growth rate of GDP at 7 per cent, and for crude oil at 5.5 per cent, and diesel at 3 per cent. These values correspond to our 'normal' or most likely scenarios for both GDP growth and price increases (see the first section of Chapter 4). The predicted values of the two energy variables using these two ways are shown in columns 2 and 3 in Table 9.5. Comparing these two different ways of prediction helps us assure the accuracy of the forecast.

Table 9.5 shows that in the case of crude oil demand, the projected value based on actual and constant growth rate reveal upward and downward bias. However, the difference is within 5 per cent level in all years except in 2009. Similarly, in the case of diesel, the per cent difference between actual and predicted value is in a reasonable range of under 5 per cent. The forecast performance of the models for diesel is somewhat better than that for crude oil, because the government regulates prices for diesel, and its movement was much more gradual than that of the crude oil prices, which are determined freely in the international markets and are much more volatile. The above results show that the predictive performance of our models is reasonably good.

**Table 9.5: Predictive performance of our ARDL long run estimation models[1]**

| | Actual | Prediction based on actual growth rate of GDP & prices | Prediction based on 'normal scenario' growth rate of GDP & prices2 | per cent difference (1) & (2) | per cent difference (1) & (3) |
|---|---|---|---|---|---|
| | (1) | (2) | (3) | (4) | (5) |
| Crude oil demand (million tonnes) | | | | | |
| 2007 | 129.0 | 127.7 | 126.9 | 1.0 | 1.6 |
| 2008 | 133.6 | 137.4 | 135.6 | −2.9 | −1.5 |
| 2009 | 137.8 | 150.5 | 140.5 | −9.2 | −1.9 |
| 2010 | 141.8 | 146.3 | 144.9 | −3.2 | −2.2 |
| 2011 | 147.2 | 140.0 | 149.1 | 4.9 | −1.2 |
| Diesel demand (million tonnes) | | | | | |
| 2007 | 48.3 | 47.8 | 46.0 | 1.1 | 4.8 |
| 2008 | 52.3 | 53.8 | 51.0 | −2.9 | 2.5 |
| 2009 | 56.7 | 55.8 | 55.1 | 1.6 | 2.8 |
| 2010 | 60.5 | 61.4 | 59.8 | −1.6 | 1.1 |
| 2011 | 63.7 | 65.2 | 63.8 | −2.4 | −0.1 |

*Notes:*

[1] We estimated ARDL long run model for the period (1970–2006) and use it to forecast for the period (2007–11) using the long run income and price elasticities and actual or specified growth rates of GDP and petroleum prices.

[2] For the predictions based on 'normal scenario', we assume constant per annum growth rate of 7 per cent for GDP, 5.5 per cent for prices of crude oil and 3 per cent for prices of diesel (also see first section of Chapter 4).

*Source:* Author's calculations.

## IMPACT OF DIESEL SUBSIDY WITHDRAWAL

Diesel is about 30 per cent cheaper than petrol in India, as it was argued that diesel is used mostly in transportation, agriculture and allied sectors and lower diesel prices will help keep prices of goods of mass consumption low. However, the under-recovery or subsidy on diesel[4] has assumed gigantic proportions over the last few years and it amounted to as much as ₹93,000 crore or about $15 billion (Figure 9.5) or almost 20 per cent of the total budget deficit for 2012–13. Simultaneously, the fiscal deficit and the current account deficit have also become much larger. The fiscal deficit implies that the government is borrowing to spend more than it is collecting in revenues, which leads to excessive aggregate demand for goods, which in turn contributes to both higher inflation and higher current account deficits (by encouraging imports to meet the excess demand). India has been suffering from both these phenomena. These are, obviously, undesirable for the economy, and underlie the need to control the fiscal deficits.

Our estimations above of the long-run demand function for diesel found a price elasticity of –0.56 (Equation 3). This suggests that reducing subsidy on the price of diesel will reduce the demand for diesel significantly. If we consider phasing out this subsidy, the dealer price of diesel before taxes would rise by about ₹10.24. Adding the VAT and other minor charges, this would raise the price to the consumer by about ₹ 11.75 per litre, or about 22 per cent. Given the price elasticity of –0.56, the demand would decline by about 12.5 per cent or about 9 million metric tonnes on an expected demand of about 72 million tonnes over the next year. This is a substantial decrease in the demand of diesel, and worth about $7.2 billion at the approximate price of about $800 per tonne. Thus, increasing the price of diesel would reduce India's current account deficit by about $7.2 billion in *each subsequent year*. This is a substantial amount, considering that the expectation of a $70 billion current account deficit in 2013–14 was creating pressure on the rupee exchange rate. A price increase of ₹10.24 per litre on the remaining compressed consumption of about 63 million metric tonnes (or about 74 billion litres) of diesel will earn the government a revenue of ₹760 billion (₹76,000 crore or about $12 billion) *in each subsequent year* that is nearly sufficient to meet the entire cost of the National food security bill!

The NFSA guarantees 5 kg of food grains per month per eligible person at a fixed per kilogram price of ₹3 for rice, ₹2 for wheat, and ₹1 for coarse cereals. Pregnant women, lactating mothers, and children aged between 6 months and 14 years are eligible for free daily meals. The total annual cost is officially estimated at ₹125,000 crore, but this is not the *additional* cost; since the government was already incurring a cost of ₹75, 000 crore on the public distribution system (PDS)

---

[4] Part of the under-recovery on diesel (40 per cent currently) is not subsidised by the government but passed on to the up-stream companies (ONGC, Oil India etc). We ignore this issue here since the up-stream companies' contribution can be alternately viewed as an equivalent royalty payment to the government that would remain at comparable level even if the diesel subsidy was withdrawn.

and other allied schemes (including mid- day meals for school-children) in the previous financial year (2012–13), the *additional* burden on the budget will be only about ₹50,000 crore per year. Thus, the additional revenue of ₹76,000 crore a year from phasing out the diesel subsidy alone is more than sufficient to meet all additional costs of the NFSA.

On the other hand, a one shot increase in diesel prices would add to inflationary pressure immediately; since diesel has a weight of about 5 per cent in the WPI, a one-time increase of 25 per cent in diesel prices would cause inflation to increase by almost 1.25 per cent. The two opposing pressures on inflation can be expected to cancel out over about 1–2 years. Thus, it turns out that the long-held argument that diesel subsidy controls inflation is only true for the immediate short run, but not if we consider a longer period of one or two years. However, even the short run spurt in inflation can be avoided by increasing the diesel prices slowly by about ₹1 per month or so, rather than a large one time increase in its price. Thus, a gradual increase in diesel prices to eliminate the diesel subsidy over a year or so is probably the optimum way to proceed.

## CONCLUSIONS

This chapter empirically estimated long-run demand relations for crude oil and diesel for India using the ARDL co-integration procedure and data from 1970 to 2011 and found long-run income elasticity of about 1 for crude oil and diesel. Thus, demand for petroleum seems to be growing about proportionately to real GDP, because GDP growth is leading to greater output of goods and services, which require more petroleum products for both production and transportation. Income levels are rising, and more people are buying automobiles, motorcycles, etc., for personal transportation, which in turn increases the demand for diesel and petrol and, thence, crude oil. Further, the price elasticity of petroleum products was found negative and statistically significant in all the models. The values of long-run price elasticities were found to be −0.41 and −0.56 for crude oil and diesel respectively, which show that demand declines moderately with rising petroleum prices.

Using the estimated long run elasticities, we projected the demand for crude oil and diesel until 2025 for three possible scenarios of GDP growth rates and oil price growth rates, based partly on past trends, etc. For the normal scenario of 7 per cent real GDP growth rate and 5.5 per cent growth rate of real crude oil price, crude oil demand in India would increase at the rate of about 4.72 per cent annually, which means a total increase of about 90 per cent between 2011 and 2025. Similarly, the demand for diesel would increase by about 5.43 per cent annually or by a total of 110 per cent between 2011 and 2025 for the normal scenario of

7 per cent real GDP growth rate and 3 per cent growth rate in real diesel price.

Thus, India has to brace not only for increasing crude oil demand, but also for possible increases in crude oil prices. For example, if India's crude oil demand increases by about 90 per cent by 2025 and crude oil price too increase by 50 per cent to 100 per cent by 2025, India's crude oil import bill (which stood at about $155 billion in 2011–12) would increase three or four times (i.e., to about $450 to $600 billion) by the year 2025. Considering that India's total exports were only $305 billion in 2011–12, this is a worrisome scenario and requires urgent action.

Our calculations also show that diesel has a price elasticity of 0.56, it implies that withdrawing the current subsidy of about ₹10 on every litre of diesel will reduce diesel demand by about 9 million metric tonnes and reduce the current account deficit by $7 billion (about 10 per cent of the deficit of $70 billion expected in 2013–14) *every year*. It will also reduce the fiscal deficit by ₹76,000 crore ($12 billion) *every year*, which is more than sufficient to meet the entire *additional* cost of the NFSA over the previous cost of the PDS. But caution must be exercised in withdrawing the subsidy on diesel (and cooking gas and kerosene), as a substantial one-time increase in the price of diesel could easily re-ignite inflationary pressures, and the consequent monetary tightening could further delay growth recovery in the economy, which would be very undesirable. On the other hand, if the decision to increase the diesel price is postponed any further, the country's fiscal balance will be destabilised and there will be severe negative consequences, including a rating downgrade that will dry up foreign investments. Therefore, the only prudent option is to introduce a small increase of about one rupee per month in the price of diesel (and comparable increases in other petroleum products), which is unlikely to materially increase the inflation rate while providing the same benefits to the current account and fiscal deficits, albeit with some lag.

## REFERENCES

Adams, F. G., and Y. Shachmurove. 2008. 'Modeling and Forecasting Energy Consumption in China: Implications for Chinese Energy Demand and Imports in 2020'. *Energy Econ.*, 30(3): 1263–78.

Altinay, G. 2007. 'Short-run and Long-run Elasticities of Import Demand for Crude Oil in Turkey.' *Energy Policy*, 35(11): 5829–35.

Chemin, Elodie Sentenac. 2012. 'Is the Price Effect of Fuel Consumption Symmetric? Some Evidence From An Empirical Study.' *Energy Policy*, 41(C): 59–65.

Ghosh, S. 2006. 'Future Demand of Petroleum Products in India.' *Energy Policy*, 34(15): 2032–37.

———. 2009. 'Import Demand of Crude Oil and Economic Growth: Evidence From

India.' *Energy Policy*, 37(2): 699–702.

——— 2010. 'High Speed Diesel Consumption and Economic Growth in India.' *Energy*, 35(4): 1794–98.

Global Economic Monitor, 2013. *The World Bank*. http://data.worldbank.org/data-catalog/global-economic-monitor

Goldar, B., and H. Mukhopadhyay. 1990. 'India's Petroleum Imports: An Econometric Analysis.' *Economic Political Weekly*, 25(42/43): 2373–77.

International Energy Agency. 2008. World Energy Statistics. France. http://www.iea.org/textbase/nppdf/free/2008/key_stats_2008.pdf.

International Energy Agency. 2009. World Energy Statistics. France.

Johansen, S., and K. Juselius. 1990. 'Maximum Likelihood Estimation and Inference on Cointegration – with Applications to the Demand for Money.' *Oxford Bulletin of Economics and Statistics*, 52(2): 169–210.

Kumar, U., and V.K. Jain. 2010. 'Timer series models (Grey-Markov, Grey Model with Rolling Mechanism and Singular Spectrum Analysis) to Forecast Energy Consumption in India.' *Energy*, 35, 1709–16.

Parikh, J., P. Purohit, and P. Maitra. 2007. 'Demand Projections of Petroleum Products and Natural Gas in India.' *Energy*, 32, 1827–37.

Pesaran, M. H, Y. Shin, and R.J. Smith. 2001. 'Bounds Testing Approaches to The Analysis of Level Relationships.' *J. Applied Econometrics*, 16, 289–326.

——— 1999. 'Bounds Testing Approaches to the Analysis of Long-run Relationships.' *Cambridge Working Papers in Economics*, No. 9907, Faculty of Economics, University of Cambridge.

Ramanathan, R. 1999. 'Short- and Long-run Elasticities of Petrol Demand in India: An Empirical Analysis Using Co-integration Techniques.' *Energy Econ*, 21(4): 321–30.

Rao, R., D. Parikh, and K. Jyoti. 1996. 'Forecast and Analysis of Demand for Petroleum Products in India.' *Energy Policy*, 24(6): 583–92.

Sa'ad, S. 2009. 'An Empirical Analysis of Petroleum Demand for Indonesia: An Application of the Cointegration Approach.' *Energy Policy*, 37(11): 4391–96.

Suganthi, L. and Samuel, A. Anand. 2012. 'Energy Models for Demand Forecasting – A Review.' *Renewable and Sustainable Energy Reviews*. 16, 1223–40.

# 10

# Social and Physical Infrastructure in India: Constraints to Rapid Growth

## Pradeep Agrawal

## INTRODUCTION

A country's level of human and economic development is closely related to its levels of achievement in physical and social infrastructure. While physical infrastructure is an important determinant of domestic production, good social infrastructure is vital for human development as well as economic progress through better educated, better skilled and healthier citizens.

Education and health are the main constituents of social infrastructure. Many studies document the contribution of education and health to economic development in which they are considered investments in human capital comparable to physical means of production, such as factories and machines. The economic attainments of Europe, North America, Japan and East Asia are inconceivable without their attainments in human capital; hence, the importance of social infrastructure. Therefore, it can be surmised that investment in human capital through education, training, health and medical facilities yields additional output and economic returns. Economic growth theory also sees human capital as an important source of economic growth. Further, to achieve rapid economic growth, it is essential that the population should be well-educated and trained to be able to work effectively. It is also essential for reducing poverty. No amount of welfare measures can help a poor illiterate person the way education can by enabling him to become more productive and skilled. Therefore, effective education for the masses is crucial for reducing poverty and sustaining high rates of economic growth over long periods by providing a well-skilled labour force. The role of physical infrastructure in promoting economic development has been well-documented in the literature [Estache (2006), Sahoo and Dash (2008, 2009)]. Physical infrastructure not only contributes to enhance productivity, but it also assists in the realization of the potential ability of human capital and creates situations in which the potential can fully function. It also directly and indirectly contributes towards improving the quality and safety of people's lives. Within the scope of infrastructure, roads, railways, air transportation, seaports, electric power and telecommunications and information technology are often used as services and intermediate goods essential for the productive processes of the manufacturing, agriculture and services sectors.

In spite of some improvements in infrastructure in recent years, India still ranks 89th in basic infrastructure as per the Global Competition Report 2011–12. This indicates poor development compared to other countries of the world. The poor state of infrastructure, stretched to limits by the growing population and increasing regional and rural–urban disparities, implies that major improvement in physical and social infrastructure is absolutely essential to sustain further progress and high rate of economic growth. To meet this need for infrastructure improvement, the Government of India raised the investment in infrastructure from 4.7 per cent of GDP to around 7.5–8 per cent of GDP in the Eleventh Five Year Plan, and further plans to double the investment in infrastructure from INR 20.5 trillion to INR 40.9 trillion during the Twelfth Plan period, raising the share of infrastructure investment in GDP to more than 10 per cent. If these infrastructure investment plans are properly implemented; they can propel India's economic growth to a higher trajectory.

Given the importance of infrastructure in the economy, we compare the levels of development of the social and physical infrastructure in India with those in other major emerging countries as well as the developed countries (taken as a benchmark for achievement). We, then, try to identify challenges and shortcomings in key social and physical infrastructure sub-segments, including education, health, transportation, electricity, and telecommunication and information technology. We, next, discuss some possible ways in which some of these challenges can be addressed to help India achieve its infrastructure goals.

## CHALLENGES IN SOCIAL INFRASTRUCTURE

Endogenous growth theory argues that both poor physical infrastructure and human capital can constrain economic growth (see Romer 1992). Social infrastructure, such as education and health, is essential to promote better utilization of human resources and physical infrastructure, thereby improving economic growth and quality of life (Hall and Jones 1999; De and Ghosh 2003). For example, Hall and Jones (1999) argue that international differences in levels of output per worker are determined by differences in human capital and in physical and social infrastructure. Wagstaff (2002) notes that up to 1.7 per cent of annual economic growth in East Asia between 1965 and 1990 can be attributed to massive improvements in public education and health. Improvement in human capital could be critical for India in sustaining its service-led growth, which depends mainly on the availability of skilled manpower. Given this backdrop, there have been some efforts in recent years to improve both physical and social infrastructure facilities in India. To assess the impact of the government's efforts on social infrastructure, we discuss various indicators pertaining to education and health in the next two subsections and compares India's performance with that of other major emerging countries. Then, we try to point out challenges and shortcomings in these efforts and suggest some solutions that can enhance education and health levels in India.

## *The state of education infrastructure in India*

India has a vast population of young people. Even after 66 years of independence, a surprisingly large proportion of our youngsters are not getting sufficient education or vocational training. On the one hand, this keeps a large number of them in poverty and misery for lack of productive skills; on the other hand, it reduces the rate of economic growth because of the lack of enough sufficiently skilled workers in many areas, which reduces our international competitiveness. Thus, India requires strong educational infrastructure to keep pace with the growing economy and provide it with quality manpower. Education can accelerate economic growth and investment and is a key indicator to quality of life and the Human Development Index (HDI).

Over the past decade or so, both central and state governments have implemented new initiatives and increased spending to encourage greater enrolment and attendance at the school level. This has led to some improvement. Despite this, the performance of the education sector has been woefully inadequate. In April 2010, the Right to Education (RTE) Act was passed. With its implementation, the universalization of primary (standards one to eight) education was given new impetus. The RTE Act makes education a fundamental right of every child between the ages of 6 and 14 and specifies minimum norms in elementary schools. It requires all private schools to reserve 25 per cent of seats for poor children (to be reimbursed by the state). It also prohibits donation or capitation fees. The RTE Act requires surveys that will monitor all neighbourhood, identify children requiring education and set up facilities for providing it.

In higher education too, there is need to implement major reforms as rising affluence and aspirations spur strong demand for education at all levels and the traditional dominance of the public sector as a provider of education recedes. Now, the dual challenge is to build upon the progress made in improving participation and try to improve the quality of education, which remains poor. To meet these objectives, the reform momentum needs to be maintained and broadened, given especially the pace of development in the Indian economy, the changing needs of households and businesses, and the considerable lags between changes in education policies and outcomes.

Table 10.1 provides data on education sector characteristics measured by enrolment, literacy rate, pupil–teacher ratio, public spending, etc., to take stock of the current situation in India and compare it with international standards and achievements. First, we look at adult literacy rates. Even in 2011, India's adult literacy rate (only 63 per cent) was way behind that of China, East Asia and BRCS countries (about 94 per cent) and developed countries (98 per cent). India's literacy rate gap with China and East Asia has stayed nearly the same for the last 10 years. The gap is narrower among the youth but still substantial–81 per cent for India but about 99 per cent for the rest of the emerging and developed countries. In addition to literacy rate, average years of schooling per adult is an important and commonly used indicator to measure educational attainment; it was only 4.4 years in India, about half of the average for other emerging countries (China at 7.5, East Asia at 8.5 and BRCS countries averaging 8.8 years) and even less than half of the developed countries (about 10.7 years of schooling per adult on average).

These poor outcomes are partly due to low levels of public expenditure on education and partly due to weak institutions and governance. Thus, public expenditure on education as a fraction of GDP was again lower at 3.3 per cent in India as compared to 4.3 per cent in East Asia and about 5.3 per cent in BRCS and developed countries. Similarly, expenditure per student as a percentage of GDP per capita in primary and secondary education was significantly lower in India at 7 per cent and 14 per cent but many times higher in BRCS and developed countries (though not in China). However, the expenditure on students in the tertiary sector is significantly higher in India than in East Asia, BRCS countries and even developed countries (with China even higher than India). This seems to be the result of continuing practically free education even at the tertiary level in India and China while the costs go up sharply. It, however, seems a misplaced subsidy since the benefit goes largely to the middle and upper classes rather than the poor. Instead, the urgent need in India is to expand the tertiary education opportunities (even if it means raising its costs to some extent) and to improve the institutional structure to better reward excellence, which seems to be taking a back seat.

Despite the public expenditure not increasing much as a proportion of GDP, it has increased in real terms as the real GDP has more than doubled over the past decade and there have been some efforts at increasing enrolment and access to education. There has also been a court-mandated free mid-day meal for children in elementary schools (standards 1 to 8). These have contributed to improving enrolment rates in elementary education, which have improved significantly; the gross enrolment ratio (number of students as share of all children of the relevant age group) grew from 94 per cent in 2001 to 112 per cent in 2011 (the number can exceed 100 per cent due to the presence of older children or adults in lower classes). This number looks large, and is so – in comparison with all the other groups of countries – but the transition has been very slow. For example, the gross primary enrolment rate in China has exceeded 100 per cent since 1985, but India reached that figure only in 2000.

The enrolment rate in secondary education (standards 9 to 12) was about 45 per cent for India in 2000 and has increased since then, but was still only around 63.2 per cent in 2011 This compares to average figures of about 85 per cent for other emerging countries and 104 per cent for developed countries. The tertiary enrolment rate has increased from 9 per cent in 2000 to 18 per cent in 2011. This compares to average figures of about 37 per cent for other emerging countries and 68 per cent for developed countries. Thus, while there has been some progress in India over the past decade, more needs to be done as enrolment at the secondary and tertiary level remains low boy international standards, particularly the latter.

The teaching staff represents a vital aspect of education. The pupil–teacher ratio (PTR) is one of the critical indicators of education and may provide insight to measure its quality. The table reveals that the PTR is quite low at the primary and middle levels – figuring at 30.2 and 25.3, respectively – about twice that of China and other groups of countries, and needs improvement. Thus, it is imperative to improve PTR and to strengthen the institutional framework of the schools and colleges to enhance quality of education and to make human resources globally competitive.

Growth in private institutions has been significant during the Eleventh Plan period, with 98 private state universities, 13 private deemed universities, 6,335 private colleges and 2,321 private diploma institutions being set up during this period. In 2012, 28.3 per cent of all primary students (age group 6–14 years) enrolled in schools attended private schools, in comparison to 18.7 per cent in 2006. Most institutions of secondary and higher education are driven by the private sector; private institutions make up 60 per cent of all secondary schools in 2010–11, and 63 per cent of all higher education institutes with 52 per cent of the share of students in 2010. The privatization of education sector is adding to the financial burden on the overburdened lower and middle income families.

However, in spite of the significant progress made during the past few years, India's education sector is still plagued with several challenges, e.g., its relatively low GER, inequitable access to higher education by community, gender and geography and lack of high-quality research and education institutions, resulting in sub-optimal outcomes. Another serious shortcoming has been the failure to ensure good quality elementary education. While all academic facilities in the school such as library, teaching; learning material, and so on, have a significant influence on the quality dimension, there is very limited systematic and specialized data on how much children learn in schools. However, studies indicate that states

**Table 10.1: India and the world comparison of the access to and quality of education**

| Indicators | Year | India | China | East Asia | BRCS | Developed Countries |
|---|---|---|---|---|---|---|
| Literacy rate, adult total (% of people ages 15 and above) | 2010–11 | 62.8 | 94.3 | 94.9 | 93.2 | 98.3 |
| Literacy rate, youth total (% of people ages 15–24) | 2010–11 | 81.1 | 99.4 | 98.5 | 98.6 | 99.5 |
| School enrolment, primary (% gross) | 2010–11 | 112 | 111.2 | 104.5 | 112.5 | 104.7 |
| School enrolment, secondary (% gross) | 2010–11 | 63.2 | 81.4 | 82.0 | 92.4 | 104.1 |
| School enrolment, tertiary (% gross) | 2010–11 | 17.9 | 26.8 | 49.0 | 35.9 | 67.7 |
| *Average years of schooling* | 2010–11 | 4.4 | 7.5 | 8.5 | 8.8 | 10.7 |
| Public spending on education, total (% of GDP) | 2010–11 | 3.3 | – | 4.3 | 5.3 | 5.2 |
| Public expenditure per student, primary (% of GDP per capita) | 2010–11 | 7.3 | 6.0 | 15.9 | 53.2 | 21.4 |
| Public expenditure per student, secondary (% of GDP per capita) | 2010–11 | 13.8 | 11.5 | 17.3 | 45.7 | 26.9 |
| Public expenditure per student, tertiary (% of GDP per capita) | 2010–11 | 69.8 | 90.0 | 23.3 | 47.7 | 26.3 |
| Pupil-teacher ratio, primary | 2010–11 | 30.2 | 16.8 | 19.4 | 21.7 | 15.8 |
| Pupil-teacher ratio, secondary | 2010–11 | 25.3 | 15.2 | 20.2 | 16.3 | 13.3 |
| Research and development expenditure (% of GDP) | 2010–11 | 0.8 | 1.7 | 0.95 | 1.34 | 2.6 |
| Researchers in R&D (per million people) | 2010–11 | 136 | 863.0 | 1265.8 | 1263.0 | 4269 |

*Source:* World Development Indicators, 2012

are rushing to achieve enrolment targets but providing substandard education in the process. The results of a recent effort to assess learning achievements facilitated by

Pratham – a non-governmental organization – highlight the poor state of affairs. In Annual Survey of Education Report (ASER) – Rural, 2012, children were assessed on three bases – reading and comprehension ability in native language and in English and ability in basic arithmetic (Table 10.2). Across rural India, the percentage of children who could read standard 2 books was only 10 per cent of standard 2 students, 47 per cent of standard 5 students and only 76 per cent of standard 8 students. As many as 51.1 per cent children enrolled in standard 5 could not read even simple English words, and as many as 77.5 per cent could not read simple English sentences. Among all children enrolled in standard 8, 53 per cent could not read simple English sentences. Coming to mathematics, 55.6 per cent of standard 2 students could not even recognize two-digit numbers (10–99), and 75.2 per cent of standard 5 and as many as 51.9 per cent of even standard 8 students could not do simple division problems.

**Table 10.2: Assessment of children's reading and numeric skills in rural India**

| Standard | Cannot read words in native language | Cannot read standard two text | Cannot read simple words in English | Cannot read easy sentences in English | Cannot recognize numbers 10–99 | Cannot divide |
|---|---|---|---|---|---|---|
| 2 | 43.8 | 89.9 | 81.1 | 93.8 | 55.6 | 97.2 |
| 5 | 83.4 | 53.2 | 51.2 | 77.5 | 17.9 | 75.2 |
| 8 | 94.3 | 23.6 | 26.7 | 53 | 6.2 | 51.9 |

*Source*: Pratham, Annual Survey of Education Report (ASER), 2012

Not only is the quality of education for the masses shockingly bad, it is getting worse over time. Comparing the cohort of children who were in government schools in standard 5 in 2011 with the cohort in standard 5 in 2012, there is evidence of a drop of more than 10 per cent in almost all states in the ability to do basic subtraction. The proportion of all children enrolled in standard 5, who could not do division problems, has increased from 63.8 per cent in 2010 to 72.4 per cent in 2011 and further to 75.2 per cent in 2012. In 2010 nationally, 46.3 per cent of all children in standard 5 could not read a standard 2 level text on their own language. This proportion increased to 51.8 per cent in 2011 and further to 53.2 per cent in 2012.

This reflects, among other things, teachers' inability to explain even simple concepts that students understand. It is also reported that school dropout rates are highest in early grades. This indicates the need for dramatically improving the teaching–learning methods adapted in standards 1 to 5 so that students attain at least basic reading and numeric skills failing which ensuring standards in higher grades becomes difficult.

Further, the quality of learning is equally bad across all levels of the education system. All surveys unanimously point to 'extremely poor learning outcomes across-the-board. Urban schools are not significantly better than rural schools and the vast majority of private schools are not much better than government schools. While about half the primary school students are three classes below the levels they ought to be in reading and even more in arithmetic. These appalling outcomes continue or are even exacerbated at the secondary and higher levels. High school children do not have basic conceptual understanding. Students entering the workforce have very low employability. Clearly, raising the quality of education is the biggest challenge in our educational system. An urgent action is needed in this regard, including redesigning the basic institutional framework of schools and colleges and creating greater accountability.

## Higher education

The emphasis in the past decade was on enhancing supply and increasing access to higher education. Consequently, the Indian higher education witnessed particularly high growth in the last decade, with the number of institutions growing at 9 per cent per annum and the enrolment of students growing at 10.8 per cent per annum. Table 10.3 provides detailed data on the expansion of higher education in India over 2000–12. The GER for higher education (both degree and diploma programmes) as a percentage of the population in the eligible age cohort of 18–23 years has increased from 13.1 per cent in 2007–08 to 18 per cent in 2011–12. Even though our higher education system is one of the largest in the world, the GER is far below the average for emerging and developed economies. Increased enrolments in the Eleventh Plan have enabled Indian higher education to cross the threshold of 15 per cent GER, moving the country from an 'elite' towards a 'mass' higher education system. Despite this growth, the unmet demand for access to higher education remains significant, indicating that access to higher education needs further expansion. Even though the national level GER is 20 per cent, there are wide inter-state variations. Delhi, Chandigarh and Puducherry, which attract a large number of students from outside their states, have GERs exceeding 25 per cent, while states like Bihar, Jharkhand, Assam, Rajasthan, Orissa and West Bengal have significantly lower GERs. This suggests a need for state-specific strategies in addressing issues of expansion of higher education during the Twelfth Plan period.

When we look at other characteristics of the higher education system, we find that it lacks on other fronts as well. For example, the Planning Commission estimates faculty shortages of about 40 per cent in state universities and 35 per cent in central universities, respectively. It also faces lower enrolment of female students over male students and lower enrolment of lower caste, Muslim, scheduled caste and scheduled tribe students over those from the general categories.

**Table 10.3: Expansion in higher education in India, 2000–12**

|  | 2000–01 | 2006–07 | 2011–12 |
|---|---|---|---|
| Number of Universities | 256 | 387 | 659 |
| Number of Colleges | 12,086 | 21,170 | 33,023 |
| Student Enrolment Colleges/Universities (in million) | 8.4 | 16.6 | 25.9 |
| GER (Gross Enrolment Ratio) of Colleges and Universities (%) | 10 | 12.3 | 17.9 |
| Number of Distance Education Institutions | 74 | 144 | 197 |
| Student Enrolment in Distance Education (in million) | 1.38 | 2.74 | 4.2 |

The quality of higher education is also a major issue. Barring a few Indian institutes of technology, which are ranked 50th to 100th worldwide in various rankings, no Indian university or institute is listed among the top 200 universities/institutions in the world. Around 62 per cent of universities and 90 per cent of colleges in India were average or below average in 2010 on the basis of their NAAC accreditation. India's relative citation impact is as low as half the world average. Part of the problem lies in the weak institutional structure and in poor evaluation and promotion procedures where excellence in teaching or research does not get rewarded sufficiently and the teaching staff does not have much stake in teaching outcomes or student performance.

Despite the significant progress made during the past few years, India's higher education sector is still plagued with several challenges, e.g., its relatively low GER, inequitable access to higher education by community, gender and geography, and lack of high-quality research and education institutions, resulting in sub-optimal outcomes.

## Vocational education and training (VET)

Vocational education and training (VET) consists of practical courses through which one gains skills and experience directly linked to a career and employment opportunities. These training courses are parallel to other conventional courses of study (like B.Sc., M.Sc., etc) and give students some work-related experience, which many employers look for. However, considering the availability of manpower, high unemployment rates and need to create more employment opportunities, VET (except in computer-related courses) is surprisingly underdeveloped in India.

Vocational training institutions can be categorized into (a) government, (b) local body, (c) private aided, (d) private unaided and (e) not known. According to an NSSO report (2009–10), only 10 per cent of persons aged 15–29 years received vocational training, only 2 per cent of them received formal training, and only 3 per cent of those formally trained are employed. Computer-related training is most sought after. Vocational training is imparted mainly by (a) public Industrial Training Institutes (ITIs) and (b) privately owned Industrial Training Centres (ITCs).

According to the Planning Commission Report for the Eleventh Five Year Plan, there are about 5,114 ITIs imparting training in 57 engineering and 50 non-engineering trades. Of these, 1,896 are state-government-run ITIs, while 3,218 are private. The total seating capacity in these ITIs is a mere 7.42 lakh (4 lakh seats in government ITIs and the remaining 3.42 lakh in private ITCs). However, only 20 per cent of formal vocational training is received from ITI/ITCs.

Though there is a growing demand for vocationally trained workers, the segment per se has not really picked up in India because of a variety of reasons. One is that vocational education and training for manual or industrial jobs were perceived as low paying and meant for the lower strata of society. Good trainers have always been an issue with vocational education in India. Because of societal pressures, the segment has failed to attract good mentors. The salaries of teachers in VET have been at the lower end of the spectrum and this may have also discouraged some teachers.

In some states, the course curriculum has not been updated for 20 or more years, so even if students have completed VET qualifications, they may not be employable in modern industry. Of the trained candidates, the labour market outcomes as seen from placement/absorption rates are reportedly very low, perhaps due to the outdated curriculum of VET courses.

There is an urgent need to expand vocational training in India in a big way and to make it more oriented to current labour market needs. As the Indian economy becomes knowledge-based, new and revised courses that fulfil the requirement of modern industries become all the more imperative. Thus, the private sector, which is more adaptable in this respect, should be allowed and supported to play a larger role. Public–private partnership can also be a good option in this sector. In addition to the degree and diploma programmes in vocational courses, we also need shorter and more informal training facilities. In fact lower level vocational training in fields like carpentry, masonry, plumbing, electrician, electrical and electronic goods repairs, basic computer related training, etc., could easily be offered in schools (perhaps after normal school hours and extended to non-students alike) to all those with basic education as per the course requirement. This may be particularly suitable for rural areas and smaller towns where the share of students being able to go to degree colleges is limited and could create a lot of semi-skilled manpower at very low cost.

### Key challenges in education

Investment in public education still limited

The government of India spends far less on education than other emerging and developed countries and less than even its own assessment calls. For example, the Central Advisory Board on Education (reconstituted by the Government of India in 2004) has consistently argued that average annual expenditure on education from the public exchequer has to be in the range of 6 per cent of GDP, at least half of which should be for primary and secondary schools.

Elementary education still not universal

While close to 93 per cent (NER) children in the 6–11 age group are formally enrolled in primary schools, nearly 40 per cent drop out at the primary stage. About 38.41 per cent boys and 51.88 per cent girls in the 6–14 age group are not attending school. The enrolment ratios of scheduled castes and tribes (SC, ST) and Muslim children still remain far lower than the national average, even more so for girls.

The most socially disadvantaged in most rural areas have been allocated single-teacher, single classroom Education Guarantee Scheme (EGS) kind of schools where dysfunctional education including frequent teacher absenteeism and poor infrastructure discourages students and leads to large share of dropouts.

Further, there are still significant costs that the poor have to bear even in government schools where the tuition fee is generally not charged. Families have to still pay for uniforms, stationery, transport, etc. Poor school infrastructure, lack of things like toilets, safe drinking water in the schools, poorly paid teachers burdened with multiple tasks and little accountability and hardly any stakes in the system, frequent teacher absenteeism, and generally poor level of governance add to the misery of the children and to high dropouts.

Thus, the data in Table 10.4 shows that while the net enrolment ratio (NER) in primary (standard 1–5) was about 93 per cent, it dropped sharply to 62 per cent in upper primary, even in 2011. Nonetheless the table also gives hope for the future since the NER for upper primary has increased considerably from 48 per cent in 2006–07 to 62 per cent in 2010–11, and an additional 167,000 schools have been established with additional 590,000 teachers have been employed in government-run schools over the same period. We should certainly aim for near universal education up to standard 8, and then standard 10.

**Table 10.4: Progress in Net Enrolment Ratio (NER) in elementary education**

|  |  | 2006–07 | 2009–10 | 2010–11 |
|---|---|---|---|---|
| NER: Primary (standard 1–5) | (in %) | 93 | 94 | 93 |
| NER: Upper primary (standard 6–8) | (in%) | 48.4 | 58.3 | 61.8 |
| No. of schools | (in thousands) | 1,195 | 1,304 | 1,362 |
| Teachers in govt. school | (in thousands) | 3.600 | 3.900 | 4.190 |

*Source*: UNESCO, http://www.uis.unesco.org/DataCentre and Ministry of Human Resource Development, GoI

Education quality remains low

Notwithstanding the rapid gains in enrolment and attendance, average levels of educational attainment and basic skill acquisition, including reading, writing and basic arithmetic, remain very low by international standards. Overtime, the stock of educated workers will rise. However, cognitive skill formation, rather than education attainment per se, is what matters the most for both the earnings potential of the individual as well as their contribution to economic growth at the aggregate level (Handshake and Woessmann, 2008). The extent to which increases in participation translate into improvements in skills and ultimately better social and economic outcomes will depend heavily on the quality of education provided. As participation rates continue to rise, the priority will need to shift to focus on learning outcomes of students.

To summarize, while the central and state governments have been devoting substantial funds and public effort towards provision of education, these efforts have not been adequate nor have they yielded the desired results. The aspects of policy failure could be categorized as follows:

(a) Attention to the challenges posed by the rapidly increasing population has been inadequate.
(b) Delivery mechanisms are poorly designed.
(c) Implementation of policies and schemes is poor.
(d) Appropriate institutional mechanisms to bridge need gaps are absent.
(e) Institutions do not appear to be adequately answerable for the failure of the delivery system.

*Overcoming the challenges in education*

Listed below are some of the points which can help in overcoming the challenges faced in education.

## Improvement in infrastructure and institutions

Improvements are not possible if the quality of physical infrastructure is poor, but they are even more unlikely if institutions are weak. Studies reveal that the public infrastructure for both education and healthcare in India is of poor quality and very inadequate to meet the full demand. Therefore, improvements can be brought about by expanding facilities and improving the delivery mechanism.

## Offer school health programmes

Along with mid-day meals, health programmes should also be introduced in schools to cover basic healthcare including de-worming and iron supplementation. The World Health Organization (WHO) has identified worm infections as the greatest cause of disease among 5–14-year-old children, and programmes ensuring health of students increase school attendance and raise scores on tests of cognition or school achievement.

## Educating girls and mothers

Educating girls and mothers leads to sustained increases in education attainment from one generation to the next. It can change a society in which not sending one's children to school are socially acceptable into one in which the expectation is that every child completes school. Multiple studies find that a mother's level of education has a strong positive on their children's enrolment. The effect on daughters' enrolment is stronger than the effect on sons' enrolment, and it is significantly greater than the effect of fathers' education on children.

Increasing girls' educational attainment is essential to fulfilling education's potential for positive social transformation. Given the barriers to girl's education specific interventions are needed to make schools more accessible and secure for them. Providing female teachers for girls, decreasing the distance to school and provision of toilet in the school may address some security concerns.

## Address special needs

It is also important to go beyond averages and disaggregate results by region, gender, ethnic group and socioeconomic status to identify weaknesses within a particular segment of the population. This will help in formulating directed policies aiming to bring improvement in the identified segments such as the Davits, the Muslims, people with disabilities, etc.

## Evaluate learning outcomes

The ability to measure what the education sector produces – that is, learning outcomes – is weak. Instead, the focus is typically on the number of children in seats or even children's names on class rosters. Indian education system should be subjected to full international learning assessment which provides international comparability. We will be able to improve by comparing ourselves with better countries and reviewing the fields where we lack.

Create better institutional mechanism for more effective delivery

The institutional mechanism does not seem to be functioning well and needs major overhauling and improvement. Teachers and higher management officers have to be made more accountable for actual delivery and students' performance.

Challenges in higher education

Higher education sector also needs improved management and a major expansion in capacity by establishing new colleges and universities. Improve quality in existing colleges by increasing salaries, promoting research and encouraging private participation. Ensure access for all deserving students through scholarships and promote distance education. Reform in professional education is crucial in building a knowledge society. Therefore, reform in governance, accreditation mechanisms and curriculum revisions should be done to promote quality. Colleges should provide credit and non-credit courses in the form of employment-oriented programmes.

*The state of healthcare infrastructure in India*

Despite some improvements over the last decade or so, India's healthcare infrastructure is woefully inadequate and has not kept pace with the country's requirements. While India has several centres of excellence in healthcare delivery, these facilities are limited in their ability to drive healthcare standards because of the poor condition of the infrastructure in the vast majority of the country. This is reflected in the numbers of physicians per 1,000 persons which has hardly risen from 2,000 and remains rather low at only 0.65 compared to 1.8 in China, 2.2 in BRCS and 2.8 in developed countries (see Table 10.5). The situation with the number of hospital beds per 1,000 persons is even worse at 0.9 in the year 2011. These numbers are about four times smaller than that in China, East Asia and BRCS countries. It is, therefore, not surprising that India's life expectancy at birth at 61.6 years is considerably lagging behind not only the average for developed countries (78.5 years), but also BRCS (65.4 years), East Asian countries (70.6 years) and China (70.6). The main reason for the formidable challenges faced by healthcare system in India is low public spending on public health in India which is much below what is required. Between 1996–97 and 2005–06, total government spending on health was stagnant at about 1 per cent of GDP, and the public expenditure elasticity with respect to GDP was at 0.94 per cent, lower than the average for low-income countries (1.16) for the same period (Tandon and Cashin, 2010). Despite efforts to increase public spending after 2005–06 including the adoption of the National Rural Health Mission (NRHM), under which spending on healthcare is expected to increase to 2–3 per cent of GDP, the actual expenditure has actually declined slightly from 1.3 per cent of GDP in 2000 to 1.2 per cent of GDP in 2011. This compares with public health expenditure as per cent of GDP at 2.2 per cent in East Asia, 2.9 per cent in China, 3.7 per cent in BRCS countries and a whopping 8.7 per cent in developed countries. This has resulted in poor quality of preventive care and poor health status of the population. The inadequate level of public health provision has forced the population to seek private health providers resulting in high out of pocket spending. Out of pocket spending in India is over four times higher than the public spending on healthcare.

**Table 10.5: Health indicators for India and other emerging and developed countries**

| Indicators | Year | India | China | East Asia | BRCS | Developed |
|---|---|---|---|---|---|---|
| Life expectancy at birth, total (years) | 2011 | 66 | 75 | 73.5 | 67.1 | 80.5 |
| | 2000 | 61.6 | 71.2 | 70.6 | 65.4 | 78.5 |
| Physicians (per 1,000 people) | 2011 | 0.65 | 1.82 | 0.99 | 2.2 | 2.8 |
| | 2000 | 0.6 | 1.1 | 0.61 | 1.7 | 2.6 |
| Hospital beds (per 1,000 people) | 2011 | 0.9 | 4.2 | 3.8 | 4.7 | 7.02 |
| | 2000 | 0.6 | 2.5 | 2.3 | 5.3 | 7.9 |
| Health expenditure, public (% of GDP) | 2011 | 1.2 | 2.9 | 2.2 | 3.7 | 8.7 |
| | 2000 | 1.3 | 1.8 | 1.6 | 2.8 | 6.7 |
| Health expenditure, public (% of government expenditure) | 2011 | 8.1 | 12.5 | 9.9 | 11.0 | 18.4 |
| | 2000 | 3.9 | 11.1 | 7.5 | 9.7 | 16.2 |
| Health expenditure per capita, PPP (constant 2005 international $) | 2011 | 141.0 | 432.0 | 677.6 | 933.4 | 4679.6 |
| | 2000 | 69.4 | 107.0 | 272.9 | 380.5 | 2741.9 |
| Improved water source (% of population with access) | 2011 | 91.6 | 91.7 | 94.0 | 94.4 | 99.5 |
| | 2000 | 81.0 | 80.0 | 89.8 | 88.8 | 99.2 |
| Improved water source, rural (% of rural population with access) | 2011 | 89.5 | 84.9 | 89.9 | 85.2 | 97.5 |
| | 2000 | 77 | 70 | 82.2 | 76.0 | 97.1 |
| Improved sanitation facilities (% of population with access) | 2011 | 35.1 | 65.1 | 84.4 | 72.6 | 99.8 |
| | 2000 | 25.0 | 44.0 | 79.0 | 66.3 | 99.5 |
| Improved sanitation facilities, rural (% of rural population with access) | 2011 | 23.9 | 55.8 | 80.7 | 55.1 | 99.3 |
| | 2000 | 14.0 | 35.0 | 74.0 | 48.8 | 98.1 |

*Source*: World Development Indicators, 2012

Not just medical facilities but even drinking water supply and especially sanitation in India continue to be inadequate though there is some improvement. The share of Indians with access to improved sources of water has increased from 72 per cent in 1990 to 81 per cent in 2000 to 91.6 in 2011. Although these numbers do not look so bad by international comparison (averaging from 91 per cent for China to 99 per cent for developed countries – see Table 10.5), it has to be noted that even those with access to improved water in India typically get water supplies for only a few hours a day (only two Indian cities have continuous water supply) and even the 'improved source' is often not entirely safe for drinking.

However, it is the level of sanitation that is a real cause of concern and requires a major effort by various levels of government and communities for improving coverage. Thus, at the national level, improved sanitation facilities were available to only 17 per cent of population in 1990, 25 per cent in 2000, and even in 2011 it was only at 35 per cent (compared with about 70 per cent in other emerging economies and 99 per cent in developed countries – Table 10.5). Poor sanitation is particularly dangerous to health as it is very likely to lead to infection of water sources and water supplies reaching the poor – leading to a large number of water-borne diseases like diarrhea, cholera, typhoid, etc. (endemic in India) and endless health problems including poor absorption of nutrients from food. This leads to a large number of health problems for the poor. Combine this with highly inadequate public health facilities and you get the nightmare that the poor in India face – poor health, malnutrition, frequent infections and resulting acute medical and financial distress. Thus, poor sanitation facilities (lack of toilets, poor waste disposal) are a major source of misery for the poor and in very urgent need of serious attention from all levels of governments (local, state and national). Additional financial and managerial resources need to be provided for this are needed as India's level of investment in water, sanitation and public health has been low by international standards.

## *Key challenges facing the healthcare sector*

Health services in India are characterized by (a) inadequate and inferior infrastructure; (b) poor public service delivery; (c) lack of quality choices for consumers and (d) lack of access especially for the poor due to a high dependence on relatively expensive privately provided services. In this subsection we will discuss some of the challenges faced by health sector and how they undermine the impact expected.

Public expenditure on health too low

The WHO calls for a 7.5 per cent allocation of GDP for health. Today, India allocates only about 1 per cent, which is less than that of even Nepal and Thailand, and reaching its avowed target of even 3 per cent of GDP seems difficult. Western countries allocate 6 per cent and above to their health sectors. Calculations by the United Nations show that India's spending on public health provision as a share of GDP is the eighteenth lowest in the world.

Adverse impact of user fees and privatization of health services

Possibly the single largest cause of putting health services out of the reach of the poor is the introduction of user fees in public hospitals by the government (user fees keep expanding into admission fee, pathological tests and diets, and follow different patterns across states). Since 1990, the privatization and penetration of the market into the health sector have had damaging consequences for the poor. Rising costs are greatly limiting their access to health services.

Focus on women is needed

The patriarchal functioning has ensured that health for women normally means maternity services, excluding basic health services that lay at the root of many a problem. Along with gender budgeting, services need to be integrated into a comprehensive primary healthcare system as conceived by the Alma Ata declaration. According to the latest National Rural Health Mission (NRHM) surveys, more than 50 per cent women of this country are anemic. 40 per cent of the maternal deaths during pregnancy and childbirth occur due to anaemia and under-nutrition. This points further towards the vicious cycle of poverty and ill health following each other in a socially oppressive system.

Poor institutional structures

The institutional mechanism does not seem to be functioning well and needs major overhauling and improvement. Doctors and higher management officers have to be made more accountable for actual delivery performance.

### Overcoming the challenges in healthcare

Improvement in infrastructure and institutions

Improvements are not possible if the quality of physical infrastructure is poor, but they are even more unlikely if institutions are weak. Studies reveal that the public infrastructure for both healthcare in India is of poor quality and inadequate to meet the full demand. Therefore, improvements can be brought about by expanding facilities and altering the delivery and institutional mechanisms to improve their quality.

## Public expenditure on health

The government should aim to increase public expenditure on health to 2–3 per cent of the GDP from the current 1 per cent as one of the strategies to meet the growing need. However, we also need to undertake institutional reforms to improve effectiveness in delivery of services.

## Planning around the poorest

The government must prioritize the needs of traditionally marginalized groups in planning its investments and outreach. The poorest districts of the country and the most vulnerable groups including women, children, people with disabilities, and communities like the *dalits*, *adivasis*, de-notified tribes and Muslim minorities – must be the focus while planning for infrastructure and allocating resources. The introduction of user fees in public hospitals has further added to the burden of the costs borne by poor in accessing public health facilities and should be eliminated for the very poor.

## Uniform quality of service

The quality of health is a crucial factor in ensuring the achievement of the human development outcomes intended through these services. The quality of health services even in the poorest areas of the country should be commensurate with the standards and norms envisaged by the National Development Goals at the very least, and encourage further improvisation and enhancement through active local participation, information sharing and accountability.

## CHALLENGES IN PHYSICAL INFRASTRUCTURE

For India to maintain the growth momentum, it is essential to strengthen infrastructure facilities such as transportation, energy, communication and so on. However, performance of physical infrastructure in Indian economy in the last one and a half decades has been mixed and uneven. As well as being in short supply, India's infrastructure in most cases is also of poor quality by world standards. In fact, India's high rate of economic growth will be difficult to sustain if infrastructure development does not increase and keep pace with demand. Therefore, a number of measures are needed to address the various infrastructure constraints that the country faces and improve the productivity of infrastructure sector.

At this juncture, it should be useful to take stock of the current infrastructure situation in India and to compare with other countries, especially other major emerging economies like China, other BRICS countries and East Asia with whom we are competing in exports and in attracting foreign investment. Thus, in this section, we benchmark India's infrastructure development (in transportation, electricity, information and communication technology) against other major countries of the world. We do this by comparing India's infrastructure development with that of China which is perhaps the most relevant comparison given its large and comparable size to India's and other country groups like East Asian countries (this classification includes Malaysia, South Korea, Indonesia, Thailand and Philippines), other major emerging economies – BRCS (average over Brazil, Russia, China and South Africa, i.e., BRICS countries other than India), and the average over the developed countries. We believe that such comparison will be helpful in understanding where we stand compared to the rest of the world and in setting reasonable goals for the future. We then consider various challenges to infrastructure development in India and how to overcome these.

### The state of physical infrastructure in India

Transportation

In the transportation sector, comparison with other country groups reveals somewhat mixed picture for India. India's performance regarding railways and road transportations look better for air transportation and seaports. However, in this sector, it is rather difficult to compare across countries or country groups because of different geographies, climates and population densities. Thus, comparisons of, say, road or rail kilometers per unit area or per unit population have their limitations in providing an accurate comparison across countries. Nevertheless, for want of better measures, we use these measures since they still provide some indication of the real situation of transportation infrastructure (Table 10.6).

India is doing well in terms of road density by population (road-km/1,000 people). For the year 2010, road density for India was 3.3 which compares well with 3.0 for China and 2.8 for East Asia. However, India lags behind other BRICS countries, which were around 6.6 and way behind the developed countries which were at 12.1 in the year 2010. Given its relatively high population density and low forest cover, India also fares better in term of road density by land area (road-km per 1,000 sq km of land area) and stands at a better position compared to China, BRCS and East Asian countries, though behind the developed countries.

**Table 10.6: India and the world: Comparison of access to and quality of transportation**

| Indicators | Year | India | China | East Asia[1] | BRCS[2] | Developed Countries[3] |
|---|---|---|---|---|---|---|
| **Roadways** | | | | | | |
| Road density by population | 2010 | 3.3 | 3 | 2.8 | 6.6 | 12.1 |
| (road km per 1,000 people) | 2000 | 3.1 | 2.6 | 2.4 | 6.7 | 13.3 |
| Road density by land area | 2010 | 1250 | 417 | 545.6 | 221.3 | 1390 |
| (road km per 1,000 sq. km) | 2000 | 1100 | 190 | 530 | 185 | 1790 |
| Paved roads | 2010 | 49.5 | 53.5 | 72.2 | 38.8 | 89.5 |
| (% of total roads) | 2000 | 47.5 | 40.8 | 63.2 | 37.7 | 88.9 |
| **Railways** | | | | | | |
| Railways, goods transported | 2011 | 0.5 | 1.9 | 0.1 | 2.9 | 2.22 |
| (million ton-km per year per 1,000 people) | 2000 | 0.3 | 1.1 | 0.1 | 1.8 | 1.99 |
| Railways, passengers carried | 2011 | 0.8 | 0.6 | 0.18 | 0.6 | 1.02 |
| (million passenger-km per year per 1,000 people) | 2000 | 0.4 | 0.3 | 0.17 | 0.4 | 0.92 |
| **Air Transport and Seaports** | | | | | | |
| Air transport, freight | 2012 | 1.4 | 13.08 | 80.15 | 18.14 | 111.6 |
| (1,000 ton-km per 1,000 people) | 2000 | 0.53 | 3.09 | 55.38 | 8.9 | 87.1 |
| Air transport, passengers carried | 2012 | 57.7 | 200.9 | 489.8 | 332.6 | 1479.5 |
| (per 1,000 people) | 2000 | 16.6 | 49 | 367.6 | 132.7 | 1196.2 |
| Commercial perception of seaports (1= poor, 7= world's best) | 2009 | 3.47 | 4.27 | 4.3 | 3.6 | 5.3 |

Notes: 1. East Asia refers to average over Indonesia, Korea, Rep.; Malaysia, Philippines, Thailand
2. BRCS refers to average over Brazil, Russia, China and South Africa
3. Developed countries refer to average over the USA, the UK, France, Germany and Japan

*Source*: World Development Indicators, 2012

This indicator shows India has better road density than many relatively developed regions. However, the quality of Indian roads is relatively inferior. For example, in India only half of the total roads are paved which is much lower than 73 per cent for East Asia, 84 per cent for the developed countries. When we compare India with China, we discover that though China was behind India in the year 2000, the percentage of paved roads has increased rapidly in China since then, thus, leaving behind India in 2011 with 53.5 per cent of paved roads.

Indian Railways is the world's fourth largest railway network in the world after the US, Russia and China, comprising 115,000 km of track over a route of 65,000 km and 7,500 stations. As of year 2011, railways in India transported 0.8 million passenger – km per year per 1,000 people – this number is better than that for China, East Asia and BRCS but below that for developed countries. However, for volume of good transported, India at 0.5 million ton-km of goods per year per 1,000 people in 2011 fares better than East Asia only, while it is considerably behind China, BRCS countries and developed countries which were at 1.9, 2.9 and 2.2 million ton-km per 1,000 people in 2011.

India's relatively decent performance in roads and railways by international comparisons is partly due to the fact that other countries, such as East Asia, BRCS and especially the developed countries make much greater use of air transportation. This is evident from the data of air transport (Table 10.6). India is still trailing behind all the countries in our dataset both in the case of freight million ton-km per 1,000 people and passengers carried per 1,000 people per year. Thus, in India, only 57.7 persons per 1,000 people travelled by air in 2012 compared to 201 in China, 490 in East Asia, 333 in BRCS countries and a whopping 1480 in the developed countries. In terms of air transportation of freight, India's volume was only 1.4 (1,000 ton-km per 1,000 people in 2012) compared to 13 for China, 18 for BRCS countries, 80 for East Asia and a huge 111 (or about 100 times India's volume per 1,000 people) for the developed countries. Finally, India is also behind these countries in the volume of sea transportation as well as in the quality and efficiency of its seaports.

## Electricity

Electricity is a very important form of energy used in homes, offices and industries for production, efficiency and productivity enhancement, as well as for personal comforts. Regarding this sector, we have data on three indicators: per cent of population with access to electricity network, electricity consumption per capita (kilowatt hours per year), electricity power transmission and distribution loss. While the first two indicators measure access and average consumption of electricity, the third indicator measures efficiency of distribution in power transmission and the viability of the electricity networks.

The data for India and other countries on these variables is provided in Table 10.7. In India, only 75 per cent people have access to the electricity network. This compares to 86 per cent for the East Asian countries and 94 per cent for the BRCS countries, while it is almost 100 per cent for China and the developed countries. Comparison with China, with almost 100 per cent access, shows that India has a lot of work to do in this crucial area as lack of access to electricity seriously affects output and productivity. Next, if we look at electricity power consumption per capita, India again comes out at the bottom of the ladder with a per capita consumption of only 626 kilowatt hours. Compared to India's level, the per capita consumption of electricity is about five times higher in China, 6 times in East Asia, 7.5 times in BRCS and 15 times in the developed countries. This comparison again shows how far India has to catch up in this crucial aspect. At the same time, it is worth noting that China tripled its per capita consumption of electricity between 2000 and 2010, (while India only managed to increase it by 63 per cent over the same period) showing that it is possible to raise performance on this count much more rapidly than India has been able to achieve.

Electric power transmission losses reflect the technical efficiency in transmission, while distribution losses largely represent theft of electricity in the form of unauthorized use and under-reporting of usage.

**Table 10.7: Quality of electricity networks in India and other emerging and developed countries**

| Indicators | Year | India | China | East Asia | BRCS | Developed Countries |
|---|---|---|---|---|---|---|
| Access to electricity network (% of population) | 2010 | 75.0 | 99.7 | 85.9 | 93.6 | 99.9 |
| | 2000 | – | – | – | – | – |
| Electric power consumption (kwh per year per capita) | 2010 | 641.0 | 2943.0 | 3505.8 | 4101.9 | 8493.6 |
| | 2000 | 391.0 | 993.3 | 2456.0 | 3195.0 | 8326.4 |
| Electric power transmission & distribution losses (% of output) | 2010 | 20.3 | 6.1 | 7.5 | 10.6 | 5.53 |
| | 2000 | 27.63 | 6.9 | 8.44 | 11.08 | 6.02 |

*Source*: World Development Indicators, 2012

Such losses are usually larger in public distribution systems than in the private ones as the latter have a much stronger incentive to check such losses. In India, the transmission and distribution losses were 20.3 per cent in 2010, implying that more than one fourth of the electricity output was wasted or stolen. India stands at the bottom in this regard too with the transmission and distribution losses at 10.6 per cent for BRCS, 7.5 per cent for East Asian countries and about 6 per cent for China and developed countries.

Thus, India's electricity infrastructure is seen to be one of the weakest. It fares badly not only in comparison to the developed countries, but also in comparison to other emerging countries, like China, East Asia and BRCS. China seems to hold important lessons for India in this regard as it has provided access to electricity to almost all its citizens, has a per capita consumption of electricity about five times India's and transmission and distribution losses less than one-third of India's losses.

## Information and Communication Technology (ICT)

Access to ICT is crucial for productivity enhancement not only now but also in the future as the younger generation's exposure to ICT helps to prepare them for more productive jobs in the future. Access to ICT can be measured in terms of number of telephone and Internet subscribers per 1,000 persons, number of computers per 1,000 persons, and per capita expenditure on telephone, Internet, etc. The data on these indicators for India and other selected countries is shown in Table 10.8.

**Table 10.8: Access to and quality of ICT in India and other emerging and developed countries**

| Indicators | Year | India | China | East Asia | BRCS | Developed |
|---|---|---|---|---|---|---|
| **Telephone access** | | | | | | |
| Landline telephone subscribers | 2012 | 20 | 210 | 214 | 135 | 591.6 |
| (per 1000 inhabitants) | 2000 | 29 | 114 | 182 | 155 | 542 |
| Cellular telephone subscribers | 2012 | 690 | 810 | 1186 | 1312 | 1153.3 |
| (per 1000 inhabitants) | 2000 | 6 | 68 | 188 | 103 | 546.8 |
| Total telephone subscribers | 2012 | 710 | 1020 | 1400 | 1448 | 1744.9 |
| (per 1000 inhabitants) | 2000 | 35 | 182 | 370 | 258 | 1098 |
| Telecommunication revenue | 2008 | 2.01 | 2.87 | 3.96 | 4.37 | 3.11 |
| (% of GDP) | 2000 | 1.52 | 3.21 | 3.07 | 3.44 | 2.88 |
| **Computers and internet access** | | | | | | |
| Personal computers | 2007 | 33 | 57 | 192 | 109 | 650 |
| (per 1,000 inhabitants) | 2000 | 6 | 20 | 49 | 109 | 392 |
| International Internet bandwidth | 2008 | 32 | 483 | 1583 | 808 | 19337 |
| (bits per person) | 2000 | 1 | 2 | 16 | 9 | 240 |
| ICT expenditure per capita (current US $) | 2008 | 46 | 195 | 594 | 403 | 2902.2 |
| | 2002 | 17.8 | 100.4 | 398.2 | 172.7 | 2075.8 |
| ICT expenditure | 2008 | 4.5 | 6 | 7 | 6.2 | 6.2 |
| (% of GDP) | 2002 | 3.2 | 7.9 | 6.8 | 6.4 | 6.3 |
| Internet users | 2012 | 125 | 423 | 456 | 466 | 828 |
| (per 1,000 people) | 2000 | 5 | 18 | 145 | 80 | 482 |

*Source*: World Development Indicators, 2012, Econstat, 2012

Data on total telephone subscribers reflects a somewhat lower access rate in India in comparison to other countries. India's situation regarding the number of landline telephone subscribers is dismal with only 20 subscribers per 1,000 inhabitants in 2012. This compares with 210 subscribers per 1,000 inhabitants in 2012 in China, 214 in East Asia, 135 in BRCS and 592 for developed countries. However, the situation is better in terms of the cellular telephone indicators, the latest available data for comparison purposes is from 2012, which shows that per 1,000 inhabitant, there were 690 cellular phones in India, while the number was 810 for China, 1,186 for East Asian economies, 1,312 for BRCS and 1,153 for the developed countries. The total telephone subscribers in India was 710 per 1,000 inhabitants in the year 2012, which is lower than most other emerging and developed economies (Table 10.8), although the difference is not very huge. In terms of total revenue of the telecommunication sector, it is about 2 per cent for India as compared to about 3 per cent in China and developed countries and about 4 per cent in East Asia, BRCS countries.

Data on access to computers and Internet show that India lies far below China, East Asia and BRCS countries. The number of personal computers per 1,000 inhabitants in India was only 33 compared to 57 in China, 192 in East Asia, 109 in BRCS and a whopping 650 in developed countries. India is also well behind in the access to Internet services with the Internet information accessed per person being a mere 32 bits per year. It was about 15 to 50 times higher for other emerging economies and a whopping 500 times higher for the developed countries. Similarly, number of Internet users per 1,000 people in India is at least four times less when compared to China, East Asia and BRCS countries – for example, for the year 2012, the number for India was 125 per 1,000 persons but it was 423 for China, 256 for East Asia, 466 for BRCS and 828 for the OECD countries. However, when we look at the rate of growth for India over the period of time, we find that India has done a commendable job in increasing the base from 5 per 1,000 at the beginning of the decade to 125 in just 12 years. Therefore, it is crucial for India to invest more in this crucial sector and enable the faster optical fibre Internet connectivity within the country and with other countries. This will not only increase the user base of the country but also increase the expenditure on Internet and contribute to enhancement of productivity and growth.

India's overall performance regarding ICT seems to be mixed – it is unfavourable in terms of number of subscribers and technical efficiency, at the same time it has cheaper call rate and better telephony and Internet quality perception than many comparable groups and economies.

## Challenges to infrastructure development

There are multiple challenges that are likely to hamper any move to accelerate development of infrastructure. Funding constraints, land acquisition issues, delays related to identification and award of projects and shortage of skilled manpower are some of the major reasons that are currently causing delays in infrastructure projects.

### Land acquisition

Land acquisition has been the single largest roadblock for the development of infrastructure. Several projects have been stalled or delayed due to land acquisition issues. There are multiple reasons that lead to delays in land acquisition. One primary reason has been the resistance from farmers or local communities whose land is being acquired. There was generally a huge difference between the price offered by the government agency forcibly acquiring the land under some archaic laws and the prevailing market value, which resulted in major disputes and litigation. In addition, lack of well-planned, efficient and demonstrable rehabilitation packages for the displaced persons added to the distrust of the local communities.

The Government of India has recently (in 2013) passed a new law, the Land Acquisition and Rehabilitation & Resettlement Act (LARR), to resolve disputes relating to land acquisition. This law will help the farmers, who were being exploited earlier. However, this law now promises to pay farmers four times the existing market price for their land and requires the approval of 80 per cent of the landowners in the affected area, making it much more difficult for corporations to acquire land. This could be detrimental to private investments in the long term since the viability of projects may be affected.

### Delay in regulatory and environmental clearance

There are various categories of approvals required across the project cycle at every stage, right from the pre-tendering stage to post-construction. For instance, at the pre-tendering stage, there are substantial delays in inviting bids. Moreover, approval is required from multiple layers of the government at the central, state and local levels. In most cases, there is lack of coordination between the different agencies, leading to standoffs on critical approvals, which seriously affect the execution of projects.

Environmental safeguards and guidelines are evolving that are similar to the scale and complexity of infrastructure projects. While new projects need to comply with these regulations, even a project under construction may sometimes need to comply with revised standards midway through the execution stage (or because some concerned government department or agency had 'overlooked' its duties and wrongfully issued required approvals). Clearly, better governance will be a big help in mitigating long delays in infrastructure projects.

### Funding constraints

Funding is another major roadblock in implementation of infrastructure projects. There is increasing reliance on the private sector for developing and maintaining infrastructure. The private sector, however, needs funds to develop infrastructure projects that are often capital intensive and have a high-gestation period. Typically, private investments in infrastructure projects are mainly in the form of debt raised by developers. Often, most large developers have over-leveraged their balance sheets to raise debt and their cash flow does not permit them to raise fresh debt to fund new projects. Equity markets are also not favourable for financing projects because of uncertainties involved in the execution and returns from the project due to various regulatory requirements limiting exit options and other vagaries of the equity markets (such as various unpredictable global economy issues that can have substantial impact on prices of any given share). These issues still remain unresolved and continue to create problems in financing infrastructure financing.

### Capacity of private players

Given the above-mentioned problems, another emerging challenge for achievement of the large infrastructure projects is the capacity of the private sector to undertake or implement such projects. Today, most large companies in India are integrated players executing projects as developers. However, the total number of such players is low and they have already secured several projects, which limits their capacity to undertake new ones, given the financing and other issues mentioned above.

Infrastructure projects in India are, however, becoming larger in size and complexity, and such projects require financial patronage and additional project management skills, which most medium-to-small Indian companies currently lack. Foreign players can bring in investments and technical expertise to undertake large and complex projects. There is, therefore, a need to speed up ongoing efforts to simplify the approval and the regulatory processes to attract foreign developers to invest.

### *Overcoming the challenges*

### Land acquisition

The government is expected to follow up with policies or guidelines on land acquisition for project authorities or sponsoring agencies. The government has taken a positive step to resolve land issues by relaxing land transfer regulations for government-owned lands. It had earlier made it mandatory for specific approval of the cabinet being sought before leasing, licensor transferring land. This led to long delays in concessions being awarded for infrastructure projects. The government's recent initiative is, therefore, encouraging since the likelihood of projects getting delayed due to procedural issue should now be resolved and complement the guidelines.

### Fast-track policy and regulation reforms for enhanced implementation

There needs to be a concerted effort from sponsoring agencies to develop strong performance management systems to drive timely execution of the projects. This includes defining performance standards for nodal agencies and creating a transparent and accurate tracking mechanism as well as performance-linked incentives and penalties. One of the methods of doing this is by having independent third-party audits conducted for infrastructure projects. This will ensure greater transparency in public contracts and enhanced compliance on project execution. Moreover, additional expert opinions could help in improving project engineering. Third-party audits should become a mainstream activity for planning and execution of infrastructure projects.

### Dispute resolution

At present, disputes between parties are one of the major causes of the delay in projects. The arbitration clause is poorly defined or is one-sided. Furthermore, arbitration is generally not binding. This leads to the majority of the cases going into further litigation, which can be a long drawn-out process given the extremely slow pace of Indian courts. The government may also consider setting up a single quasi-judicial authority for all the infrastructure sectors. This authority would have statutory powers to resolve disputes between the authorities and private developers.

A large number of projects are delayed due to delayed regulatory approvals or clearances from different agencies. Government agencies often function independently, and there is no incentive or obligation to cooperate with project authorities to expedite the approval process. To eliminate this issue, a Performance Review Unit should be given powers to gather information from nodal agencies on clearances and incentivize or regulate this.

### Facilitate funding for infrastructure projects

The Twelfth Plan has aggressive investment targets with at least 50 per cent of the investment proposed to be contributed by the private sector. Setting up of Infrastructure Debt Funds (IDFs) and reduction in 'withholding tax' on the interest paid on these bonds are some other positive measures that are expected to facilitate the flow of long-term debt into infrastructure projects.

Furthermore, decisions pertaining to inclusion of lending to the infrastructure under the priority sector, exempting infrastructure lending from cash reserve requirement or at least the statutory liquidity requirement (that mandates that 24 per cent of all loans made by commercial scheduled banks in India be allocated to the purchase of government bonds) can facilitate infrastructure funding. Further, policy and regulatory reforms in the infrastructure sector as well as in financial markets can have a long-term effect on availability of funds since they create a conducive environment for investors. These need to be fast-tracked and will go long way in creating a mature financial market for facilitating investment in infrastructure.

## Public private partnership (PPP)

In some of the former fully government-owned infrastructure sectors, such as telecommunications and domestic civil aviation, the opening to the private sector has produced exemplary results. In both sectors, new private entrants now have market shares of over three quarters. Since the easing of regulatory constraints in 2004, the telecommunications network has become the third largest in the world. In both sectors, choice has expanded and prices have fallen. Even so, more needs to be done to promote competition in the fixed-line market, given the possibilities offered by broadband technology.

A significant start has been made in involving the private sector in the provision of transport infrastructure. By end 2010, the outstanding value of public–private partnerships (PPPs) had risen to an amount equivalent to 3½ per cent of GDP, with most contracts having been awarded in the previous 2 years. The government encourages private involvement in the construction and operation of ports and airports. Here, there is a need to change the tariff-setting process in a way that encourages productivity improvements, moving away from a cost-plus basis system of price determination. The government has also introduced model PPP concessions, which are awarded on the basis of competitive bids for subsidies, or payments if the concession is estimated to be commercially viable. Early experience with private involvement in these areas is generally positive, but outcomes under contracts need careful monitoring. A significant implementation problem has been the need to obtain cabinet approval for road contracts that are sufficiently large to attract private sector interest. Greater authority should be delegated to the Highways Authority to speed up the process.

# CONCLUSIONS

This chapter has argued that good social and physical infrastructure facilities are crucial for rapid economic growth, rapid human development, poverty reduction and improvement in living conditions for the people. A comparison with other emerging and developed economies shows that India's physical and social infrastructure is much poorer and requires major improvement.

Formal schooling per adult in India is appallingly poor, at only 4.4 years on average, while other emerging economies average at about 7 to 9 years. This is further compounded by the poor quality of education – survey studies show that Indian elementary school students are typically about 3 years behind the standard in which they are studying. The condition of higher education is also quite bad while vocational training which could create productive jobs for so many with limited education has simply not received the attention it deserves. A major expansion in education facilities at all levels, along with a significant improvement in the institutional structures to better deliver the promised education, is urgently needed. This has to begin with a system of regularly measuring the actual educational attainment at various levels and, then, careful monitoring and experimentation with institutional design to achieve far better performance.

In the health sector, the facilities for the vast majority of population are very poor and require urgent attention in both expansion and improvement in institutional mechanisms.

In the sphere of physical infrastructure, India's performance (for its level of per capita income) in the development of roads, railways and telephony is reasonable though significantly behind China and other emerging economies. However, in the sphere of electricity access and consumption per capita, Internet access, level of air travel and quality of seaports, India's performance is quite poor compared to other emerging economies. So, once again major efforts need to be made to expand and improve the quality of the physical infrastructure and improve the institutional mechanism for faster delivery and less leakage. The new land acquisition law of 2013 has made land acquisition for infrastructure projects too cumbersome and needs to be revised to make land acquisition for infrastructure and industrial development easier. Regulatory and environmental clearances are another source of major delay in infrastructure projects and need better governance,

If proper efforts are made in expanding and improving the quality of education and health facilities and of physical infrastructure through improved budgetary allocation and better governance, it will go a long way in reducing poverty, improving human development as well as reviving and sustaining high rates of economic growth in India.

# REFERENCES

Annual Survey of Education Report (Rural) (ASER) 2012

De, P., & Ghosh, B. 2003. *How Do Infrastructure Facilities Affect Regional Income?: An Investigation with South Asian Countries*. Research and Information System for the Non-aligned and Other Developing Countries.

Estache, A. 2006. 'Infrastructure: A Survey of Recent and Upcoming Issues'. In *World Bank ABCDE Conference* Tokyo, 29–30).

Hall, R. E. and Jones, C. I. 1999. 'Why Do Some Countries Produce so much more Output per Worker than Others'? *The Quarterly Journal of Economics* 114(1), 83–116.

Hanushek, E. A. and Woessmann, L. 2008. 'The Role of Cognitive Skills in Economic Development'. *Journal of Economic Literature* 607–68.

Mankiw, N. G., Romer, D. and Weil, D. N. 1992. 'A Contribution to the Empirics of Economic Growth'. *The Quarterly Journal of Economics* 107(2), 407–37.

Sahoo, P., and Dash, R. K. 2008. *Economic Growth in South Asia: Role of Infrastructure*, IEG Working Paper Series No. E/288/2008.

Sahoo, P., and Dash, R. K. 2009. 'Infrastructure Development and Economic Growth in India'. *Journal of the Asia Pacific Economy* 14(4), 351–65.

Tandon, A., and Cashin, C. 2010. 'Assessing Public Expenditure on Health from a Fiscal Space Perspective, Health, Nutrition and Population (HNP), Discussion Paper, World Bank, Washington DC. 1–84.Wagstaff, A. 2002. 'Poverty and Health Sector Inequalities'. *Bulletin of the World Health Organization* 80(2), 97–105.

# 11

# Infrastructure Challenges in India
## The Role of Public–Private Partnerships

### Geethanjali Nataraj

## INTRODUCTION

India is the fourth largest economy in the world. However, one factor which is a drag on its development is the lack of world-class infrastructure. In fact, estimates suggest that the lack of proper infrastructure pulls down India's Gross Domestic Product (GDP) growth by 1–2 per cent every year. Physical infrastructure has a direct impact on the growth and overall development of an economy. However, the fast growth of the Indian economy in recent years has placed increasing stress on physical infrastructure, such as electricity, railways, roads, ports, airports, irrigation, urban and rural water supply, and sanitation, all of which already suffer from a substantial deficit. The goals of inclusive growth and a 9 per cent growth in GDP can be achieved only if this infrastructure deficit is overcome. Infrastructure development will help in creating a better investment climate in India. To develop infrastructure in the country, the government is expected to revisit issues of budgetary allocation, tariff policy, fiscal incentives, private sector participation and public–private partnerships (PPPs) with resolve.

There are many issues that need to be addressed in different infrastructural fields. To begin with, the gap between electricity production and demand is affecting both manufacturing and overall growth. Then, though road transport is the backbone of the Indian transport infrastructure, it is inadequate in terms of quality, quantity and connectivity. Also, in the overall transport sector, civil aviation and ports desperately need modernization. It is expected that the public sector will continue to play an important role in building transport infrastructure. However, the resources needed are much larger than what the public sector can provide. Rest of the chapter is organized as follows. The first section of Chapter 1 gives a brief description of infrastructure development in the Twelfth

Five Year Plan. Its second section explains in detail a few important sources of infrastructure financing in the country. The second section also elucidates PPPs in India and follows it up with a case of Cochin International Airport in the first and second sections of Chapter 2 presents the approach to PPPs in India. The major challenges and impediments to infrastructure development in the country are presented in the third and the fourth section gives the concluding remarks.

## INFRASTRUCTURE DEVELOPMENT IN THE TWELFTH FIVE YEAR PLAN

Inadequate infrastructure was recognized in the Eleventh Plan as a major constraint for rapid growth. The Plan had, therefore, emphasized on the need for massive expansion on investment in infrastructure based on a combination of public and private investment, the latter through various forms of PPPs. Substantial progress has been made in this respect. The total investment in infrastructure, which includes roads, railways, ports, electricity and telecommunication, oil gas pipelines, and irrigation, is estimated to have increased from 5.7 per cent of GDP in the base year of the Eleventh Plan to around 8 per cent in the last year of the Plan. The pace of investment has been particularly buoyant in some sectors, notably telecommunication and oil and gas pipelines, while falling short of targets in electricity, railways, roads and ports. Efforts to attract private investment in infrastructure through the PPP route have met with considerable success, not only at the level of the central government, but also at the level of individual states. A large number of PPPs have taken off, and many of them are currently operational at both the centre and in the states.

The Twelfth Plan intends to continue its thrust on accelerating the pace of investment in infrastructure as this is critical for sustaining and accelerating growth. In its Twelfth Five Year Plan Document (2012–17), the Planning Commission expects investments in infrastructure projects to be worth of US$1 trillion over the five years of the plan. The total investment as a percentage of GDP is also expected to be in the range of 7–9 per cent (see Figure 11.1). Public investments in infrastructure have been the dominant form of infrastructure financing in India, but this is expected to change and the private sector will be expected to invest more in infrastructure in the coming years (see Figure 11.2). It would be necessary to review the factors which may be constraining private investment, and steps may be needed to rectify them. PPPs, with appropriate regulation and concern for equity, need to be encouraged in social sectors, such as health and education. Several state governments are already taking steps in this direction.

**Figure 11.1: Share of infrastructure in GDP**

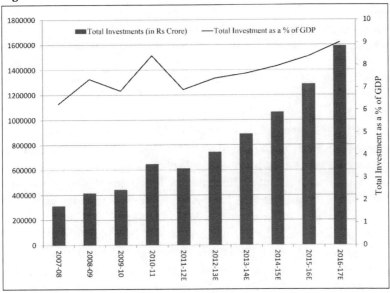

*Source:* 12th Five-Year Plan document

**Figure 11.2: Private sector share in infrastructure**

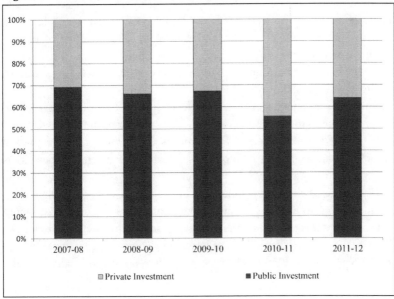

*Source:* 12th Five-Year Document

This includes Andhra Pradesh which has spent 1,069 crore INR on education-centric PPPs which include partnerships for computer education, mid-day meal, upgradation of Industrial Training Institutes (ITIs) and Information Communications Technology (ICT) in schools, skills development centre, etc.

As recently as in this year, Maharashtra has started outsourcing laboratory tests or diagnostic services in government hospitals through a PPP model. The Mumbai-based Enso Healthcare Private Limited (Ensocare) along with GE Healthcare shall be covering this aspect of medical care for 22 government hospitals for the next 10 years. They also intend to replicate this model in other states with the same partners. Punjab is a prominent example of the same.

However, public investment in infrastructure is still expected to bear a large part of the infrastructure needs in backward and remote areas for improving connectivity and expanding much-needed public services. Since resource constraints will continue to limit public investment in infrastructure in other areas, PPP-based development needs to be encouraged wherever feasible. The above chart shows the percentage component of public and private investment in infrastructure in the Eleventh Five Year Plan. As per the Twelfth Plan Document, the Planning Commission targets to achieve 50 per cent private and PPP funding in total infrastructure investments, compared to a little more than 30 per cent in the Eleventh Plan. There is a greater emphasis to initiate PPP projects in the Twelfth Plan.

In terms of number of projects, roads and highways are emerging as favoured destinations for PPP, while telecom and electricity lead in terms of private investments. Currently, there are 758 projects in the pipeline with more than 53 per cent in the roads sector, followed by urban development with 20 per cent of the projects. See Figure 11.3.

The Indian power sector has attracted much private investment in the past years. With 56 projects for a total consideration of US$12.6 billion, the sector accounts for 18 per cent of the total value of PPP projects across sectors, though only 7 per cent of the total number of PPP projects. India's total generating capacity is around 173,626.4 megawatts (MW),[1] of which the private sector accounts for the lowest (21.2 per cent). See Figures 11.4 and 11.4a.

India is expected to make great investments in the power sector due to rapid urbanization, rural electrification and industries across the country. Under the Twelfth Plan, the private sector is likely to account for a major share of the additional capacity (55.6 per cent). PPP is likely to be the preferred route for such ventures.

---

[1]   Based on PowerMin, 228.7 GW;http://powermin.nic.in/indian_electricity_scenario/
      introduction.htm

**Figure 11.3: PPP projects in India by sector (Total: 758)**

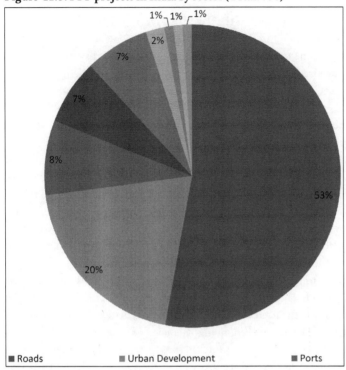

■ Roads          ■ Urban Development          ■ Ports

*Source:* 12th Five-Year Plan Document, PPP India.

**Figure 11.4: Sector-wise capacity break-up under the Twelfth Five Year Plan (in MW)**

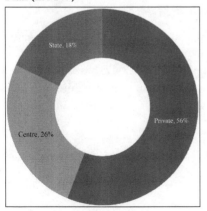

*Source:* 12th Five-Year Plan, Aranca Research

**Figure 11.4a: Sources of funding for power projects under the Twelfth Five Year Plan**

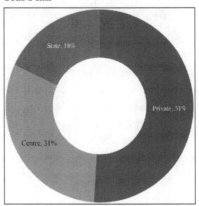

*Source:* 12th Five Year Plan, Aranca Research

# INFRASTRUCTURE FINANCING IN INDIA

According to the approach paper of the Twelfth Five Year Plan since more than two-thirds of the investment in the economy is by the private sector (households and corporate), it will be necessary to ensure that the financial system is able to translate the otherwise favourable macroeconomic investment–savings balances into effective financing of private sector investment needed for 9 per cent GDP growth. For this, a financial system capable of mobilizing household savings and allocating them efficiently to meet the equity and debt needs of the fast expanding private corporate sector is a must. This depends on the efficiency of the financial system as a whole, which at present consists of a large number of financial institutions, such as banks, non-bank finance companies, mutual funds, insurance companies, pension funds, private equity firms, venture capital funds, angel investors and micro-finance institutions. Special attention is required for the financing needs of private sector investment in infrastructure. Infrastructure investment (defined as electricity, roads and bridges, telecommunication, railways, irrigation, water supply and sanitation, ports, airports, storage, and oil gas pipelines) will need to increase from about 8 per cent of GDP in the base year (2011–12) of the plan to about 10 per cent of GDP in 2016–17. According to the Twelfth Five Year Plan, the total investment in infrastructure will have to be over ₹45 lakh crore or US$1 trillion. Financing this level of investment will require larger outlays from the public sector, but these will have to be coupled with a more than proportional rise in private investment. Private and PPP investment is estimated to have accounted for a little over 30 per cent of the total investment on infrastructure in the Eleventh Plan. Their share may have to rise to 50 per cent in the Twelfth Plan.

### Funding infrastructure in India through domestic savings

The domestic savings rate in India is very high and projected to grow consistently as presented in Table 11.1. Though infrastructure investment targets are ambitious, much of it can be financed domestically. The WSGI (2012–17) has estimated that such high rates of infrastructure investment constitute over one-third of India's financial savings and would entail as much as 21 per cent of the incremental financial savings being directed to infrastructure.

Again, The WSGI (2012–17) has opined that it is not just the adequacy of domestic financial savings that matters. These savings have to be intermediated into infrastructure to achieve these targets.

**Table 11.1: Savings and infrastructure investment needs (as per cent of GDP)**

| Year | Infra invest-ment | Gross domestic savings | o/w financial savings | Incremental infra investment | Incre-mental financial savings | Infra investment as % of financial savings | % share of incremental infra in incremental financial savings |
|---|---|---|---|---|---|---|---|
| FY10 | 7.5 | 33.7 | 22.0 | 0.3 | 2.8 | 34 | NA |
| FY13 | 9.0 | 37.8 | 24.8 | 0.6 | NA | 36 | NA |
| FY14 | 9.5 | 40.6 | 27.2 | 0.5 | 2.4 | 35 | 21 |
| FY15 | 9.9 | 42.9 | 29.1 | 0.4 | 1.9 | 34 | 21 |
| FY16 | 10.3 | 45.5 | 31.1 | 0.4 | 2.0 | 33 | 20 |
| FY17 | 10.7 | 48.2 | 33.4 | 0.4 | 2.3 | 32 | 17 |

*Source*: (1) Mid-term Appraisal Eleventh Five Year Plan, Reports submitted by Sub-Groups on Household Savings, Private Sector Corporate Savings and Public Sector Savings for 9 per cent p.a. real growth and 5 per cent p.a. inflation scenario. (2) Working Sub-Group on Infrastructure, Working Group on Savings Formulation of the Twelfth Five Year Plan, GOI.

## *Availability of debt financing*

Table 11.2 shows that the major funding was through budgetary support which constituted 45 per cent of the total infrastructure spending. The debt from commercial banks, non-banking finance companies (NBFCs), insurance companies and the External Commercial Borrowings (ECB) constituted 41 per cent of the funding, while the balance 14 per cent was through equity and FDI.

**Table 11.2: Sources of funds during first three years of the Eleventh Five Year Plan**

| Sl. No. | Sources of fund | Percentage of total infra spending |
|---|---|---|
| 1. | Commercial banks | 21 |
| 2. | NBFCs | 10 |
| 3. | Insurance companies | 4 |
| 4. | ECBs | 6 |
| 5. | Equity/FDI | 14 |
| 6. | Budgetary support | 45 |
| | **Total** | **100** |

*Source*: Compiled by author from (1) Mid-Term Appraisal Eleventh Five Year Plan, Planning Commission, GOI (2) Working Sub-Group on Infrastructure, Working Group on Savings Formulation of the Twelfth Five Year Plan, GOI.

# INFRASTRUCTURE INVESTMENT THROUGH DEBT FINANCING

There was no major demand from the financial system to fund infrastructure investment until the mid-2000s as it was fairly low being 3–5 per cent of GDP. So, infrastructure investment was financed largely by budgetary allocations and through the internal resources of public sector enterprises engaged in infrastructure. Infrastructure spending picked up substantially with an important role played by the private sector during the Eleventh Five Year Plan. Infrastructure spending relied upon the financial system significantly during this period. Most of the debt financing came from banks, NBFCs, and ECB, mutual funds, private equity funds, venture capital funds, micro-finance institutions, followed by insurance companies.

Commercial banks

Commercial banks stepped up lending to infrastructure companies largely by unwinding their excess investments in government securities maintained as Statutory liquidity ratio (SLR). SLR investments as a share of deposits came down from 47.3 per cent in 2005–06 to 29 per cent in 2010–11 as the credit–deposit ratio increased. Credit to infrastructure grew at a faster pace than total credit. Table 11.3 shows that the share of infrastructure in gross bank credit increased from 6 per cent in March 2007 to 9 per cent in March 2009 and to 11 per cent in March 2011. Similarly, share of infrastructure as non-food credit rose from 8.23 per cent in March 2007 to 10.38 per cent in March 2009 and to 14.69 per cent in March 2011. As a result, it is observed that banks were able to provide about half the debt finance needs required for infrastructure investment.

The WSGI (2012–17) has opined that this rapid growth in bank credit to infrastructure has resulted in a greater concentration of risks in banks, due to asset and liability management (ALM) mismatch and reaching exposure ceilings. The WSGI (2012–17) has a view that the banks have prudential exposure caps for infrastructure sector lending as a whole as well as for individual sectors. Most of the banks have almost reached the prudential caps for power sector; other sectors like roads may not be far behind.

The WSGI (2012–17) expects that power and road sector will face significant constraints as the exposure is already high. However, it may be worthwhile to point out that the funding gap will not be felt universally. Some of the smaller sectors will be able to get adequate funding subject to availability of commercially viable, bankable projects, but the funding gap will be much larger for power, roads, etc.

Khan (2011) in the Diamond Jubilee International Conference on Frontiers of Infrastructure Finance 2011 has a view that takeout financing offers an opportunity to the banks to free their balance sheet from exposure to infrastructure loans, lend to new projects and also enable better management of the asset liability position. In other words, takeout financing enables financing longer term projects with medium term funds. However, due to several factors the mechanism has not really emerged as a game-changer. One plausible reason is that the model does not envisage equitable distribution of risks and benefits. One of the often repeated arguments is that banks assume credit and liquidity risk since the inception of the project but once the project is economically viable, taking out of the loan results in loss of opportunity of earning returns on seasoned loans. Further, if the original lenders/bankers are required to completely part with their security interest, their residual exposure would be subordinated to the interest of the take out financier.

**Table 11.3: Commercial banks: Lending to infrastructure during FY07–11**

| As on | Gross bank credit outstanding | Non- food credit | Credit to infrastructure sector | Share of infra as a % of non-food credit | Share of infra as a % of gross bank credit in overall |
|---|---|---|---|---|---|
| FY07 Mar | 23,79,985 | 17,56,051 | 1,44,531 | 8.23 | 6.07 |
| FY08 Mar | 29,52,874 | 22,04,801 | 2,05,336 | 9.31 | 6.95 |
| FY09 Mar | 35,34,284 | 26,01,825 | 2,69,972 | 10.38 | 7.64 |
| FY10 Mar | 41,32,186 | 30,40,007 | 3,79,888 | 12.50 | 9.19 |
| FY11 Mar | 49,12,012 | 36,77,429 | 5,40,390 | 14.69 | 11.00 |
| FY11 Jun | | 37,08,927 | 5,52,682 | 14.90 | |

*Source*: (1) Reserve Bank of India (RBI) (2) Working Sub-Group on infrastructure, Working Group on Savings Formulation of the Twelfth Five Year Plan, GOI.

### Non-banking finance companies (NBFCs)

The WSGI (2012–17) has observed that the increased credit demand for power, telecom and road sector give opportunity to NBFCs to increase their lending sharply towards infrastructure projects. The key Infrastructure Finance Companies (IFC) are Power Finance Corporation (PFC), Rural Electrification Corporation Limited (REC), The Infrastructure Development Finance Company Limited (IDFC), India Infrastructure Finance Company Limited (IIFCL), L&T Infra and Industrial Finance Corporation of India (IFCI), the outstanding credit from these institutions to infrastructure sector has increased from ₹110,549 crore in FY08 to ₹140,355 in FY09 and to ₹181,595 crore in FY10 at a Compound Annual Growth Rate (CAGR) of 28 per cent. The WSGI (2012–17) has also highlighted that the PFC and REC which together constitute 80 per cent of the lending by IFCs have had their outstanding credit grown at 27 per cent p.a.

(a) Power Finance Corporation: PFC was set up on 16 July 1986 as a financial institution (FI) dedicated to power sector financing and committed to the integrated development of the power and associated sectors. The Corporation was notified as a Public Financial Institution in 1990 under Companies Act, 1956. The Corporation is registered as a Non-Banking Financial Company with the Reserve Bank of India (RBI). RBI, vide its revised Certificate of Registration no. B-14.00004 dated 28 July 2010 classified the company as an 'Infrastructure Finance Company (NBFC–ND–IFC)'. PFC, which has entered its Silver Jubilee Year in 2010, is a Schedule-A, Nav-Ratna CPSE (conferred by Govt. of India on 22 June 2007) in the Financial Service Sector, under the administrative control of the Ministry of Power. PFC was incorporated with an objective to provide financial resources and encourage flow of investments to the power and associated sectors, to work as a catalyst to bring about institutional improvements in streamlining the functions of its borrowers in financial, technical and managerial areas to ensure optimum utilization of available resources and to mobilize various resources from domestic and international sources at competitive rates.

(b) Rural Electrification Corporation Limited: REC, a Nav-Ratna Central Public Sector Enterprise under Ministry of Power, was incorporated on 25 July 1969 under the Companies Act 1956. REC a listed Public Sector Enterprise Government of India with a net worth of ₹14,745 crore as on 31 March 2012. Its main objective is to finance and promote rural electrification projects all over the country. It provides financial assistance to State Electricity Boards, State Government Departments and Rural Electric Cooperatives for rural electrification projects as are sponsored by them. REC provides loan assistance to SEBs/State Power Utilities for investments in rural electrification schemes through its Corporate Office located at New Delhi and 17 field units (Project Offices), which are located in most of the States. The Project Offices in the States coordinate the programmes of REC's financing with the concerned SEBs/State Power Utilities and facilitate in formulation of schemes, loan sanction and disbursement and implementation of schemes by the concerned SEBs/State Power Utilities.

The creation of National Electricity Fund (NEF) was announced in budget speech to mitigate the funding gap and expedite the reform process particularly in distribution sector, which requires huge capital investment. The distribution sector is the most important link in the power sector value chain, which channelizes the revenue realization to provide overall stability to the sector. The requirement of funds for the power sector for the Eleventh Plan was estimated at ₹10,59,515 crore which includes ₹5,91,734 crore for the generation sector, ₹15,875 crore for renovation and modernization of existing generation plants and ₹4,49,577 crore for the transmission and distribution (T&D) sector. The actual expenditure in the distribution sector is much below the estimates due to various reasons during the Eleventh Plan, resulting in huge funding gap. The Creation of National Electricity Fund becomes more relevant since this will encourage utility to match the investments with the planned Generation during Twelfth Plan. Government of India has approved the NEF (Interest Subsidy) Scheme to promote the capital investment in the distribution sector by providing interest subsidy, linked with reform measures, on the loans taken by public and private power utilities for various capital works under distribution projects. This scheme shall be applicable in the entire country and all distribution projects shall be considered. Ministry of Power has constituted a Steering Committee vide Office Memorandum (OM) 24 February 2012–NEF/APDRP dated 13 February 2012 for ensuring effective implementation of the scheme.

(c) The Infrastructure Development Finance Company Limited (IDFC): IDFC has been an integral part of the country's development story since 1997, when the company was formed with the specific mandate to build the nation. Since 2005, it has built on the vision to be the 'one firm' that looks after the diverse needs of infrastructure development. Whether it is financial intermediation for infrastructure projects and services, adding value through innovative products to the infrastructure value chain or asset maintenance of existing infrastructure projects, IDFC focuses on supporting companies to get the best return on investments.

IDFC Project Finance: IDFC Project Finance is a pioneer in lending for infrastructure projects. IDFC was founded with the sole objective of providing and promoting private financing of Indian infrastructure. IDFC lend to costumer through different financial instruments such as:
- Corporate loans
- Project loans
- Subordinated debt
- Loans against shares
- Mezzanine finance
- Equity

IDFC played a key role in introducing innovative financial products and structures such as takeout financing and risk participation facilities, which allow a broader cross-section of lenders and investors to participate in infrastructure financing. Undoubtedly, there is new intent on the part of Government to finance infrastructure and also motivate PPPs.

This is a sign that new intent to finance infrastructure and also motivate PPPs has been showcased by the government.

## PUBLIC–PRIVATE PARTNERSHIPS IN INDIA

In the last one decade, the government has been faced with a huge resource crunch. The combined deficit of the central and state governments is roughly 10 per cent of GDP. Government borrowing has been capped through the Fiscal Responsibility and Budgetary Management Act. This necessarily limits state participation in infrastructure financing, thus opening the door to innovative approaches, such as PPPs.

The Government of India has been encouraging private sector investment and participation in all infrastructure sectors. As the National Development Council has made clear that 'increased private participation has now become a necessity to mobilize the resources needed for infrastructure expansion and upgrading,' the PPP model has been fairly successful in many advanced countries and it is a robust model. PPPs in India are in a nascent stage, but are gaining popularity and support given the dire need to improve infrastructure in the country. A review of international best practice in PPPs suggests a number of core issues that public authorities must address when considering their use for procuring public infrastructure projects. These include:

(a) Whether PPP arrangements will result in better value for money than conventional procurement methods;

(b) Whether the project is affordable in the long term, given overall budgetary constraints;

(c) How willing is the private sector to be involved in the provision of public services; and what type of PPP arrangement is most appropriate for a particular project.

In recent years, the PPP model in India has been fairly successful with several projects being implemented across sectors. However, one of the main problems confronting infrastructure and PPPs in India is the delay in implementing and executing large-scale projects resulting in time and cost overruns. Efficiency in implementing infrastructure projects in India is a rarity. The PPP model is a complex one leading to problems at various stages of implementation and execution of the project. Box 11.1 gives the broad reasons why PPPs fail in some cases.

---

**Box 11.1: Why do some PPPs fail?**

If a contract is inadequately managed, one or more of the following problems may occur and potentially render the project unworkable:

The provider may assume control, leading to unbalanced decisions that do not reflect the interest of the public sector;

Decisions are taken at inappropriate times;

New business processes are unsuccessfully integrated with existing ones, and fail;

People within either sector may fail to understand their roles and responsibilities;

Disputes and misunderstandings may arise, some of which might be inappropriately escalated;

Progress may be slow or there might be an inability to move forward;

The desired benefits may not be achieved; and

There are a number of reasons why the public sector may fail to manage a PPP project successfully, including:

Poorly drafted contracts; contract managers assigned insufficient resources; lack of experience in either the public sector or the provider teams; a failure to adopt an attitude towards partnership; personality clashes between project team personnel; lack of understanding of the complexity, context, and dependencies of the contract; unclear identification of authority and responsibility in relation to commercial decisions; lack of measurement of performance; focus on existing arrangements rather than emphasis on potential improvements; and inadequate monitoring and management of statutory, political, and commercial risks.

---

Undoubtedly, PPPs in India have gathered significant traction in recent years, but it is said that India lacks the overall sophistication of the market in terms of innovative and diverse application of PPPs. According to a 2011 survey by the Royal Institution of Chartered Surveyors, over 240 projects with a value of US$14.5 billion have been delivered over the last 15 years which show that this model has been operational in India, with a majority of $9.4 billion having been delivered during 2005–10 alone.

Over the years, adoption of standardized documents, such as model concession agreements and bidding documents for award of PPP projects have been streamlined, and there has also been accelerated decision-making by agencies in a manner that is fair, transparent and competitive. This approach has contributed significantly to the recent strides in rolling out a large number of

PPPs in different sectors. According to the private participation in infrastructure database of the World Bank (India), with 1,017 PPPs accounting for an investment of ₹486,603 crore, India is second only to China in terms of the number of PPPs; in terms of investment, it is second to Brazil. Transport is the dominant PPP sector in India both by the number of projects and investment, mainly due to the large number of road sector projects. Further efforts are needed to mainstream PPPs in several areas, such as power transmission and distribution, water supply and sewerage, and railways where there are significant resource shortfalls and also a need for efficient delivery of services. Similar efforts will also have to be initiated in social sectors. The government has also been emphasizing the need to explore the scope of PPPs in the development of social sectors like health and education.

Some of the major PPPs undertaken so far are:

(a)  Delhi, Mumbai, Hyderabad and Bengaluru airports.
(b)  Ultra-mega power projects at Sasan (Madhya Pradesh), Mudra (Gujarat), Krishnapatnam (Andhra Pradesh), and Tilaiya (Jharkhand).
(c)  Container terminals at Mumbai, Chennai, and
(d)  Tuticorin ports.
(e)  15 concessions for operations of container trains.
(f)  Jhajjar power transmission project in Haryana.
(g)  298 national and state highway projects.

India's estimated overall infrastructure investment is pegged at US$1 trillion in the Twelfth Five Year Plan of which approximately 40 per cent is expected from the private sector. While this ensures tremendous potential opportunities for private sector investment, it is imperative that both the government and the private sectors address the issues of achieving efficiency in the tendering process, execution of projects on-time and within budgets, and streamlining structural financing problems.

### A case study of Cochin International Airport

Key facts relating to the project

Cochin International Airport (CIAL), also known as Nedumbassery Airport, is the largest and busiest airport in Kerala. The airport was the first to be developed under a PPP model. The project commenced on 21 August 1994 and was completed on 25 May 1999. The total cost of the project is estimated to be around ₹283 crore.

Fifteen hundred acres (6,100,000 m$^2$) of land was acquired for the construction of the airport. Approximately, 2,300 landowners and 872 families were resettled under a rehabilitation package. Major electric lines and an irrigation canal had to be delivered for the construction.

## Imaginative approach to financing the project

The idea of raising money to finance the project through private individuals (in this case Gulf-based NRIs) came up from a relatively junior civil servant. Private placement efforts brought in ₹15 crore as equity. A majority of the NRIs as well as domestic investors were attracted to the project through word-of-mouth publicity and news about CIAL.

## Outstanding leadership

Speedy implementation was facilitated by the key interest of the state's top political leadership. The presence of the chief minister and legislators as board members facilitated the company to work around complex governmental systems, particularly land acquisition, not to forget the dedication and supreme vision of the CEO of CIAL, Mr V. J. Kurien.

## Land acquisition process

The project CEO took charge of personally convincing the farmers and the locals during the land acquisition process. Employment was provided to all those who gave up their land during the construction of the airport and thereafter at the airport itself.

## Contribution by project to fast growth of city

The airport is the primary base for the operations of Air India Express and is a focus city for Air India, GoAir, IndiGo, Jet Airways, JetLite, SpiceJet and Kingfisher Airlines. Efficient financial mobilization and the claim on distinction of not losing even one day of project time due to labour unrest has contributed to chain effects on other developments like setting up of 'Smart City'. The Chief Minister of Kerala remains as ex-officio chairman of CIAL and elected legislators, bureaucrats, nominees of financial institutions (FIs) and investor directors are on the company board. A senior civil servant is the managing director. Contribution by the project to fast growth of the city.

## Case study of the Delhi Gurgaon Expressway[2]

With the growing vehicular density and non-segregation of traffic that led to increase in accidents, acute congestion, wastage of fuel and excessive pollution, it was decided to construct a better road infrastructure through PPP model. This project was mainly launched to convert the very busy section of NH-8 connecting Delhi to Gurgaon into a 6/8 lane access controlled divided carriageway under the responsibility of the National Highways Authority of India (NHAI). The nature of project is build operate and transfer (BOT) where Concessionaire is allowed to collect toll from the users of the project facility during the operation period to recover the investment and, then, to transfer back to the government. The expressway was commissioned late due to the confrontation of project on the ground of land acquisition and changes in the scope of work.

Now, the expressway is fully operational and is handling a significant traffic volume of more than 180,000 PCUs per day, growing at 9 per cent every year. The project has attained key efficiencies in terms of average speed, time span, capacity, etc. Average travel speed has increased from 25.65 km/h to 66 km/h. Average time taken from Delhi to Gurgaon has reduced from 65 minutes to 25 minutes, and capacity in terms of lane has enhanced from previous of 6 lane – 5 km and 4 lane – 22.7 km to 8 lane – 22.3 km and 6 lane – 5.4 km. The numbers of intersections have reduced from 20 to 10 grades separated intersections (GOI, 2010).

## Case study of the Nhava Sheva International Container Terminal (NSICT)

It is India's first private container terminal and one of the most modern container terminals (totally automated computerized container terminal) in India and located within the Jawaharlal Nehru Port across from the island of Mumbai. The 30-year license for the port was awarded in 1997 on the basis of highest Net Present Value (NPV) of royalty offered for the construction of a 600-metre long piled wharf with three approach bridges, reclamation of 20 hectares for container yards and installation of requisite container handling equipment construction of office facilities and ancillary buildings and construction of an electrical sub-station and associated electrical work.

In terms of project outcome, NSICT is fully operational and handles close to 20 per cent of India's container traffic. Significant improvements were observed in key port efficiency parameters:

[2]  GOI (December 2010). Public Private Partnership Projects in India-Compendium for case studies. Department of Economic Affairs, Ministry of Finance, Government of India.

(a) The average turnaround time dropped from 4.5 days in FY98 to about 2 days in FY09.

(b) The pre-berthing delays dropped from close to 1.5 days to 0.5 days over same period.

(c) The success of NSICT can be attributed to its superior productivity parameters as well as the state-of-the-art equipment and latest technology.

Even it was pointed out that the efficient practices of NSCIT project prompted the Jawaharlal Nehru Port Container Thermal (JNPCT) to modify their policy measures and strategy so as to compete with NSICT. More importantly, the project has been considered as a case of a successful PPP process implementation in terms of time, efficiency and cost overruns in public works (GOI, 2010).

### Case study of the Gangavaram Port

The Gangavaram Port, located on the East Coast of India, has been developed as all weather, multipurpose, deep water port with a depth of up to 21 metre, capable of handling Super Cape size vessels of up to 200,000 DWT. The master plan has a provision for 29 berths with a capacity of 200 MTPA to be developed in three phases over 15–20 years. In Phase I, five berths have been constructed with an estimated handling capacity of 35 MTPA. The port is operational since August 2008 and has handled more than 8 MT of cargo as on August 2009, including cargo such as coking coal, steam coal, iron ore, limestone, bauxite, urea, slag, steel, raw sugar, scrap and project cargo. The port has handled the largest coal vessel to call at Indian Ports, Cape size vessel MV Ocean Dragon (151,049 DWT) and has achieved high cargo discharge rates. (71,808 tons per day).

The project has been appreciated on the ground of the capital expenditure efficiency, and the ability of the concessioner company to negotiate better financing terms with the lenders is identified as the contributing factor for same (GOI, 2010).

### Case study of the Bhiwandi Electricity Distribution Franchisee

The growing number of default on power bills and a poor distribution network with a very high level of Aggregate Technical and Commercial (AT&C) losses led the setting up of distribution efficient mechanism in Bhiwandi. Torrent Power AEC Limited (TPAL) was the private entity appointed by MSEDCL for this project. TPAL has completed more than 3 years of operations as the distribution franchisee for the Bhiwandi circle. The project has generated the following key benefits:

- AT&C losses are estimated to have declined by 34 per cent in the first 2 years of the franchise to 24 per cent at the end of year 2008–09.
- The distribution transfer failure rate reduced from 40 per cent at the time of handover to 7 per cent at the end of 2009.
- The load shedding duration reduced from 6 hours a day to 3.5 hours a day.
- The percentage of acute metered sales increased from 23 per cent to 95 per cent.

The efficiency gains brought to the power distribution system through the franchisee model benefited all the stakeholders, thus creating a win–win situation. TPAL has benefited in terms of the increased revenue from reduction in losses and improvement in collection efficiency due to refurbishment of the existing network, regularizing illegal connections, metering, etc. MSEDCL benefited due to savings in terms of reduction in O&M expenditure, capital investments and interest on working capital. The consumer benefited through increased reliability of power supply and improved customer service (GOI, 2010).


## APPROACH TO PPPs IN INDIA

PPPs are still a relatively new phenomenon in India and in a nascent stage compared to the advanced models of PPPs in other countries. Until 2004, there were only 85 PPPs, but between 2004 and 2005, this figure leapt to 500, and in 2011 the number of PPPs in the country had increased to 840 as per the PPP database of the Government of India (see Table 11.4). PPPs worth billions are under development across the country, with the largest number of projects in the road and bridges sector, followed by ports. These sectors dominate PPP initiatives. The leading state users of PPPs by number of projects are Madhya Pradesh and Maharashtra, followed by Gujarat, Tamil Nadu and Karnataka. Almost all contracts have been of the BOT/BOOT-type or their close variants, which involve user payments. Tables 11.4 and 11.5 show that the largest number of PPPs in India have been in the road sector followed by urban development, energy and port sectors. Economic Survey (2008–09) noted six key hurdles faced by PPPs: policy and regulatory gaps; inadequate availability of long-term finance; inadequate capacity in public institutions and public officials to manage PPP processes; inadequate capacity in the private sector –both developer/ investor and technical manpower; inadequate shelf of bankable infrastructure projects that can be bid out to the private sector; and inadequate advocacy to create greater acceptance of PPPs by stakeholders. Undoubtedly, India has to proceed with caution with respect to PPPs, ensuring necessary checks and balances because the benefits of private sector efficiencies will come at a price.

**Table 11.4: PPP projects in central and state sectors in India**

|  | No. of projects | Project cost (₹Crore) |
| --- | --- | --- |
| National highways | 172 | 96,152 |
| Major ports | 21 | 14,735 |
| Airports | 5 | 19,111 |
| Railways | 7 | 2,418 |
| Energy | 4 | 17,500 |
| *Total* | *209* | *149,916* |
| State sector |  |  |
| Roads | 273 | 123,386 |
| Ports | 41 | 66,479 |
| Airports | – | – |
| Railways | 2 | 1,494 |
| Urban infrastructure | 166 | 84,914 |
| Energy | 65 | 56,185 |
| Tourism | 50 | 4,497 |
| Other sectors | 34 | 3,756 |
| *Total* | *631* | *340,711* |
| *Grand total* | *840* | *490,627* |

*Source*: Planning Commission and Infrastructure.gov.in

**Table 11.5: PPP projects in India**

| Sector | Number |
| --- | --- |
| Airports | 5 |
| Education | 19 |
| Health care | 8 |
| Energy | 72 |
| Ports | 62 |
| Roads | 445 |
| Railways | 9 |
| Tourism | 53 |
| Urban development | 167 |
| Total projects | 840 |

*Source*: Planning Commission

In this context and in view of ensuring project sustainability over the long term, the suggestion for independent regulatory bodies in core infrastructure sectors, such as the transport sector—comprising highways, railways, urban metros, ports and airports—is a welcome suggestion for future reforms. Measures also need to be taken to make existing regulatory agencies in the power sector more effective.

To make PPPs a success, state governments need to establish full-fledged PPP departments mandated with developing core competencies, policy frameworks and public discourse. Lessons and experiences of other emerging markets in this context would also be helpful. Rigorous assessment of the costs and benefits of large projects would also be critical for achieving broader public support for the projects. Haryana serves as a suitable example of the same. As a state government, they have their own clear PPP policy and action. They have attracted significant investment and have PPP policies well-established. This has significantly contributed to the fact that Haryana has risen amongst the Indian states at an astonishing pace. It is currently the third ranked state as per GDP indicators.

## MAJOR IMPEDIMENTS TO INFRASTRUCTURE DEVELOPMENT IN THE COUNTRY

### Financing

For a variety of reasons, the infrastructure development has been predominantly public sector. The reasons for this include the public good nature of infrastructure services which imply non-excludability, elements of natural monopoly in the sectors and the need for long-term investments before commercially viable returns could accrue given the highly capital-intensive nature of the sector. The change in the policy regime in the early 1990s also led to a change in the strategies for infrastructure development. Private sector participation in infrastructure development was actively pursued, first in the electricity and telecommunications sectors.

However, we still find infrastructure financing an underdeveloped sector in India. The Government of India has encouraged private sector investment, both domestic and foreign, in almost all infrastructure units through the PPP mode. Today the debate is no longer focused on the conflict between public and private sectors, but rather on the most efficient way of sharing risks, joint financing and achieving balanced partnership.

An essential aspect of the sustained development of infrastructure is financing arrangements for development. As per the Twelfth Five Year Plan document, as much as 50 per cent of the new investments in infrastructure are expected to be from the private sector. While private sector investors would look for the commercial viability of investments, public investments would have to look for the overall economic growth outcome of the investments to make new investments sustainable. Conserving fiscal resources for infrastructure development is essential for maintaining the momentum of infrastructure development.

The crucial role infrastructure development plays in easing supply side constraints to economic growth has well been recognized. According to the Twelfth Plan, as much as US$1 Trillion is required for investment in infrastructure. Certainly, this is not a small number and much has to be done including capital market reforms that would facilitate easier borrowings. The corporate bond market in India is still in its infancy. There is an increasing reliance on private sector for developing and maintaining infrastructure; however, such projects are largely capital intensive and have a high gestation period. Most large developers have over-leveraged their balance sheets to raise debt and their cash flows do not permit them to raise fresh debt to fund new projects. It is because of this that we are witnessing delay in achieving financial closure. In FY12, Concession Agreements were signed for more than 25 projects, but financial closure of 15 projects is still pending. This problem is further compounded with most commercial banks and financial institutions having reached their exposure limits for funding infrastructure. Their ability to lend is further constrained by the slow mobilization of deposit as compared to the growth in credit and the asset–liability mismatch in commercial banks.

### Land acquisition

One of the single largest roadblocks for development of infrastructure would be the issue of land acquisition. Resistance from local communities has proven to be a potent force and has led to delays in infra projects. There is generally a huge difference between the registered value offered and the actual market value, which results in disputes and litigation. Moreover, valuations are conducted on the basis of the current status of land, and the system does not capture the appreciation after the construction of the project.

Land being a pre-requisite for any infrastructure project, acquiring land has become a curse for many potential projects. Local communities feel cheated out from the path of development, which leads to distrust and disputes. In addition, rehabilitation packages are not planned meticulously and execution is inefficient. For instance, the National Highway Authority of India (NHAI) bids out highway projects even when it has acquired only 10–15 per cent of the land, or even less, assuming that the balance land will be acquired by the time financial closure of the project is achieved. Almost 70 per cent of PPP road projects witness delayed financial closure and commencement of construction.

Lack of proper dispute resolution mechanism adds to the delays. Disputes often lead to lengthy litigation and substantial project delays. Taking possession of land for large projects is both a contentious and time-consuming issue. There were weaknesses in the laws governing land acquisition and, right now, a process of securing political consensus on the amendment to existing legislation is in progress. There is a need to reduce the time needed for land acquisition while recognizing the competing demands on scare resource. Infrastructure projects require an efficient process of land acquisition to be in place with adequate checks and balances for considerations of equity and justice.

A new bill, the Land Acquisition and Rehabilitation & Resettlement Bill (LARR), has been passed in the Parliament and is a law. The Bill is expected to ease the process of land acquisition and reduce the number of litigations due to the government's detailed and improved provisions for compensation and rehabilitation, but this will also substantially increase the cost of acquiring land. This could be detrimental to private investments in the long term, since viability of projects may be affected.

*Regulatory framework*

Most of the infrastructure projects in India suffer from delays in completion. This is mainly due to an inadequate regulatory framework and inefficiency in the approval process. Infrastructure projects require multiple sequential clearances at various levels of government. As an illustration, more than 2 years were needed for the Gujarat Pipavav port project to receive the necessary clearances after achieving financial closure. Moreover, most of the large projects involve dealings with various ministries. Often, the perspectives of the different ministries/departments vary and coordination remains inefficient (World Bank, 2006).

The various categories of approvals required across the project cycle at every stage, right from the pre-tendering stage to post construction. While it is important to have a rigorous procedure that ensures transparency and quality, the bureaucratic complexities and the protracted procedure for securing approvals are often considered serious disincentives for developers and contractors.

Environmental safeguards and guidelines have proven to be one of the major reasons for delay in infrastructure projects, especially in the power sector. While new projects need to comply with these regulations, even a project under construction may need to comply with revised standards midway through the execution stage. While the concerned Ministry states that the delays are primarily due to non-compliance with the procedures of Environment Impact Assessment (EIA) notifications and circulars issued, the terms of compliance involve a complex and time-consuming procedure.

## Delay in clearances and implementation

Drawbacks of the regulatory framework naturally extend to the implementation of infrastructure projects. These lead to time and cost overruns, and delay in financial closure of projects.

Time is lost both before the actual physical commencement of the project work and in the course of execution. In terms of cost to the economy, delays in implementing power projects are arguably the most serious. Taking possession of land for large projects (and thermal power projects in particular require extensive land area) is both contentious and time consuming issue. Land and environment-related issues often lead to delays caused by legal procedures initiated by various stakeholders.

Among the infrastructure sectors, railway projects account for among the highest cost overruns (169 per cent escalation) caused by dragged-out projects. Much of this occurs because of a factor that we have not discussed above: the deliberate commencement of work on a far greater number of projects than the organization's financial capacity for execution.

Shortage in trained manpower in vocational skills has been highlighted in more than one context. The situation is true even in the case of infrastructure projects. The process of enlarging the facilities for vocational training across the country has to become more effective to meet the manpower needs of the growing economy. The requirement is not merely for large numbers but for large numbers which are imparted with quality skills.

These issues have no easy solutions. Transparency in procedures like contract award and setting of time limits for completing legal processes are among the obvious remedies. Imparting improved project management skills and techniques within the implementing agencies is another area that can fetch results in the short term. Removal of weaknesses in the long-standing law and setting up additional manufacturing capacity will require more time. However, introducing greater competition, including imports, requires as much attention.

To deal with this, the head of state now has a direct committee. The setting up of the Cabinet Committee under the Prime Minister has shown a significant amount of intent indicating that the government is well aware of the concerns raised while debating various clearances. This change is indicative of a potential 'fast-track' process and the fact that infrastructure projects, especially PPP projects, are vital to the national growth story.

## Slack capacity

It was pointed out that growth of electricity capacity in India has observed a substantial dip in the last decade compared to the level of the 1980–90s. The capacity growth which was at around 120 per cent in the decade of the 1980s went down to around 60 per cent in the decade of the 1990s and was only around 30.2 per cent in the period 2000–07. Generation growth was also around 120 per cent in the 1980s and so capacity use was roughly constant. In the 1990s, at around 90 per cent, it was much higher than expansion of capacity at 60 per cent, showing a substantial increase in Plant Load Factors. In this decade, the slack seems to have been used up and both capacity and generation growth are similar at around 30 to 33 per cent. Generation growth is now around 5 per cent annual as compared to around 9 per cent in the last decade and a near crisis situation is emerging.[3]

Ironically, while overall infrastructure remains inadequate, there is also slack capacity to deal with it. In the case of power, the causes are both internal and external. Internally, there is abundant scope for improving the Plant Load Factor in generating units and for reducing line losses. Both problems need targeted outlays on equipment modernization and adoption of efficient management practices. In the case of line losses, governance issues are cardinal. The external factors include fuel shortages that have caused under-utilization of capacity in coal-based as well as gas-based plants. In addition to the problems associated with the coal sector, logistic constraints attributable to the railways also contribute to this problem.

### Uneven private participation

The record so far of the infrastructure sectors in regard to private participation and even within segments of the same sector itself is very uneven. Only the telecom sector has crossed the hurdles of privatization though the allotment of spectrum for 3G services and infrastructure sharing in rural areas are yet to be resolved. The ports sector has functioning examples of fully privately owned ports. However, further scope exists for private participation in select areas of port operation. In the case of airports, Green field airports have come up in the private sector. There are also successful cases of the upgradation of metro airports under the PPP mode. To garner investments for upgrading the second tier of airports there is urgency to develop suitable PPP models. The Power sector, where the need for private investment is the greatest, provides an example of uneven progress within the sector itself. The progress is most inadequate in the distribution sector – despite some successes – and the need to overcome this drawback is of the highest priority because efficient distribution holds the key to efficient pricing as well as overall efficiency of the sector itself. The roads sector has developed a viable

---

3   Yoginder Alagh (2010). Transmission and Distribution of Electricity in India: Regulation, Investment and Efficiency. http://www.oecd.org/dev/partnerships-networks/46235043.pdf

model for private entry on the basis of BOT and its variants but faced problems of implementation. In the Railways PPP schemes like 'own your wagon' contrast with models to award concessions for passenger and freight terminals still remain to be developed.

Overall, though there is increasing number of cases of successful PPPs initiated in recent years in India, the PPP route has not been able to meet the supply–demand gap in infrastructure facilities. The uneven success of PPPs shows that difficult issues face the PPP route for infrastructure development requiring establishment of clear-cut and stable legal framework, adequate information for the private sector participants, competent institutional mechanisms to prioritize investment projects, efficient mechanisms for dispute resolution and effective financial markets.

## The National PPP (Preparation, Procurement and Management) Policy and Dispute Resolution Bill 2013

With the wide ranging experiences from the PPP models within and outside the country, the academicians proposed a well-structured legal regime for handling such issues. In this direction, the Department of Economic Affairs, Ministry of Finance has carried out Draft PPP Rules, 2012, where PPP Preparation, Penetration and Procurement have been addressed for the fuller utilization of private sector potentialities, while ensuring feasibility of the project, proper setting up of the establishment and its smooth functioning, transparency, accountability, etc. Major provisions include the Identification of a PPP Project, Designation of Project Officer and Project Management Team, Pre-Feasibility Report, Internal Clearance to Proceed with Project Development, Registration of the PPP Project with DEA, Budgeting and planning for the preparation and procurement process of the PPP Project, Appointment of consultants and advisors, Feasibility Study, Project Affordability and Expenditure Control, Value for Money Assessment, Revenue Sharing or Revenue Support Mechanisms, Developing the procurement plan, Formation of Tender Evaluation Committee, Appointment of Independent Monitor, etc.[4]

Keeping in view the holding back of big ticket projects and a discouragement to the investor in the current fiscal year, the country felt the need of setting up of institutional mechanism to redress the public contract-related problems. In this direction, the Planning Commission finalized the Public Contracts (Settlement of Disputes) Bill 2013 which is under consideration at the part of the government. The move comes as a big relief not only for the private players but also for the

---

[4] GOI (March 20, 2012). Draft PPP Rules, 2012, Discussion Report, Department of Economic Affairs, Ministry of Finance, Government of India.

government, which is burdened with delays and cost overruns arising out of disputes between the parties involved in PPP projects. At present, all disputes in public contracts are resolved through the Arbitration Act of 1996. However, the process of arbitration in India is marred by huge financial, legal and opportunity costs of locked investments because of the time taken to resolve such disputes.[5] The Bill ensures the constitution of a 'Tribunal for public contracts' which will be dealing with disputes in the public contracts exceeding ₹5 crore. It grants power for handling contract executed by central government, state government, local or statutory authority or any corporation society or trust owned and controlled by the government. Under the breach of contract, the tribunal has the power for termination, cancellation, repudiation and claims for damages. The timely settlement of disputes is also the important feature of the said bill.[6]

### Governance-related constraints

Infrastructure projects are affected by governance-related constraints in several ways. Project award process has to be transparent. It is highlighted in the existing literature that the major issue for PPP projects hinges towards the lower level of incentive-based regulation. In an empirical study, it is pointed out that project governance issues were identified across two dominant interfaces – one between the public and private sector and the other between the project and the societal stakeholders. Governance mechanisms based on providing shared incentives combined with the capacity to administer projects are effective in combating governance challenges across the public–private sector interface. Cognitive mechanisms which make the project more accountable to the societal stakeholders are most effective across the project–stakeholder interface.

The experience of contract award process in telecom should help improve the process in the other sectors. Given the wide 'rural–urban divide' in the infrastructure services, the general budgetary support in the form of measures such as tax incentives, viability gap funding or direct allocations to make infrastructure services more widely available may be necessary over the long term.

Upgrading India's infrastructure to the best global standards as a strategic requirement has provided the context for the current strategies. Recent developments in the global economy would suggest that accelerated growth of

---

5 Yogima Seth Sharma, (1 October 2013). Planning Commission finalizes PPP tribunal bill draft. The Economic Times.
6 PTI (October 02, 2013). Government to push PPP disputes resolution bill in winter session. The Economic Times.

the Indian economy not only would benefit large disadvantaged sections of the country's own population but also would be necessary for sustained global growth.

## Efficient pricing of infrastructure

There is unequivocal linkage between problems of attracting private investment in infrastructure and price fixation of infrastructure services. This represents a major challenge for the policy strategy during the Eleventh Plan and Twelfth Five Year Plan.

The broad policy approach relies on independent regulation. This is the case with the four major infrastructure sectors: telecom, power, airports and ports. Roads where pricing is of limited application and railways where all services are priced but prices continue to be set by the operator are the exceptions. Irrigation remains a complex sector, where power and water pricing for agriculture are yet to achieve resources even for maintenance of services.

The regulator in telecom is fully empowered, but as forces of competition have taken over much of the sector, the prices ruling are well below the ceilings set. The regulator for airport services has just come into position, which is a positive development. Pricing issues will come to the fore in the sector when more players enter the field through green field projects or JVs with AAI. Potential for large gains from pricing efficiencies are expected in power and railways because the pricing regime continues to be highly inefficient in both. A comparison of pricing of retail power supply in China and in India shows that the price ratio ranges between consumer groups within 1.8 in China, while in India it is as high as 7.8. The National Tariff Policy stipulates that the tariff differentials should be brought down to the range of 2 in phases, but the progress has been slow.

The global PPP experience: Successful models

Some countries have meaningful experiences regarding the functioning of PPP projects. The PPPs in UK have been highly successful and with several countries around the world trying to emulate the UK model. According to British National Audit Office, an assessment of the UK PPP policy in 2009 shows that 65 per cent of the contracts were delivered on time and within the agreed budget.[7] In Australia, the financial advantage of PPPs has been well-documented. The University of Melbourne conducted a study of 42 traditional procurement projects and 25 PPPs and concluded that PPPs provide far greater cost certainty. In related

---

[7]  FICCI and Earnest & Young (2012). Accelerating public private partnership in India.

research with the University of Melbourne, the Allen Consulting Group studied 21 PPPs and 33 traditional Australian projects and found the PPP cost advantage to be 'economically and statistically significant'.[8] Also, China's experiences in terms of infrastructure development through PPP are also appreciated. As an outcome of political and economic settings being conducive to the same, China could exploit the fullest advantage for the parties involved in the contract. China's efficient bureaucracy, fewer corruption cases, zero or minimal red tape and cheap resources have been considered as the factors contributing to the success of PPP projects. Resulting numerous SPVs (Special Purpose Vehicles; corporations set up to manage PPP projects) are efficiently bolstering the rapid growth and success of PPP projects in that country.[9] Even the US economy has experienced the limited scope of PPP projects' potentialities. It is pointed out that the United Kingdom financed $50 billion in transportation infrastructure via PPPs between 1990 and 2006, the United States, an economy more than six times as large as that of the United Kingdom, financed only approximately $10 billion between those years. However, the use of PPPs to provide the U.S. infrastructure increased fivefold between 1998–2007 and 2008–10.[10]

In UK, the private sector's project management skills, innovation and risk management expertise, such as ensuring buildings, are delivered to a high quality on time and budget and those assets are maintained to a high standard throughout their lives, are the major factors for effective functioning of UK private finance investment (PFI). Also, the UK Government's approach of utmost transparency, launching the Operational PFI Savings Programme to improve the cost effectiveness, providing a helping hand to the PFI projects through financial assistance, introducing new arrangements for the assurance and approval of major projects to strengthen scrutiny and control, etc. are the few prominent steps in the direction of contributing to the successful experience of PFIs.[11]

It is observed that UK and Australia have already been enjoying the better legal framework and, hence, the factors such as favourable legal framework and commitment and responsibility of public and private sectors emerged as the medium ranking factors for contributing the PPPs success. Whereas the factors like strong and good private consortium, stable macroeconomic condition and appropriate

---

8    PwC (June 2010). Public Private Partnership: The US perspective. PricewaterhouseCoopers.
9    Arindam Chaudhary (7 February 2013). Why the public-private partnership model has failed in India. The Sunday Indian.
10   Eduardo Engel, Ronald Fischer, Alexander Galetovic (February 2011). Public-Private Partnerships to Revamp U.S. Infrastructure, the Hamilton Project, Brookings.
11   HM Treasury (December 2012), A new approach to public private partnerships, Government of UK.

risk allocation and risk sharing have been considered the most important factor for enhancing the performance of U.K. and Australian PPP infrastructure projects.[12]

The PPP projects in India have certain limitations as the share of PPP in the total infrastructure development has been minuscule.[13] Besides, these projects have been facing the wide ranging challenges as stated above. Additionally, in this context, the ability of PPP projects to deliver the best services is limited. The PPP model even in the developed countries also got confrontation. However, the existing gap from the targeted output puts forth the scope for learning the lessons from past experiences emanating within and outside the country, and moving ahead seems the prudent decision for India to enhance its infrastructure base, a key pillar for the Twelfth Five Year Plan of India.

With the limited success of PPP projects in India (where several projects being cancelled and renegotiated), it is pointed out that further institutional reforms, such as the appointment of an independent regulator in several sectors, the setting up of dispute resolution mechanisms and so on can address the growing challenges of PPP projects. In this direction, the setting up of the Public Contract Bill 2013 is a landmark step to deal with the bottlenecks of infra projects.

## CONCLUSIONS

India is the fourth largest economy in the world. However, one factor which is a drag on its development is the lack of adequate infrastructure. In fact, there are estimates suggesting that the lack of proper infrastructure pulls down India's GDP growth by 1–2 per cent every year. Physical infrastructure has a direct impact on the growth and overall development of an economy. While strategies to accelerate economic growth did anticipate the need for faster development of infrastructure as well, the fast growth of the Indian economy in recent years has placed increasing stress on physical infrastructure. Sectors such as electricity, railways, roads, ports, airports, irrigation, and urban and rural water supply and sanitation continue to experience the pressure of rising demand for services even as they suffer from a substantial initial deficit. The goals of inclusive and high level of economic growth can be achieved only if this infrastructure deficit is overcome. Infrastructure development would also help in creating a better investment climate in India. To develop infrastructure, there is a continuing need to revisit the issues of budgetary

---

[12] Cheung, Esther, Chan, Albert and Kajeswki, Stephe, L. (2012). Factors contributing to the successful public private partnership projects: comparing Hong Kong, with Australia and the United Kingdom. Journal of Facilities Management, 10(1), pp. 45-58.

[13] L. Lakshmanan, (Summer 2008). *Public-Private Partnership in Indian Infrastructure Development: Issues and Options, Reserve Bank of India Occasional Papers, Vol. 29(1).*

allocation, tariff policy, fiscal incentives, private sector participation and PPPs to ensure that required infrastructure development takes place.

The public sector is expected to continue to play an important role in building transport infrastructure. However, the resources needed are much larger than the public sector can provide and public investment will, therefore, have to be supplemented by private sector investments, in PPP mode. This strategy was followed in the Eleventh Plan and it has begun to show results. PPPs are still a relatively new phenomenon in India and in a nascent stage compared to the experience in a number of other countries. However, PPPs have compensated for the budgetary and borrowing constraints of the governments. They also imply efficiency gains, efficient use of resources, availability of modern technology and better project design. They have also led to faster implementation, reduced lifecycle costs and more optimal risk allocation. The private sector has responded to the government's attempts to encourage private-sector-led growth and investment for meeting infrastructure deficit. Projects in the roads sector now attract far more bidders than they did five years ago. Apart from the projects surveyed in the study, some of the projects such as Coimbatore Bypass, Mumbai–Pune Expressway, Pipavav and Mundra ports, Delhi and Hyderabad airports, Mundra and Sasan UMPP demonstrate the efficacy of the PPP model in India. The Economic Survey (2008–09) noted six key hurdles faced by PPPs: policy and regulatory gaps; inadequate availability of long-term finance; inadequate capacity in public institutions and public officials to manage PPP processes; inadequate capacity in the private sector – both developer/investor and technical manpower; inadequate shelf of bankable infrastructure projects that can be bid out to the private sector; and inadequate advocacy to create greater acceptance of PPPs by the stakeholders.

It is too early to give the conclusion statement regarding the success of the PPP model in India. As defining success is multidimensional – it can be considered in light of fulfilment of the targeted output, comparison with other public sector undertakings, societal welfare, etc. Overall, the outcome for PPP projects in India has remained mixed so far as few identify the successful story for highway PPP projects, whereas the outcome for Metro rail projects through PPP has remained disappointing. The Union Urban Development Ministry's report on 'Innovative Financing of Metro Rail Projects' suggests that PPP has not been very successful in Metro rail projects. It is also mentioned that there has been the dominance of public sector mode in developing metro infrastructure worldwide.[14] The poor delivery of PPP projects in Metro rail infrastructure may be attributed to the functioning of

---

[14] In 113 cities across the world having Metro rails, 88 per cent have been developed and are being operated in public sector mode whereas in only 12 per cent cities some form of PPP exists.

PPP model at substantial smaller scale compared to the public sector, and having infancy in this sector. It is added in the existing literature that measuring success of PPP projects at this stage is difficult as these projects are usually having 20–30 year contracts period. The success of a PPP can be measured only once it has been operational for 10–15 years and can be judged if it is delivering its intended societal benefits. Indian agreements are in a nascent stage, and it is not possible to determine whether its PPPs have been successful thus far.[15]

India has to proceed with caution with respect to PPPs, ensuring necessary checks and balances because the benefits of private-sector efficiencies will come at a price. In this context, the suggestion for independent regulatory bodies in core infrastructure sectors such as the transport sector – comprising highways, railways, ports and airports – is a welcome suggestion for future reforms. Measures also need to be taken to make existing regulatory agencies in the power sector more effective. To make PPPs a success, state governments need to establish full-fledged PPP departments mandated with developing the core competencies, policy framework and public discourse. Rigorous assessment of the costs and benefits of the large projects would also be critical for achieving broader public support for the completion of projects to show results in both the Centre and the State sectors.

In sum, the infrastructure development in India will continue to be mainly demand led and, therefore, efficient use of existing infrastructure and efficient construction of new assets will be critical in the pursuit of higher economic growth. Fiscal support will continue to be dominant for infrastructure development but equally important would be the enabling policies that could lead to streamlining of procedures and protecting interests of both investors and consumers.

## REFERENCES

Asian Development Bank: Study on Public–Private Partnerships. 2011.

Banerji, S., K. Gangopadhyay, I. Patnaik, and A. Shah. 2011. 'New Thinking on Corporate Bond Market in India'.

Competition Issues in Regulated Industries: Case of Indian Transport Sector (TERI, 2009).

Department of Economic Affairs, Ministry of Finance, Government of India. 2009. 'Position Paper on the Power Sector in India'.

Department of Land Resources, Ministry of Rural Development, GOI. 2011. 'The Land Acquisition, Rehabilitation and Resettlement Bill'. 31st report. http://www.unescap.org/ttdw/common/TPT/PPP/text/ppp_guidebook.pdf.

Economic Survey of India. 2011–12.

---

[15] NBAR (May 2012). Collaborating to construct India: The role of public-private partnerships in infrastructure development. National Bureau of Asian Research.

FICCI KPMG Report on Urban Transport. 2012. Getting Urban Transport on Track.

FICCI Ernst & Young Report. 2012. Accelerating Public–Private Partnerships in India.

IDFC Infrastructure Report. 2012.

India Electricity. 2011 (A Ministry of Power – FICCI report).

India – Building Capacities for Public–Private Partnerships – World Bank. 2006.

indiawaterreview.com

jnnurm.nic.in

Key Features of Budget. 2012–13. http://indiabudget.nic.in.

Khan, H. R. 2011. *Infrastructure Financing in India – Progress and Prospects*. Diamond Jubilee International Conference on Frontiers of Infrastructure Finance, Vinod Gupta School of Management & RCG School of Infrastructure Design and Management, Kharagpur: Indian Institute of Technology.

Nataraj, G. 2007. *Infrastructure Challenges in South Asia: The Role of Public–Private Partnerships*. ADB Institute Discussion Paper No. 80.

pppinindia.com

PPP Cell, Department of Economic Affairs Ministry of Finance, Government of India. 2008. 'Criticality of Legal Issues & Contracts for Public–Private Partnerships, Position Paper and Workshop Report, New Delhi'. www.pppinindia.com.

Planning Commission, Government of India, Eleventh Five Year Plan. 2007–12. 'Rural Development, Industry, Services, and Physical Infrastructure' 3.

Planning Commission, Government of India, Faster, Sustainable and More Inclusive Growth. 2012–17. *An Approach Paper to the Twelfth Five Year Plan*.

Reports of Working Groups for the Twelfth Plan. 2012–17. Power, Coal & Lignite, Urban Transport, Railways, Urban & Industrial Water, Roads & Highways.

Report of the Expert Group for Modernization of Indian Railways. 2012.

Raghuram, G., and R. Gangwar. 2010. 'Lessons from PPPs of Indian Railways and Way Forward'.

The 21st Century Public Policy Institute. 2011. 'Asian Bond Markets Development and Regional Financial Cooperation'.

The Secretariat for the Committee on Infrastructure, Planning Commission, Government of India. 2006. 'Guidelines for Financial Support to Public–Private Partnerships in Infrastructure'. wwwinfrastructure.gov.in.

The World Bank. 2006. 'Financing Infrastructure: Addressing Constraints and Challenges'.

Vaidya, C., and H. Vaidya. 2008. 'Creative Financing of Urban Infrastructure in Indiathrough Market-based Financing and Public–Private Partnership Options'.

Working Sub-group on Infrastructure. 2012–17. 'Working Group on Savings Formulation of the Twelfth Five Year Plan'. *Infrastructure Funding Requirements and Its Sources over the Implementation Period of the Twelfth Five Year Plan*.

# Section 5

# Emerging issues in growth: The labour and capital markets

# 12

# Issues in Labour Cost and Employment

## Arup Mitra
## Chandan Sharma

## INTRODUCTION

In the backdrop of globalization, developing countries are trying desperately to reduce the cost of production in a significant manner so that it can help them achieve an edge over others in terms of competitiveness. Labour costs are usually thought to be highly significant. Hence, constant and continuous efforts to pursue capital intensive methods of production are made to attain significant labour productivity gains and to reduce the labour costs. As labour intensive methods also involve a huge range of uncertainties due to labour unrest, capital intensive technological progress is thought to be an obvious solution. No doubt, productive employment generation is an important challenge for most of the developing countries. Thus, keeping in view several rigidities including unionisation and the lack of flexibility that pose major constraints and hamper the smooth functioning of firms, labour market reforms have been suggested on a large scale in order to improve the competitiveness of the countries. Economic reforms in various spheres have already been introduced to remove bureaucratic and other structural rigidities in the system and enhance economic growth, which in turn is thought to reduce poverty by generating gainful job opportunities. However, in the Indian context of example, the lack of labour market deregulations is viewed to be a major constraint in generating productive employment in the formal manufacturing sector and attaining other desirable goals in terms of attracting FDI and rapid industrialization. This is because globalization and shifts in the production activities are expected to impact the labour market outcomes such as wages, employment and labour productivity. Secondly and most importantly, for other reforms, in the area of trade for example, to be successful, labour market reforms are considered as essential prerequisites. It is generally viewed that the labour markets in developing countries are rigid in terms of work practices, wages, hiring and firing policies, etc, and all these have been attributed to the existing labour laws (Fallon and Lucas, 1991)[1].

On the whole, sluggish employment growth or the absence of significant effects of growth on living standards through productive employment generation is viewed as an outcome of strict labour market regulations. For example, Botero, et. al. (2004) noted that countries that have tough labour-market regulations have lower rates of labour-market participation and higher levels of unemployment. In India's case, findings of Amin (2008) reveal that the labour regulation has sizable and negative effects on employment growth. Focusing on the Indian states, Almeida and Carneiro (2008) found that inflexible labour regulations not only constrain the size of the firm but also reduce employment. Ahsan and Pagés (2008) argued that employment protection diminishes output and employment without benefiting workers much. In the case of Colombia, Kugler (2004) finds that a reduction in firing costs reduces the level of unemployment.[2] Findings of Connell et al. (2008) suggest that labour market reforms have several beneficial effects on employment and the quality of life of labours. In an important study, Hasan, et al. (2003) observed that labour demand elasticity increases with reductions in protection. Providing evidence from a panel of 48 developing countries, his findings suggested that trade liberalization is more likely to have a beneficial impact when labour markets are flexible and vice versa. More regulated and rigid labour markets are associated with higher real wages, which, however, come at the expense of employment.

Some of the studies also indicate that flexibility in the labour market with reforms in other sectors of the economy is expected to raise employment and also the real wages in the long-run, if not in the short-run (Fallon and Lucas, 1991). Reforms in trade sector, for example, provide reorientation in production towards exports, which is expected to have a favourable impact on employment (Krueger, 1983; Balassa, 1986).[3] Evidence on limited benefits from trade liberalisation for the typical worker largely refers to the Latin American experience. Some argue that trade does have the potential to benefit workers at large though the nature

---

[1]  The World Bank report on "Doing Business in 2005" estimated that India is ranked at 48th in terms of 'Rigidity in Employment Index'[1] compared to China's rank of 30.

[2]  For a detailed review of the related literature, in the case of developing countries, can be seen in Djankov and Ramalho (2008).

[3]  Despite the generally favourable expectations of job creation as a result of the reforms, various theoretical considerations, experience show that the impact of the reforms on the labour markets generally negative in an initial phase. Liberalization impairs import competing activities, while the policies of State reform tend to constrain public sector growth. Both factors have a negative short-term impact on employment in the initial years (see Weller, 2001).

of labour market regulations actually play an important role in giving a tangible shape to these benefits (Edwards and Edwards, 1994). Hence, one important view, as mentioned above, is that with the presence of regulated labour market, the overall impact of economic policy may not necessarily have positive impact on employment generation. While there may be a case for removing labour market rigidities by discouraging the political patronization of the unions and relaxing the strict labour laws that prohibit employment growth, attention also needs to be given to the labour welfare issues. There is a fear that flexibility may expand employment but affect wages and social security support to the labour adversely. Hence, the debate continues as to whether labour market deregulations are to be pursued aggressively or the national governments should be more careful in recommending major flexibility to the employers.

Given the vast stretches of underemployment and poverty, developing countries cannot afford to have rapid growth that does not benefit labour in a significant way. Hence, there has emerged a strong case for speedy reforms in the labour market together with reforms in other segments of the economy. But it is a well-known fact that in the process of economic reforms there are certain social costs particularly for the existing labour force, and any such reforms without addressing these costs would only have adverse impact on the labour market and economy. For example, Besley and Burgess (2004) estimate that 'pro-worker' labour reforms in India have adversely affected employment and productivity and increased poverty in the country. Goldar (2004) argued that the unions in India have become weaker in the reform period, which caused a slow-down in the growth rate of real product wage rate in the organized manufacturing in the nineties. Further, the ILO-SAAT study (ILO-SAAT, 1996) emphasizes that although labour market reforms could reduce the social costs of structural adjustments, it cannot minimize the social costs of stabilization. Though deregulation might be desirable in the context of increasing integration of a particular economy with the global economy, any reform in the labour market, the study argues, needs to be a gradualist one and it has to be accompanied by appropriate social safety nets and some institutional innovations that help the job losers in the process of labour reallocation. Hasty reforms would only reduce the social welfare. Moreover, given the fact that the organized labour market in several developing countries like India accounts for only a small fraction of the work force, it is legitimate to wonder if labour market reform can be of much consequence in such context (ILO-SAAT, 1996). But there is a need for a balanced view on this issue as both labour and capital have been pushed to the market forces following the reforms. Furthermore, it is also important to take into account that labour market reforms cannot be viewed in isolation but rather as a component of a comprehensive program of structural reforms (see e.g., Agénor, et al., 2007).

Against this background, in this chapter, we attempt to provide answers to several important questions related to employment, wage rate, labour market reforms and productivity. Specifically, the analyses of this study have five important objectives. First, in a cross country framework, we attempt to examine how responsive employment is in relation to wages in the manufacturing sector. Second, we compare the elasticity of employment with respect to growth and wages for a set of countries. Third, our analysis seeks to quantify how much of productivity growth actually gets transferred to the workers. Fourth, in order to evaluate the case of labour market deregulation, we attempt to estimate the cost of labour in production process in a set of countries. Finally, focusing on an interesting case of India, we attempt to analyse the wage-productivity nexus in the manufacturing sector.

The outline of the rest of the chapter is as follows. Section 2 examines the employment elasticity with respect to wages and the wage-productivity linkage based on key indicators of labour market statistics for the manufacturing sector. Section 3 uses different indicators of labour market deregulation in order to examine its effect on employment. Section 4 focuses on Indian organized or formal manufacturing sector as a case study and section 5 summarises the major findings.

## WAGE ELASTICITY OF EMPLOYMENT AND WAGE – PRODUCTIVITY RELATIONSHIP

Since much of the focus of labour market deregulation lies on introducing wage flexibility or in other words, removal of downward stickiness of wages so as to expand employment opportunities in the high productivity sector we may like to examine how responsive employment is in relation to wages in the manufacturing sector. Specifically, we are interested to know whether change in wage rate affect the level of employment in developing countries. For this purpose, we utilize information from 'The Key Indicators of the Labour Market' (KILM).[4] For knowing the inter-linkage, we have computed wage elasticity of employment, which is presented in Table 12.1-A in the appendix. The table also gives the rate of growth of employment in industry (manufacturing and allied activities) and the rate of growth of wage in the manufacturing sector. Wage elasticity of employment defined as the ratio of the rate of growth of employment to that of wages turns out to be close to unity or more than unity with a negative sign only in the case of Cambodia, Mexico and Uruguay. Though in some of the other countries the magnitude is high, the elasticity is seen to have a wrong (or

---

[4] KILM is of the International Labour Office (ILO)'s research tool for labour market information. The first KILM was released in 1999. It has since become a flagship database of ILO and is used on a daily basis by researchers and policy-makers throughout the world.

positive) sign and in the rest of the countries the elasticity is quite low even when it is negative. This piece of evidence may be taken to suggest that deregulation in terms of wage flexibility does not have a strong standing across countries. In other words, raising employment substantially through wage reduction does not seem to be promising in a large majority of the developing countries. However, it would be interesting to examine if similar patterns emerge from the United Nations Industrial Development Organization (UNIDO) data as well.

Next we attempt to analyse the elasticity of employment with respect to growth and wages and the elasticity of wages with respect to labour productivity. Wage elasticity of employment is computed as the ratio of the rate of growth of employment to the rate of growth of wages. For this purpose, we utilized the UNIDO data[5] for the manufacturing sector. We present this ratio in Table 12.2-A in the appendix, which turns out to be negative in a number of countries[6], (Table 12.2-A). However, it is high (i.e., more than -0.5) only in India, Senegal, Vietnam and Bangladesh and Botswana (in descending order of magnitude). Econometric estimation of elasticity of employment with respect to wages also confirms a high magnitude with a negative sign only in the case of Brazil, Japan[7], Macau, Madagascar, Malaysia, Mauritius and Philippines (see Table 12.3-A in the

---

[5]  For the manufacturing sector information on employment, value added, wages and salaries and gross fixed capital formation have been compiled by UNIDO. The INDSTAT4 2007 ISIC Rev.3 database reports time series data for currently 113 countries. From this we picked up those which fall into the South and East Asian regions, African and Latin American countries for the period starting from 1990 to 2004. The nominal variables are available both in terms of national currency and US dollars. We preferred the later as it would make international comparison easier. The time series of nominal variables reflect (a) the effect of exchange rate fluctuations, (b) price movements in respective countries and (c) the real changes. UNIDO used the average period exchange rates as given in the International Financial Statistics to convert the series in dollar terms. This way the effect of changes in the exchange rate are neutralised. As far as the country specific price inflations are concerned we have taken the Gross Domestic Product (GDP) deflators from the World Development Indicators. Since different countries have different bases we have tried to convert the series of GDP deflators with respect to a common base for all the countries (1990) though this has not been possible for some of the countries which started the series at a later date. The GDP deflators have been used to neutralise the price effect in the series of nominal variables. The deflated wage bill has been divided by the total number of employees to work out the real wage rate. Needless to add that information on all the variables are not reported for each of the years. For some of the countries only one or two variables and that too for only a few years this information is available. Hence, the computation of growth rate of a particular variable does not necessarily reflect the movement from 1990 through 2004.

[6]  India, Senegal, Vietnam, Bangladesh, Botswana, Panama, Peru, Malaysia, Ethiopia, Brazil, Mexico, Singapore, Mauritius and Uruguay.

[7]  Japan has been included though it is not a developing country.

appendix). Hence, UNIDO data like the KILM data do not provide any significant evidence on the basis of which the argument for employment expansion through wage reduction can be built strongly.

In the related literature, effects of productivity growth on wage and employment are a debatable issue (e.g., see Phelps 1994, Blanchard and Wolfers, 2000, Krueger and Solow, 2002 and Pissarides, 2000). Considering the contrary evidence on the issue, next we pose the question how much of productivity growth actually gets transferred to the workers. In the neoclassical framework the benefits of productivity growth gets shared between the entrepreneurs and the employees.

To analyse the issue, using the KLIM data, we estimate the elasticity of wage with respect to productivity in manufacturing for a set of developing countries. Interestingly, the elasticity turns out to be positive only in China and Korea during the nineties (Table 12.1). In Brazil and India it is negative during the same period, suggesting no transfer of benefits to the workers. However, this coefficient could be estimated only for a few countries and hence, it may not be appropriate to deduce any strong conclusion. We, therefore, turn to the UNIDO data. The elasticity of wage with respect to labour productivity as given in Table 12.2 for the manufacturing sector is positive and high in a number of countries with a few exceptions: Bolivia, Senegal, India, Mongolia and Macau and Malaysia, where elasticity is less than 0.5. Econometric estimation also conforms to this pattern as a large number of countries reveal strong links between labour productivity and wage. This would possibly indicate that labour is already able to get its due share in a number of countries. However, before concluding in this direction we need to carry out country and industry specific detailed analysis which is attempted for India as a case study in section 4.

**Table 12.1: Rate of growth of labour productivity and elasticity of wage with respect to productivity in manufacturing (KILM data)**

| Country | Period | Rog of Lab. Prod. in Mfg (2) | Elasticity of Mfg Wage with respect to Lab Prod. |
|---------|--------|------------------------------|--------------------------------------------------|
| Brazil | 80–91 | −2.92 | |
| | 91–04 | 1.44 | −2.62 (1994–02, $N = 9$, −1.68**) |
| China | 80–91 | 4.82 | 0.31 |
| | 91–05 | 10.15 | 0.79 (1990–03, $N = 14$, 0.71*) |
| India | 80–91 | 3.75 | −0.93 |
| | 91–05 | 3.02 | −1.43 (1990–03, $N = 14$, −2.04*) |

*Table 12.1 Continued*

*Table 12.1 Continued*

| Indonesia | 80–91 | 4.07 | 0.51 |
|---|---|---|---|
| | 91–05 | 2.43 | (1995–01, $N$ = 7, 0.52) |
| Korea, Rep | 80–91 | 5.35 | 0.79 |
| | 91–05 | 8.19 | (1993–05, $N$ = 13, 0.52*) |
| Mexico | 80–91 | −0.33 | 2.82 |
| | 91–05 | 1.99 | (1991–04, $N$ = 12, −0.66) |
| Taiwan, China | 80–91 | 5.09 | |
| | 91–05 | 3.05 | |

*Note:* (1) Growth rate of labour productivity is calculated from GDP per person employed (1997 US$, at PPP) in the manufacturing sector with 1980 as the base for the index. (2) The base year for real manufacturing wage indices are as follows: Brazil, 1996; China, 2000; India, 2000; Indonesia, 2000; Korea, 2000; Mexico, 2000. (3) Figures in the last column within the parentheses are based on econometric estimation. The period over which the estimation has been done, the number of observations ($N$) used, and the elasticity figures are shown within the brackets. * and ** represent significance at 5 and 10 per cent levels, respectively.

*Source:* Based on KILM Data, ILO.

## LABOUR MARKET DEREGULATION AND EMPLOYMENT

Those who support labour market deregulation believe that the cost of labour is too high. In the context of globalisation firms need to become more competitive by cutting cost, and high labour cost is thought to be one of the major sources of inefficiency (see e.g., Slaughter and Swagel, 1997). Labour rules and strong unions are believed to push the wage rate artificially much above the market clearing wage rate, which in turn suppresses employment. Hence, labour market deregulation is expected to reverse the attitude of the employers against expanding employment since it empowers them to hire and fire labour as per requirement and offer wages that allow product prices to remain competitive.

With this viewpoint, we are set to analyse the cost of labour in order to evaluate the case of labour market deregulation. For this purpose, based on the UNIDO data, we measure the average labour cost (real wage rate multiplied by total employment) as a per cent of real value added for the period 1990–2004 in the manufacturing sector for a set of developing countries. Surprisingly, 36 countries for which this ratio could be calculated only eight countries have the labour cost more than 35 per cent (see Table 12.2). To begin with, high cost of labour argument, therefore, does not seem to have a strong basis to build a case for labour market deregulation. Therefore, these findings corroborate the argument of Gorter and Poot, (1999) that the benefits of labour market deregulation should not be exaggerated.

**Table 12.2: Average labour cost as a percentage of real value added in manufacturing: 1990–2004**

| Country | Labour cost (%) | Country | Labour cost (%) | Country | Labour cost (%) |
|---------|-----------------|---------|-----------------|---------|-----------------|
| Ecuador | 12.49 | Bangladesh | 22.01 | Vietnam | 30.68 |
| Sudan | 13.34 | Rwanda | 23.08 | Mongolia | 30.71 |
| Colombia | 14.39 | Cambodia | 23.34 | Uruguay | 30.80 |
| Bolivia | 14.63 | Korea, Re | 23.71 | Gambia | 31.16 |
| Philippines | 17.11 | Zimbabwe | 23.73 | Singapore | 34.06 |
| Indonesia | 17.37 | Brazil | 24.34 | Argentina | 35.01 |
| Ghana | 17.87 | Malaysia | 24.58 | Senegal | 35.19 |
| Peru | 18.37 | India | 24.73 | Egypt | 35.42 |
| Eritrea | 18.65 | Madagascar | 25.11 | Panama | 36.70 |
| Nepal | 18.75 | Botswana | 25.96 | Morocco | 39.93 |
| Mexico | 18.79 | Japan | 27.73 | South Africa | 41.11 |
| Ethiopia | 19.10 | Thailand | 29.03 | Mauritius | 44.40 |
| | | Malawi | 29.24 | Macau, China | 60.72 |

*Source*: Based on UNIDO Data.

Next, we examine if there is any connection between labour absorption in manufacturing sector and labour market regulation across countries[8]. World Development Indicators report the per cent of managers indicating labour regulations (LABREG) as a major business constraint and the per cent of manager indicating labour skill as a major business constraint (LABSKILL) for various countries. The higher the per cent, higher is the probability that labour market regulations and skill factor affect employment adversely. We have tried to relate these skill and regulation specific responses to the ratio of labour to real value added (LTORVA) estimated from UNIDO data for the aggregate manufacturing sector. The coefficients in the estimated equations, however, turn out to be highly insignificant (Table 12.3). Even when we control for real wage rate in the manufacturing sector (RWAGE), GDP per capita (GDPPC) at the national level

---

[8] Berg and Cazes (2007) point out the serious conceptual and methodological problems associated with the World Bank's Employing Workers Index of the Doing Business indicators and risks of formulating policies on the basis of these indicators.

and the share of manufactures in total imports (MFGIM) taken as a proxy for imported technology, neither the labour skill variable nor labour market regulation turns out to be significant. Alternate estimate of labour absorption (or dependent variable) have been tried in the equation, i.e., the rate of growth of employment (ROGEMFG) in the manufacturing sector from UNIDO data. Interestingly the skill factor is seen to affect employment growth in the manufacturing sector negatively. In other words, the higher is the per cent of managers who feel skill has been affecting business adversely, lower is the rate of growth of employment in the manufacturing sector. This implies that poor skill base of the work force in the developing countries reduces the pace of labour absorption as labour demand is possibly rising only for the high skilled variety. However, the effect of the labour market regulation is not statistically significant on the alternate form of the dependant variable. Though the sample is quite small, at least this much is evident that the labour market regulations do not retard labour absorption.

**Table 12.3: Employment, skill and regulations: Regression results**

| Variable | Dep. Var. LTORVA | Dep. Var. LTORVA | Dep. Var. LTORVA | Dep. Var. ROGEMFG |
|---|---|---|---|---|
| LABSKILL | 0.00004 (0.83) | | | −0.47 (−1.93)** |
| LABREG | | −0.00001 (-0.25) | | |
| REALW | −1.24e-06 (−2.08)* | −1.74e-06 (−2.53)* | −1.02e-09 (−2.41)* | |
| GDPPC | 1.29e-06 (3.05)* | 8.52e-07 (1.83)** | | |
| MFGIM | −0.0001 (−2.56)* | −0.0001 (−1.65) | | |
| WFUIN | | | 2.06e-06 (13.07)* | |
| INTER | 0.01 (2.70)* | | −7.03e-06 (−0.45) | 14.30 (2.60)* |
| Adj. $R^2$ | 0.40 | 0.23 | 0.98 | 0.11 |
| N | 22 | 24 | 13 | 22 |

*Note: N* stands for the number of observations. * and ** represent significance at 5 per cent and 10 per cent levels, respectively.

*Source*: Based on data from UNIDO, World Development Indicators and ILO Bureau of Statistics.

ILO's data on the per cent of workers registered with the unions has also been tried as a proxy for labour market condition[9]. Interestingly higher is the per cent of Work force registered with unions (WFUIN) higher is the ratio of labour to real value added in the manufacturing sector. This is, however, based only on 13 observations and, therefore, needs to be cited with caution (Table 12.5)

## EVIDENCE FROM THE INDIAN MANUFACTURING SECTOR

In this section we focus on the Indian manufacturing (organized) sector. The country has witnessed a set of reforms particularly in relation to this sector. However, the labour regulations (including labour related) that are applicable only to the organized sector are quite rigid and they seem to constrain the employers' choice as far as the labour demand is concerned.

In order to elaborate on some of the labour market issues, we analyse the elasticity of employment with respect to wages and also the wage-productivity nexus, using the state level data in India for different groups of industries. Keeping in view the wide divergence in the industrialisation experience of the Indian states this exercise has been undertaken pooling the data across states. Based on the panel data over the period 1979–80 through 1997–98 employment elasticity with respect to wages and value added has been estimated for each of the two digit manufacturing industry groups and the aggregate manufacturing in the organized or formal sector[10]. The following functions have been estimated to reflect on the elasticity coefficients:

$$lnEMP = f(lnVA, lnEML) \qquad (1)$$

$$lnEMP = f(lnVA, lnMANE) \qquad (2)$$

where, *ln* stands for natural log, EMP for employees, VA for value added, EML for emoluments per employee, and MANE for man days per employee. Given the man days per employee (worker) and emoluments (wages) per worker, increase in value added is expected to raise the labour demand though with adoption of capital-intensive technology rise in employment may not be significant. Labour

---

[9] Trade union members as a percentage of total paid employees has been calculated by ILO Bureau of Statistics.

[10] We may refer to it as ASI-sector or the component of the manufacturing sector which is covered by the Annual Survey of Industries. More recent years could not be included in the analysis as the comparability problem between NIC, 1998 and NIC, 1987 is quite serious, particularly at the state level. The value added figures have been deflated by the wholesale price index of the corresponding industrial group. The wages are deflated by the consumer price index of the industrial workers corresponding to different states.

demand is expected to vary inversely with wages. On the other hand, given the value added and wages per worker, any rise in the number of man days per worker may actually reduce the number of workers[11].

The slope dummy with respect to value added has been introduced for the years, 1991–92 to 1997–98, to examine if the reforms changed the employment elasticity of growth. This equation has been estimated for each of the industry groups including the aggregate manufacturing sector, based on the panel data across fourteen major states. However, it is not uniformly a balanced panel across each of the industry groups.[12]

Table 12.4 reports the results of the employment functions estimated in reference to total employees, which include workers as well as educated and skilled staff. Gross value added is an important determinant of employment across all the two digit industry groups and at the aggregate level of manufacturing sector too. Except wood (27), paper (28), leather (29), non-metallic minerals (32), basic metal (33), metal products (34), transport equipment (37) and other manufacturing (38) and the aggregate manufacturing the estimates are indicative of a change in the employment elasticity of growth during the nineties compared to the eighties. Only in the case of cotton textile (23), wool, silk etc. (24) and jute (25) the employment elasticity declined in the reform period and in the rest of the industry groups it showed signs of improvement compared to the eighties. However, the extent of change is only nominal and in general the employment elasticity of growth turns out to be much below unity: only in jute (25) and textile (26) the employment elasticity has been above 0.7 and 0.6, respectively whereas at the aggregate level it turns out to be only around 0.35. By and large similar patterns are noted when we estimated the employment function by replacing the employees by workers.[13]

Though the employment elasticity with respect to emoluments per employee is significant in a large number of two-digit industry groups, the magnitude is not very high except in food (20–21), beverages (22), jute (25), textile (26), paper (28),

---

[11] Nagaraj (1994) and Balhotra (1998) noted that the growth in man days per worker was the cause of stagnation in employment in the eighties. Goldar (2000), however, did not find this variable to be significant.

[12] It may be noted that at the state level the figures corresponding to each of the industry groups have not been stated explicitly for some of the years, i.e., two industry groups have been merged at times. In such cases, on the basis of the information for the previous or the succeeding year an attempt has been made to separate out the figures. However, for some of the years even this approximation could not be carried out; hence those years had to be dropped.

[13] However, the results from the panel data used in our analysis, are expected to capture much larger variations than what a pure time series or cross-sectional data set can, and hence, from this point of view the estimates based on panel data may assume greater reliability.

non-metallic mineral (32) and other manufacturing (38), where it turns out to be at least around 0.5 in one of the two alternative specifications (with and without man-days per employee). At the aggregate level the wage elasticity of employment is estimated at only 0.24.

Is not then economic policy over-stretching the wage rigidity argument? As the empirical results show, reduction in wage rates cannot bring in miraculous increase in employment[14]. Besides, labour market flexibility in terms of the changes in the mode of employment, i.e., from regular wage employment to contractual, casual and piece rate employment, has serious implications in terms of the social costs and welfare losses (see Uchikawa, 2003, Datta, 2003, Dutt, 2003, Hasan, Mitra and Ramaswamy, 2003).

**Table 12.4: Employment function (total employees)**

| Ind. | LnVA | DLnVA | LnEML | LnMANE | Adj. R2 | Model | N |
|------|------|-------|-------|--------|---------|-------|---|
| 20–21 | 0.32 | 0.005 | −0.18 | −0.74 | 0.98 | FE | 252 |
| | (12.03)* | (4.35)* | (−2.30)* | (−7.44)* | | | |
| | 0.30 | 0.008 | −0.65 | | 0.97 | FE | 266 |
| | (10.19)* | (6.19)* | (−14.33)* | | | | |
| 22 | 0.30 | 0.01 | −0.58 | −0.14 | 0.97 | FE | 251 |
| | (10.13)* | (6.50)* | (−7.98)* | (−0.97) | | | |
| | 0.31 | 0.01 | −0.67 | | 0.97 | FE | 265 |
| | (10.50)* | (6.72)* | (−10.20)* | | | | |
| 23 | 0.33 | −0.005 | −0.35 | 0.006 | 0.97 | FE | 252 |
| | (10.26)* | (−4.47)* | (−2.75)* | (0.03) | | | |
| | 0.31 | −0.005 | −0.31 | | 0.97 | FE | 266 |
| | (10.13)* | (−4.64)* | (−2.74)* | | | | |
| 24 | 0.23 | −0.005 | 0.27 | −0.28 | 0.96 | FE | 239 |
| | (7.82)* | (−2.29)* | (2.88)* | (−1.08) | | | |
| | 0.32 | −0.009 | −0.02 | | 0.96 | FE | 253 |
| | (10.20)* | (−3.72)* | (−0.21) | | | | |
| 25 | 0.74 | −0.004 | −0.77 | 0.80 | 0.98 | FE | 192 |
| | (23.62)* | (−1.25) | (−5.30)* | (3.59)* | | | |
| | 0.76 | −0.007 | −0.32 | | 0.98 | FE | 206 |
| | (25.07* | (−2.19)* | (−3.70)* | | | | |

*Table 12.4 Continued*

---

[14] Besley and Burgess (2004) meticulously examined if labor regulation can hinder economic performance.

*Table 12.4 Continued*

| | | | | | | | |
|---|---|---|---|---|---|---|---|
| 26 | 0.60 (17.85)* | 0.005 (1.86)** | −0.46 (−4.02)* | −0.48 (−1.25) | 0.95 | FE | 249 |
| | 0.64 (19.90)* | 0.004 (1.47) | −0.53 (−5.04)* | | 0.95 | FE | 265 |
| 27 | 0.41 (13.58)* | 0.002 (1.17) | −0.32 (−3.25)* | −0.31 (−1.32) | 0.95 | FE | 252 |
| | 0.45 (14.81)* | 0.003 (1.42) | −0.38 (−4.13)* | | 0.94 | FE | 266 |
| 28 | 0.37 (12.43)* | −0.0003 (−0.183) | −0.30 (−3.20)* | −0.81 (−3.64)* | 0.95 | FE | 252 |
| | 0.36 (12.23)* | 0.002 (1.60) | −0.51 (−6.13)* | | 0.95 | FE | 266 |
| 29 | 0.44 (13.09)* | 0.003 (1.02) | −0.23 (−1.64) | −0.47 (−2.37)* | 0.95 | FE | 245 |
| | 0.45 (14.21)* | 0.003 (1.02) | −0.35 (−2.59)* | | 0.95 | FE | 258 |
| 30 | 0.19 (7.58)* | 0.004 (2.90)* | −0.03 (−0.396) | −0.34 (−2.18)* | 0.97 | FE | 249 |
| | 0.18 (7.17)* | 0.005 (3.48)* | −0.12 (−1.59) | | 0.97 | FE | 262 |
| 31 | 0.36 (12.15)* | 0.01 (5.18)* | 0.26 (2.04)* | −0.92 (−5.33)* | 0.93 | FE | 249 |
| | 0.40 (13.85)* | 0.01 (5.53)* | −0.21 (−2.22)* | | 0.92 | FE | 262 |
| 32 | 0.30 (12.42)* | 0.001 (0.97) | −0.38 (−5.24)* | −0.15 (−3.04)* | 0.86 | FE | 252 |
| | 0.31 (12.56)* | 0.001 (0.86) | −0.48 (−6.83)* | | 0.97 | FE | 265 |
| 33 | 0.18 (6.36)* | 0.0006 (0.41) | −0.037 (−0.37) | −0.37 (−2.02)* | 0.96 | FE | 252 |
| | 0.18 (7.04)* | 0.001 (0.96) | −0.15 (−1.92)** | | 0.95 | FE | 266 |
| 34 | 0.44 (13.57)* | −0.0002 (−0.14) | 0.23 (2.66)* | −0.69 (−2.55)* | 0.97 | FE | 252 |
| | 0.44 (13.88)* | −0.0003 (−0.26) | 0.13 (1.69)** | | 0.97 | FE | 266 |

*Table 12.4 Continued*

*Table 12.4 Continued*

| | | | | | | | |
|---|---|---|---|---|---|---|---|
| 35–36 | 0.33 (12.92)* | 0.003 (3.19)* | −0.18 (−2.74)* | −0.18 (−1.14) | 0.99 | FE | 228 |
| | 0.38 (14.85)* | 0.0003 (0.44) | −0.26 (−3.85)* | | 0.99 | FE | 266 |
| 37 | 0.22 (8.23)* | −0.002 (1.26) | 0.14 (1.26) | −1.22 (−4.72)* | 0.98 | FE | 251 |
| | 0.24 (8.80)* | −0.002 (−0.89) | −0.12 (−1.15) | | 0.98 | FE | 265 |
| 38 | 0.35 (12.00)* | 0.001 (0.50) | 0.02 (0.23) | −0.51 (−1.96)* | 0.97 | FE | 251 |
| | 0.37 (13.28)* | 0.15 (0.67) | −0.75 (−0.90) | | 0.97 | FE | 265 |
| Agg. Mfg (ASI) | 0.35 (11.54)* | −0.0001 (−0.18) | −0.24 (−3.26)* | −0.63 (−4.26)* | 0.98 | FE | 252 |
| | 0.37 (13.28)* | 0.001 (0.67) | −0.07 (−0.90) | | 0.97 | FE | 265 |

*Note:* $N$ stands for the number of observations and * and ** for 5 per cent and 10 per cent levels of significance. FE represents Fixed Effect Model, RE Random Effect Model and CR Classical Regression Model. Based on the Lagrange Multiplier statistic and the Hausman statistic the appropriateness of the model is chosen.

The other exercise tried in the analysis relates to wage per worker function. The main motivation to carry out this exercise is to examine the effect of labour productivity on wages along the line of neoclassical argument:

$$lnWAG = G(lnGVEM, DlnGVEM, lnCAPEM) \qquad (3)$$

$$lnWAG = f(lnGVEM, DlnGVEM, lnCAPEM\ lnCAPEM) \qquad (4)$$

where, *ln* is the log transformation, WAG is the wage per worker, GVEM is gross value added per employee, and CAPEM is the capital per employee ratio[15]. Wage per worker is taken as a function of productivity and capital-employee ratio. To allow for the change in the effect of labour productivity on wage in the nineties relative to the eighties the slope dummy DlnGVEM has been introduced. Higher levels of productivity are likely to raise the wages, as part of the productivity gains may be transferred to the workers. The sources of productivity rise are rise

---

[15] The nominal values of capital have been deflated by the combined price index of machinery and metal products.

in capital intensity, technological change or improved organization efficiency (see Tendulkar, 2000). If higher levels of capital-labour ratio are indicative of a mere rise in capital intensity and not technological improvement, this may reduce labour demand and thus, wages. However, if higher levels of capital-labour ratio reflect higher levels of technology, suggesting improved performance of labour, wages may then actually increase. In an alternative specification, man-days per worker (lnMANW) has also been introduced hypothesizing that with a rise in the man days per worker wage per worker would go up. If labour is used on part time or piece rate basis, higher levels of man days per worker would mean more work opportunities, and hence, earnings are expected to increase. In the context of labour market reforms with larger possibilities of recruiting workers on part time and piece rate basis, this variable is expected to be of great importance. Even for the full-time workers the provision for over-time remuneration would cause a positive effect of man-days per worker on wages per worker. Only when for the full time workers there exists no scope for over-time payment, rise in man-days per worker cannot make any impact on wages per worker. If full-time workers are under-utilized, strict work conditions in terms of more intensive utilization of work force may also raise the man days per worker, but this will not enhance earnings. On the other hand, when full-time workers are utilized to the full extent, rise in man days per worker can result in rise in over time employment and thus, over time payment.

As shown in Table 12.5, productivity is a significant determinant of wages per worker across a large number of two digit industry groups. However, the partial elasticity of wage with respect to productivity for the aggregate manufacturing sector turns out to be 0.27 and 0.19 depending upon whether man days per worker is or is not included in the function, suggesting that only a small fraction of productivity gains is transferred to workers in terms of wage benefits. Except wool (24), jute (25), textile (26) and basic metal (33) in the rest of the industry groups the effect of productivity on wage rose in the reform period compared to the pre-reform period, as the coefficient of the slope dummy turns out to be significant. However, the magnitude of rise is only nominal. At the aggregate level, for example, it is increased by 0.008 point.

Capital-employee ratio reveals a mixed picture: it raised wages in a number of industries while it affected wages adversely or remained insignificant in some other, consequently showing an insignificant effect on wages at the aggregate level. Corresponding to the following industry groups food (20–21), beverages (22), wool and silk (24), wood (27), paper (28), rubber (31), non-metallic minerals (32), metal (34), machinery (35–36), transport equipment (37) the capital-employee ratio reveals a positive effect on wages. Only in cotton textile (23), the effect is seen to be negative and in textile products (26) and basic metal (33) it is positive when

Table 12.5: Determinants of wages per worker

| Ind. Code | Constant | LnGVEM | DLnGVEM | LnCAPEM | LnMANW | Adj. R2 | Model | N |
|---|---|---|---|---|---|---|---|---|
| 20–21 | 1.42 (8.10)* | 0.11 (5.04)* | 0.01 (6.97)* | 0.04 (1.65)** | 1.01 (20.18)* | 0.77 | RE | 252 |
|  | 3.24 (12.49)* | 0.33 (10.33)* | 0.002 (0.65) | 0.21 (5.95)* |  | 0.68 | RE | 266 |
| 22 | 0.82 (1.30) | 0.18 (7.48)* | 0.005 (2.03)* | 0.08 (4.31)* | 0.90 (7.70)* | 0.74 | RE | 251 |
|  | 5.35 (22.41)* | 0.22 (8.28)* | 0.005 (1.92)** | 0.11 (5.46)* |  | 0.63 | RE | 265 |
| 23 | 4.72 (8.11)* | 0.05 (2.30)* | 0.004 (2.46)* | -0.02 (-1.26) | 0.69 (6.65)* | 0.17 | RE | 252 |
|  | 8.46 (37.09)* | 0.09 (3.81)* | 0.005 (2.93)* | -0.04 (-2.19)* |  | 0.51 | RE | 266 |
| 24 |  | 0.05 (1.85)** | 0.003 (-0.75) | 0.11 (3.98)* | 0.98 (4.10)* | 0.77 | FE | 239 |
|  |  | 0.08 (2.80)* | -0.004 (-1.18) | 0.12 (4.49)* |  | 0.77 | FE | 253 |
| 25 | 0.77 (1.30) | 0.14 (4.14)* | 0.004 (1.30) | 0.20 (0.95) | 1.14 (12.45)* | 0.43 | RE | 192 |
|  | -29.90 (-0.34) | 1.42 (0.15) | 0.76 (0.67) | 1.93 (0.34) |  | -0.01 | OLS | 206 |
| 26 |  | 0.18 (5.92)* | 0.004 (1.16) | 0.06 (2.09)* | 0.82 (3.09)* | 0.83 | FE | 249 |
|  | 37.08 (0.64) | 0.147 (2.10)* | 1.38 (1.60) | -18.91 (-3.05)* |  | 0.03 | RE | 265 |

*Table 12.5 Continued*

*Table 12.5 Continued*

| | | | | | | | | |
|---|---|---|---|---|---|---|---|---|
| 27 | −0.83 (−0.57) | 0.13 (5.34)* | 0.01 (5.12)* | 0.04 (2.56)* | 1.35 (5.06)* | 0.48 | RE | 252 |
| | 6.58 (30.98)* | 0.15 (6.00)* | 0.01 (5.50)* | 0.05 (2.87)* | | 0.33 | RE | 266 |
| 28 | 4.15 (4.43)* | 0.18 (7.42)* | 0.02 (8.05)* | 0.02 (1.32) | 0.51 (2.95)* | 0.41 | RE | 252 |
| | 6.28 (24.40)* | 0.25 (11.40)* | 0.01 (7.03)* | 0.04 (2.15)* | | 0.43 | RE | 266 |
| 29 | 4.00 (4.17)* | 0.13 (6.36)* | 0.02 (3.86)* | −0.02 (−1.12) | 0.66 (4.0)* | 0.27 | RE | 245 |
| | 0.75 (26,89)* | 0.12 (5.98)* | 0.009 (3.52)* | −0.18 (−0.81) | | 0.27 | RE | 258 |
| 30 | 2.13 (3.30)* | 0.09 (3.81)* | 0.01 (5.77)* | −0.03 (−1.60) | 1.15 (10.11)* | 0.36 | RE | 249 |
| | 7.99 (23.30)* | 0.14 (5.49)* | 0.01 (5.79)* | −0.02 (−0.84) | | 0.17 | RE | 262 |
| 31 | 1.99 (5.79)* | 0.11 (5.54)* | 0.01 (5.40)* | 0.04 (2.36)* | 0.94 (17.84)* | 0.53 | RE | 249 |
| | 6.88 (23.21)* | 0.19 (6.25)* | 0.02 (5.42)* | 0.008 (0.31) | | 0.34 | RE | 262 |
| 32 | | 0.14 (6.48)* | 0.006 (3.62)* | 0.07 (4.65)* | 0.04 (1.17) | 0.86 | FE | 252 |
| | | 0.14 (7.05)* | 0.006 (3.51)* | 0.07 (5.12)* | | 0.86 | FE | 265 |
| 33 | 1.08 (1.10) | 0.09 (2.99)* | −0.004 (−1.61) | 0.09 (3.28)* | 1.09 (6.17)* | 0.47 | RE | 252 |

*Table 12.5 Continued*

Table 12.5 Continued

| | | | | | | R² | Model | N |
|---|---|---|---|---|---|---|---|---|
| 34 | 5.61 (8.06)* | 0.19 (7.29)* | 0.0002 (0.17) | -0.16 (-2.74)* | | 0.95 | FE | 266 |
| | 6.10 (16.94)* | 0.21 (5.14)* | 0.009 (3.72)* | 0.10 (3.68)* | 0.04 (0.37) | 0.42 | RE | 252 |
| 35–36 | 4.50 (5.13)* | 0.18 (4.70)* | 0.01 (4.24)* | 0.1 (3.62)* | | 0.42 | RE | 266 |
| | | 0.18 (5.33)* | 0.005 (2.75)* | 0.12 (3.99)* | 0.28 (1.95)** | 0.45 | RE | 228 |
| 37 | 3.02 (3.14)* | 0.17 (5.43)* | 0.004 (2.50)* | 0.13 (5.04)* | | 0.86 | FE | 266 |
| | 8.01 (36.30)* | 0.58 (2.93)* | 0.009 (4.97)* | 0.05 (3.08)* | 0.92 (5.35)* | 0.40 | RE | 228 |
| | | 0.09 (4.24)* | 0.01 (4.74)* | 0.04 (2.53)* | | 0.36 | RE | 265 |
| 38 | | 0.19 (7.65)* | 0.006 (2.25)* | -0.03 (-1.46) | 0.45 (3.09)* | 0.81 | FE | 251 |
| | | 0.19 (7.54)* | 0.008 (2.76)* | -0.03 (-1.18) | | 0.79 | FE | 265 |
| Agg. | 0.08 (0.11) | 0.27 (8.16)* | -0.0006 (-0.36) | -0.03 (-1.10) | 1.15 (7.57)* | 0.62 | RE | 252 |
| | | 0.19 (7.54)* | 0.008 (2.76)* | -0.03 (-1.18) | | 0.79 | FE | 265 |

*Note:* N stands for the number of observations and * and ** for 5 per cent and 10 per cent levels of significance. FE represents Fixed Effect Model, RE Random Effect Model and CR Classical Regression Model. Based on the Lagrange Multiplier statistic and the Hausman statistic the appropriateness of the model is chosen.

man-days per worker is included; otherwise it turns out to be negative with the exclusion of this variable. In the rest of the industry groups, the effect is statistically insignificant. On the whole, in a large number of industry groups capital-labour ratio tends to raise wages indicating improved performance of labour with higher levels of capital per head. However, in most of the cases the elasticity of wage with respect to capital-labour ratio turns out to be extremely low except wool and silk etc. (24) and machinery (35–36) where it ranges from 0.11 to 0.13; (also in the case of 20–21 it is 0.21 when man-days per worker is dropped).

Finally, man-days per worker turns out to be an important determinant of wage in most of the industry groups–except non-metallic minerals (32) and metal products (34). And interestingly the elasticity of wage with respect to man-days appears to be around unity except paper (28), leather (29), machinery (35–36) and other manufacturing (38). Man-days per worker being a significant determinant of earnings, the decline in the rate of growth of wages in the nineties, relative to that of the eighties, might be an outcome of the decline in the rate of growth of man days per worker, which virtually did not grow during the nineties.

On the whole, what we note is that elasticity of employment with respect to wages is quite moderate though much has been talked about labour market deregulation and wage flexibility with a view to expanding employment. In other words, reduction in wages through labour market deregulation does not seem to promise any significant increase in employment. Productivity gains did not get substantially transferred to the workers and there has been a decline in the wage growth during the reform period. However, part of this decline in wage growth might have resulted from sub-contracting, outsourcing, and piece rate payment, which are increasing in response to labour market flexibility. Also, man-days per worker being an important determinant of the wage rate, the stagnancy in the former during the nineties possibly resulted in a decline in the rate of growth of wages compared to the pre-reform period. Wage-productivity linkage exists but the elasticity of wages with respect to productivity is miniscule. However, the only consolation is that the elasticity coefficient did not deteriorate further after the reforms were initiated.

Goldar (2011) argues that employment in India's organized manufacturing sector increased in recent years at the very rapid rate of 7.5 per cent per annum between 2003–04 and 2008–09. He further rationalizes it in terms of labour market deregulation, contributing to manufacturing employment growth. The value added growth also picked up to a double-digit figure during the same period (13.7 per cent per annum). However, as Nagaraj (2011) argued that the fine print of exemptions and loopholes built into the labour laws provide sufficient flexibilities to the industrial firms and hence, labour regulations could not be the cause of deceleration in employment growth in the past. By the same logic labour market deregulation, therefore, could not be treated responsible for rapid employment growth in the recent period. He argues that the recent manufacturing employment boom could be merely a recovery of the employment lost over the previous nine years. He also points out that the correlation coefficient between employment elasticity and labour reforms index across states is not statistically significant (Nagaraj, 2011). Another way of rationalizing this employment boom could be in terms of regional change in the industrial employment growth. Some of the states which have not been industrialized registered a rapid employment growth rate during the recent period. The states like Chattisgarh, Haryana, Punjab, Goa, Jammu and Kashmir, Himachal Pradesh, Orissa and Uttarakhand witnessed a double-digit employment growth whereas most of them (except Goa) had experienced either a sluggish or negative employment growth in the earlier years (1998–99 through 2003–04).

## CONCLUSIONS

The argument of high cost of labour does not seem to have a strong basis to build a case for labour market deregulation. Based on the UNIDO data the average labour cost as a per cent of real value added over the period 1990 through 2004 has been estimated for the manufacturing sector. Out of the 36 countries for which this ratio could be calculated, only eight reported a figure of more than 35 per cent. Empirical findings do not favour labour market regulations affecting employment adversely and, hence the arguments for labour market deregulations need to be viewed carefully. Unionisation rather seems to have a favourable effect on labour absorption though the number of observations is very small. Skill factor, however, has shown a negative impact on employment. In other words, the higher is the response of the managers perceiving skill as a major business constraint, the lower is the employment growth. All this would tend to suggest that instead of labour market deregulation, focus has to lie on improvement in skill and training. The available technology rather seems to be incompatible with the quality of labour available in the developing countries. The modern technology is both capital and skill intensive and hence, incompatibility between the two can hardly enable firms to benefit in the context of globalization.

The wage elasticity of employment does not turn out to be high across countries. Hence, the argument favouring wage flexibility through labour market deregulation does not seem to be empirically justified for employment generation. Wage-productivity links exist but these may get weakened with labour market deregulations, and thus, the due share to labour may not get delivered. Detailed country specific studies need to be pursued before recommending labour marker deregulations.

Our case study of the Indian organized manufacturing sector based on panel data shows that though the employment elasticity with respect to emoluments per employee is statistically significant in a large number of two-digit industry groups, the magnitude is not very high except in food, beverages, jute, textile, paper, non-metallic mineral and other manufacturing, where it turns out to be at least around 0.5. At the aggregate level the wage elasticity of employment is estimated at 0.24. Is not then the economic policy over-stretching the wage rigidity argument? As the empirical results show, reduction in wage rates cannot bring in miraculous increase in employment. Besides, labour market flexibility in terms of the changes in the mode of employment, i.e., from regular wage to contractual, casual and piece rate basis, has serious implications in terms of the social costs and welfare losses.

The results are also indicative of a weak relationship between productivity and wage even before the economic reforms were initiated. The partial elasticity of wage with respect to productivity for the aggregate manufacturing sector turns out to be 0.27 and 0.19 depending upon whether man days per worker is or is not included in the function, suggesting that only a small fraction of productivity gains is transferred to workers in terms of wage benefits. Except some of the industries groups the effect of productivity on wage rose in the reform period compared to the pre-reform period. However, the magnitude of rise is only nominal. If we were to believe in these results, then labour market deregulations would further weaken these links, introducing gross inequality in income. The recent employment boom in the organized manufacturing sector is not necessarily an outcome of labour market deregulation. It could be due to recovery from an employment deceleration that occurred prior to 2003. Besides, the regional shift in the employment structure could have contributed to the employment boom.

In the name of economic reforms neither labour should be marginalized nor should growth-maximizing strategy should be pursued without ensuring that its positive benefits accrue to those located at the lower echelons. From this point of view, the role of institutions in getting fair share to labour and in minimizing the social cost is important while steps are initiated to reallocate labour. It is of great significance to assure that mechanisms that make labour market more flexible are accompanied by measures that protect labour from welfare-loss. Besides, the innovation of technology that can enhance productivity without leading to employment-loss is of considerable importance in an economy faced with large underemployment and poverty.

# APPENDIX

**Table 12.1-A: Employment growth, wage growth and wage elasticity of employment in industry (KILM data)**

| Country | Emp. Gr. in industry(1) 1993–05 | Country | Period | Wage growth in Mfg. (2) | Wage elasticity(3) |
|---|---|---|---|---|---|
| Algeria | 1.45 | Algeria | 92–96 | −7.67 | −0.19 |
| Angola | 0.28 | | | | |
| Argentina | 5.33 | Argentina | 90–01 | 1.07 | 4.98 |
| Bangladesh | 1.29 | | | | |
| Belize | 0.51 | | | | |
| Benin | 1.12 | | | | |
| Bhutan | 1.26 | | | | |
| Bolivia | 0.63 | Bolivia | 96–00 | 5.26 | 0.12 |
| Botswana | 0.011 | Botswana | 2004–05 | −4.71 | −0.002 |
| Brazil | 0.89 | Brazil | 94–02 | −3.77 | −0.24 |
| Burkina Faso | 1.55 | | | | |
| Cambodia | 11.9 | Cambodia | 96–01 | −4.48 | −2.66 |
| Cameroon | 0.93 | | | | |
| Cape Verde | 0.61 | | | | |
| Central African Republic | 0.32 | | | | |
| Chad | 0.85 | | | | |
| | | Chile | 80–91 | 5.6 | |
| Chile | 0.005 | | 91–05 | −2.2 | −0.002 |
| | | China | 86–91 | 1.51 | |
| China | 0.009 | | 91–03 | 8.04 | 0.001 |
| Colombia | 14.16 | Colombia | 2002–04 | 5.31 | 2.67 |
| Comoros | 1.96 | | | | |
| Congo | 0.67 | | | | |
| Congo, Democratic Republic of | 0.49 | | | | |

*Table 12.1-A Continued*

*Table 12.1-A Continued*

| | | | | |
|---|---|---|---|---|
| | | Costa Rica | 80–91 | 2.87 |
| Costa Rica | 0.2 | | 91–05 | 4.74 | 0.04 |
| Côte d'Ivoire | 0.28 | | | |
| Ecuador | | Ecuador | 95–04 | −8.45 |
| | | Egypt | 82–91 | −5.37 |
| Egypt | 0.15 | | 91–03 | 2.88 | 0.05 |
| | | El Salvador | 80–91 | −13.96 |
| El Salvador | 0.23 | | 91–05 | 2.56 | 0.09 |
| Equatorial Guinea | 0.47 | | | |
| Eritrea | 0.42 | | | |
| Ethiopia | 6.49 | | | |
| Gabon | 0.97 | | | |
| Gambia | 1.34 | Gambia | 93–99 | −3.84 | −0.35 |
| Ghana | 2.09 | Ghana | 83–91 | 13.56 | 0.15 |
| | | Guatemala | 84–91 | −6.95 |
| Guatemala | 0.87 | | 91–02 | 2.24 | 0.39 |
| | | Guinea | 87–91 | 18.95 |
| Guinea | 0.77 | | 91–96 | 3.84 | 0.20 |
| Guinea–Bissau | 0.52 | | | |
| Honduras | 0.74 | | | |
| | | Hong Kong | 81–91 | 5.07 |
| | | | 91–05 | 0.88 |
| | | India | 80–91 | −3.5 |
| India | 0.52 | | 91–03 | −4.31 | −0.12 |
| Indonesia | 0.50 | Indonesia | 95–01 | 2.06 | 0.24 |
| | | Kenya | 80–91 | −1.07 |
| Kenya | 1.46 | | 91–97 | −9.61 | −0.15 |
| Korea, Republic of | 0.014 | Korea, (Re) | 93–05 | 4.25 | 0.003 |
| Lao People's Democratic Republic | 3.42 | | | |

*Table 12.1-A Continued*

*Table 12.1-A Continued*

| | | | | | |
|---|---|---|---|---|---|
| Lesotho | 0.204 | Macau, China | 98–05 | 4.65 | 0.04 |
| Madagascar | 1.55 | | | | |
| Malawi | 1.11 | Malawi | 90–94 | −2.35 | −0.47 |
| | | Malaysia | 81–91 | 1.81 | |
| Malaysia | 0.204 | | 91–01 | 4.23 | 0.05 |
| Mali | 3 | | | | |
| Mauritania | 1.703 | | | | |
| Mauritius | 0.03 | Mauritius | 99–05 | 2.02 | 0.01 |
| Mexico | 1.5 | Mexico | 91–04 | −0.93 | −1.61 |
| Mongolia | 0.05 | Mongolia | 2000–05 | 2.96 | 0.02 |
| Morocco | 0.54 | | | | |
| Mozambique | 0.65 | | | | |
| Namibia | 2.72 | | | | |
| Nepal | 15.69 | | | | |
| Nicaragua | 2.88 | Nicaragua | 2003–04 | −8.01 | −0.36 |
| Niger | 1.28 | | | | |
| Nigeria | 2.13 | | | | |
| | | Pakistan | 82–90 | 4.66 | |
| Pakistan | 1.16 | | 93–02 | 0.25 | 4.64 |
| Panama | 0.56 | Panama | 2003–05 | 11.28 | 0.05 |
| Paraguay | −1.26 | Paraguay | 2000–03 | −8.54 | 0.15 |
| Peru | 0.08 | Peru | 95–05 | −1.44 | −0.05 |
| Philippines | 0.53 | Philippines | 2001–04 | −3.06 | −0.17 |
| Rwanda | 1.17 | Rwanda | 96–97 | −10.54 | −0.11 |
| Senegal | 0.79 | | | | |
| | | Seychelles | 86–91 | −0.01 | |
| | | | 91–04 | 0.21 | |
| Singapore | 0.048 | Singapore | 86–91 | 7.41 | 0.01 |
| | | | 91–05 | 4.72 | |
| South Africa | 12.43 | South Africa | 90–02 | 1.18 | 10.54 |
| | | Sri Lanka | 80–91 | 1.01 | |
| Sri Lanka | 0.402 | | 91–05 | −0.02 | −20.10 |
| | | St. Helena | 94–02 | 3.35 | |

*Table 12.1-A Continued*

*Table 12.1-A Continued*

| | | | | | |
|---|---|---|---|---|---|
| Sudan | 0.78 | Sudan | 88–92 | –33.85 | –0.02 |
| Swaziland | 0.504 | | | | |
| Tanzania, United Republic of | 0.735 | | | | |
| | | Thailand | 89–91 | 4.73 | |
| Thailand | 0.36 | | 91–03 | 1.07 | 0.34 |
| Togo | 0.84 | | | | |
| Tunisia | 1.59 | | | | |
| Uganda | 0.415 | | | | |
| | | Uruguay | 84–91 | 2.38 | |
| Uruguay | 6.65 | | 91–99 | –2.62 | –2.54 |
| Venezuela | –0.033 | | | | |
| Viet Nam | 1.68 | | | | |
| Zambia | 0.86 | | | | |
| Zimbabwe | 0.21 | Zimbabwe | 95–01 | –2.16 | –0.10 |

*Note:* (1) Industry refers to manufacturing and other allied activities. (2) Growth rates are based on real manufacturing wage indices. The base year varies from country to country. (3) Wage Elasticity of Employment is defined as the ratio of employment growth to wage growth.

*Source*: Based on KILM data, ILO.

**Table 12.2-A: Elasticity of employment with respect to wages and wage-productivity links in manufacturing sector (UNIDO data, 1990–2004)**

| Period | Country | Emp. Elas. w. r. t growth | Emp. Elas. w. r. t wages | Rate of growth of lab. prod. | Rate of growth of real wages | Elas. of wages w. r. t lab. prod. |
|---|---|---|---|---|---|---|
| 1993–02 | Argentina | 0.09 | 0.11 | –10.07 | –8.90 | 0.88 (0.98)* |
| 1995–98 | Bangladesh | –1.23 | –0.62 | –12.39 | –10.97 | 0.89 |
| 1995–01 | Bolivia | 0.10 | 0.75 | –6.81 | –0.96 | 0.14 (0.14)** |
| 1995–04 | Botswana | –1.62 | –0.52 | –8.01 | –9.60 | 1.20 |
| 1996–04 | Brazil | –0.29 | –0.16 | –13.31 | –18.65 | 1.40 (1.39)* |

*Table 12.2-A Continued*

*Table 12.2-A Continued*

| | | | | | |
|---|---|---|---|---|---|
| 1993–00 | Cambodia | 0.98 | 5.39 | 1.23 | 9.31 | 7.56 (0.52) |
| 1995–04 | Ecuador | 0.63 | 0.90 | 1.70 | 3.18 | 1.87 (–0.06) |
| 1990–04 | Ethiopia | –0.64 | –0.23 | –4.18 | –7.09 | 1.69 (1.26)* |
| 1992–04 | Eritrea | 0.01 | 0.01 | –11.74 | –9.99 | 0.85 (0.81)* |
| 1998–03 | India | –3.23 | –2.58 | 1.15 | 0.34 | 0.30 (0.22) |
| 1998–03 | Indonesia | 0.21 | 0.15 | 3.33 | 6.09 | 1.83 (0.61) |
| 1994–02 | Japan | 0.82 | 2.76 | –0.66 | –1.12 | 1.69 (0.91)* |
| 1990–02 | Korea, Re | 2.17 | 0.82 | 0.74 | –1.68 | –2.27 (0.93)* |
| 1997–04 | Macau, China | 0.18 | 0.45 | –3.51 | –1.72 | 0.49 (0.44)* |
| 1998–03 | Madagascar | –0.43 | 5.36 | 54.78 | –3.08 | –0.06 (1.18)* |
| 1999–01 | Malawi | 0.16 | 0.24 | –30.41 | –24.04 | 0.79 (0.80)* |
| 2001–03 | Malaysia | –0.18 | –0.30 | 4.67 | 2.32 | 0.50 (0.47) |
| 1997–03 | Mauritius | –0.10 | –0.07 | –3.66 | –4.98 | 1.36 (1.06)* |
| 1994–00 | Mexico | –0.16 | –0.13 | –13.74 | –14.93 | 1.09 (1.22)* |
| 1992–00 | Mongolia | 0.69 | 5.46 | –1.93 | –0.79 | 0.41 (0.25) |
| 2000–04 | Morocco | 0.25 | 0.20 | 4.09 | 6.93 | 1.70 (1.63)* |
| 1996–02 | Nepal | 0.40 | 0.79 | –2.38 | –2.02 | 0.85 |
| 1992–01 | Panama | –0.32 | –0.40 | –5.67 | –3.44 | 0.61 (0.27) |
| 1995–96 | Peru | –1.41 | –0.40 | –6.93 | –10.11 | 1.46 |

*Table 12.2-A Continued*

*Table 12.2-A Continued*

| 1996–03 | Philippines | 0.16 | 0.21 | −10.80 | −9.69 | 0.90 (0.92)* |
|---------|-------------|------|------|--------|-------|--------------|
| 1998–02 | Senegal | −0.63 | −2.04 | −9.84 | −1.87 | 0.19 (0.37)* |
| 1991–03 | Singapore | −0.23 | −0.11 | 1.93 | 3.21 | 1.66 (0.71)* |
| 1998–04 | Vietnam | 0.84 | −1.59 | 3.73 | −12.20 | −3.27 |
| 1991–04 | South Africa | 0.23 | 0.11 | −5.66 | −15.93 | 2.81 (1.06) |
| 1996–00 | Thailand | 0.06 | 0.11 | −19.54 | −11.01 | 0.56 (0.66)* |
| 1998–03 | Uruguay | −0.07 | −0.06 | −57.22 | −63.78 | 1.11 (1.07)* |

*Note:* Figures in parentheses in the last column give the econometric estimates of elasticity of wages with respect to labour productivity. * and ** represent significance at 5 per cent and 10 per cent levels, respectively.

*Source*: Based on UNIDO data.

**Table 12.3-A: Regression results for the manufacturing sector from UNIDO data (Dep. Var. ln EMP)**

| Country | Intercept | lnVA | lnW | N | Adj R² |
|---------|-----------|------|-----|---|--------|
| Argentina | 12.16 (4.93)* | 0.02 (0.10) | 0.11 (0.73) | 10 | 0.21 |
| Bolivia | 8.10 (2.22)** | 0.12 (0.92) | 0.04 (0.06) | 7 | −0.04 |
| Botswana | 11.52 (1.71) | −0.07 (−0.18) | | 7 | −0.19 |
| Brazil | 1.69 (0.64) | 0.77 (5.46)* | −0.58 (−7.11) | 9 | 0.93 |
| Cambodia | −7.79 (−1.52) | 1.00 (3.66)* | | 3 | 0.86 |
| Ecuador | 5.42 (4.49)* | 0.07 (1.76) | 0.64 (5.43)* | 10 | 0.78 |
| Eretria | 8.77 (3.25)* | 0.05 (0.28) | −0.0001 (−0.28) | 13 | −0.19 |

*Table 12.3-A Continued*

*Table 12.3-A Continued*

| | | | | | |
|---|---|---|---|---|---|
| Ethiopia | 7.63<br>(6.89)* | 0.29<br>(4.09)* | −0.28<br>(−5.85)* | 15 | 0.72 |
| Indonesia | 14.61<br>(6.31)* | 0.02<br>(0.15) | 0.05<br>(0.44) | 6 | 0.13 |
| India | 13.96<br>(4.94)* | 0.16<br>(1.15) | −0.30<br>(−0.67) | 6 | −0.15 |
| Japan | −3.27<br>(−1.66) | 1.15<br>(9.72)* | −1.23 ₁<br>(−6.58)* | 9 | 0.93 |
| Korea, Re | 19.20<br>(6.11)* | −0.47<br>(−2.57)* | 0.83<br>(4.52)* | 13 | 0.78 |
| Macau, China | 6.77<br>(2.48)* | 0.45<br>(0.72) | −0.59<br>(−0.39) | 8 | 0.06 |
| Madagascar | −2.64<br>(−1.05) | 1.04<br>(6.59)* | −0.85<br>(−4.34)* | 4 | 0.93 |
| Malawi | 8.80<br>(2.71)* | 0.16<br>(7.9)* | | 3 | 0.95 |
| | 10.56<br>(11.0)* | | 0.23<br>(8.57)* | 3 | 0.94 |
| Malaysia | 12.46<br>(2.23)** | 0.38<br>(2.23)** | −0.91<br>(−3.22)* | 4 | 0.82 |
| Mauritius | 3.13<br>(0.50) | 0.69<br>(1.71) | −0.71<br>(−2.59)* | 6 | 0.61 |
| Mexico | 28.74<br>(2.14)* | −0.81<br>(−1.07) | 0.57<br>(1.01) | 7 | −0.09 |
| Mongolia | 5.94<br>(0.56) | 0.41<br>(0.58) | −0.46<br>(−0.38) | 5 | −0.70 |
| Morocco | 4.06<br>(1.03) | 0.47<br>(1.87) | −0.18<br>(−0.87) | 5 | 0.92 |
| Panama | 10.75<br>(5.72)* | 0.08<br>(0.92) | −0.22<br>(−1.87) | 9 | 0.18 |
| Philippines | 4.93<br>(4.82)* | 0.55<br>(7.96)* | −0.52<br>(−5.93)* | 6 | 0.94 |
| Senegal | 18.13<br>(7.32)* | −0.48<br>(−1.32) | 0.13<br>(0.20) | 5 | 0.76 |
| Singapore | 10.33<br>(12.96)* | 0.18<br>(3.86)* | −0.18<br>(−3.31)* | 13 | 0.53 |

*Table 12.3-A Continued*

*Table 12.3-A Continued*

| | | | | | |
|---|---|---|---|---|---|
| South Africa | 11.40 | 0.101 | 0.05 | 10 | 0.60 |
| | (10.51)* | (1.98)** | (1.79) | | |
| Thailand | 11.06 | 0.15 | | 3 | 0.35 |
| | (4.48)* | (1.44) | | | |
| | 12.50 | | 0.28 | 3 | 2.33 |
| | (10.15)* | | (1.72) | | |
| Uruguay | 6.57 | 0.38 | −0.40 | 6 | 0.83 |
| | (3.54)* | (2.71)* | (−3.29)* | | |
| All countries pooled (random effect model) (1) | 6.03 (8.9)* | 0.41 (10.48)* | −0.29 (−5.56)* | 212 | R2 = 0.87 |

*Note:* (1) Based on the Lagrange Multiplier statistic and Hausman test the RE model has been chosen over the classical regression model and the Fixed Effect model. (2) ln stands for logarithmic transformation, VA is value added, EMP is employment and W is real wage per worker.

*Source:* Based on UNIDO data (1990–2004).

## REFERENCES

Agénor, P. R., Nabli, M. K., Yousef, T., and Jensen, H. T. 2007. 'Labor Market Reforms, Growth, and Unemployment in Labor-exporting Countries in the Middle East and North Africa'. *Journal of Policy Modeling* 29(2): 277–309.

Ahsan, A., and C. Pagés. 2009. 'Are All Labor Regulations Equal?: Evidence from Indian Manufacturing'. *Journal of Comparative Economics*, 37(1): 62–75.

Almeida, R., and P. Carneiro. 2009. 'Enforcement of Labor Regulations, Labor Demand, Em-ployment, Productivity'. *Journal of Comparative Economics*, 37(1): 28–46.

Amin, M. 2008. 'Labor Regulation and Employment in India's Retail Stores'. *Journal of Comparative Economics*, 37(1): 91–105.

Balassa, B. 1986. 'The Employment Effects of Trade in Manufactured Products between Developed and Developing Countries'. *Journal of Policy Modeling*, 8(3).

Berg, J., and S. Cazes. 2007. 'The Doing Business Indicators: Measurement Issues and Political Implications', Economic and Labour Market Papers 6, Employment Analysis and Research Unit, Economic and Labour Market Analysis Department, International Labour Office, Geneva.

Besley, T., and R. Burgess. 2004. 'Can Labor Regulation Hinder Economic Performance? Evidence from India'. *Quarterly Journal of Economics*, 119(1): 91–134.

Bhalotra, S. 1998. 'The Puzzle of Jobless Growth in Indian Manufacturing'. *Oxford Bulletin of Economics and Statistics*, 60(1): 5–32.

Blanchard, O., and J. Wolfers. 2000. 'The Role of Shocks and Institutions in the Rise of European Unemployment: The Aggregate Evidence'. *The Economic Journal*, 110, 1–33.

Botero, J.C., S. Djankov, R. L. Porta, F. Lopez-de-Silanes, and A. Shleifer. 2004. 'The Regulation of Labor'. *Quarterly Journal of Economics* 119(4): 1339–82. Chicago: University of Chicago Press.

Connell, J., J. Burgess, Z. Hannif. 2008. 'Job Quality: What Does It Mean, What Does It Matter?' *Comparisons between Australia and the UAE, International Journal of Employment Studies*, 16(1): 59–78.

Datta, R.C. 2003. 'Labour Market – Social Institution, Economic Reforms and Social Cost'. In *Labour Market and Institution in India*, edited by ShujiUchikawa, Manohar Publications.

Dutt, P. 2003. 'Labor Market Outcomes and Trade Reforms: The Case of India'. In *The Impact of Trade on Labor: Issues, Perspectives and Experiences from Developing Asia*, edited by Hasan, R. and D. Mitra. Elsevier Science B.V.

Edwards, A.C., and S. Edwards. 1994. 'Labour Market Distortions and Structural Adjustment in Developing Countries'. In *Labour Market in an Era of Adjustment* edited by S. Horton, R. Kanbur, and D. Mazumdar, *EDI Development Studies*, 1, 105–45. Washington, DC: World Bank.

Fallon, P.R., and R.E.B. Lucas. 1991. 'The Impact of Changes in Job Security Regulations in India and Zimbabwe'. *The World Economic Review*, 5(3).

Goldar, B. 2011. 'Growth in Organized Manufacturing Employment in Recent Years'. *Economic and Political Weekly*, February 12, 46(7).

——— 2004. 'Trade Liberalisation and Real Wages in Organized Manufacturing Industries in India'. In *Economic Policies and the Emerging Scenario: Challenges to Government and Industry*, edited by Ajit Karnik and L. G. Burange. Mumbai: Himalaya Publishing House.

——— 2000. 'Employment Growth in Organized Manufacturing in India'. *Economic and Political Weekly*, April 1, 1191–95.

Goldar, B., and S. C. Agarwal. 2005. 'Trade Liberalisation and Price Cost Margin in Indian Industries'. *The Developing Economies*, 43(3): (September), 346–73.

Gorter, C., and J. Poot. 1999. '*The Impact of Labour Market Deregulation: Lessons from the "Kiwi" and "Polder" models*'. Tinbergen Institute Discussion Papers, 99-001/3, Tinbergen Institute, Netherlands, 1–38.

Gunter, B. G., and R. van der Hoeven. 2004. 'The Social Dimension of Globalization: AReview of the Literature'. Working Paper No. 24, Policy Integration Department, World Commission on the Social Dimension of Globalization, International Labour Office, Geneva.

Hasan, R. 2003. 'The Impact of Trade and Labour Market Regulations on Employment and Wages: Evidence from Developing Countries'. In *The Impact of Trade on Labour: Issues, Perspectives and Experiences from Developing Asia*, edited by R. Hasan and D. Mitra. Amsterdam, North Holland: Elsevier.

Hasan, R., D. Mitra, and K.V. Ramaswamy. 2003. 'Trade Reforms, Labor Regulations and Labor Demand Elasticities: Empirical Evidence from India'. *NBER Working Paper*, No. w9879.

ILO-SAAT 1996, *Economic Reforms and Labour Policies in India,* New Delhi, 1996.

International Labour Office. 2007. *Key Indicators of the Labour Market,* 5th Edition, International Labour Office, Geneva.

International Monetary Fund. 2005. *World Economic Outlook,* World Economic and Financial Surveys.

Krueger, A. B., and R. Solow, eds. 2002. *The Roaring Nineties: Can Full Employment be Sustained?* New York: Russell Sage Foundation.

Krueger, A. O. 1983. *Trade and Employment in Developing Countries,* vol. 3, Chicago: University of Chicago Press.

Kugler, A. D. 2004. The Effect of Job Security Regulations on Labour Market Flexibility: Evidence from the Colombian Labour Market Reform, In *Law and Employment: Lessons from Latin America and the Caribbean,* edited by James Heckman and Carmen Pagés. University of Chicago Press.

Nagaraj, R. 2011. 'Growth in Organised Manufacturing Employment in Recent Years'. *Economic and Political Weekly,* February 12.

———— 1994. 'Employment and Wages in Manufacturing Industries: Trends, Hypotheses and Evidence'. *Economic and Political Weekly,* January 22, 177–86.

———— 2004. 'Fall in Organised Manufacturing Employment: A Brief Note'. *Economic and Political Weekly,* July 24, 2004, 3387–90.

Phelps E. S. 1994. Structural Slumps, The Modern Equilibrium Theory of Unemployment, Interest and Assets, Cambridge MA: Harvard University Press.

Pissarides, C. A. 2000. Equilibrium Unemployment Theory, Cambridge, Mass: MIT Press.

Tendulkar, S. D. 2000. 'Employment Growth in Factory Manufacturing Sector during pre and post-Reform Periods', Paper Presented in the Conference in Honour of K.L. Krishna, Delhi School of Economics, Delhi, December.

Tendulkar, S.D. 2004. 'Organised Labour Market in India: Pre and Post Reform', Paper Presented at the Conference on Anti Poverty and Social Policy in India, Alwar, January 2–4.

Uchikawa, S. 2003. *Labour Market and Institution in India,* New Delhi: Manohar Publications.

Weller, J. 2001. Economic Reforms, Growth and Employment: Labour Markets in Latin America and the Caribbean, United Nations. Economic Commission for Latin America and the Caribbean.

# 13

# Financing Structure and Growth
## A Study of Firms in the Indian Private Corporate Sector

Prabhakaran Nair V. R.

## INTRODUCTION

Issues regarding the interface between corporate financial structure and corporate growth have gained prominence in the recent years, especially in the context of the fast changing institutional framework in the financial markets in many countries. More importantly, the institutional set-up within corporate houses operated in the regulated era has undergone substantial transformation over the last two decades. The move toward market-driven allocation of resources, coupled with the widening and deepening of financial markets, including the capital market, and the stringent disclosure and transparency practices consequent upon initial public offerings, have provided greater scope for the corporates to determine their financing structure and introduce better growth enhancing practices. A fast growing literature has analysed the relationship between financial structure and corporate growth [see among others, Fazzari et al. (1988), Whited (1992), Rajan and Zingales (1988) Devereux and Schiantarelli (1989) Hoshi et al. (1991) Mills et al. (1994)]. For instance, Fazzari et al. (1988) have empirically shown that while capital market informational problems arise at the level of the firm, financial constraints have a clear macroeconomic dimension because fluctuations in firms' cash flow and liquidity are correlated with movements of the aggregate economy over the business cycle, and that in general unlike the neoclassical investment theory, financial factors do affect investment decisions. In other words, according to the financial constraints hypothesis by Fazzari et al. (1988), financial structure of firms in terms of cash flow and debt affects investment when there exists a wedge between the costs of internal and external finance[1] in an imperfect financial market. The question of the financing choice of firms is critical in this regard because the cost of capital and hence the value of a firm depends upon its debt-equity mix (Pagano 1993).

A large volume of research has tested this hypothesis by focusing on the sensitivity of cash flow on firms' investment and growth [see, among others, Devereux and Schiantarelli (1989) Hoshi et al. (1991) Mills et al. (1994)], Bond et al. (2003), Fagiollo and Luzzi (2006) Harris et al. (1994)]. These studies based their empirical analysis on the idea that financial markets, especially those of developing countries, are imperfect in nature in the sense that the suppliers of funds have less information about the profitability and risks of investment projects than what the firms have. Under such financial constraints, investment decisions depend on the availability of internal funds. Furthermore, the heterogeneity of firms implies that investment of financially constrained firms' is more likely to be affected by the availability of internal funds (cash flow). In an attempt to examine the endogenous interaction between financial structure and real activity, Calomiris and Hubbard (1987) concluded that with credit market imperfections, borrower's investment decisions will be 'excessively sensitive' to current cash flow that changes with financial liberalization.

Kaplan and Zingales (2000), however, suggest that simple positive investment/cash flow sensitivities do not necessarily reflect the financial constraints, since investment may react positively to investment even under no financial constraints, with cash flow providing adequate degrees of freedom to finance investment. Based on this, many studies have emphasized that different dimensions of financing patterns is determined by various institutional factors such as tax and bankruptcy law investors' protection rules, legal legacy, role of banks in the economic system [Rajan and Zingales (1998), La Porte al. (1998)]. These studies are thought to have emphasized that the type of financing structure (as a part of financial strategy) chosen by the firm has a definite impact on the future expansion decisions and growth. The financial structure of a firm will influence its investment decision and shocks to the balance sheet will alter the evolution of growth over time. The crux of these studies is that the type of financial strategy (financial structure) chosen by the firm is not neutral for the firm's future growth, as it importantly shapes the managers' incentives.

This chapter investigates whether and how different debt financing ratios impact the firm growth using a large sample of Indian manufacturing firms

---

[1] A firm can mobilize resources for investment mainly from two sources viz., internal and external. While internal sources mainly include retained earnings, external sources include debt (borrowings from Banks and Development Financial Institutions), equity (paid-up capital), debentures, trade dues and current liabilities etc.

in the private corporate sector. Using panel regression analysis we estimate the relationship between financial structure and the growth of firms during the period 1991–2013. In the context of the ongoing reforms in the financial markets, it is pertinent to analyse whether the expected benefits of the liberalization and promotion of banking sector and stock market have translated into better financing choices at firm level and thereby determining real growth of firms. We shall address mainly two issues in this regard. First, was there any discernible change in the financing structure of firms? Second, how was the financing structure and real growth of firms in the private corporate sector related? Specifically, the chapter makes an improvement over the existing literature by throwing light on the aspects of the relation between financial structure and debt maturity structure on one side and growth of firm on the other. Our results reveal that, on an average, Indian manufacturing firms in the private corporate sector do not depend on capital market resources including equity to finance economic growth, rejecting the contribution of capital market liberalization in fostering growth. Instead, firms depend heavily on debt to finance their expansion. Interestingly enough, the study found that, on an average, the growth pattern of Indian manufacturing firms is highly fragile, since it is negatively related with the increase of non financial debt. Rather, the negative relationship of the share of short term debt suggests that increase in the debt levels of firms is not sustainable as far as the growth of firms is concerned.

The study is organized into five sections. Following the introductory section, in the second section, we discuss the theoretical literature. The third section analyses the changes in the financing structure (financing pattern) of the selected sample of firms in the private corporate sector. The fourth section empirically estimates the relationship between financial structure and growth. The fifth section concludes the chapter.

## THEORETICAL LITERATURE

During 1950s, studies on corporate finance argued that under perfect financial market setting, financial structure does not affect the investment decision of firms. However, the emergence of the popular Modigliani-Miller irrelevance proposition observes that, in a perfectly functioning capital market, the method of choosing the financing of a firm will not affect the cost of capital and the firms will not face any constraints since they have access to unlimited sources of funds (Modigliani and Miller 1958). This is because they assume that the capital markets being perfect in nature, there is neither transaction nor information costs, internal and external funds are perfect substitutes in terms of financing investment and growth, and firms have access to unlimited sources of funds. In other words, the role of financial intermediaries (financial factors) in financing of firms was generally ignored during 1960s.

The neutrality of financial factors, however, was confronted with criticisms after the emergence of theoretical and empirical studies [Stiglitz (1988), Fazzari (1992), Beckaert et al. (2005)], which emphasized the relationship between finance and investment and provided a framework for analysing the impact of financing structure on real activities. It was pointed out that financial markets, especially those of developing countries are imperfect in nature, in the sense that, the suppliers of funds have less information about the profitability and risks of investment projects than firms. During the 1980s and 90s, many studies that linked the financial structure and investment behaviour based on the economics of information asymmetry and incentives argued that, under information asymmetry, the financial structure of firms affects investment through a wedge between the costs of external and internal finance in an imperfect financial market. Akerlof (1970) argued that the, 'lemon problem', and the existence of risk in debt and capital markets prevent the system from reaching the efficient general equilibrium.

Myers and Majluf (1984) demonstrate that the cost of external funds is higher than that of internal funds owing to information asymmetry between lenders and borrowers. Second, managerial agency problems arise when managers who are not owners pursue their own interests (Jensen and Meckling 1976). Managers who may prefer riskier projects have an incentive to issue a new debt senior to the existing one, by therefore increasing the risk of existing creditors. The external investors who are unable to participate in designing contracts would then try to offset moral hazards by asking for a higher price for the issuance of risk. The firm is then required to pay a premium for external financing if outside investors suspect the managers who are not owners pursuing the interests of shareholders. Finally, transaction costs associated with the issuance of debt and equity might raise the cost of external financing. The combined effects of asymmetric information, managerial agency problems and transactions costs will raise the costs of external finance and bring a disparity between the cost of internal and external funds.

The above theoretical consideration is at the heart of the 'pecking order' and, 'financial hierarchy' hypotheses, which have argued that under imperfections in financial markets, internal and external sources are no longer equivalent in undertaking real activities of firms. In other words, financial constraint hypothesis suggests that firms prefer internal funds to external funds and if external financing is needed, debt is preferred to equity. This is known as the *pecking order hypothesis* as developed by Myres and Majluf (1984). Under financial constraints, investment decisions depend on the availability of internal funds. Furthermore, the heterogeneity of firms implies that investment of financially constrained firms is more likely to be affected by the availability of internal funds. In a nutshell, firms adopt a hierarchical order of financing source preferences and the combination of internal and external sources is the result of financial strategies emerging from the characteristics of firms adopting it. The 'pecking-order hypothesis' in capital choices of firms postulates that firms prefer internal finance to external finance; in case the latter is required, debt is preferred over equity. In essence, it says that when internal funds are insufficient, the manager will prefer debt to equity because debt is less sensitive to information asymmetries and results in a 'pecking order' in debt equity mix. The 'pecking order' theory suggests that the firms' financing patterns begin with retained earnings, followed by riskless debt, and then new equity[2] (Myers 1977; Myers and Majiluf 1984). The pecking order theory and the information asymmetries introduced further analytics in to the debt structure (leverage) debate in developing countries.

What emerges from the above discussion is that the status of capital structure or debt structure is significant for the managers of firms to determine the real business decisions of investment and growth, since it is argued that different forms of debts in the governance path of firms carry different effects on investment and growth, as they produce different motivations to firm managers. The recent theoretical and empirical studies pointed out that different dimension of financial structures (financing ratios) of firms may be associated with the firms' value and growth. The link between the combination of internal and external funds and firms' real variables has been widely discussed in voluminous literature. According to the financial constraints and pecking order hypotheses, the internal liquidity through cash flow and retained earnings is an important factor in investment and hereby determining the desired growth targets of firms. Calomiris and Hubbard (1987) concluded that with credit market imperfections, borrower's investment decisions will be 'excessively sensitive' to internal funds. A better functioning of the financial system would imply that investment is less determined by the firm's internal resources and less negatively affected by leverage (debt), which in turn, would imply significant and non-negative magnitude on the coefficient of debt (borrowing) [Fazzari et al. (1988), Almeida et al. (2004)].

It is evident that shifts in cash flow (profit) and debt (leverage) may influence the dynamics of investment growth profile of firms. While profitability should have a positive effect, the degree of financial leverage should have a negative effect on the level of investment under market imperfections. If the financial market is imperfect, the additional cost of external funds increases at an ever-increasing

---

2   Because of the information problems, there can be under pricing of equity, which therefore makes equity issues unattractive. Mackie Mason (1990), however, argued that if benefits of information asymmetry outweigh the costs, the choice of pecking order may not be the course that a firm would follow.

rate. Therefore, an increase (decrease) in internal funds will lower (raise) the cost of funds that the firm uses to invest, thereby increasing (decreasing) its investment. This means that investment of the firm is positively correlated with its internal funds. Moreover, if the measure of cash flow has a positive impact on investment; it implies the existence of constrained access to credit markets. Due to the absence of constrained access to resources, firms would borrow as much as needed to maximize profits, and cash flow would not be constraining. All these suggest that financial factors do affect investment decisions.

Jenson (1986) expressed the view that external debt is an effective tool to reduce the agency cost problems but may result in underperformance of firms. Moreover, if cash flow is high under organizational inefficiencies, prevalence of conflicts of interests may cause managers to undertake unprofitable investment. In such a situation, it would be better for the managers to resort to external financing so that they would become aware to avoid cash wasting tendencies, and thus eventually lead to better performances and growth. As similar to debt, maturity structure of debt (share of short term over long term debt) plays a pivotal role in reducing the agency problems between the users and suppliers of funds. As Myers (1977) rightly pointed out, the dominance short term debt provides a deeper commitment of managers of the firms not to alter the end use of the funds and distort growth profile. Barclay et al. (2003) further added that short-term finance allows pursuing projects with net present value, while suspending unprofitable ones. Many empirical studies show that maturity structure of debt positively affects investment, profitability, and growth of firms [see for instance Schianterelli and Sembenelli (1997)].

In recent times, as a significant departure from studying the finance growth nexus with aggregate time series, a large volume of literature has attempted to study how the growth of financial institutions are related with the growth activity using firm level data. Using industry level data Rajan and Zingales (1998) found that industries with greater need of external sources for financing grow faster in more financially developed countries. It is pointed out by Demirguc-Kunt and Maksimovic (1998) that firms grow at faster rate, relative to benchmark growth rate that would hold in the absence of external finance, in countries with a more developed financial system. Regarding external financing, Stulz (2001) found that staged financing of banks would reduce asymmetric information and opportunistic behaviour of firms, since staged finance allows the loans to be renewed and expanded as and when the firms ask for more financing. The role of bank debt on the liability structure of the banks could be either high or low depending on a number of demand and supply side factors. Indeed, the relation between the amount of bank debt and growth of a firm is important since it reveals the dynamics of growth of manufacturing firms. Some studies have also discussed the role of non-financial debt in real performance of firms and showed that trade debt relaxes financial constraints and expand their spending capacity and growth [Petersen and Rajan (1996), Demirguc-Kunt and Maksimovic (2001)].

## FINANCING STRUCTURE AND ECONOMIC GROWTH: EMPIRICAL ANALYSIS

### The sample data

In this section, we analyse the financing pattern of a panel of Indian private corporate manufacturing firms selected for the study. Slightly less than half of the companies in the corporate sector are from manufacturing. And the bulk of the corporate sector's value added originates in registered manufacturing. The firm level data is obtained from the electronic database PROWESS provided by Centre for Monitoring Indian Economy (CMIE). The analysis is carried out for the period 1991–92 to 2012–13. The panel is unbalanced. It contained detailed information on the financial performance of the companies culled from their profit and loss accounts. 'PROWESS' database includes data on more than 20,000 non-financial firms in the private corporate sector covering 23 industries for the period 1991–2013. We have included manufacturing firms existing for the period 1991–2013 under analysis due to two reasons. First, since we included lagged values in the model, we cannot utilize the observations for the initial year. Second, the selection of the period coincides with the liberal financial regime since 1991, when one expects to find an increase in the financial resources from both debt and equity markets for firms in the private corporate sector. We have excluded those observations having implausible values for main variables such as output, equity, debt, cash flow etc. After checking for the consistency of the data throughout the whole sample period, deleting firms that have implausible values and permanently negative profit rates, and omitting outliers, we have obtained 20,836 observations on 2017 manufacturing firms in the private corporate sector. The PROWESS data does not allow us to undertake a comparative analysis of pre and post liberalization for sample firms due to the lack of data in the pre-reform period. Thus, we attempt to classify the entire period in to two equal periods 1991–92 to 2001–02 and 2002–03 to 2012–13 to see whether there is any discernable change within the post liberalization period.

### Financing structure

Sources of funds: Trends and patterns

The evidence from the Table 13.1 supports the idea that our sample manufacturing firms in the corporate sector depend heavily on external finance throughout the period. On an average, external finance constitute around 61 per cent of firms' total finance during the period 1991–92 to 2012–13. On the other hand, in the case internal resources, it stood around 39 per cent of the total sources. Internal sources of a firm generally involve retained profits and depreciation allowances (depreciation). These are used to meet the fixed or working capital requirements of firms. Retained profit is the amount of net profits, which are retained within the company, and are not distributed as dividend. Depreciation allowance is the amount provided to firms to finance the wearing out, consumption or loss of value of depreciable asset arising from use, effluxion of time or obsolescence through technology and market changes. The competitive business firms keep a proportion of their earnings for future investment. The increase in retained profit results in accumulation of reserves and surplus that determines the firm's future growth prospects. However, if the financing of investment from the internally generated funds may be difficult for a firm, external financing becomes necessary. Though internal resources have increased in the post liberalization period, external resources still form the major source.

**Table 13.1: Sources of internal and external funds for sample firms (per cent share in total)**

| Source | 1991–92 to 2001–02 | 2002–03 to 2012–13 | 1991–92 to 2012–13 |
|---|---|---|---|
| **Total** | **100** | **100** | **100** |
| Internal sources | 37.2 | 40.9 | 39.05 |
| External sources (1+2+3) | 62.8 | 59.1 | 60.95 |
| *1. Funds from capital market* | *13.47* | *7.14* | *10.31* |
| a. Fresh capital* | 3.63 | 1.94 | 2.79 |
| b. Share premium* | 6.29 | 2.16 | 4.23 |
| c. Debentures/bond | 3.06 | 1.85 | 2.46 |
| d. Fixed deposits | 0.49 | 1.19 | 0.84 |
| *2. External debt (borrowings)* | *41.12* | *46.57* | *43.85* |
| a. Bank borrowings | 24.76 | 36.23 | 30.50 |
| b. Institutional borrowings | 16.36 | 10.34 | 13.35 |
| *3. Other debt* | *8.21* | *5.39* | *6.80* |

*Source:* Author's Calculation using CMIE PROWESS Database

*Note:* (1) * and ** are equity related instruments.

    (2) Other debt includes borrowing from government, borrowing from promoters, hire purchase, public borrowings (commercial papers and debentures), sundry creditors, etc.

In Table 13.1, an item-wise analysis of external sources in the financial liberalization regime is also given. It gives the share of different components of external sources as a percentage of total sources. External finance includes funds from capital markets, external debt (borrowings), other debt, etc. It is seen from Table 13.1 that though external sources have declined towards the second half of the reform period, the share of different components of external finance have changed over the years. Two main external sources, viz. funds from capital markets, and external borrowings are analysed to understand the changes in the financing structure. In PROWESS database, 'capital market' is the summation of funds mobilized from four channels such as fresh capital, share premium, debentures/ bond and fixed deposits. Table 13.1 reveals that the percentage of funds mobilized through capital markets, which was relatively high, has come down to 7.14 per cent in 2002–13 from 13.47 per cent during 1991–2002. Rather, the high percentage in first half of reforms may simply reflect the temporary stock market boom driven by the liberalization of stock prices during 1993–95 period. This is evident from the fact that, for the entire period 1991–2013, on an average, funds mobilized from capital markets was 10.31 per cent, which was less than the average of 13.47 per cent in 1991–2002 period. From this, it could generally be observed that, the capital market has not performed on a sustained basis as a source of finance in the financial liberalization regime, and this pattern is similar across almost all the instruments of capital market funds. The only exception is fixed deposits. However, its contribution to the capital market funds is slightly more than 1 per cent. In the breakups of instruments for capital market given in Table 13.1, fresh capital and share premium are the most important components of capital market resources. These two represents external equity components. The share of external equity (fresh capital + share premium) increased significantly during 1991–2002. However, its share has declined in the later years, which was sufficient to make overall decline in the share of funds from capital markets.

Borrowings (debt) continued to be the most important source of external finance. It is seen from Table 13.1 that borrowings have increased from 41.12 per cent in 1991–2002 to 46.57 per cent in 2002–13 period. A close examination of different components of borrowings reveals that the increase in borrowings solely contributed by the increase in bank borrowings. More specifically, there has been a shift away from equity related instruments to external debt, especially bank borrowings in the post liberalization period. In other words, firms have substituted external equity by external debt over the years as their most important source of external finance. This increase was mainly due to a substantial increase in bank borrowings on the face of a drastic decline in institutional borrowings. While bank borrowings increased from 24.76 per cent in 1991–2002 to 36.23 per cent during 2002–13, institutional borrowings have declined from 16.36 in

1991–2002 to 10.34 during 2002–13 (Table 13.1). To conclude, the sources of funds for the sample firms gives an indication that, they have a higher dependence on bank borrowings for meeting their requirements compared to both internal funds and other sources within external sources. The analysis shows that firms have a clear preference for internal resources with increased dependence on bank borrowings indicating a financing hierarchy in financing pattern of firms in the private corporate sector.

### External financing structure: A size-wise analysis

As noticed, firms depend heavily on external funds, particularly external debt, from banks. Thus, we analyse the changes in the external financing pattern using some key financing ratios calculated for different size groups firms to see if this pattern was uniformly true for all firms. We would hypothesize that the elimination of credit ceilings and interest rate controls along with other structural reforms in the financial markets will have different effects on different size firms depending upon their differential capabilities to raise external finance. How is this regime change at the macro level reflected in our sample of firms? Since we are unable to make a comparison with pre-liberalization data for our sample, we only study the differences in the financial ratios between large and small firms in the post liberalization period.

The classification of the total sample into different size categories is based on our analytical framework that the extent of information asymmetry and agency problems are likely to be reflected in the characteristics of the firms.[3] For our analysis, firms are divided into small and large categories according to size. We have used the variable gross fixed asset as a base to classify the total sample in to different size categories. We have calculated financial ratios by averaging the values across the firms in each year. Measures of debt ratios for different size categories and total sample are reported in Table 13.2. The external financing ratios used are the ratio of domestic debt to total debt, the ratio of foreign debt to total debt, total bank debt to total debt, short term bank debt to total bank debt, long term bank debt to total bank debt, debt from financial institutions to total debt, public debt to total debt and other debt to total debt. The difference in these debt ratios is a partial indication of the differential access to types of external finance. Total debt refers to all kinds of debt, interest bearing or otherwise. Therefore, it includes debt

---

[3]  Similar to macro level studies establishing link between finance and growth (see Beck, Levine and Loayza 2000a, 2000b), recent studies produced evidence at the firm level also (see Beck, Demirguc-Kunt and Maksimovic 2003). The micro level study particularly stressed that firms financial constraints tend to reduce growth.

from banks (short-term and long-term) and financial institutions, inter-corporate loans, fixed deposits, foreign loans, government loans etc. Bank borrowings refer to total loans from banks, e.g., cash credit, bank overdraft facilities, term loans etc. Short-term bank borrowings refer to bank loans with maturities of less than one year; the rest are long-term bank borrowings. Long-term bank debt is one minus short-term bank debt.

**Table 13.2: Debt structure of firms: All firms and size-wise, 1991–2002 to 2003–13 (as ratio of total debt)**

| Debt ratios | All firms | Small | Large |
| --- | --- | --- | --- |
| Domestic debt/total debt | 0.94 | 0.97 | 0.92 |
| Foreign debt/total debt | 0.06 | 0.03 | 0.08 |
| *Total* | *100* | *100* | *100* |
| Total bank debt/total debt (a + b) | 0.49 | 0.53 | 0.45 |
| *a. Short-term bank debt/total bank debt* | *0.39* | *0.45* | *0.33* |
| *b. Long-term bank debt/total bank debt* | *0.12* | *0.09* | *0.15* |
| Debt from financial institutions/total debt | 0.21 | 0.12 | 0.30 |
| Debt from corporations/total debt | 0.12 | 0.14 | 0.10 |
| Public debt/total debt | 0.02 | 0.01 | 0.03 |
| Other debt/total debt | 0.16 | 0.20 | 0.12 |

*Source*: Computed from CMIE PROWESS database

*Note:* Other debt includes borrowing from government, borrowing from promoters, hire purchase, public borrowings (commercial papers and debentures), etc.

In Table 13.2, we separately consider the percentage of total debt coming from bank borrowings, foreign borrowings, borrowing from non-bank financial institutions, debt from corporation and the catch-all category 'other debt' that includes government loans, promoters, hire purchase and other residual borrowings. We find that bank borrowings represent by far the largest category among different debt financing sources. On average, over the period 1991–2013, bank borrowings represented 49 per cent of total debt. The next largest category is borrowing from other financial institutions[4], which averaged 21 per cent of total debt and other borrowing that average 16 per cent of debt. Borrowing from corporations is also a relatively large proportion of total borrowing–the average

---

[4]    This includes borrowing from all non-bank Indian financial institutions as well as insurance companies, such as Life Insurance Corporation, General Insurance Corporation, and Unit Trust of India.

over the period was 12 per cent. On the other hand, public borrowing and foreign borrowing were relatively small fractions of total borrowing, averaging less than 1 per cent of total borrowing, respectively. In total debt both bank debt and debt from financial institutions together constitute secured debt. Accordingly, approximately 70 per cent of all debt held by our sample firms is secured or collateralized.

We now investigate the composition of debt by firm size by looking at the percentage of total debt (i.e., borrowing) coming from different sources. We find that small firms have a higher proportion of bank debt relative to large firms. This difference is driven by differences in short-term bank debt, since long-term bank debt (only 0.06 per cent more for large firms) is almost similar across firm sizes. On the other hand, large firms are able to borrow proportionately more from non-bank financial institutions relative to small firms. Compared to small firms larger firms have more than 2 times of debt from financial institutions. Adding up the share of debt from bank and non-bank financial institutions (secured debt), we see that small firms are able to rely less on formal financial intermediaries. At the same time, large firms have more public borrowing (commercial papers and debentures) and more foreign borrowing, though these comprise relatively small portions of total borrowing. While small firms have only 3 per cent foreign borrowings, it is 8 per cent in the case of large firms.

Perhaps not surprisingly, we find that small firms borrow significantly more from other corporations, which is 4 per cent more than large firms do. It may be possible that, much of this financing comes from companies with the same business groups. Thus, it appears that, for small firms, intra group corporate financing serves as substitute for financing from formal financial institutions and public debt markets. Finally, we find that small firms have less secured borrowings (bank and financial institutions) than larger firms. The secured or collateralized debt is 75 per cent for larger firms and 65 per cent for small firms. Smaller firms are less likely to have the appropriate assets that could be used as collateral or are less able/willing to pay the fixed costs of registering such collateral (i.e., in relative terms the costs of collateralizing assets tend to be higher for firms).[5] Compared to small firms, large firms seem to have benefited from expensive domestic credit with cheaper foreign credit since they are unlikely to face informational asymmetries. This is because quite often, large firms with direct relations with foreign markets

---

[5] According to Smith and Warner (1979) secured debt lowers the total costs and enforcement costs by ensuring that the lender has clear title to the assets and by preventing the lender's claim from being jeopardized if the borrower subsequently issues additional debt. However, it is also argued that secured debt involves out of pocket costs (e.g., required reports to the debt-holders, filing fees, and other administrative expenses). Securing debt also involves opportunity costs by restricting the firm from potentially profitable dispositions of collateral.

may have increased access to offshore credit and international equity markets (Harris et al., 1994).

Size-wise financing ratios

Having analysed the differences in the debt structure for various size groups, we now attempt to understand the financing patterns by analysing some key financing ratios. Our main variable of interest is the ratio of debt (borrowings) to assets. In addition to looking at the aggregate debt ratio, we also examine the interest coverage ratios of our sample firms. It is defined as the share of earnings before depreciation, interest and taxes to interest payments. The interest coverage ratio measures the number of times that firms' earnings exceed its interest payments. This ratio shows the ease with which a firm can meet its debt payments or it measures the repayment capacity. In other words, it provides an indication of how far a company's cash flows could fall before the company will have difficulties meeting its interest payments. Measures of financial ratios for different size categories are reported in Table 13.3. As noted earlier, total debt includes bank borrowing, foreign borrowing, and borrowing from non-bank financial institutions, public borrowings (debentures and commercial borrowings), government borrowing, and hire purchase. It is seen from the Table 13.3 that in the post financial reform period the mean debt-to-assets ratio (D/K) has shown slight increase for all firms in the sample. From 0.40 in 1991–2002 it has increased to 0.41 in 2003–13. However, in the case of debt-assets-ratio (leverage ratio), the effects are not homogeneous across different size categories. It is evident that the leverage ratio for small firms has decreased (from 0.37 in 1992–2002 to 0.34 in 2003–13) towards the later years of financial liberalization. On the other hand, large firms significantly improved the leverage ratio from 0.42 in 1991–2002 to 0.48 in 2003–13 period (Table 13.3).

Table 13.3: Financing ratios: All firms and sizes

| Ratios | Small | | Large | | All firms | |
|---|---|---|---|---|---|---|
| | 1991–2002 | 2003–13 | 1991–2002 | 2003–13 | 1991–2002 | 2003–13 |
| Debt/total assets (D/K) | 0.37 | 0.34 | 0.42 | 0.48 | 0.40 | 0.41 |
| Cash-flow/interest payments (CF/int) | 4.92 | 6.65 | 4.11 | 5.86 | 4.52 | 6.25 |
| Profit/total assets (P/K) | 0.19 | 0.28 | 0.24 | 0.36 | 0.21 | 0.32 |

Source: Computed from CMIE PROWESS Database

Regarding the average interest coverage ratio (cash flow/interest payments) across firm sizes, we observe an increasing pattern. For all firms it has increased from 4.52 in 1991–2002 to 6.25 in 2002–13. This means that on an average interest coverage ratios during the post reform period were relatively high. Though for both size groups interest coverage ratio has increased over the reform period, throughout the period small firms have slightly higher mean interest coverage ratio than large firms (Table 13.3). This suggests that, on average, small firms have better repayment capacity than large firms, relative to their respective debt levels. In other words, small firms are able to support larger interest payments with their cash flows. This means that small firms' debt level is low compared to their interest paying capacity. This in turn gives an indication of a possibility that small firms suffer from credit constraints since they are unable to raise more debt.

The shifts in the policy regime clearly have different impacts on the profitability of different categories of firms. During the period 1991–2002, the measure of total returns to total assets (P/K) show highest returns for large firms and lowest returns for small firms. Though this pattern continued to exist even in the later period, i.e., 2003–13, there emerged a reversal of profit rates in all size categories. After the reforms, there was a dramatic increase in P/K both small and large firms (Table 13.3). The increased ratios of P/K ratios for small and large firms, demonstrate that rates of profitability have increased substantially, that may increase the capacity of firms to expand investment through internal financing also. It is pertinent to note that high interest coverage ratios we have seen earlier also are contributed by the increase in profitability of both small and large firms.

One of the most striking aspects of trends in sources of funds for firms in the private corporate sector is the increasing dependence of firms on internal funds rather than external funds in the post reform period. However, in the post liberalization period external financing has shown different patterns over the years. After a boom in the initial years, the funds from capital market sources have drastically declined. A similar picture is seen in the case of total borrowings also. The sharp decline in the share of borrowings (debt) in the post reform period is contributed by drastic decline in institutional borrowings (FIs). The only notable feature of external financing is the re-emergence of bank borrowings as a major source of external financing over the years. However, this upward bias is to be seen in the context of a declining share of external sources of funds of firms. It is interesting to see that a booming stock market has not witnessed any significant increase in money raised by firms from the capital market.

In terms of differences across firms, it is seen that debt levels increase with firm size. We find that large firms are able to borrow proportionately more than 2 times of debt from financial institutions. Adding up the share of debt from bank and non-bank financial institutions (secured debt), we see that small firms able to rely less on formal financial intermediaries. It is also noted that large firms seems to be benefited by substituting the more expensive domestic credit with cheaper foreign credit. The analysis provides suggestive evidence of strong credit constraints for small firms. Having analysed the behaviour of cost of debt and leverage ratios of different size categories, it is to be concluded that, given the institutional structure of Indian Manufacturing, conditions of access to financial resources (credit) significantly vary across different size categories of firms. This picture is inconsistent with the picture of small firms (less well connected) experiencing increased access to credit after reforms, albeit at higher interest rates, a result predicted by the conventional literature on financial repression and reform. From the analysis of debt ratios for size categories, it is not wrong to conclude that small firms are credit constrained in the financial liberalization period.

The sound financing practices of the corporate sector in terms of the implication for future financing and thereby investment and growth depend on financial structure. The external stimuli in the post financial liberalization period, whether in the form of fiscal or financial system (institutions), may give rise to a pattern of financing, whereas what ultimately matter to a firm is the proportion of borrowed to internal funds-the debt structure, which is an internal decision of firms. If financial liberalization increases supply of external finance and integrates financial markets, then, debt structure would reflect the true value. Given the increase in debt and its variations among different size groups, it is our interest to study the impact of financing structure on growth of firms. It is important to know what factors determine growth, because debt structure has implications for the value of a firm and thereby its ability to raise funds for future growth of firms. We intend to undertake an empirical analysis towards the end of the next section.

## FINANCING STRUCTURE AND GROWTH: ECONOMETRIC ANALYSIS

### The model specification

We conducted the estimation of growth function by using data obtained on non-financial firms in the Private Corporate Sector from the electronic database 'PROWESS' provided by Centre for Monitoring Indian Economy (CMIE). In recent years, there have been several studies on the role of financing structures in growth of firms. Following (Fagiolo and Luzzi 2006) we estimate the growth equation in which various financing ratios form regressors in the model. Based on the theoretical literature and the context of our study, adding cash flow and six financial indicators viz., equity, total debt, financial debt, bank debt, and short term bank debt, we specify an augmented growth equation where the dependent variable is output growth. Dependent variable $GROWTH_{i,t}$ is the growth rate of output computed as $GROWTH_{i,t-1} = \dfrac{OUTPUT_{i,t} - OUTPUT_{i,t-1}}{OUTPUT_{i,t-1}}$ . Among regressors, as a measure of internal liquidity, we added cash flow. The cash flow measures the liquidity position of the firm and its ability to depend on internal sources of funds to finance its investment decisions (Fazzari et al., 1988). In case a firm faces constraints on external financing, its investment and thereby growth will be determined partly by its internal resources. We use the ratio between gross cash flow before interest and tax and sales (gross operating surplus) in the analysis denoted as cashflow (CF).

Regarding external financing liability structure, various debt indicators are used to account for leverage of the firms. In the first place, total debt (all liability items excluding equity) to asset ratio (*TOTDEBT*) is used as the degree of leverage. It is likely that the cost of outside finance is positively correlated with debt, which is referred as agency cost in the literature on investment and credit constraints. As pointed out by the theory, asymmetric information and imperfections implies that the unavailability of finance, in terms of debt (borrowings) may constrain the investment decisions and thereby growth of firms. Second, we take debt from financial institutions to capture the role of financial debt in the growth of firms, as a ratio between debt from financial institutions to total debt (FINDEBT). Third, we capture the relative importance of bank debt in determining growth, as a ratio of bank debt to total debt of firms (BANKDEBT). Finally, we account for the role of debt maturity structure in the growth of firms. The debt maturity structure is taken as the ratio of short term bank debt to total bank credit (SHORTBANKDEBT).

The statistical specification for our regression equation estimated form is:

$$\text{GROWTH}_{i,t} = \beta_0 + \beta_1 \log(\text{CF}_{i\,t-1}) + \beta_2 \log(\text{CF}_{i\,t-2}) + \beta_3 \log(\text{EQ}_{i\,t-1}) + \beta_4 \log$$
$$(\text{TOTDEBT}_{i\,t-1}) + \beta_5 \log(\text{FINDEBT}_{i\,t-1}) + \beta_6 \log(\text{BANKDEBT}_{i\,t-1}) + \beta_7$$
$$\log(\text{SHORTBANKDEBT}_{i\,t-1}) + u_{it}$$

where, $\beta_0 \ldots \ldots \ldots \beta_7$ are parameters, the $i$ subscript denotes the firm and $t$ subscript denotes the time period and $u_{it}$ is the disturbance term. $u_{it} = \varepsilon_{it} + \lambda_i$ in which $\lambda_i$ in is the firm specific fixed effect, and $\varepsilon_{it}$ is a random error term. The use of logarithmic forms will help to account for potential non-linearities in the relationships between the explanatory variables and the growth. Regarding the effects on growth, we included the lagged value of $\text{OUTPUT}_{i\,t-2}$ to allow for possible dynamic effects in the model.

The data used in estimating growth equation in this section is the same we used to analyse trends and patterns of financial structure in the third section. Using firm level data provides us with several advantages. This helps us to avoid the substantial serial correlation problem, which typically arises when using aggregate time series data. Since the firm level data has substantial cross-sectional variation, it gives more precise estimates of the parameters. We have included a firm in the sample if it has at least 5 years of observations after cleaning for the missing values for the independent variables used in the study. Summary statistics of the variables used is given in Table 13.4.

**Table 13.4: Summary statistics**

| Variables | Mean | Std. Dev. |
|---|---|---|
| CF | 0.096 | 0.967 |
| EQ | 0.215 | 0.734 |
| TOTDEBT | 0.940 | 1.990 |
| FINDEBT | 0.210 | 0.489 |
| BANKDEBT | 0.497 | 0.768 |
| SHORTBANKDEBT | 0.390 | 0.456 |

In the case of panel data, the estimation of the model using the Ordinary Least Squares (OLS) may yield unsatisfactory results, because dynamic models are likely to suffer from endogeneity problem. The endogeneity problem arises mainly due to the fact that in a dynamic model, there is the presence of lagged dependent variable. The presence of lagged dependent variable makes the estimates inconsistent. In order to overcome this problem, the generalized method of moments (GMM) estimation is widely used for dynamic panel data models.

The growth equation in our empirical analysis has been estimated in first differences to eliminate the fixed effects in the model. This will help us to control the firm specific effects including both time-specific effects and firm-specific effects. We have used the GMM to allow for the potential endogeneity of the independent variables. The appropriate lagged values of the right hand side variables are used as instruments. We have used full instruments of second lag onwards as instruments in the models estimated. The consistency of the GMM estimator depends on whether the lagged values of the micro variables are valid instruments in the regression procedure. A necessary condition for the validity of such instruments is that the error term be serially uncorrelated. If the model has been transformed to first difference as we do in our estimation, first order serial correlations are to be expected but not second order. In the absence of higher-order serial correlation, the GMM estimator provides consistent estimates of the parameters.

To address these issues, we presented two specification tests suggested by Arellano and Bond (1991). The first is the Sargan test of over-identifying restrictions, which tests for the overall validity of the instruments by analysing the sample analog of the moment conditions used in the estimation process. The second test examines the hypothesis that the error term differentiated regression is not second order serially correlated, which implies that the error term in the level regression is not serially correlated. The failure to reject the null hypotheses in all cases provides support to model estimation. From the Regression, we report m1 test of the existence of first-order serial correlation, m2 test of the second order serial correlation, and a robust Sargan test of the over identifying restrictions that the estimator exploits. For the estimation of our unbalanced panel data on Indian private corporate manufacturing firms we have used the Dynamic Panel Data (DPD) technique (Arellano and Bond 1988). The estimation is carried out using the OX Package.

### Estimation results

In our empirical analysis, our central question is what are the financial structure variables that are most likely to determine a firm's growth? We have estimated the model for all manufacturing firms in the private corporate sector and two sub categories viz., large and small within manufacturing. A firm is considered to be large if the size of its total assets is in the upper 10 per cent distribution of the total assets for the sample. On the other hand, if the size of its total assets is in the lower 25 per cent distribution of the total assets for the sample it is considered as small. The results are given in Table 13.5.

It is interesting to note that the amount of cash flow is positively correlated with economic growth for all manufacturing firms and both size categories. The positive and significant impact of cash flow on growth represents liquidity constraints as per the 'financial constraints' or financing hierarchy (Pecking Order) hypothesis. However, how far this reflects actual liquidity constraints needs to be analysed in the context of the results obtained while controlling for the effects of financial structure variables. The negative and significant coefficients of equity-to-assets ratio for all manufacturing firms suggest that capital market resources do not contribute to the growth of these firms. However, interestingly enough, the estimated coefficient of equity-to-assets ratio for the large sized manufacturing firms is positive and significant. This suggests that firms that grow more are more reliant on internal resources (cash flow), but raise more external funds relative to their assets than the low growth small firms do. The analysis regarding cash flow and equity variables lend credence to the argument that financial constraints play a crucial role in the growth of firms.

With regard to the financial structure analysis in the last section, we pointed out that the reform intended to boost the mobilization of resources from the capital markets had not produced any significant impact and the external financing is still depends on borrowings of firms including banks. Different types of debt are being used by firms to mobilize resources for investment and it is presumed that different types of debt will contribute differently to the growth of firms. Among different types of debt, the variable debt-to-assets ratio is used as a proxy for the long-term robustness of the firms. While for large firms, debts show positive and significant coefficient, small firms conform to a negative and significant relationship predicted by the theory of asymmetric information and agency costs. According to the theoretical expectations, due to imperfections in the market, the leverage coefficient is expected to be negative and significant. However, our result seems to suggest that for larger firms, having a higher degree of leverage increases their capability to mobilize external funds. One possible explanation for this is that, having obtained debt in the past years may act as a signal to financial intermediaries like banks and other institutions about the firm's credit worthiness. Once they found that a particular firm is able to repay the debt without much transaction cost for the intermediaries, they will be ready to lend them without formalities as required in the former times. However, for small firms, they faced an increasing cost of external funds as their leverage increased, as suggested by the negative and significant coefficients of the leverage coefficient.

**Table 13.5: Dynamic panel data regression: Dependent variable-GROWTH$_{it}$**

| Dependent Variable: GROWTH$_{i,t}$ | Manufacturing | | |
|---|---|---|---|
| | All | Large | Small |
| $log$ OUTPUT$_{i\,t-2}$ | 0.064*** | 0.037*** | 0.014*** |
| | (3.86) | (2.98) | (4.23) |
| $log$ CF$_{i\,t-1}$ | 0.143*** | 0.096*** | 0.014*** |
| | (3.94) | (3.01) | (2.89) |
| $log$ EQ$_{i\,t-1}$ | −0.055** | 0.042* | −0.013*** |
| | (−2.23) | (−1.65) | (3.17) |
| $log$ TOTDEBT$_{i\,t-1}$ | −0.196** | 0.089** | −0.382** |
| | (−2.12) | (2.31) | (2.21) |
| $log$ FINDEBT$_{i\,t-1}$ | −0.011* | −0.043*** | 0.008*** |
| | (−1.63) | (−4.18) | (3.67) |
| $log$ BANKDEBT$_{i\,t-1}$ | 0.179*** | 0.216*** | 0.407*** |
| | (4.23) | (−3.87) | (−2.99) |
| $log$ SHORTBANKDEBT$_{i\,t-1}$ | 0.345 | 0.369 | 1.012 |
| | (1.14) | (1.32) | (0.98) |
| m1 | −2.306 [0.000] | −2.167 [0.000] | −0.365 [0.000] |
| m2 | −1.096 [0.173] | −0.1280 [0.230] | −2.824 [0.156] |
| Sargan Test | 139.2 [0.538] | 207.6 [0.469] | 115.74 [0.298] |
| Firms | 2017 | 323 | 816 |

*Notes:* (1) * means significance at 10 per cent, ** significance at 5 per cent and ***significance at 1 per cent. (2) Figures in parantheses are '*t*' values except for m1, m2 and Sargan tests.

It is interesting to notice that the impact of financial debt on growth is negative for firms irrespective of their sizes. As against this, the results show a positive and significant relationship between bank debt and growth in all estimations. Having occupied a lion's share in the financial debt, it suggests that firms in our sample predominantly use credit from banks to expand their growth. Reading in lines with the positive effect of cash flow on growth, it has to be viewed that firms borrow from banks to grow by using the liquidity emanates from large cash flows as platform to ensure the firm solvency even by small firms. In our analysis absolutely no impact is seen to be exerted by debt maturity structure on firm growth. Though the relation is positive it is very weak by significant levels. Another interesting result is that the growth of firms is not sustained by a long term maturity structure. This tends to suggest that growth profile of firms could be highly fragile, as they increase short term debt levels to finance economic growth. The increased levels of short term debt may be an indication of future financial distress in the corporate sector, though the interest coverage in terms of cash flow seems to be higher for the firms in our sample.

## CONCLUSIONS

In our study, we have undertaken the analysis of the relationship between financial structure and growth instead of the traditional tests of investment cash flow sensitivities. Specifically, the chapter makes an improvement over the existing literature by throwing light to the aspects of the relation between financial structure and debt maturity structure on one side and growth of firm on the other. Our results reveals that, on an average, Indian manufacturing firms in the private corporate sector do not depend on capital market resources including equity to finance their expansion. Instead, firms depend heavily on debt to finance their expansion. From the positive impact of total debt on the growth of firms applicable only for large firms in the estimation shows that the debt per se do not impact on growth for all firms. Similarly, the positive impact of financial debt was only for small firms in the model. Nevertheless, the positive and significant impact of the share of bank debt in total for all three categories of firms suggests that the corporate financing strategy of Indian firms is still bank-based in nature. Interestingly enough, the study found that, on average, growth pattern of Indian manufacturing firms is highly fragile, since it is negatively related with the increase of non financial debt. Rather, the negative relationship of the share of short term debt suggests that increase in the debt levels of firms is not sustainable as far as the growth of firms is concerned.

To conclude, market imperfections exist in the financial markets that prevent an economy wide efficiency in the post liberalization period. What do these results suggest for the financing practices of the corporate sector? It would be useful to recall that the underlying factor for firm financing is found to be information asymmetry, more specifically the operation of moral hazard and adverse selection. In such a situation one may argue that relative cost principle is not in operation even after financial reforms. In the context of the need to augment total resources available to corporate sector it implies that there is a need for greater role of the state to intervene in the financial markets in terms of evolving suitable accounting standards, regulation on insider trading, strengthening fraud laws, and improving provisions for investors' protection. It should be recognized that the legal, informational, and incentive frameworks need reform. Such reforms will also involve a much greater private role in the banking sector and, correspondingly will require much stronger regulation and supervision to limit moral hazard. Generally speaking, Indian regulation and supervision is not as strong as in many other developing countries, in terms of income recognition and provisioning. Thus, Indian banking needs not only more private management and ownership, appropriate incentives for sound banking that will contribute to development, but much better regulation and supervision to limit the moral hazard associated with private owners and high deposit insurance. Small borrowers often suffer from lack of access because they cannot demonstrate their willingness to pay due to lack of collateral. Thus, to improve credit access, the credit registry should include information on small-sized borrowers from non-banking institutions that serve them. Improving the development contribution of India's financial system will require a reduction in fiscal deficit and a clear focus on improving institutional, informational and incentive frameworks. The study has brought out certain findings on the relationship between financing patterns and growth and concluded that a present the external financing structure of firms do not contribute to growth of firms. The study, however, suggests certain areas for further research with particular focus on industry variations and variation in terms of other characteristics such as age, ownership etc., to get a deeper understanding of the dynamic relationship between financing patterns and growth in the post reform period.

## REFERENCES

Akerlof, G. 1970. 'The Market for "Lemons": Qualitative Uncertainty and the Market Mechanism'. *Quarterly Journal of Economics,* 84, 488–500.

Almeida H., M. Campello., and M. Weisbach. 2004. 'The Cash-flow Sensitivity of Cash'. *Journal of Finance,* 9, 1777–1804.

Arellano, M., and S. R. Bond. 1988. *Dynamic Panel Data Using DPD: A Guide for Users,* Working Paper No.15, London: Institute of Fiscal Studies.

—— 1991. 'Some Tests of Specification for Panel data: Monte Carlo Evidence and an Application to Employment Equations'. *Review of Economic Studies*, 58, 277–97.

Barclay, M., L. Marx, and C. Smith. 2003. 'The Joint Determination of Leverage and Maturity'. *Journal of Corporate Finance*, 9, 149–67.

Beck, T., R. Levine, and N. Loayza. (2000a). 'Finance and the Sources of Growth'. *Journal of Financial Economics*, 58, 261–300.

—— (2000b). 'Financial Intermediation and Growth: Casuality and Causes'. *Journal of Monetary Economics*, 46, 31–77.

Beck, T., D.-K Asli, and V. Maksimovic. 2003. 'Law, Endowments, and Finance'. *Journal of Financial Economics*, 70, 2.

Beckaert, G., C. Harvey, and C. Lundbald. 2005. 'Does Financial Liberalization Spur Growth?' *Journal of Financial Economics*, 77, 3–56.

Bernanke, B.S., and M. Gertler. 1987. 'Banking and Macroeconomic Equilibrium'. In *New Approach to Monetary Economics*, edited by Barnett, W.A. and K.J Singleton. 89–111. Cambridge: Cambridge University Press.

Bernanke, B.S. and M. Gertler. 1990. 'Financial Fragility and Economic Performance'. *Quarterly Journal of Economics*, 105, 88–114.

Bond, S., J. Elston, J. Mairesse, and B. Mulkay. 2003. 'Financial Factors and the Investment in Belgium, France, Germany, and the United Kingdom: a comparison using company panel data'. *The Review of Economics and Statistics*, 85, 153–65.

Calomiris, C.R., and G. Hubbard. 1987. *Price Flexibility, Credit Availability, and Economic Fluctuations: Evidence from the United States, 1879–1914*, Northwestern University.

Centre for Monitoring Indian Economy (CMIE). *Prowess*, Economic Intelligence Service, Electronic Database, CMIE, Mumbai.

Coen, R. M., and E. Robert. 1987. 'Investment'. In *The New Palgrave Dictionary of Economics*, edited by Eatwell J., Milgate M. and Newman P. *The macMillan Press Limited*, 980–86.

Demirguc-Kunt, A., and V. Maksimovic. 1998. 'Law, Finance, and Firm Growth'. *Journal of Finance*, 3, 2107–37.

—— 2001. Firms as Financial Intermediaries: Evidence from Trade Credit Data. The World bank Policy Research Working Paper No. 2696.

Devereux, M.P., and F. Shiantarelli. 1989. 'Investment, Financial Factors and Cash Flow from UK Panel Data'. In *Information, Capital Market, and Investment*, edited by Genn, Hubbard. Chicago: University of Chicago Press.

Fagiolo, G., and A. Luzzi. 2006. 'Do Liquidity Constraints Matter in Explaining in Explaining Firm Size and Growth?' Some Evidence From the Italian Manufacturing Industry, Industrial and Corporate Change, 15, 1–39.

Fazzari, S.M. 1992. 'Keynesian Theories of Investment and Finance: Neo, Post, and New'. *In Financial Condition and Macroeconomic Performance: Essays in Honour of Hyman*

P. Minsky, edited by Fazzari S.M. and Dimitri B Papadimitriou. New York: M E Sharpe, Inc. Armond, 121–32.

Fazzari, S.M., R.G. Hubbard, and B.C Petersen. 1988. 'Financing Constraints and Corporate Investment'. *Brooking Papers on Economic Activity*, 19, 141–95.

Harris, J.R., F. Schiantarelli, and S.G. Miranda. 1994. 'The Effect of Financial Liberlisation on Firms Capital structure and Investment Decisions: Evidence from Panel of Indonesian Manufacturing Establishments, 1981–88'. *The World Bank Economic Review*, 8(1): 17–47.

Hoshi, T., A. Kashyap, and D. Scharfstein. 1991. 'Corporate Structure, Liquidity and Investment: Evidence from Japanese Industrial Groups'. *Quarterly Journal of Economics*, 106, 33–60.

Jensen, M., and W. Meckling. 1976. 'Theory of the Firms: Managerial Behaviour, Agency Costs and Ownership Structure'. *Journal of Financial Economics*, 3, 305–60.

Jensen, M.C. 1986. 'Agency Costs of Free Cashflow, Corporate Finance, and Takeovers'. *American Economic Review*, 76, 323–29.

Kaplan, S.N., and L. Zingales. 2000. 'Investment-cashflow Sensitivities are not Valid Measures of Financial Constraints'. *The Quarterly Journal of Economics*, 115, 707–12.

LaPorta R., F. Lopez-de-Silanes, A. Shleifer, and R.W. Vishny. 1998. 'Law and Finance'. *Journal of Political Economy*, 106, 1113–55.

Mackie Mason, J.K. 1990. 'Do Taxes Affect Corporate Financing Decisions'. *Journal of Finance*, 45, 1471–93.

Mills, K., S. Morling, and W. Tease. 1994. The Influence of Financial Factors on Corporate Investment, Research Discussion paper, 9402, Economic Analysis Department, Reserve Bank of Australia.

Modigliani, F., and M. Miller. 1963. 'Corporate Income Taxes and the Cost of Capital: A Correction'. *American Economic Review*, 53, 433–43.

Myers, S.C. 1977. 'Determinants of Corporate Borrowing'. *Journal of financial Economics*, 5, 146–17.

Myers, S. C., and N.S. Majluf. 1984. 'Corporate Financing and Investment Decisions When Firms have Information that Investors do not'. *Journal of Financial Economics*, 13, 187–221.

Pagano, M. 1993. 'Financial Markets and Growth: An Overview'. *European Economic Review*, 37, 613–22.

Petersen, M.A., and R.G. Rajan. 1996. Trade Credit: theories and Evidenc. NBER Working Paper 602.

Rajan, R., and L. Zingales. 1998. 'Financial Dependence on Growth'. *American Economic Review*, 88, 559–86.

Schianterelli, F., and A. Sembenelli. 1997. The Maturity Structure of deb. Determinants and Effects on firms' Performance: Evidence from the United Kingdom and Italy. The World bank Policy Research Working Paper 1699.

Smith, C., and J. Warner. 1979. On Financing Contracting: An Analysis of Bond.

Stiglitz, J.E. 1988. 'Why Financial Structure Matters'. *Journal of Economic Perspectives*, 2(4):121–26.

Stiglitz, J.E., and A. Weiss. 1981. 'Credit Rationing in Markets with Imperfect Information, Part-I'. *American Economic Review*, 71(3), 393–410.

Stulz, R. 2001. Does Financial Structure Matter for growth? A corporate finance perspective. In *Financial Structure and economic growth*, edited by A. Demigurc-Kunt and R. Levine. Cambridge: The MIT Press.

Whited T.M. 1994. 'Debt, Liquidity Constraints, and Corporate Investment: Evidence from Panel Data'. *Journal of Finance*, 47, 1425–60.

# 14

# Export Intensity and Dividend Policy of Indian Firms

Elena Goldman

Viswanath P. V.

## INTRODUCTION

Export-led growth has been a time-honored strategy for many developing countries, most recently in China and in India. The argument is that exports can be an engine for faster growth. Exports allow a country to produce at larger and more efficient scales and to exploit its comparative advantages; furthermore, the development of the export sector could also generate employment opportunities.[1] However, this line of thinking assumes that firms in the export sector are managed efficiently. There is increasing evidence that exporting and profitability are indeed positively correlated.[2] However, most of this research looks at operational characteristics of exporting firms; little research has been done regarding the financial policies of exporting firms.[3]

Exporting firms could also generate resources for further investment from their profits. Nair (2013) documents the increasing dependence of Indian corporate investment on retained earnings. According to corporate finance

---

[1] See Athreye (2005) and Arora et al. (2001) for details on employment in the software industry; and Pradhan (2007) for a discussion of Indian outward FDI and domestic employment.

[2] Navaretti et al. (2002) find a positive relationship between export shares of Indian firms and productivity gains. So do Chibber and Majumdar (1998) and Aulakh, Kotabe and Teegen (2000). On the other hand, Demirbas, Patnaik and Shah (2009), suggest that the direction of causality is reversed – the more productive Indian firms gravitate to export markets.

[3] Demirbas, Patnaik and Shah (2009) document the financial leverage of different kinds of exporting and non-exporting firms. However, this is not their primary interest. Goldman and Viswanath (2011) look at financial leverage of exporting Indian firms.

theory, a firm's decision to retain earnings rather than pay them out in dividends is due to information asymmetry and other capital market frictions. However, arguably recycling of corporate earnings through payment of dividends and subsequent reinvestment is more desirable; the payment of dividends provides more information to the market and allows market participants to value the existing assets of the firm better, leading to more efficient resource allocation. This connection between exports, dividends, and reinvestment suggests the importance of examining the dividend behaviour of exporting firms.

There are many reasons why dividend payout ratios at the firm level should be related to export intensity. First of all, the cashflow volatility theory suggests that more stable firms should be able to pay higher dividends.[4] Shareholders prefer predictability in their dividends and cashflow stability means that firms will not need to cut dividends because of lower profits; given the low correlation between economic activities in developed and developing countries,[5] exporting firms with a mix of domestic and foreign sales would tend to have lower cashflow volatility.

Second, the Investment Opportunities Hypothesis suggests that firms with greater investment opportunities would retain more of their earnings. Once firms have made the necessary investments needed to access export markets, they have the ability to exploit market opportunities that are closed to non-exporting firms. This line of reasoning would, therefore, suggest that exporting firms would have lower dividend payouts.

Firms' export status might also be negatively correlated with dividend policy because of their asset structure. There is some evidence that exporting firms are better and more efficient than other firms.[6] If so, these firms probably have a lot of human capital incorporated in their value. Such intangible assets are indicators of information asymmetry between the firm and financial markets. This would make it more difficult for exporting firms to raise external funds and would lead to a tendency to retain more funds. According to this theory, exporting firms would have lower payout ratios.

---

[4] Support for this is provided by Bradley, Capozza and Seguin (1998) and Chay and Suh (2008).

[5] The recent global recession speaks to this. While all countries have been affected to some extent, countries like China and India have been affected a lot less than developed regions like the US, Europe and Japan. For research on this point, see Fadhlaoui, Bellalah, Dherry and Zouaouil (2008).

[6] See, for example, Ganesh-Kumar, Sen and Vaidya (2003) and Bernard, Jensen, Redding and Schott (2007). On the other hand, Navaretta et al. (2002) find that large Indian exporters are not necessarily more human capital intensive.

Furthermore, exporters have greater exposure to foreign markets and so foreign investors are more familiar with them. As such, their ability to raise capital abroad through External Corporate Borrowings (ECBs) is greater. This, again, would allow them to reduce their reliance on internal equity. In line with many other developing countries, India, too, has erected barriers against the free inflow and outflow of foreign capital. To the extent that exporting firms are able to raise foreign funds more cheaply, they are more likely to use them, compared to non-exporting firms.[7] This is even more likely to be the case if the Indian government moves forward with plans to auction entitlements for Indian corporations to borrow abroad.[8]

In this chapter, we look at how the export intensity of Indian firms is related to their dividend payout policies. Investigating exporting firms' dividend policies is useful from many points of view : one, it can be used to examine the connection between financial policies and export performance; two, it can be used to test theories of exporting firms;[9] and, finally, as suggested above, it can be used to explore one part of the link between exports and corporate investment. Finally, we look at the effect of firms' exporting behaviour on their stock market valuation. We discuss the data and methodology in the next section.

## DATA AND METHODOLOGY

### Data

Data was obtained from the Prowess database marketed by Centre for the Monitoring of the Indian Economy (CMIE). While CMIE data is available from the 1990s, there are a lot of policy changes in the earlier years; furthermore, firms are still responding to the new economic environment in these years.[10] Hence, we

---

[7]  This seems to be the view in the popular press, as well. A recent Economic Times article (April 30, 2013) opined that, "borrowers who have a natural foreign currency edge tend to borrow from the overseas market. Such firms are typically engaged in exports. A top-rated export-oriented firm can get rates up to 250 bps over Libor, with borrowing costs working out to around 3 per cent."

[8]  See recent article in the Economic Times (Nov. 19, 2009; http://economictimes.indiatimes.com/news/economy/finance/Govt-set-to-auction-ECB-entitlements/articleshow/5245563.cms). On the other hand, Kumar et al. (2008) present evidence that Indian firms that have listed on foreign exchanges have not seen any reduction in the sensitivity of their investments to internal cashflows.

[9]  See, for example, Cavusgil (1982)Czinkota (1982), Moon and Lee (1990), Rao and Naidu (1992), Wortzel and Wortzel (1981) and Bernard and Jensen (2004).

[10]  There is some evidence even in the earlier years that exporting firms are already different from other firms (see Ganesh-Kumar, Sen and Vaidya, 2003).

used data from a more recent time period. We chose firms on the A and B lists of the Bombay Stock Exchange with available data from the years 2000–09. Table 14.1 shows the number of firms, by year, for which we have data.

As discussed in the introduction, we are interested in the determinants of the dividend payout ratio (defined as dividends paid divided by after-tax profits) and its relation to export activity. We measure export activity in the following way. We first compute the conventional measure of export intensity, i.e., the ratio of exports to sales (expintensity); we then define ExpIntenRel = $1-2|$expintensity$-0.5|$.[11] If a firm's sales are equally divided between exports and domestic sales, such a firm would score the maximum of 1 on this measure. Firms that rely entirely on the domestic market or entirely on the foreign market for their sales would score the minimum of zero; other firms would score between zero and one. Given the low correlation between developing and developed economies, it makes sense to use a measure of export activity that captures this diversification effect on cashflow variance. Suppose $var_x$ is the variance of cashflows derived from foreign sales and $var_d$ is the variance of domestic sales. Then, assuming $var_d = var_x$, the optimal proportion of sales to be derived from exports in order to minimize the variance of total cashflows would be 0.5. Hence, ExpIntenRel measures the distance of expintensity from this optimal value; the higher the distance, the higher the cashflow variance. In principle, we could estimate $var_d$ and $var_x$ for each firm, but the estimation error would be large. Hence we use the simple assumption that $var_d = var_x$ as a reasonable prior and as a convenient approximation to the true variance numbers.

**Table 14.1: Number of firms in sample, by year**

| Year | Number of firms |
| --- | --- |
| 2000 | 1,495 |
| 2001 | 1,525 |
| 2002 | 1,612 |
| 2003 | 1,631 |
| 2004 | 1,621 |
| 2005 | 1,658 |
| 2006 | 1,730 |
| 2007 | 1,798 |
| 2008 | 1,832 |
| 2009 | 1,738 |

---

[11] This measure was also used in Goldman and Viswanath (2011)

We performed all our estimations using both export intensity and our new measure, ExpIntenRel. The results are similar in all cases; hence, in what follows, we report results with ExpIntenRel alone. ExpIntenRel has the additional attractive feature that it can be considered a reasonable proxy for cashflow volatility, since it is effectively the absolute distance of expintensity from the value 0.5, as explained above. We now discuss determinants suggested by competing theories of the dividend payout ratio.

### Theories of dividend determination

Investment opportunities and information asymmetry

It has been hypothesized that firms with investment opportunities would have lower payout ratios so as to conserve retained earnings, given that information asymmetry causes external funds to be more expensive than internal funds. This follows from Myers' (1984) Pecking Order Hypothesis. Empirically, Woolridge and Ghosh (1985) found that the market penalized firms that cut dividends; however, when the firms simultaneously announced investment opportunities, the negative market reaction was much lower, and it was more than overturned in the next quarter. Soter, Brigham and Evanson (1996) reported similar results with the Florida Power and Light's dividend cut in 1994. Although the negative market reaction at the time of the dividend cut announcement is troubling, the overall market response is positive.[12] Abbott (2001) looks at firms whose investment opportunity sets have changed and tries to correlate this with their financing policies: he finds that firms with improved investment opportunities decrease their dividend payouts. This evidence implies that firms with higher investment and growth opportunities would have lower payout ratios.

We use several measures of growth: the ratio of Intangibles to Total Assets is usually positively correlated with growth opportunities; the Book-to-Market ratio and the ratio of fixed assets to total assets (capital intensity) are usually negatively correlated with growth opportunities; hence high book-to-market firms, having low investment and growth opportunities should pay high dividends.[13] These variables are also associated with information asymmetry.

---

[12] One possible explanation for the immediate negative market reaction is that the market did not have enough information to confirmation the firms' announcement of better investment opportunities.

[13] R&D could also be used as a measure of investment opportunity, since its purpose is to generate investment ideas. In our regressions, however, it was consistently unrelated to payout ratio, and hence we do not report results of regressions including this variable.

## Access to funding

We looked at both internal and external access to funds. As a measure of internal fund availability, we used CashflowAssets (the ratio of cashflow to assets).[14] The higher the level of internal funds available, the higher the payout ratio the firm can tolerate and still fund internally generated projects. Hence, we would expect a positive relationship between payout ratio and measures of cashflow. Financial leverage may also indicate the availability of free cashflow to be paid out as dividends; the higher the financial leverage, the lower the free cashflow.

In addition, as mentioned above, access to external funds might be an important determinant of dividend policy, since the payment of dividends increases dollar-for-dollar the need to raise funds externally, as long as there are positive NPV investment projects available for the firm. Access to domestic capital markets is similar for all firms. However, not all firms have equal access to foreign capital markets. We measure access to foreign capital markets by looking at foreign currency borrowings, normalized by total borrowings.[15] On the other hand, the greater a firm's borrowing, the lower the free cashflow available to be paid out as dividends. Hence the effect of this variable on dividend payouts could be either positive or negative.

Second, it has also been conjectured that business groups in India function like chaebols or keiretsus and provide access to capital to their group members.[16] Using data on group membership, we created six different categories, based on ownership-type. Table 14.2, below, lists the ownership categories (Owncat) and indicates the relative proportion of membership of firms in our sample in each of the ownership categories:

**Table 14.2: Relative proportion of firms in sample by ownership category**

| Group | Description | Proportion in sample |
|-------|-------------|----------------------|
| Owncat 1 | Government companies | 3.83% |
| Owncat 2 | Private Indian group companies | 33.70% |
| Owncat 3 | Private foreign group companies | 2.08% |

*Table 14.2 Continued*

---

[14] See Myers (1984) for a static version and Viswanath (1993) for a dynamic version of the Pecking Order Hypothesis that suggests the importance of this category of variable. Byoun (2008) presents a recent test of this hypothesis.

[15] We also have data on GDR/ADR issues; however, it turns out that most firms did not take advantage of this method of raising foreign equity capital. Hence we do not include this variable in our analysis.

[16] See Khanna and Palepu (1999, 2000) and Hansoge and Marisetty (2011), for example.

*Table 14.2 Continued*

| Owncat 4 | Joint sector companies and NRIs | 0.50% |
| Owncat 5 | Private Indian non-group companies | 55.54% |
| Owncat 6 | Private foreign non-group companies | 4.35% |

We first provide evidence, in Table 14.3, regarding the importance of this variable in explaining dividend payout behaviour.

**Table 14.3: Ownership category status and dividend payout ratios**

| OwnCat | Ownership category | Obs | Payout ratio Mean | Standard deviation |
|---|---|---|---|---|
| 1 | Government companies | 638 | 0.2455 | 0.1769 |
| 2 | Private Indian group companies | 5,607 | 0.1705 | 0.2124 |
| 3 | Private foreign group companies | 346 | 0.3307 | 0.2520 |
| 4 | Joint sector companies and NRI companies | 84 | 0.0691 | 0.1344 |
| 5 | Private Indian non-group companies | 9,242 | 0.0817 | 0.1752 |
| 6 | Private foreign non-group companies | 723 | 0.2261 | 0.2577 |

We see that the average payout ratio varies quite a bit from one ownership category to another. In fact, a Hotelling test confirms this [$F(4,16636) = 709.24$; Prob > F = 0.0000]. Next, we combined private Indian companies into one category and private foreign companies into another category. We then conducted another Hotelling test for the four categories of government, private Indian, private foreign, and joint sector companies [Hotelling $F(3,16637) = 2144.85$; Prob > F = 0.0000]. The test statistic shows conclusively that considering these distinctions is useful in explaining payout ratio and that it is not just the group versus non-group characteristic of companies that makes their payout ratios vary (whether they are private or foreign companies). We tested for equality of mean payout ratio for private Indian group and non-group companies; and similarly, for foreign group and non-group companies. We could not reject the hypothesis of equality. This suggests that even though group affiliation might not be useful in explaining payout ratio, ownership affiliation might. Henceforward, we consider the following ownership categories : OwncatInd, OwnCatFrn, OwnCatGov and OwnCatJt, where OwncatInd includes all private Indian firms (OwnCat 2 plus OwnCat 5) and OwnCatFrn includes all private foreign firms (OwnCat 3 and OwnCat 6). OwnCatGov is the same as OwnCat 1, while OwnCatJt is the same as OwnCat 4.

Cashflow Volatility

Cashflow variability is measured directly as the variance of Operating Cashflow before Working Capital Changes (VarCashFlow) for each company over the past five years, normalized by total assets. In addition, larger firms and older firms tend to be more stable; hence also we use Size (measured as the log of Total Assets) and Firm Age as additional measures of cashflow stability.[17] Furthermore, as suggested in the Introduction, the correlation between domestic and foreign sales can also be used as an indicator of cashflow volatility.

Before presenting our results, we provide in Table 14.4, summary statistics for our measures of payout and our independent variables.

## RESULTS

### *Payout ratios for exporters and non-exporters*

We first present information on the behaviour of the payout ratio over time for exporters versus non-exporters in Table 14.5. Figure 14.1 shows this behaviour graphically. In particular, the payout ratio, averaged over firms is clearly greater for exporters than for non-exporters, for each year and for the entire sample. This difference is strongly statistically significant, as well, as can be seen from Table 14.5. Of course, as is clear from Table 14.6, exporters and non-exporters differ in terms of other variables that affect dividend payment behaviour, as well. For example, we see that exporters tend to be larger, invest more in R&D, have higher average but less volatile cashflows, higher capital intensity, and also tend to borrow more abroad. Many of these variables are related to investment opportunities, as well as to funding access; hence a simple test of differences in payout ratios between exporters and non-exporters could not be interpreted as evidence that exporting firms qua exporters pay higher dividends. We, therefore, include different determinants of dividend payout ratios as control variables in the regressions presented below. Table 14.7 below summarizes the expected signs of the explanatory variables in the payout regressions.

---

17  We considered including the firm's asset beta as an explanatory variable, on the assumption that beta and return volatility would be positively correlated. However, this variable was not significant, and so we do not report the associated regression coefficients. Part of the problem was that we did not have enough data to compute the asset beta directly using asset returns. Instead, we took the measure of equity beta provided by Prowess and adjusted for the weight of equity in the capital structure of the firm by multiplying the equity beta by the ratio of the market value of equity to total assets, implicitly assuming a debt beta of zero. To complicate the issue, Prowess only provides the most recent estimate of a firm's equity beta.

**Figure 14.1: The behaviour of the payout ratio over time**

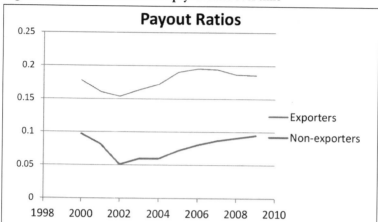

**Table 14.4: Summary statistics for selected firm-specific variables**

ExpIntensity is the ratio of exports to sales; ExpInten Rel is $1-2|\text{expintensity}-0.5|$; Dummy Exports = 1 for firms which export and = 0 for firms which do not export; Payout Ratio is the payout ratio or dividends paid/profit after taxes. Profit Margin is the ratio of operating cash flow before working capital to sales. CapInt is the ratio of Net Fixed Assets to Total Assets. Intangibles is the ratio of Net Intangible Assets to Total Assets; MarketCap is defined as the market price of the stock at the end of March (which is the end of the financial year for most firms in India) times the number of shares outstanding; Book Value is defined as Assets minus Total Borrowings ; Bkto Mkt is the ratio of Book Value to MarketCap; Cashflow ToAssets is Operating Cash flow before Working Capital Changes as a ratio of Total Assets; R&D is the ratio of R&D expenses on Capital Account to Sales; Size is the natural logarithm of Total Assets; Asset beta is the equity beta times (MarketCap/MktValAssets), where MktValAssets is computed as Total Assets − Net Worth + MarketCap; Age is 2010 minus the year of incorporation; Ltdebt is (Total Borrowings - Short-term Borrowings)/ (MktValAssets); VarCashFlowis the Variance of OpCashFlow/Totassets, computed using observations for the previous 5 years; Corsalesexports is Corr (Sales, Exports), the correlation between sales and exports using data from the previous five years; Forexborrow is the ratio of unsecured foreign currency borrowings to total borrowings.

| Variable | No. of obs. | Mean | Std. dev. |
|---|---|---|---|
| Exp Intensity | 14,489 | 0.149 | 0.259 |
| DummyExports | 16,640 | 0.512 | 0.500 |
| ExpIntRel | 14,489 | 0.168 | 0.262 |
| Payout Ratio | 16,640 | 0.129 | 0.203 |
| CapInt | 16,639 | 0.337 | 0.246 |
| Intangibles | 16,639 | 0.015 | 0.106 |

*Table 14.4 Continued*

*Table 14.4 Continued*

| | | | |
|---|---|---|---|
| MarketCap | 16,640 | 1121.628 | 7739.520 |
| CashflowToAssets | 16,639 | 0.075 | 0.762 |
| BktoMkt | 16,636 | 4.768 | 14.925 |
| Size | 16,639 | 4.405 | 2.294 |
| Age | 16,640 | 30.501 | 19.759 |
| R&D | 14,489 | 0.001 | 0.011 |
| Assetbeta | 14,805 | 0.257 | 4.764 |
| Ltdebt | 16,640 | 0.194 | 0.204 |
| VarCashFlow | 7,457 | 0.156 | 5.798 |
| Lvar | 7,420 | −6.840 | 0.0245 |
| Corsalesexports | 4,764 | 0.536 | 0.548 |
| Forexborrow | 14,675 | 0.025 | 0.111 |

**Table 14.5: The behaviour of the payout ratio over time for exporters and non-exporters**

| Year | | Non-exporters | Exporters | Total | T-stat* |
|---|---|---|---|---|---|
| | Mean | 0.0774 | 0.1789 | 0.1293 | −33.4 |
| 2000–09 | Std. Dev. | 0.1742 | 0.2164 | 0.2033 | |
| | No. of obs. | 8125 | 8515 | 16640 | |
| 2000 | Mean | 0.0971 | 0.1778 | 0.1377 | −7.20 |
| | Std. Dev. | 0.2073 | 0.2261 | 0.2206 | |
| | No. of obs. | 743 | 752 | 1495 | |
| 2001 | Mean | 0.0817 | 0.1604 | 0.1212 | −7.50 |
| | Std. Dev. | 0.1907 | 0.2182 | 0.2087 | |
| | No. of obs. | 758 | 767 | 1525 | |
| 2002 | Mean | 0.0508 | 0.1536 | 0.1014 | −10.98 |
| | Std. Dev. | 0.1436 | 0.2225 | 0.1935 | |
| | No. of obs. | 819 | 793 | 1612 | |
| 2003 | Mean | 0.0596 | 0.1636 | 0.1115 | −10.60 |
| | Std. Dev. | 0.1660 | 0.2257 | 0.2047 | |
| | No. of obs. | 817 | 814 | 1631 | |

*Table 14.5 Continued*

*Table 14.5 Continued*

| | | | | | |
|---|---|---|---|---|---|
| 2004 | Mean | 0.0598 | 0.1722 | 0.1174 | −11.93 |
| | Std. Dev. | 0.1558 | 0.2197 | 0.1993 | |
| | No. of obs. | 790 | 831 | 1621 | |
| 2005 | Mean | 0.0719 | 0.1905 | 0.1314 | −12.55 |
| | Std. Dev. | 0.1625 | 0.2185 | 0.2015 | |
| | No. of obs. | 826 | 832 | 1658 | |
| 2006 | Mean | 0.0806 | 0.1956 | 0.1389 | −12.44 |
| | Std. Dev. | 0.1701 | 0.2124 | 0.2010 | |
| | No. of obs. | 853 | 877 | 1730 | |
| 2007 | Mean | 0.0871 | 0.1944 | 0.1423 | −12.05 |
| | Std. Dev. | 0.1714 | 0.2057 | 0.1972 | |
| | No. of obs. | 873 | 925 | 1798 | |
| 2008 | Mean | 0.0910 | 0.1867 | 0.1416 | −10.64 |
| | Std. Dev. | 0.1803 | 0.2048 | 0.1994 | |
| | No. of obs. | 862 | 970 | 1832 | |
| 2009 | Mean | 0.0950 | 0.1858 | 0.1448 | −9.56 |
| | Std. Dev. | 0.1846 | 0.2112 | 0.2046 | |
| | No. of obs. | 784 | 954 | 1738 | |

*Notes:* T-stat is the t-statistic for the difference between the payout ratios for non-exporters and exporters, under the assumption that the observations for the exporting and non-exporting subsets are independent.

**Table 14.6: Differences between exporters and non-exporters**

| Variable | Non-exporters | | | Exporters | | | |
|---|---|---|---|---|---|---|---|
| | Obs | Mean | Std. Dev. | Obs | Mean | Std. Dev. | t-stat |
| BktoMkt | 8,121 | 5.5539 | 18.4428 | 8,515 | 4.0190 | 10.4729 | **6.6** |
| R&D | 5,974 | 0.0002 | 0.0039 | 8,515 | 0.0015 | 0.0145 | **−7.8** |
| Size | 8,124 | 3.5460 | 0.0259 | 8,515 | 5.2240 | 1.9278 | **−50.5** |
| Cashflow Assets | 8,124 | 0.0408 | 1.0816 | 8,515 | 0.1079 | 0.1333 | **−5.6** |
| Profit Margin | 5,974 | 6.2784 | 346.0028 | 8,515 | 0.2655 | 5.7157 | 1.3 |

*Table 14.6 Continued*

*Table 14.6 Continued*

| | | | | | | | |
|---|---|---|---|---|---|---|---|
| CapInt | 8,124 | 0.2930 | 0.2736 | 8,515 | 0.3799 | 0.2084 | **−23.0** |
| Intangibles | 8,124 | 0.0156 | 0.1328 | 8,515 | 0.0146 | 0.0729 | 0.6 |
| VarCashFlow | 3,422 | 0.3330 | 8.5569 | 4,035 | 0.0051 | 0.0247 | **2.2** |
| Ltdebt | 8,125 | 0.1932 | 0.2204 | 8,515 | 0.1955 | 0.1878 | −0.7 |
| Forexborrow | 6,652 | 0.0181 | 0.0929 | 8,023 | 0.0310 | 0.1245 | **−7.2** |

*Note:* Values in bold indicate t-test is significant at 5 per cent

**Table 14.7: Expected signs of variables in payout-ratio regression**

| Factor | Variable | Expected sign in payout-ratio regression | Dominant theory |
|---|---|---|---|
| Firm size | Log(total assets) | + | Cashflow Volatility |
| Age | Age | + | Cashflow Volatility |
| R&D | | − | Investment Opportunities |
| Log (variance of the ratio of Operating Cashflows to Total Assets) | Lvar | − | Cashflow Volatility |
| Ratio of intangibles to total assets | Intangibles-to-assets | − | Investment Opportunities |
| Book-to-Market | | + | Investment Opportunities |
| Capital intensity | Fixed assets/total assets | + | Investment Opportunities |
| Ratio of CashflowtoAssets | Cashflow-to-assets | + | Access to Funds |
| Ratio of cashflow to sales | Profit-margin | + | Access to Funds |
| Ltdebt | | − | Access to Funds |
| Correlation between total sales and exports | Corr(Sales, Exports) | − | Cashflow Volatility |

*Table 14.7 Continued*

Elena Goldman, Viswanath P. V.

*Table 14.7 Continued*

| Ratio of unsecured foreign currency borrowings to total borrowings | Forexborrow | +/– | Access to Funds |
|---|---|---|---|

*Note:* Results for Capital Intensity and R&D are not reported in the regressions below because they were consistently insignificant. Results of cashflow to sales are also not reported because this variable is uniformly insignificant in the regressions.

### Regression evidence

We now go on to investigate the relationship between export intensity and dividend policy. We regress the payout ratio, defined as the ratio of dividends to profit after taxes, on a measure of export intensity, as well as on several explanatory variables.[18] Tables 14.8 and 14.9 provide the results of these regressions.[19]

**Table 14.8: Payout ratio as a function of firm characteristics and export intensity variables**

OLS regression; variables are as defined above in Table 14.4

| Variable | Coef. | Robust Std. Err | t | P > |t| |
|---|---|---|---|---|
| ExpIntenRel | 0.028989 | 0.006345 | 4.57 | 0 |
| intangiblestoassets | –0.04646 | 0.018273 | –2.54 | 0.011 |
| BktoMkt | –0.00137 | 0.000156 | –8.75 | 0 |
| Size | 0.033301 | 0.000879 | 37.9 | 0 |
| forexborrowing | –0.03587 | 0.015036 | –2.39 | 0.017 |
| cashflowtoassets | 0.010423 | 0.007014 | 1.49 | 0.137 |
| age | 0.001125 | 9.55E-05 | 11.78 | 0 |
| Ltdebt | –0.1979 | 0.00775 | –25.54 | 0 |
| Constant | –0.00845 | 0.004733 | –1.78 | 0.074 |

Number of obs = 13169
F(8,13160) = 444.84; Prob> F = 0.0000
R-squared = 0.1848 Root MSE = .18653

---

[18] The Prowess database records some negative values for this variable, which clearly does not make any sense. As a result, we delete all negative values (there were 129 such observations).
[19] We also included capital intensity and R&D as independent variables; however, they were not significant, and, hence, the results are not reported.

**Table 14.9: Payout ratio as a function of firm characteristics and export intensity variables, with ownership variables**

OLS regression; variables are as defined above in Table 14.4. Ownership Category variables are as described in Table 14.3 and in the text below; OwnCatJt is used as a reference variable.

| Variable | Coef. | Robust Std. Err | t | P > \|t\| |
|---|---|---|---|---|
| ExpIntenRel | 0.02628 | 0.00643 | 4.09 | 0 |
| intangiblestoassets | −0.05099 | 0.018865 | −2.7 | 0.007 |
| BktoMkt | −0.00134 | 0.000154 | −8.69 | 0 |
| Size | 0.033047 | 0.000909 | 36.36 | 0 |
| forexborrowing | −0.0371 | 0.015381 | −2.41 | 0.016 |
| cashflowtoassets | 0.010222 | 0.006864 | 1.49 | 0.136 |
| age | 0.001069 | 9.45E-05 | 11.3 | 0 |
| Ltdebt | −0.19062 | 0.007718 | −24.7 | 0 |
| OwnCatGov | 0.055367 | 0.016301 | 3.4 | 0.001 |
| OwnCatInd | 0.073931 | 0.012881 | 5.74 | 0 |
| OwnCatFrn | 0.130015 | 0.015181 | 8.56 | 0 |
| Constant | −0.08323 | 0.013592 | −6.12 | 0 |

Number of obs = 13169
$F_{(11, 13157)}$ = 337.13; Prob > F = 0.0000
R-squared = 0.1902 Root MSE = .18594

We see from Table 14.8 that Size and Age are significant and positively related to the payout ratio, which is not surprising since they are measures of stability. However, BktoMkt, which in US data is also associated with stability is negatively related to the payout ratio; one possibility might be that the causation goes in the other direction; firms with high dividends are valued highly by the markets.[20] Higher leverage is correlated with lower payout ratios; this can be interpreted as a reflection of the fact that with higher leverage, free cashflow available to pay out as dividends is lower. Forexborrow also has a negative relationship with payout ratio and can also be interpreted similarly. We see, however, that ExpIntenRel, our measure of export activity is also significant. Table 14.9, which includes

---

[20] The demonstrated ability to pay dividends is taken by investors as proof of valuation creation, according to the Signaling Hypothesis. One thing to keep in mind is that the tax regime has changed over time, even during the decade that we analyse. For part of this period it was taxed in the hands of investors, as in the US, and for part, a dividend tax was paid directly by the company. In the latter instance, there is less of an incentive to retain funds. However, due to the lack of consistency in dividend taxation policy over this period, chances are that tax policy will not have any predictive power, on average.

ownership category variables, has similar results. The ownership category of a company does seem to make a difference. Foreign companies pay much higher dividends than other companies. This may, indeed, be because they have easier access to foreign capital as hypothesized, compared to other companies. On the other hand, it may be that they wish to repatriate capital. We note, however, that the payout ratio cannot take values less than zero, and should properly be treated as a censored variable.[21] This can be seen in the Figure 14.2. Hence we redo the regressions using Tobit analysis.

**Figure 14.2: Frequency distribution of all dividend payout ratios**

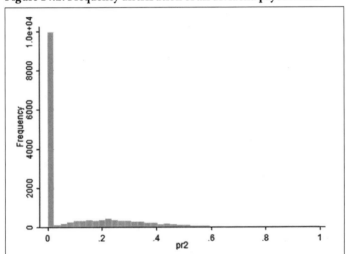

---

[21]  In the Prowess database, there were 3808 observations with negative dividends; these were removed from our analysis. 562 observations were deleted because the computed payout ratio was greater than 1. Most of the very high payout ratio observations were either for government companies or for foreign companies. Foreign companies might have high payout ratios, if they're trying to repatriate funds out of the country, as mentioned in the text. Government companies might also have some kind of requirement to pay high dividends; alternatively, the government may want to access liquidity. If this is true, then the payout ratios greater than one might be valid observations; our results do not change much whether we exclude or include these observations. Note, however, that in most of the regressions (see, for example, Table 14.9), average conditional payout ratios for government firms are low, while that for foreign companies is high; private Indian firms occupy an intermediate position. Joint sector and NRI firms have the lowest average conditional payout ratio though it's not clear why. In the Tobit analysis, we left-censor at zero, but we do not right-censor at unity.

The Tobit analysis results are presented in Table 14.10. Note that the same variables continue to be significant. The export measure continues to be positive and significant, indicating that exporting firms have higher payout ratios. As far as the ownership category variables are concerned, the tendency of foreign firms to pay higher dividends is again evident.

**Table 14.10: Payout ratio as a function of dependent vars, ownership categories: Tobit regression**

Number of obs = 13169
F(11,13158) = 427.09
Prob > F = 0.0000
Log pseudolikelihood = -5452.1067 Pseudo R2 = 0.2849

| Variable | Coef. | Robust Std. Err | $t$ | $P > |t|$ |
|---|---|---|---|---|
| ExpIntenRel | 0.082997 | 0.012744 | 6.51 | 0 |
| intangiblestoassets | −0.28582 | 0.065758 | −4.35 | 0 |
| BktoMkt | −0.00409 | 0.000657 | −6.22 | 0 |
| Size | 0.098045 | 0.00204 | 48.05 | 0 |
| forexborrowing | −0.09009 | 0.02501 | −3.6 | 0 |
| cashflowtoassets | 0.029715 | 0.017602 | 1.69 | 0.091 |
| age | 0.001816 | 0.000166 | 10.93 | 0 |
| Ltdebt | −0.56052 | 0.02129 | −26.33 | 0 |
| OwnCatGov | 0.084523 | 0.04226 | 2 | 0.046 |
| OwnCatInd | 0.215696 | 0.039073 | 5.52 | 0 |
| OwnCatFrn | 0.255625 | 0.040864 | 6.26 | 0 |
| Constant | −0.67328 | 0.041025 | −16.41 | 0 |
| /sigma | 0.341229 | 0.004071 | | |

Obs. summary: 7506 left-censored observations at pr 2 < = 0
5663 uncensored observations 0 right-censored observations

Up to this point, we have not distinguished firms by industry affiliation. While the analysis this far supports our general thesis that exporting firms pay higher dividends, we must recognize that there are likely to be differences across industries that are not sufficiently captured by the firm-specific variables that we have already taken into account.[22] In order to check this, we examine if mean payout ratios vary by industry; if so, we should allow for industry fixed effects in

---

[22] Industry affiliation often turns out to be a significant explanatory variable in studies of financial policies, for example in capital structure models (Frank and Goyal, 2009).

our regression of payout ratio on firm-specific characteristics. Industry membership for the companies was obtained from the PROWESS database, using the NIC classification variable. We used the industry classification shown below in Table 14.11.

**Table 14.11: Distribution of observations across industries**

| Industry | NIC numbers | per cent observations | Variable indicator |
|---|---|---|---|
| Agriculture and Mining | 10000–14999 | 2.35% | agric |
| Manufacturing | 15000–36999 | 52.37% | manuf |
| Electricity | 40000–44999 | 0.93% | electr |
| Construction | 45000–45301 | 2.76% | constr |
| Trade and Hotel | 50000–55000 | 6.13% | trade |
| Transport and Telecom | 60000–64202 | 1.88% | transpt |
| Business Services | 65000–75000 | 19.99% | busserv |
| Community Services | 80000–92200 | 1.72% | comserv |
| Miscellaneous | 93000–97000 | 11.87% | |

**Table 14.12: Payout ratios by industry**

| Industry | Obs | Mean | Standard dev |
|---|---|---|---|
| Agriculture and mining | 391 | 0.1105 | 0.1726 |
| Manufacturing | 8,714 | 0.1507 | 0.2130 |
| Electricity | 155 | 0.2229 | 0.1809 |
| Construction | 460 | 0.1271 | 0.1799 |
| Trade and hotel | 1,020 | 0.1233 | 0.2236 |
| Transport and telecom | 313 | 0.1550 | 0.2003 |
| Business services | 3,327 | 0.1133 | 0.1900 |
| Community services | 287 | 0.1290 | 0.2194 |
| Miscellaneous | 1,973 | 0.0579 | 0.1551 |

We also added year dummies to allow for the possibility that payout ratios might vary over time, maybe over the business cycle; the export variable may be capturing this effect. Since the agriculture industry includes very few observations, it has been commingled with the miscellaneous category. This commingled category is left out from the regression to prevent multi-colinearity; hence all industry effects are relative to the agriculture industry. From the results below in Tables

14.12 and 14.13, we see that payouts do vary by industry. In fact, we conducted a Hotelling F test, and found that the statistic was highly significant [$F(8,16632) = 550.42$; Prob > $F_{0.05} = 0.0000$]. Furthermore, although in almost every industry, exporters pay out more than non-exporters, the importance of export status varies from industry to industry. Hence, we need to include industry affiliation in our regressions, to ensure that export status is not proxying for asset characteristics as reflected in industry affiliation.

**Table 14.13: Payout ratios by industry: Exporters vs non-exporters**

| Industry | Non-exporters | | Exporters | | |
|---|---|---|---|---|---|
| | Obs | Mean | Obs | Mean | T-stat |
| Agriculture and Mining | 148 | 0.0462 | 243 | 0.149661 | **−6.0** |
| Manufacturing | 2795 | 0.072912 | 5919 | 0.187377 | **−24.19** |
| Electricity | 104 | 0.203043 | 51 | 0.263309 | **−1.97** |
| Construction | 310 | 0.090978 | 150 | 0.201627 | **−6.45** |
| Trade and Hotel | 601 | 0.053605 | 419 | 0.223253 | **−12.85** |
| Transport and Telecom | 193 | 0.148571 | 120 | 0.165421 | **−0.72** |
| Business Services | 2604 | 0.099412 | 723 | 0.16333 | **−8.08** |
| Community Services | 170 | 0.057575 | 117 | 0.232874 | **−7.22** |
| Miscellaneous | 1200 | 0.032658 | 773 | 0.097147 | **−9.2** |

Table 14.13 shows that payout ratios vary between exporters and non-exporters, for most industries. We also jointly tested for the equality of means between exporters and non-exporters and were able to reject it strongly. (Wald $\chi^2(16) = 1533.24$; Prob > $\chi^2_{0.05} = 0.0000$). It is clear that while exporters pay higher dividends in every industry, still the nature of this difference varies from industry to industry. This means that introducing industry affiliation as an independent variable will increase the explanatory power of our model. Accordingly, Table 14.14 provides the results from a Tobit analysis similar to that in Table 14.10; however, these results now include year fixed effects and industry affiliation variables. Export Intensity continues to be as significant, as in Table 14.10.

Table 14.15 replicates the results from Table 14.14; however, it includes, in addition, our direct measure of cashflow volatility, Lvar. Unfortunately, as we need to use the data for the first five years to compute Lvar, we only have observations from 2005–09 in these regressions. Table 14.15 provides results for 2005–09 including Lvar, while Table 14.16 provides results for the same subperiod, but without Lvar.

**Table 14.14: Payout ratio as a function of independent variables, ownership categories, industry affiliation and year fixed effects: Tobit regression. (ind_Misc left out, as is OwnCatJt) Year fixed effects coefficients not shown**

Number of obs = 13,169
$F(27, 13142) = 181.33$
Prob > $F = 0.0000$
Log pseudolikelihood = −5352.4609 Pseudo R2 = 0.2980

| Variable | Coef. | Robust Std. Err | $t$ | $P>|t|$ |
|---|---|---|---|---|
| Expintenrel | 0.080077 | 0.012954 | 6.18 | 0 |
| intangiblestoassets | −0.2893 | 0.067693 | −4.27 | 0 |
| BktoMkt | −0.00432 | 0.000685 | −6.31 | 0 |
| Size | 0.098352 | 0.00212 | 46.4 | 0 |
| forexborrowing | −0.0923 | 0.025604 | −3.6 | 0 |
| cashflowtoassets | 0.031184 | 0.017008 | 1.83 | 0.067 |
| age | 0.001707 | 0.000172 | 9.95 | 0 |
| Ltdebt | −0.56712 | 0.021621 | −26.23 | 0 |
| ind_manuf | 0.132559 | 0.012185 | 10.88 | 0 |
| ind_electr | 0.157529 | 0.026432 | 5.96 | 0 |
| ind_constr | 0.081286 | 0.021179 | 3.84 | 0 |
| ind_trade | 0.15744 | 0.020035 | 7.86 | 0 |
| ind_transport | 0.106563 | 0.028457 | 3.74 | 0 |
| ind_busserv | 0.126718 | 0.016826 | 7.53 | 0 |
| ind_comserv | 0.150231 | 0.030852 | 4.87 | 0 |
| OwnCatGov | 0.099629 | 0.042028 | 2.37 | 0.018 |
| OwnCatInd | 0.231605 | 0.038321 | 6.04 | 0 |
| OwnCatFrn | 0.25836 | 0.040226 | 6.42 | 0 |
| Constant | −0.73404 | 0.043368 | −16.93 | 0 |
| /sigma | 0.337852 | 0.00404 | | |

7506 left-censored observations at pr2 < = 0
5663 uncensored observations
0 right-censored observations

Results in Tables 14.15 and 14.16 are very similar, except of course that Table 14.15 includes Lvar, which turns out to be significant, showing conclusively that cashflow volatility is an important determinant of dividend payout ratio. Forex borrowing, which was significant in the earlier regressions for the full sample, now turns out to be insignificant. Except for this variable, all other variables behave similarly in the second subperiod to their behaviour in the whole sample. ExpIntenRel is significant in both regressions, except that the coefficient is slightly smaller and slightly less significant when Lvar is included. This indicates that even after adjusting for the influence of all the other variables, export intensity continues to be important in determining a firm's payout ratio.

**Table 14.15: Payout ratio as a function of industry affiliation, ownership category, years and Lvar 2005–09; year fixed effects coefficients not shown: Tobit regression**

Number of obs = 5,843
$F(23,5820)$ = 92.87
Prob > $F$ = 0.0000
Log pseudolikelihood = -2060.5706 Pseudo R2 = 0.3216

| Variable | Coef. | Robust Std. Err | $t$ | P > $|t|$ |
|---|---|---|---|---|
| ExpIntenRel | 0.056987 | 0.015567 | 3.66 | 0 |
| intangiblestoassets | −0.36973 | 0.092356 | −4 | 0 |
| BktoMkt | −0.00318 | 0.000863 | −3.69 | 0 |
| Size | 0.070709 | 0.002525 | 28.01 | 0 |
| forexborrowing | −0.01932 | 0.026218 | −0.74 | 0.461 |
| cashflowtoassets | 0.018697 | 0.01843 | 1.01 | 0.31 |
| Age | 0.001447 | 0.000209 | 6.92 | 0 |
| Ltdebt | −0.51038 | 0.028475 | −17.92 | 0 |
| ind_manuf | 0.131037 | 0.015127 | 8.66 | 0 |
| ind_electr | 0.173943 | 0.02854 | 6.09 | 0 |
| ind_constr | 0.071357 | 0.025492 | 2.8 | 0.005 |
| ind_trade | 0.177494 | 0.025006 | 7.1 | 0 |
| ind_transport | 0.077696 | 0.031544 | 2.46 | 0.014 |
| ind_busserv | 0.166549 | 0.020625 | 8.08 | 0 |
| ind_comserv | 0.165361 | 0.039517 | 4.18 | 0 |
| Lvar | −0.01538 | 0.002432 | −6.32 | 0 |
| OwnCatGov | 0.109906 | 0.030694 | 3.58 | 0 |
| OwnCatInd | 0.20851 | 0.025295 | 8.24 | 0 |
| OwnCatFrn | 0.258808 | 0.030474 | 8.49 | 0 |
| Constant | −0.71145 | 0.036269 | −19.62 | 0 |
| /sigma | 0.289752 | 0.005022 | | |

Obs. summary: 2,737 left-censored observations at pr2 < = 0
3,106 uncensored observations; 0 right-censored observations

**Table 14.16: Payout ratio as a function of ExpIntenRel, ownership categories, industry affiliations, and years (w/o Lvar) 2005–09: Tobit regression; year fixed effects coefficients not shown**

Number of obs = 5,843
$F(22,5821) = 94.61$
Prob > $F$ = 0.0000
Log pseudolikelihood = -2076.9382 Pseudo R2 = 0.3163

| Variable | Coef. | Robust Std. Err | $T$ | $P > |t|$ |
|---|---|---|---|---|
| ExpIntenRel | 0.074798 | 0.017241 | 4.34 | 0 |
| intangiblestoassets | −0.40407 | 0.0955 | −4.23 | 0 |
| BktoMkt | −0.00265 | 0.000775 | −3.42 | 0.001 |
| Size | 0.072913 | 0.00246 | 29.64 | 0 |
| forexborrowing | −0.02505 | 0.026259 | −0.95 | 0.34 |
| cashflowtoassets | 0.019613 | 0.017767 | 1.1 | 0.27 |
| age | 0.0016 | 0.000212 | 7.54 | 0 |
| Ltdebt | −0.49016 | 0.028734 | −17.06 | 0 |
| ind_manuf | 0.137013 | 0.015038 | 9.11 | 0 |
| ind_electr | 0.173532 | 0.028174 | 6.16 | 0 |
| ind_constr | 0.081473 | 0.025461 | 3.2 | 0.001 |
| ind_trade | 0.190275 | 0.024809 | 7.67 | 0 |
| ind_transport | 0.082434 | 0.031894 | 2.58 | 0.01 |
| ind_busserv | 0.153273 | 0.020861 | 7.35 | 0 |
| ind_comserv | 0.172429 | 0.039939 | 4.32 | 0 |
| OwnCatGov | 0.111096 | 0.031554 | 3.52 | 0 |
| OwnCatInd | 0.213686 | 0.026283 | 8.13 | 0 |
| OwnCatFrn | 0.257629 | 0.031326 | 8.22 | 0 |
| Constant | −0.63575 | 0.034399 | −18.48 | 0 |
| /sigma | 0.290963 | 0.005018 | | |

Obs. summary: 2737 left-censored observations at pr2 < = 0
3106 uncensored observations
0 right-censored observations

## Export intensity and cashflow volatility

Our results up to this point suggest that exporters pay higher dividends, even after controlling for other firm-specific variables. This raises the question as to why exporters would be so generous as regards dividend payment. We now present some evidence that export activity and cashflow volatility are closely related. In other words, the seeming greater propensity of exporters to payout more in dividends may be due to their lower cashflow volatility, which in turn is closely related to their export activities.

**Table 14.17: Log (variance of cashflows) as a measure of the correlation between domestic sales and foreign sales, ExpIntenRel and other control variables**

Number of obs = 4,327
$F (12,4314) = 21.04$
Prob > $F$ = 0.0000
R-squared = 0.0726
Root MSE = 1.6507

| Variable | Coefficient | Std Error | T-value |
|----------|-------------|-----------|---------|
| Corsalesexports | 0.169899 | 0.050443 | 3.37 |
| ExpIntenRel | −0.36226 | 0.093909 | −3.86 |
| intangiblestoassets | 1.299937 | 0.644375 | 2.02 |
| BktoMkt | −0.02844 | 0.006705 | −4.24 |
| Size | −0.16546 | 0.015253 | −10.85 |
| forexborrowing | 0.658097 | 0.152277 | 4.32 |
| cashflowtoassets | −0.1266 | 0.066728 | −1.9 |
| Age | −0.00621 | 0.001323 | −4.7 |
| Ltdebt | −0.16946 | 0.16807 | −1.01 |
| OwnCatGov | −0.17495 | 0.228007 | −0.77 |
| OwnCatInd | −0.59233 | 0.178809 | −3.31 |
| OwnCatFrn | −0.197 | 0.190553 | −1.03 |
| Constant | −5.06278 | 0.199247 | −25.41 |

We first test to see whether cashflow volatility is significantly different for exporters and non-exporters. We find that that cashflow volatility (VarCashFlow) is significantly lower for exporters (mean for exporters = 0.0051258, mean for non-exporters = 0.3329574, t-value of difference = 2.2412). A simple regression of Lvar on ExpIntenRel confirms this result; ExpIntenRel is indeed significant in explaining cashflow variance (t-statistic of −2.56). We now need to answer the question as to what might be the cause of this lower cashflow volatility for exporters. Table 14.17 reports the results of the regression of Lvar on various determinants of cashflow volatility. We see that Lvar is significantly positively related to Corsalesexports (the correlation between sales and exports using data from the previous 5 years). This suggests that exporting firms achieve lower cashflow volatility by virtue of the fact that their domestic sales are imperfectly correlated with foreign sales. However, we note that even after controlling for Corsalesports,ExpIntenRel is still significantly negatively related to Lvar. It may be, then, that there are other, as yet uncovered, reasons why exporters pay higher dividends. On the other hand, it may very well be that cashflow volatility is really the only reason, and that the Corsalesexports variable simply does not fully capture the entire diversification effect. A more detailed firm-level analysis that goes into firm operating strategies would be needed to tease out the solution to this problem; we leave this for future research.

## EXPORT INTENSITY AND VALUATION

We have just shown that export intensity is desirable in that it allows firms to reduce their cashflow volatility and pay higher dividends. At this point, it is reasonable to ask if such desirability is valued by the market. We try to answer this question by looking at the relationship between a firm's P/E ratio and its exporting behaviour. We first looked at the average P/E ratio of exporting firms compared to that of non-exporting firms.[23] We found a mean P/E ratio of 15.089 for non-exporters (n = 4649, s.d. 18.673), and a mean ratio of 14.00684 for exporting firms (n = 6709, s.d. = 14.736); the difference was statistically significant with a p-value of 0.0005. Given our recent demonstration of the desirability of exporting behaviour, one might have expected a positive relationship between P/E ratios and export intensity; our result, thus, might seem somewhat strange.

However, the P/E ratio is analogous to the inverse of a required rate of return and would normally be negatively related to equity beta, according to the CAPM; hence our results may simply be the result of exporting firms having higher betas.

---

[23]    We restrict our analysis to firm-years with positive earnings, defined as, "profits after tax." Looking at the frequency distribution of the P/E ratio, we see that it is extremely positively skewed. Although this is not entirely surprising given that a low earnings number would generate a very large P/E ratio, we excluded observations with P/E ratios greater than 100 for our analysis. When we use the full sample, we find that the average P/E ratio for non-exporting firms is 131.300 (n = 5184, s.d. = 1795.967), while that for exporting firms is 22.127 (n = 6860, s.d. = 104.761). The difference is statistically significant with a p-value of 0.000.

Accordingly, we run a regression of the log of the P/E ratio on equity beta and relative export intensity (n = 9710).[24] The slope coefficient on beta is insignificant (0.0017, p = 0.305), and so is the slope coefficient for expintenrel(0.0409, p = 0.311). While we could infer from this that exporting firms are not different from non-exporting firms in terms of their valuation in the stock market, such a test would have very little power. The reason for such low power might be our reliance on the CAPM, which has not been very successful in simple empirical tests. Post-CAPM asset pricing theories suggest other determinants of the required rate of return, as well. For example, in the presence of trading costs,[25] or if, for whatever reason, investors cannot hold the market portfolio; the required rate of return may be positively related to idiosyncratic volatility.[26] Similarly, according to Fama and French (1993), various other firm-specific variables, such as size and book-to-market could be empirically related to the required rate of return. The definition of the P/E ratio also suggests a positive relation to measures of earnings growth; furthermore, in a world where variables are measured imprecisely, proxies for risk measures, such as industry affiliation might well be related to the required rate of return, as well.

Following this literature, we first regress the P/E ratio on intangibles-to-assets ratio and book-to-market ratio (growth measures), size, equity beta, industry dummies, ownership category dummies, year dummies as well as expintenrel. Sure enough, the explanatory power of our regressions increases quite a bit. Not only that, most of the coefficients are as expected (reported in Table 14.18). The coefficient for the equity beta is significantly negative (CAPM prediction); intangibles-to-assets is positively related to the P/E ratio while the book-to-market ratio is negatively related (as predicted because of their status as measures of earnings growth); and size is positively related (consistent with the empirically-observed size effect).[27] Firms in the services industry which have been growth firms in the Indian context have higher P/E ratios, while manufacturing firms have lower P/E ratios. Foreign-domiciled firms also tend to have higher P/E ratios, for some reason. ExpIntenRel, however, has no statistically significant relationship to firm P/E ratio.

---

[24] We use the log of the P/E ratio as our dependent variable because of the above-noted skewness. After transformation, the P/E ratio has a nice, bell-shaped distribution. In any case, the qualitative conclusions in this section obtain even when we run our regressions using the raw P/E ratio.

[25] See Levy (1978)

[26] See Malkiel and Xu (2006)

[27] See Banz (1981) and Reinganum (1981) who find that the expected rate of return on small stocks is higher; however, the size effect has decreased considerably in recent years.

**Table 14.18: Log (P/E Ratio) as a function of growth variables, measure of firm risk, ExpIntenRel and other control variables**

Linear regression           Number of obs   =   9,710
$F_{(24, 9,685)} = 66.13$
Prob > $F$ = 0.0000
R-squared = 0.2021

|  | Coef. | Robust Std. Err. | t | P > \|t\| |
|---|---|---|---|---|
| ExpIntenRel | −0.03398 | 0.036296 | −0.94 | 0.349 |
| Beta | −0.00253 | 0.000826 | −3.06 | 0.002 |
| Intangibles-to-assets | 0.620504 | 0.21957 | 2.83 | 0.005 |
| BktoMkt | −0.04317 | 0.003427 | −12.6 | 0 |
| Size | 0.035021 | 0.005523 | 6.34 | 0 |
| ind_manuf | −0.15749 | 0.039014 | −4.04 | 0 |
| ind_electr | −0.1008 | 0.078732 | −1.28 | 0.2 |
| ind_constr | 0.022186 | 0.062312 | 0.36 | 0.722 |
| ind_trade | 0.125916 | 0.056846 | 2.22 | 0.027 |
| ind_transport | −0.05382 | 0.066487 | −0.81 | 0.418 |
| ind_busserv | 0.106762 | 0.04889 | 2.18 | 0.029 |
| ind_comserv | 0.533212 | 0.076652 | 6.96 | 0 |
| group_gov | 0.219384 | 0.138924 | 1.58 | 0.114 |
| group_indian | 0.225647 | 0.133532 | 1.69 | 0.091 |
| group_foreign | 0.62831 | 0.135594 | 4.63 | 0 |
| y2001 | −0.25761 | 0.051779 | −4.98 | 0 |
| y2002 | −0.10906 | 0.052572 | −2.07 | 0.038 |
| y2003 | −0.21509 | 0.052577 | −4.09 | 0 |
| y2004 | −0.10457 | 0.049357 | −2.12 | 0.034 |
| y2005 | 0.222234 | 0.047779 | 4.65 | 0 |
| y2006 | 0.343432 | 0.046519 | 7.38 | 0 |
| y2007 | 0.259719 | 0.046355 | 5.6 | 0 |
| y2008 | 0.195704 | 0.044989 | 4.35 | 0 |
| y2009 | −0.19733 | 0.046787 | −4.22 | 0 |
| constant | 1.918103 | 0.147687 | 12.99 | 0 |

One variable that we have not included, yet, is cashflow volatility, which we showed plays an important role in explaining the dividend behaviour of exporting firms. Accordingly, we repeat the regression of Table 14.18, now including Lvar (the log of the variance of cashflows), but simultaneously restricting ourselves to the second subperiod. The signs of the variables mentioned above are quite similar. However, we see, in addition, that Lvar is significantly negatively related to the P/E ratio. This is consistent with the Levy (1978) and Malkiel and Xu (2006) findings cited above. ExpIntenRel, however, continues to be insignificant. We can conclude, therefore, that a firm's export intensity is, indeed, reflected in its equity valuation, but indirectly through its salubrious effect on firm volatility.

**Table 14.19: Log (P/E Ratio) as a function of cashflow volatility, growth variables, measure of firm risk, ExpIntenRel and other control variables**

Linear regression
F (20,4966) = 32.02
Prob > F = 0.0000
R-squared = 0.1690

Number of obs = 4987

| | Coef. | Robust Std. Err. | t | P > |t| |
|---|---|---|---|---|
| **ExpIntenRel** | **0.06216** | **0.045389** | **1.37** | **0.171** |
| beta | −0.00767 | 0.002451 | −3.13 | 0.002 |
| Intangibles-to-assets | 0.822744 | 0.259353 | 3.17 | 0.002 |
| BktoMkt | −0.05471 | 0.007893 | −6.93 | 0 |
| Size | 0.033422 | 0.007173 | 4.66 | 0 |
| lvar | −0.0599 | 0.008917 | −6.72 | 0 |
| ind_manuf | −0.21223 | 0.053506 | −3.97 | 0 |
| ind_electr | −0.11668 | 0.082716 | −1.41 | 0.158 |
| ind_constr | −0.09303 | 0.075625 | −1.23 | 0.219 |
| ind_trade | −0.00232 | 0.07226 | −0.03 | 0.974 |
| ind_transport | −0.05266 | 0.093166 | −0.57 | 0.572 |
| ind_busserv | -0.04844 | 0.065044 | −0.74 | 0.456 |
| ind_comserv | 0.384614 | 0.093948 | 4.09 | 0 |
| group_gov | 0.454504 | 0.162465 | 2.8 | 0.005 |
| group_indian | 0.412174 | 0.15614 | 2.64 | 0.008 |
| group_foreign | 0.711158 | 0.159166 | 4.47 | 0 |
| y2006 | 0.14282 | 0.042064 | 3.4 | 0.001 |
| y2007 | 0.037692 | 0.042646 | 0.88 | 0.377 |
| y2008 | −0.00465 | 0.041223 | −0.11 | 0.91 |
| y2009 | −0.37817 | 0.045433 | −8.32 | 0 |
| _cons | 1.629879 | 0.18225 | 8.94 | 0 |

## CONCLUSIONS

In this chapter, we examine payout policies of Indian corporates and find that firms that export more tend to pay higher dividends. Our primary finding is that this may be due to the fact that exports are imperfectly correlated with domestic sales, thus, providing exporting firms with a kind of diversification effect leading to lower cashflow volatility: according to corporate finance theories, lower cashflow volatility allows firms to make higher dividend payouts. We also find evidence that this reduction in cashflow volatility has a positive effective on exporting firms' valuation in the stock market.

Our results provide mixed support for the Investment Opportunities hypothesis – while firms with higher intangibles seem to pay lower dividends, firms with higher book-to-market ratios seem to pay lower dividends. There is also mixed support for the Funding Access Hypothesis. Average Cashflow is unrelated, at the margin, to the payout ratio, as is forexborrowings (foreign currency borrowings). Foreign firms, whether they belong to a group or not, have higher payout ratios than other firms; if we believe that foreign firms have better access to foreign capital, then this can be interpreted as support for the Funding Access Hypothesis. On the other hand, foreign firms may simply be trying to repatriate capital. The negative relationship between payout ratio and long-term debt does conform to the predictions of the Funding Access Hypothesis; the greater the debt, the lower the free cashflow available for the payment of dividends.

Our primary finding that cashflow diversification through exports leads to higher dividend payouts can be interpreted as support for Indian government efforts to improve exports.[28] While dividend payouts don't impact growth or employment directly, they do indirectly improve allocational efficiency by allowing the market a greater say in the reinvestment of corporate earnings. This is all the more important given recent findings that Indian corporations are increasingly dependent on retained earnings for their financial resources.

## REFERENCES

Alessandrina, G., and H. Choi. 2007. 'Do Sunk Costs of Exporting Matter for Net Export Dynamics?'. *The Quarterly Journal of Economics*, MIT Press, 122(1): 289–336.

Arora, A., V.S. Arunachalam, J. Asundi, and R. Fernandes. 2001. 'The Indian Software Services Industry'. *Research Policy*, 30(8): 1267–87.

Athreye, S. S. 2005. 'The Indian Software Industry and its Evolving Service Capability'. *Industrial and Corporate Change*, 14(3): 393–418.

---

[28] Details on government efforts can be obtained on the website of the Federation of Indian Export Organizations set up by the Ministry of Commerce (http://www.fieo.org).

Aulakh, P. S, M. Kotabe, and H. Teegen. 2000. 'Export Strategies and Performance of Firms From Emerging Economies: Evidence From Brazil, Chile, and Mexico'. *Academy of Management Journal*, 43(3): 342–61.

Banz, R. 1981. 'The Relationship between Return and Market Value of Common Stock'. *Journal of Financial Economics*, 9, 3–18.

Bernard, A. B., and J. B. Jensen. 2004. 'Why Some Firms Export'. *Review of Economics and Statistics*, 86(2): 561–69.

Bernard, A. B., J. B. Jensen, S. J. Redding, and P. K. Schott. 2007. 'Firms in International Trade'. *Journal of International Perspectives*, 21(3): 105–30.

Bradley, M., D. Capozza, and P. Seguin. 1998. 'Dividend Policy and Cash Flow Uncertainty'. *Real Estate Economics*, 26(4): 555–80.

Cavusgil, S. T. 1982. 'Some Observations on the Relevance of Critical Variables for Internationalization Stages'. In *Export Management: An International Context*, edited by M.R. Czinkota and G. Tesar. 276–85. New York: Praeger.

Chay, J.B., and J. Suh. 2008. 'Payout Policy and Cash-flow Uncertainty'. *Journal of Financial Economics*.

Chibber, P., and S. Majumdar. 1998. 'Does it Pay to Venture Abroad? Exporting Behaviour and the Performance of Firms in Indian Industry'. *Managerial and Decision Economics*, 19(2): 121–26.

Czinkota, M. R. 1982. *Export Development Strategies: U.S. Promotion Policy*. New York: Praeger.

Demirbas, D., I. Patnaik, and A. Shah. 2009. 'Graduating to Globalisation: A Study of Southern Multinationals'. Working Paper, National Institute of Public Finance and Policy.

Fadhlaoui, K., M. Bellalah, A. Dherry, and M. Zouaouil. 2008. 'An Empirical Examination of International Diversification Benefits in Central European Emerging Equity Markets'. *International Journal of Business*, 13(4): 331–48.

Frank, M. Z., and V. K. Goyal. 2009. 'Capital Structure Decisions: Which Factors Are Reliably Important?' *Financial Management*, 38(1): 1–37.

Ganesh-Kumar, A., K. Sen, and R. R. Vaidya. 2003. *International Competitiveness, Investment and Finance : A Case Study of India*, New York: Routledge.

Goldman, E., and P.V. Viswanath. 2011. 'Export Intensity and Financial Leverage of Indian Firms'. *International Journal of Trade and Global Markets*, 4(2): 152–71.

Hansoge, N., and V. Marisetty. 2011. 'Economic Transition and the Value of Business Group Affiliation: Evidence from the Indian Market,' Working Paper, Indian Institute of Management, Bangalore, India.

Jakob S. H., and R. Johannes. 2008. 'Dividend Determinants in Denmark'. Management Working Paper, 2008-3. University of Aarhus, Denmark.

Jensen, J.B., S. Redding, and P. Schott. 2007. 'Firms in International Trade'. *Journal of Economic Perspectives*, 21(3): 109–30.

Khanna, T., and K. Palepu. 1999. 'Policy Shocks, Market Intermediaries, and Corporate Strategy: The Evolution of Business Groups in Chile and India'. *Journal of Economics and Management Strategy*, 8(2): 271–310.

———— 2000. 'Is Group Affiliation Profitable in Emerging Markets? An Analysis of Diversified Indian Business Groups'. *Journal of finance*, 55(2): 867–91.

Kumar, M., L.M. Bhole, and S. Saudagaran. 2008. 'How International Listings by the Indian Firms affect their Access to the External Capital Markets and Investment-Cash Flows Sensitivity?' Working Paper, accessed at http://ssrn.com/abstract=951388

Levine, R., and S. Zervos. 1998. 'Stock Markets, Banks, and Economic Growth'. *The American Economic Review*, 88(3): 537–58.

Levy, H. 1978. 'Equilibrium in an Imperfect Market: A Constraint on the Number of Securities in the Portfolio'. *American Economic Review*, 68, 643–58.

Malkiel, B., and Y. Xu. 2006. 'Idiosyncratic Risk and Security Returns'. Working Paper, Princeton University.

Mohanty, P. 1999. 'Dividend and Bonus Policies of Indian Companies: An Analysis'. 24(4): October–December, 35–42. http://www.vikalpa.com/pdf/articles/1999/1999_oct_dec_035_042.pdf

Moon, J., and H. Lee. 1990. 'On the Internal Correlates of Export Stage Development: An Empirical Investigation in the Korean Electronics Industry'. *International Marketing Review*, 7(5): 16–26.

Nair, V. R. P. 2013. *'Dynamics of Resource Mobilisation and Investment in the Indian Private Corporate Sector'*, paper presented at the Institute of Economic Growth (IEG) workshop on Sustaining High Growth in India, New Delhi, 1–38.

Navaretti, G., M. Galeotti, and A. Tucci. 2002. 'Do not get Trapped into Crossing: Indian Firms and Foreign Markets'. Development Studies Working Paper, Centro Studi Luca D'Agliano.

Pradhan, J. P. 2007. 'Growth of Indian Multinationals in the World Economy: Implications for Development'. Working Paper, Institute for Studies in Industrial Development, New Delhi, India.

P. V. Viswanath. 'Strategic Considerations, The Pecking Order Hypothesis and Market Reactions to Equity Financing.' *Journal of Financial and Quantitative Analysis*, 28, no. 2, June 1993.

Rajan, R. G., and L. Zingales. 1998. 'Financial Dependence and Growth'. *The American Economic Review*, 88(3): 559–86.

Rao, T. R., and G.M. Naidu. 1992. 'Are the Stages of Internationalization Empirically Supportable?' *Journal of Global Marketing*, 6(1–2): 147–70.

Reinganum, M.R. 1981. 'Misspecification of Capital Asset Pricing: Empirical Anomalies based on Earnings' Yields and Market Values'. *Journal of Financial Economics*, 9, 19–46.

S. C. Myers, 1984, 'The Capital Structure Puzzle,' *Journal of Finance*, Vol. 39(3), 575–92.

Sinani, E., and B. Hobdari. 2008. 'Export Market Participation with Sunk Costs and Firm Heterogeneity'. *Applied Economics*.

Wortzel, L. H., and H.V. Wortzel. 1981. 'Export Marketing Strategies for NIC and LDC-based Firms'. *Columbia Journal of World Business*, Spring, 51–60.

# Contributors

**Pradeep Agrawal** (editor) is Reserve Bank of India (RBI) Chair Professor of Economics and Head of the RBI Endowment Unit at the Institute of Economic Growth (IEG), New Delhi. He has taught at several universities in USA and has also been a faculty at Indira Gandhi Institute of Development Research. He holds a PhD in economics from Stanford University.

**Bishwanath Goldar** is Professor at the Institute of Economic Growth (IEG) and Centre for International Trade and Development (CITD), School of International Studies, JNU, New Delhi.

**Ashima Goyal** is Professor at Indira Gandhi Institute of Development and Research (IGIDR), Mumbai.

**Pravakar Sahoo** is Associate Professor at the Institute of Economic Growth (IEG), New Delhi.

**Ranjan Kumar Dash** is Fellow for Policy, Wadhwani Foundation, New Delhi.

**Prabhu Prasad Mishra** is Junior Consultant, Institute of Economic Growth, Delhi.

**Sushanta K. Mallick** is Professor at Queen Mary University of London, School of Business and Management, UK.

**Amaresh Samantaraya** is Associate Professor at the Department of Economics, Pondicherry University.

**Nilabja Ghosh** is Associate Professor at the Institute of Economic Growth (IEG), New Delhi.

**Anita Kumari** is Assistant Professor at the Institute of Economic Growth (IEG), New Delhi.

**Shruti Tripathi** is Economist, National Institute of Public Finance and Policy, New Delhi.

**Geethanjali Nataraj** is Senior Fellow at Observer Research Foundation, New Delhi.

**Arup Mitra** is Professor at the Institute of Economic Growth (IEG), New Delhi.

**Chandan Sharma** is faculty of Business Environmental at Indian Institute of Management, Lucknow, India.

**Prabhakaran Nair V. R.** is Assistant Professor at Sanatana Dharma College, Alappuzha, Kerala.

**Elena Goldman** is Associate Professor in the Department of Finance and Economics at the Lubin School of Business, Pace University.

**Viswanath P. V.** is Professor, Graduate Program Chair, at the Department of Finance and Economics in Lubin School of Business, New York.

# Index